Text and Context in the Modern History of Chinese Religions

Religion in Chinese Societies

Edited by

Kenneth Dean (*National University of Singapore*)
Richard Madsen (*University of California, San Diego*)
David Palmer (*University of Hong Kong*)

VOLUME 16

The titles published in this series are listed at *brill.com/rics*

Text and Context in the Modern History of Chinese Religions

Redemptive Societies and Their Sacred Texts

Edited by

Philip Clart
David Ownby
Wang Chien-chuan

BRILL

LEIDEN | BOSTON

Cover of the *Ten Thousand Buddha Scripture* (1928 edition), photo provided by Wang Chien-chuan.

The Library of Congress Cataloging-in-Publication Data is available online at http://catalog.loc.gov
LC record available at http://lccn.loc.gov/2019053102.

Typeface for the Latin, Greek, and Cyrillic scripts: "Brill". See and download: brill.com/brill-typeface.

ISSN 1877-6264
ISBN 978-90-04-42413-5 (hardback)
ISBN 978-90-04-42416-6 (e-book)

This book is printed on acid-free paper and produced in a sustainable manner.

Contents

On the Contributors

Chung Yun-Ying 鍾雲鶯

completed her M.A. and Ph.D. at National Chengchi University 國立政治大學, Taiwan, and is currently Professor in the Department of Chinese Literature and Linguistics of Yuan Ze University 元智大學, Taiwan. Her research focuses on two main thematic fields: the ways Confucian classics are appropriated and interpreted by Chinese sectarian movements, and the doctrines and history of Yiguandao 一貫道 in Taiwan. Since 2011, she has been conducting fieldwork on Vietnamese popular sects. Among other works, she is the author of *Qingmo Minchu minjian Rujiao dui zhuliu Ruxue de xishou yu zhuanhua* (*The Reception and Transformation of Mainstream Confucianism by Popular Confucianism in the Late Qing and Early Republican Periods*) 清末民初民間儒教對主流儒學的吸收與轉化 (2008) and of *Minguo yilai minjian jiaopai Daxue, Zhongyong sixiang zhi yanjiu* (*The Great Learning and the Doctrine of the Mean in Sectarian Religious Thought since the Republican Period*) 民國以來民間教派大學、中庸思想之研究 (2000).

Philip Clart

is Professor of Chinese Culture and History at Leipzig University, Germany. He received his Ph.D. in Asian Studies from the University of British Columbia, Canada, in 1997; prior to coming to Leipzig he taught at the University of British Columbia (1996–1998) and at the University of Missouri-Columbia (1998–2008). He is the editor of the *Journal of Chinese Religions*. His main research areas are popular religion and new religious movements in Taiwan, religious change and state/religion relations in China, as well as literature and religions of the late imperial period (10th–19th c.). His monographs include *Han Xiangzi: The Alchemical Adventures of a Daoist Immortal* (University of Washington Press, 2007) and *Die Religionen Chinas* (Vandenhoeck & Ruprecht, 2009). His most recent edited volume is *Religious Publishing and Print Culture in Modern China: 1800–2012* (De Gruyter, 2015; co-edited with Gregory Adam Scott).

Fan Chun-wu 范純武

(Ph.D. in History, National Taiwan Normal University, 2003), is currently a professor of history at Tunghai University in Taiwan. Past research has focused on the various roles of the religious rituals and organizations in modern Chinese society, and the changes in the beliefs of the Shuangzhong 雙忠 deities (Zhang Xun 張巡, Xu Yuan 許遠) since the Song Dynasty in the process of the localization of Daoism. Since then, his academic interests have expanded to explore the development of the modern Chinese redemptive society Daode xueshe 道德學社, with particular attention to religious printing and publishing; among other topics, he currently studies the impact on religious activities of modern photography, as it developed from the nineteenth century, as well as the meditation and vegetarian movements of the early Republican period. He is the author of *Qingmo minjian cishan shiye yu luantang yundong* (*Popular Charitable Associations and the Phoenix Hall Movement in the Late Qing Period*) 清末民間慈善事業與鸞堂運動 (Boyang, 2015), and of many scholarly articles.

Barend J. ter Haar
received his doctorate at the University of Leiden in 1990. He taught at the Universities of Leiden, Heidelberg and Oxford and teaches Chinese history at the University of Hamburg. He has published on a variety of topics, including most recently *Guan Yu: The Religious Afterlife of a Failed Hero* (Oxford University Press, 2017). He is currently preparing books on violence within Chinese religious culture, and on accusations of witchcraft in social conflict in China past and present.

Jeremy Jammes
is a social anthropologist and has completed his Ph.D. research on Caodaism in 2006 (Paris X Nanterre). He has widely published book chapters and articles on religious and ethnic issues in Vietnam and Cambodia. He has recently published a book on the Vietnamese religion Cao Đài and its global networks (Les Indes savantes, 2014) and co-edited a volume on Evangelical Protestantism in Southeast Asia (Presses Universitaires de Rennes, 2016) and a special issue on this topic (*Social Compass*, 2013). Between 2010 and 2014, he served in Bangkok as Deputy Director of the Research Institute on Contemporary Southeast Asia (IRASEC, Bangkok), for which he has (co-) edited three regional geopolitics outlooks. He currently serves as Associate Professor and Director of the Institute of Asian Studies in the Universiti Brunei Darussalam, and he is Editor-in-Chief of the academic book series, *Asia in Transition* (Springer).

David Ownby
completed his M.A. and Ph.D. at Harvard University, and is presently Professor of History at the Université de Montréal, where he served as Director of the Center for East Asian Studies for ten years (2001–2011). His work has focused on the history of popular movements and popular religion in modern China. He has published widely on the history of secret societies and helped to create

the field of "redemptive societies." He has also translated religious scriptures and Chinese scholarship on the history of Chinese religion. He is the author of *Falun Gong and the Future of China* (2008), co-editor of *Making Saints in Modern China* (2017), and editor and translator of *China at the Crossroads: Xu Jilin on China's Rise* (forthcoming).

David A. Palmer
is an Associate Professor in the department of Sociology and the Hong Kong Institute for the Humanities and Social Sciences at the University of Hong Kong, which he joined in 2008. He graduated from McGill University in Anthropology and East Asian Studies. After completing his Ph.D. in the Anthropology of Religion at the Ecole Pratique des Hautes Etudes in Paris, he was the Eileen Barker Fellow in Religion and Contemporary Society at the London School of Economics and Political Science, and, from 2004 to 2008, director of the Hong Kong Centre of the French School of Asian Studies (Ecole Française d'Extrême-Orient), located at the Institute for Chinese Studies at the Chinese University of Hong Kong. His books include the award-winning *Qigong Fever: Body, Science and Utopia in China* (Columbia University Press, 2007); *The Religious Question in Modern China* (University of Chicago Press, 2011, co-authored with Vincent Goossaert; awarded the Levenson Book Prize of the Association for Asian Studies); *Daoism in the 20th Century: Between Eternity and Modernity* (University of California Press, 2012, co-edited with Xun Liu), and *Dream Trippers: Global Daoism and the Predicament of Modern Spirituality* (University of Chicago Press, 2017, co-authored with Elijah Siegler).

Matthias Schumann
is working as a postdoctoral research fellow at the International Consortium for Research in the Humanities "Fate, Freedom and Prognostication" at the University of Erlangen-Nürnberg. Previously, he served as the scientific co-ordinator of the interdisciplinary research project, "Protecting the Weak: Entangled Processes of Framing, Mobilisation and Institutionalisation," at Goethe University Frankfurt am Main. He completed his Ph.D. in Sinology at Heidelberg University in 2017 with a thesis on spirit-writing organizations in early Republican China. Working on the religious history of nineteenth and early twentieth century China, his main research interests include redemptive societies, spirit-writing, spiritualism, and human-animal relations. He is co-editor of the recently published volume *Protecting the Weak in East Asia: Framing, Mobilisation and Institutionalisation* (Routledge, 2018).

Wang Chien-chuan 王見川
received his Ph.D. in History from National Chung Cheng University, Taiwan, in 2003. He is Assistant Professor at the Southern Taiwan University of Science and Technology. His research focuses on Chinese popular religion (Guandi 關帝, Xuantian shangdi 玄天上帝, Wenchang 文昌, Mazu 媽祖), prophetic texts, late imperial popular religion, and contemporary Daoism, Buddhism, spirit-writing, and charity. He has authored *Zhang tianshi zhi yanjiu: Yi Longhushan yixwi wei kaocha zhongxin* (*Studies on the Celestial Master Zhang: with a Focus on the Longhushan System*) 張天師之研究:以龍虎山一系為考察中心 (Boyang, 2015), *Hanren zongjiao, minjian xinyang yu yuyanshu de tansuo* (*Chinese Religion, Popular Belief, and Prophetic Texts*) 漢人宗教、民間信仰與預言書的探索 (Boyang, 2008), and edited (among others) *Mingqing minjian zongjiao jingjuan wenxian* (*Popular Religious Scriptures of the Ming and Qing Periods*) 明清民間宗教經卷文獻 (Xinwenfeng, 2006), and *Zhongguo minjian xinyang, minjian wenhua ziliao huibian* (*Materials on Chinese Popular Beliefs and Popular Culture*) 中國民間信仰、民間文化資料彙編 (Boyang, 2011).

Introduction

Philip Clart and David Ownby

"Redemptive societies" is the term employed by some scholars to refer to the organized expression of salvationist religious activity in Republican-period China (1912–1949). The best known of such groups is surely the Yiguandao 一貫道 (I-Kuan tao, the "Way of Pervasive Unity"), which remains extremely popular in Taiwan and elsewhere in the Chinese diaspora, but there were many similar groups in the Republican period, with nation-wide organizations and millions of members. In their path-breaking volume, *The Religious Question in Modern China*, Vincent Goossaert and David Palmer argued that these groups constituted "the most significant religious phenomenon of the Republican era."[1] At the same time, redemptive societies are a recent scholarly discovery, and almost no mention is made of them in standard textbook treatments of modern and contemporary Chinese history. How might we explain this paradox?

In China, as elsewhere, "historical" questions are often driven by contemporary issues. When Deng Xiaoping set China on the path of "reform and opening" after the death of Mao Zedong, it was an admission that communism and revolution were no longer the sole watchwords for China's future. This sea change in China's future direction also impacted the study of China's past, which to that point had largely focused on China's political revolution, understood as the central phenomenon of China's twentieth-century history. Foreign historians of China especially began to reevaluate China's Republican period, which to this point had been largely dismissed as a corrupt failure that inevitably gave way to the victorious forces of communism. At the same time, contemporary China's reform and opening, the goal of which was rapid economic development, was accompanied by a large-scale religious revival, totally unexpected because it was believed that religion had been largely eradicated under Mao. A major element in the religious revival was the *qigong* boom, in which charismatic masters attracted millions of followers by preaching a mixture of pseudo-science and Chinese traditional "cultivation" practices. When scholars looked for antecedents to the *qigong* boom, they found the Republican-period redemptive societies.

1 Vincent Goossaert and David A. Palmer, *The Religious Question in Modern China* (Chicago: University of Chicago Press, 2011), 121.

© KONINKLIJKE BRILL NV, LEIDEN, 2020 | DOI:10.1163/9789004424156_002

Actually, the term "redemptive society" is new as well, another reason why there are no references to the groups in standard histories. It was coined by historian Prasenjit Duara in the context of his research on Manchukuo, the "puppet state" founded by Japan in (formerly Chinese) Manchuria in 1931. In his work, Duara discovered that groups like Wanguo daodehui 萬國道德會 (Universal Morality Society) were extremely widespread in Manchukuo, in large measure because the Japanese had decided to view such groups as representatives of "Eastern religion" (there were Japanese equivalents of such groups, and collaboration between certain Chinese and Japanese groups), and hence worthy of protection in their effort to create a Greater East Asia Co-Prosperity Sphere. This posture stood in significant contrast to that of the Chinese Nationalists, who were at best ambivalent about the groups, and often condemned them as "superstitious" or "rebellious," even as the groups flourished and membership expanded. Duara subsequently coined the term "redemptive societies" to describe groups like the Wanguo daodehui, emphasizing their common message of salvation, or redemption, instead of their political coloration.

Prior to Duara's work, Western scholars had been generally unaware of redemptive societies; little or nothing had been written about them, hence there was no felt need to name the phenomenon. Duara's idea was rather to challenge the prevailing Chinese historiography of the groups. The most frequently used Chinese term for these organizations since the 1940s is *huidaomen* (會道門, "sects and secret societies"), short for *fandong huidaomen* (反動會道門, "reactionary sects and secret societies"). This term, obviously political in nature, was invented by CCP authorities in the 1940s and applied broadly to the "sects and secret societies" targeted on the mainland in the early 1950s for suppression as a part of the consolidation of Communist rule; no collective noun for the groups had existed in Chinese prior to this point. Subsequently, the label was affixed retroactively to the forerunners of the groups suppressed in the 1950s, or to other supposedly similar groups ("heterodox sects" and "secret societies" are conflated in the formulation). Consciously or not, the discourse drew heavily on imperial condemnation of *xiejiao* 邪教 ("heterodox teachings") and *yiduan* 異端 ("extremism," "heterodoxy"), often employed in campaigns against "White Lotus" sectarians and similar groups. The result (often the goal) was to dismiss the religious nature of redemptive societies and to cast the groups as real or potential enemies of the state who use pseudo-religion to camouflage their political intentions. In this discourse, society leaders are condemned as evil con artists who manipulate the ignorant masses with "feudal" nonsense about healing powers and salvation in paradise, eventually mobilizing them to rise up against their true representatives, the Communist Party. The Guomindang (GMD) employed similar arguments without, of course, endorsing the Communists. This view of redemptive societies remains broadly dominant in both China and Taiwan, although younger scholars in Taiwan have moved toward acceptance of the redemptive society paradigm.

The result of this series of conjunctures and confluences was a minor "wave" in studies of Chinese redemptive societies, particularly but not exclusively in the West, beginning in the 2000s, building on Duara's central insight and dovetailing with the scholarly re-evaluation of the role of religion in modern and contemporary Chinese history over the past twenty years or so. The field is really quite young, and small, and in English consists largely of synthetic overviews, some better than others, but most covering the same material in more or less the same way.[2] There are of course articles on individual redemptive societies, but there are as yet no English-language monographs outside those on Yiguandao, which are not necessarily focused on the Republican period, but remain relevant nonetheless.

In any event, most Western and some Chinese scholars (particularly in Taiwan) now see redemptive societies as religious groups (or "new religious movements") whose central message was a culturally conservative insistence on the pertinence and utility of traditional, often Confucian, values, although redemptive society teachings combined Confucian, Buddhist, and Daoist themes—as well as Christian and Muslim, of which more later.[3] Society leaders were often the sort of "holy men" who have appeared throughout Chinese (and world) history with tales of mysterious births, penetrating insights, and healing powers. They preached a return to traditional values in order to halt social decline and perhaps avert a possible apocalypse. Some groups were part of a consciously "Confucian" revival, spearheaded by Kang Youwei 康有為 (1858–1927) and others in an attempt to rescue Chinese state and society after the failure of the first republic. Many redemptive societies began as local spirit-writing cults, a popular elite practice since the Song period organized around the reception and distribution of divinely inspired texts addressing moral concerns. Another source was the late imperial period sectarian tradition; sectarian deities and discourses appear in the texts of many redemptive societies. Although not always politically reactionary (or even politically active,

2 Major syntheses include: David A. Palmer, "Chinese Redemptive Societies and Salvationist Religion: Historical Phenomenon or Sociological Category?", *Minsu quyi* 民俗曲藝, no. 172 (2011): 21–72; David Ownby, "Redemptive Societies in the Twentieth Century," in *Modern Chinese Religion II: 1850–2015*, ed. Vincent Goossaert, Jan Kiely, and John Lagerwey (Leiden: Brill, 2016), 685–727; Goossaert and Palmer, *The Religious Question in Modern China*, ch. 4.

3 For a critical voice, see Nikolas Broy, "Syncretic Sects and Redemptive Societies," *Review of Religion and Chinese Society* 2, no. 2 (2015): 145–185.

in some cases), redemptive societies appealed to that part of China that was not attracted to the iconoclastic, radical May Fourth/New Culture movements (which were occasionally denounced explicitly in redemptive society texts), a China that has been until fairly recently largely ignored by historians, Chinese and foreign, who, understandably, have focused on China's central narratives of social decline, war, and revolution.

If the message was largely traditional, the package was not. As already mentioned, most redemptive societies added Christianity and Islam to Confucianism, Buddhism, and Daoism, suggesting that all five were different expressions of the same basic truth. They also included generally positive discussions of science. Depending on the group, the message can be read either as a bold statement announcing a possible new version of modernity (with Chinese—or East Asian—characteristics), or as an undigested New Age jumble. Still, we should not see redemptive societies as hopelessly antiquated cultural relics, but instead as men and women in touch with the issues of the twentieth century, even as their message remained generally conservative and pride of place was consistently accorded to Chinese "truths."

What was really new was the organizational form of many of the redemptive societies: region- and even nation-wide societies that expanded to include tens of millions of people, mostly in the cities but to some extent in rural areas as well.[4] Redemptive societies were generally organized under national headquarters (*zongshe* 總社) and regional, provincial, or municipal offices that administered the "inner" and "outer" dimensions of society activities. The inner dimension generally involved some combination of spirit-writing and *qigong* healing or self-cultivation, practices that often originated in the Daoist *neidan* 内丹 tradition before being popularized by figures such as Jiang Weiqiao 蔣維喬 (1873–1958) in the 1920s. Parts of the inner dimension were secret, involving mantras or other codes or practices not shared with non-members. The outer dimension involved charitable activities and thus was thoroughly public. Best symbolized by the World Red Swastika Society (Shijie Hongwanzihui 世界紅卍字會), the philanthropic wing of the Daoyuan 道院 (School of the Dao), redemptive societies were major players in the fields of social reform and charity throughout the Republican period, making particular contributions during wartime. One group, the Wanguo daodehui, also built free schools for girls in

4 Some groups, like Tongshanshe, which existed prior to the Republican period, built on existing organization and membership. See Wang Chien-chuan (Wang Jianchuan), "An Exploration of the Early History of the Tongshanshe (1912–1945)," *Chinese Studies in History* 44, nos. 1–2 (2010/11): 121–131.

Manchuria in the 1920s and 1930s, a surprising innovation given the generally patriarchal tone of society teachings.[5]

It is not immediately obvious how or why redemptive societies grew so quickly. Formal religious organizations, generally subject to stricter state scrutiny, did *not* grow quickly during this period, and village religion was under intermittent attack as part of the ongoing campaign against superstition. Perhaps redemptive societies grew *because* other religions did not, or perhaps the growth of redemptive societies was a more general part of the growth of civil society in a rapidly changing and modernizing society. The goal of establishing national organizations was in any event a reflection of the nationalism of the age, and of the existence of a national religious market—created in part by the redemptive societies themselves. The initial expansion of redemptive societies in the Beiyang 北洋 period (1912–1927) may have been helped by the endorsement of the societies by certain militarists and government figures, for whom redemptive societies' claims to moral leadership may have been appealing. Yet the societies continued to grow, despite some setbacks, even after 1927 under GMD rule, despite the Nationalists' general distrust of the societies. The chaos of the wartime period probably stimulated society expansion, in some cases. The state was preoccupied with other concerns, philanthropy was much in demand, and the end of the world may well have seemed close at hand. Some groups wound up, of necessity, working with the forces of the Japanese occupation, which of course earned them the label "collaborators" once the war was over, a handy pretext justifying their suppression.

Redemptive societies also flourished as active participants in the rise of "print capitalism" in early twentieth-century China, another novelty in their organizational development.[6] Many societies became "textual machines," often establishing their own printing houses to publish spirit-writing texts, the master's teachings, society journals, and much more. The circulation of such texts surely fostered a spirit of regional and perhaps national identification among society members which likely did not exist under the dynasties. To the extent that societies came to be defined by mass media and market for religious literature, they perhaps came to cater to popular preferences even as they still sought to express the vision of a founding master.

Whatever the reasons for the rapid rise and expansion of redemptive societies, their history came to a rapid (temporary?) conclusion in the years

---

5 Melissa Inouye of the University of Auckland is currently completing a study of the Wanguo daodehui that pays particular attention to its apparent "feminism."

6 On this general topic, see Philip Clart and Gregory Adam Scott, eds., *Religious Publishing and Print Culture in Modern China: 1800–2012* (Boston: De Gruyter, 2015).

immediately following the establishment of the People's Republic. A campaign against the groups resulted in the arrest of more than 800,000 society leaders and public statements by some 13 million followers that they had cut their ties with the societies.[7] All of the conditions that had given rise to the redemptive societies during the Republican period were now in danger: freedom of movement, print capitalism, the growth of civil society. The national project was seized by a group, the Chinese Communist Party, which was jealous of any organization that might compete for loyalty or legitimacy. Most redemptive societies went into a slow decline in the Chinese diaspora, and only one, Yiguandao, managed to flourish after decades of suppression and harassment on Taiwan, finally becoming an accepted religion on the island after the lifting of martial law, as well as an important part of Chinese religious life elsewhere in the diaspora.[8] The continuing popularity of the Yiguandao, as well as the similarity of *qigong* groups to redemptive societies, suggests that redemptive societies, in one form or another, may well have a future as well as a past.

The present volume principally addresses one of the central issues of the redemptive society "field," that of texts. Needless to say, texts have long been a central feature of most if not all religious groups and activities in China (and elsewhere). Texts were central to spirit-writing cults and the late imperial sectarian tradition, two important antecedents to modern redemptive societies. Spirit-writing cults were an elite practice based in large measure on the literary skills of cult members; spirit-writing was a widespread practice in which deities communicated with the human realm through mediums who transcribed their texts in boxes of sand, at altars set up specifically for the purpose. Although technically illegal, the practice had been popular since the Song dynasty, and was widely used as a source of divination for personal use, as well as supplying texts for "morality books," collections of texts that were widely distributed throughout society in an effort to influence popular morality. Hence, texts and literacy were at the heart of spirit-writing cults. In sectarian traditions, texts played different roles, as elucidated by Barend ter Haar's typology developed in his chapter to the present volume: for some groups they had a more talismanic character, while others emphasized text study and recitation (see more below). As already mentioned, the spread of modern print technology and print capitalism to China in the early twentieth century had a major impact on Chinese

7 Shao Yong 邵雍, *Zhongguo huidaomen* 中國會道門 (Shanghai: Shanghai renmin chubanshe, 1997), 452–455.

8 Other redemptive societies remain functional but not as influential as Yiguandao. On Taiwan, the Tiandijiao 天帝教 is one such group. Other groups survive in the Chinese diaspora in Southeast Asia, one example of which is the Dejiao 德教.

religion, and on redemptive societies as the fastest growing part of Chinese religion during the Republican period.

What happens when religious groups can suddenly produce and distribute more texts than was previously possible, particularly when religion had been largely personalized and community-based to this point? Although it is easy to imagine that this would be a game-changer, the effects were probably gradual and limited in most cases, consisting mainly of changing the size of the imaginary playing field. For a charismatic master, or for a devoted lieutenant, the possibility of reaching new believers (new markets) at a distance, was surely electrifying, even if much work was required to identify those new believers. New believers might have been equally intrigued by the possibility of belonging to something larger than the local community. Imagining that his texts might be read by an audience beyond his devoted followers surely changed the nature of the texts a charismatic master might circulate. The need to recruit "staff" to produce the scriptures, journals, and pamphlets the new market required surely "professionalized" the process to a certain degree. A smart master would keep his eyes open for personnel who understood the market and knew how to make it grow.

The question of texts is central for Republican-period redemptive societies, as texts shaped their identities and fueled their rapid expansion, but our volume also examines contextual issues dealing with historical antecedents to Republican-period groups as well as the textual practices of redemptive societies in Vietnam.

Barend J. ter Haar opens the volume by establishing a historical backdrop for the following chapters; he provides a typology of pre-twentieth century popular religious movements according to the significance of texts in their organization and propagation. In a *tour de force* of late imperial religious movements, he makes a fundamental distinction between horizontally connected groups and vertically connected networks. In the former, religious texts play a much more central role than in the latter, as it is in this written form that knowledge is encoded and shared among the group. In vertically connected networks, by contrast, knowledge is primarily dispensed orally and piecemeal from teachers to disciples (i.e., vertically) and not made generally accessible (i.e., spread horizontally). Teachers may and usually do possess texts, but these are primarily "legitimating treasures." Their possession bolsters the teacher's authority, but they are not intended for general circulation. The knowledge ("lore") that is passed on from teachers to disciples in such networks typically consists of concrete ritual methods to address specific problems, such as healing and protection against evil spirits, and membership in the network is usually motivated by the desire to obtain such methods. Therefore, such networks typically do not form stable religious communities with a comprehensive program of cultivational and liturgical practices, as such a program is neither imparted by the teachers nor sought after by their disciples. Horizontally connected groups, on the other hand, have the potential for such community formation and usually possess written charters in the form of scriptures, precious scrolls, and liturgical manuals, which provide the doctrinal foundation for communal practice and are freely shared among the membership. Groups and networks are, of course, ideal types, and their features may merge in practice; however, as ideal types they emphasize two fundamentally different modes of generating and propagating religious knowledge which assign very different valance to sacred texts in the resulting social structures.

Against the late imperial historical background limned by chapter 1, Wang Chien-chuan's chapter addresses the fluid nature of sacred texts in an early Republican-period redemptive society, the Tongshanshe 同善社 (Society for Goodness), which had strong roots in the Xiantiandao 先天道 sectarian tradition of the Qing dynasty. Its charismatic leader Peng Huilong 彭迴龍 (1873–1950?) officially established the Tongshanshe as a separate religious organization in 1912 and gained legal recognition for it in 1917. Focused as it was on its charismatic founder, the movement did not at first produce any sacred scriptures of its own, but compiled various collections of Peng's sayings and treatises to be studied by its members. In addition, various widely available Confucian, Buddhist, Daoist, and Xiantiandao texts were given Peng's blessing, and some Tongshanshe-affiliated spirit-writing cults produced new texts of the morality book type. Up to now, scholars had assumed that the first formal scripture of the Tongshanshe, the *Liaodaojing* 了道經 (The Scripture of the Completion of the Way), did not appear until 1932, twenty years after the movement's founding. In his contribution to the present volume, the author picks up on references in pre-1932 Tongshanshe sources to the high importance of another scripture, the *Wanfojing* 萬佛經 (Ten Thousand Buddha Scripture), and seeks to determine its role and functions in the early Tongshanshe. Comparing several editions of the text, the author demonstrates that the earliest version, published 1925, contained a text produced probably by a Xiantiandao-affiliated group that evinced significant, but not complete overlap with Peng's teachings. A close reading of the subsequent editions allows the author to sketch the process through which this text was gradually appropriated by the Tongshanshe by adding references to Peng as a divine being and to his teachings. Also, new segments were added to the *Ten Thousand Buddha Scripture*, significantly expanding it in size and turning it into a Tongshanshe canonical scripture, which the organization spread through the distribution channels of the burgeoning publishing industry of the Republican period. The author traces this process of the creation of a corpus of canonical texts for a new religious movement in relation to various factors and events in its historical context, which included the political pressure faced by the Tongshanshe as well as efforts by other religious groups to propagate and strengthen the cult of the deity Guandi 關帝.

Fan Chun-wu's chapter on the textual modernization of the Daode xueshe 道德學社 (Moral Study Society) seeks to interrogate the received notion that Republican-period redemptive societies were mere conservative backlashes to the various challenges of Western modernity. While not denying the emphasis on traditional morality in founder Duan Zhengyuan's 段正元 (1864–1940) scriptures, the author notes that Duan also discusses the theory of evolution, notions of progress, and of women's rights, suggesting the hybridity of the society's message. And the author focuses particularly on the "imagined community" of Daode xueshe practitioners through a detailed discussion of the group's engagement in publishing, photography, and the development of visual aspects of group practice. One of the author's key arguments, which largely echoes those of other chapters treating the Republican period, is the extent to which the narrow, secretive atmosphere that characterized salvationist movements under the dynasties has been left behind. Of course, part of this was the change in the legal environment, and part was the relative disorganization of the Beiyang government, both of which accorded considerable space to these movements. But the author notes that this change was more important: transmission of knowledge in traditional salvationist societies was generally a secret exchange between a master and a small number of select disciples. "Precious scrolls," which did circulate more widely, were still closely guarded for their sacred (and sometimes dangerous) character. The publishing activities of the Daode xueshe—and other redemptive societies—exploded these traditional practices by circulating their texts widely and without restriction; anyone who could afford the subscription could obtain what had heretofore been "secret knowledge," suggesting the evolution of a very different "religious economy."

At the same time, the widespread use of photographs—generally of Master Duan Zhengyuan himself—personalized what might have been an impersonal market relationship (the practitioner who receives a Daode xueshe journal in the mail), establishing a modern, mediatized charisma made possible by use of modern technologies. For example, followers were directed to make use of Duan's images in their ritual practice and meditation. In addition, photographs were used to illustrate psychic phenomena in a manner similar to what chapter 4 found for the Lingxuehui (see below), as well as to signal the Master's transformations over time. In this sense, photographs can be considered a new "religious text" produced by new technological possibilities. Such visual elements were further developed in the memorial garden set up after Duan's death in 1940. Chapter 3 argues that all of this constitutes a "modernization" of the salvational tradition.

Matthias Schumann's essay on science and spirit-writing examines the case of the Lingxuehui 靈學會 (Spiritualist Society) in early Republican-period Shanghai, illustrating the multiple impacts of a new global "scientific spirituality" on Chinese elites, particularly in Shanghai. This scientific spirituality, prominent examples of which include Theosophy, New Thought, and psychical research, arose in Europe and the United States as alternatives to the burgeoning scientific materialism of the modern era. In China, as in the West, scientific spirituality contained both a "conservative" assertion of the importance of the spirit as well as a "modern" embrace of science as providing new evidence of the validity and utility of spiritual pursuits. The goal was to establish a "spiritual science" that would prove the existence of the soul and spiritual beings, thus providing a "source for the moral rectification of humanity," seen as particularly pertinent in the wake of the horrors of the First World War. For Chinese practitioners, the concept of *ling*, or spiritual energy, was thus understood *both* as part of traditional Chinese discourses on the resonance between the human and divine spheres based on the principle of "stimulus and response," *and* as the object of study in such modern disciplines as psychology and psychical research. On a more practical level, the embrace of science also shielded practitioners from charges of engaging in superstition.

Redemptive societies have often been portrayed as middle-brow, conservative reactions to the iconoclasm and radicalism of the May Fourth movement, vehicles for the "lost virtues" of Confucianism or traditional "Chineseness" in general. The case of the Lingxuehui, however, reveals how misleading, or incomplete, this characterization can be. Lingxuehui activists were well-educated, wealthy (membership was expensive), and well-informed of scientific developments, and consciously sought to imitate the activities of spiritualist societies elsewhere in the world. Defense of a unique "Chineseness" seems not to have been a particular concern; indeed, Lingxuehui activists hoped that their activities would be part of an innovative world-wide movement.

Yet the specific nature of the spiritualist practices of the Lingxuehui led it back into the intricacies of Chinese religious culture. Many of the activities of the Lingxuehui revolved around spirit-writing, which the Lingxuehui sought to "scientize" by eliminating discussion of personal matters (health, wealth, etc.) and concentrating on higher-order concerns such as morality and philosophy. Whatever the scientific validity of this approach, it alienated those who had sought guidance for personal concerns in spirit-writing, and thus limited the potential of the Lingxuehui as a vehicle for mass cultural change. Indeed, the Lingxuehui is not generally included in lists of Republican-period redemptive societies, at least in part because of its narrow social base.

David Ownby's chapter on Xiao Changming 蕭昌明 (1897–1943) and Li Yujie 李玉階 (1901–1994) explores similar themes as chapter 4 from a somewhat different perspective, examining Li's efforts to modernize and "scientize" the "White Lotus" scriptures of his master, Xiao Changming. Xiao Changming was the founder of the Tiandejiao 天德教, an important redemptive society from the early Republican period. Xiao's persona was that of a traditional holy man: he presented himself—at least in some contexts—as a god returned from heaven to save the world as the apocalypse approached. His scriptures—the primary focus of the author's analysis—can be divided into three categories. The first is what the author calls a "foundational public text," a text meant to establish a group's basic "brand." Xiao's foundational public text was entitled *The Compass of Life*, and consisted of Xiao's personal glosses on the twenty Chinese characters he considered to be at the center of China's civilization and his own spiritual teachings. In this text, Xiao called on Chinese to return to traditional morality so as to divert the coming apocalypse (with much more emphasis on morality than on the apocalypse). The text, composed in fairly formal classical Chinese, does not seek to innovate, but rather to return China to the proper path. The second category of texts are those designed to recruit followers for practical reasons. These writings emphasize Xiao's skills at spiritual healing and offer explanations for those powers, which illustrate Xiao's awareness of contemporary discourses on biomedicine and on superstition. The third category of texts are those offered in secret, to proclaimed followers, in which Xiao reveals his self-identification as a god and his embrace of "White Lotus" figures and vocabulary. Together, the texts reveal much about the politics of building a redemptive society in Republican-period China.

Li Yujie was a very different figure from Xiao Changming. He received a modern education, served as student leader in the Shanghai May Fourth movement, joined the GMD, and ultimately worked as a technocrat in the Ministry of Finance. Yet he took Xiao Changming as his master at their first meeting, subsequently became one of Xiao's most important lieutenants, and, ultimately, Xiao's successor after his death in 1943. Prompted by the urgings of Tiandejiao gods, Li had abandoned his government post and retired from Xi'an to Huashan, the Daoist sacred mountain, in 1937, where he remained until the end of the Sino-Japanese War. While there, with the help of disciple Huang Zhenxia 黄震遐 (1909–1974), he set out to write a new "foundational public text" for the society. This text, ultimately entitled *The Ultimate Realm* in its English translation, sought to purge "White Lotus" elements and replace them with a new scientific discourse that, in ways that recall the activities of the Lingxuehui, provided material explanations for many of the beliefs and practices at the core of the Tiandejiao.

Li's embrace of Xiao's teachings, and his efforts to rewrite the group's public foundational text, reveal the attraction, to at least a part of the educated members of Republican-period society, of both the salvationist ideas and practices associated with the White Lotus, and of scientific discourse. For Li Yujie, there was no contradiction between the two.

The next two chapters expand the present volume's purview beyond China to Vietnam and the links of Vietnamese religious movements of the nineteenth and twentieth centuries with Chinese texts and contexts. Both chapters seek to uncover the Chinese textual origins of Vietnamese religious movements and their assimilation in and into a Vietnamese cultural context of the nineteenth and early twentieth century characterized by folk-Buddhist religiosity and by a colonial situation engendering both violent resistance and cultural influences.

The Vietnamese religious movement studied by Chung Yun-Ying exemplifies the merging of the ideal types defined in chapter 1: The Tứ Ân Hiếu Nghĩa is clearly a horizontally connected organization with a substantial body of sacred texts, but at the same time these texts are divided into inner and outer corpora, with 47 generally available texts and 36 texts exclusively available to the movement's leadership. The main analytical thrust of Chung's chapter, however, is directed not at the linkage of texts and power, but at the Tứ Ân Hiếu Nghĩa's use and adaptation of Chinese religious texts, in other words: the translingual practice that also stands at the center of David Palmer and Jeremy Jammes' work in chapter 7.

Having been founded in the second half of the nineteenth century, before the adoption of the modern romanized Vietnamese script, the Tứ Ân Hiếu Nghĩa's corpora of sacred texts are composed in Chinese script, blurring at first sight the boundary lines between Chinese and Vietnamese texts. The close reading implemented by chapter 6, however, reveals the Vietnamese cultural contextualization of Chinese sacred texts by means of framing them with Buddhist liturgical formulae and supplementing them with texts newly produced by the Tứ Ân Hiếu Nghĩa founding figures. The resulting textual hybrids represent a remarkable localization of Chinese scriptural traditions.

This phenomenon is also addressed by David A. Palmer and Jeremy Jammes in chapter 7 in their study of a key sacred text of the Cao Đài movement, the *Đại Thừa Chơn Giáo* or "La Bible du Grand Cycle de l'Ésotérisme," as it was rendered into French. This text was revealed by means of spirit-writing from 1936 until 1950, with most portions (51 out of 73) composed in late 1936. The original revelations were given in romanized Vietnamese; the standard edition, dated 1950, is bilingual, juxtaposing the Vietnamese text with a French translation. Thus, simply by virtue of its bilinguality this is obviously a translingual text, and the authors devote much attention to the modes of translation from Vietnamese into a French idiom dominated by Catholic and Spiritualist terminology. However, the *Đại Thừa Chơn Giáo* is translingual in yet another way, one less immediately noticeable. By means of the experimental (and innovative) procedure of transposing the romanized Vietnamese into Chinese characters, the authors demonstrate the presence of a conceptual framework derived from texts of the Xiantiandao tradition that became influential in Vietnam in the nineteenth century. This Cao Đài scripture thus is the product of serial and highly complex contextualizations of originally Chinese religious language: first into romanized Vietnamese, which obscured the original Xiantiandao frame of reference, and then by translation into French, which involved a thorough rephrasing in Catholic and Spiritualist terms.

While the research collected in this volume is primarily historical in orientation, Philip Clart's chapter rounds it off with a methodological reflection on the ethnographic context of religious texts. Drawing on his studies of Taiwanese spirit-writing cults, he argues that since the religious identity of spirit-writing cults is based on and their ritual activities revolve around the production of texts, the study of these groups requires a unique combination of philological and ethnographic approaches. Only this combination allows us to place spirit-writing texts in their ritual and institutional contexts, without which an accurate reading of the texts or of the groups that produce them is not possible. He illustrates this argument with reference to the revelation of sacred scriptures (*jing* 經) by a network of interrelated cult groups in central Taiwan from the 1970s to the early 2000s, concluding that the philological analysis of such scriptures produces insights into systematized belief systems, which in turn can help formulate ethnographic questions and approaches for the investigation of the groups that generate the texts in question. In return, the ethnographic study of the groups and individuals involved in the production of the texts produces contextual knowledge to help interpret the texts and gauge their role and impact in the group.

The present volume thus takes a fresh angle from which to assess the contribution of redemptive societies to the complex evolution of religious life in modern and contemporary China and Vietnam, by foregrounding questions of the production, circulation, appropriation, and utilization of texts by redemptive societies.

Texts were a major feature of virtually all redemptive societies, and were produced via spirit-writing, other modes of revelation, composition by group leaders, photography, and transcription of oral lectures. Often seen as sacred writings that legitimize authority and guide individual and collective action, many texts have been carefully preserved by redemptive societies (some of which have their own libraries, "archives," and publishing houses). Spiritually authoritative or sacred texts play a number of crucial roles within redemptive societies. First and foremost, of course, they record and codify a redemptive society's beliefs and rituals and are thus key sources for the analysis of these aspects of a specific religious system. As obvious as this may appear, such analyses have not been carried out for many of these texts, which more commonly have served as quarries in which to collect data on the organizational structure or social and political history of a particular group. Research that takes the doctrinal systems encoded in modern redemptive societies' sacred texts seriously has been fairly rare.

In addition to the exegesis and critical study of the production, adaptation, and reception of often newly revealed sacred texts in redemptive societies, the perspective espoused in the present volume includes within its purview issues such as the problem of establishing sacred authority for new scriptures (canon formation), the creation and use of sacred texts as cultural capital, and the reflections of social, cultural, and more specifically religious changes in redemptive societies' sacred texts. In other words, in addition to taking this vast, but also vastly understudied, textual tradition seriously as a carrier of complex religious doctrine, we have also sought to embed it within the sociocultural context provided by the redemptive society that produced the texts, other societies that adopted them (because such texts often spread beyond the group of origin), as well as within the field of tension between religious groups and society at large. We hope that the present volume will thereby make a significant contribution to the study of religion in modern Chinese (and Vietnamese) societies, and specifically to the study of redemptive societies as religious movements rather than mere epiphenomena of the social history of the twentieth century.

Acknowledgments

The research for the chapters in this volume was completed as part of the project "Text and Context: Redemptive Societies in the History of Religions of Modern and Contemporary China," which was funded by the Chiang Ching-kuo Foundation for International Scholarly Exchange from 2010 to 2014 (research grant #RG008-U-09). We express our sincere gratitude for this support, without which this collection would not have been possible.

A special thank you goes to Ms. Chen Ling 陳玲 of Leipzig University; as editorial assistant, she caught and corrected many mistakes, big and small. Any remaining errors are, of course, strictly the responsibility of the editors and authors of this volume.

Bibliography

Broy, Nikolas. "Syncretic Sects and Redemptive Societies." *Review of Religion and Chinese Society* 2, no. 2 (2015): 145–185.

Clart, Philip, and Gregory Adam Scott, eds. *Religious Publishing and Print Culture in Modern China: 1800–2012*. Boston: De Gruyter, 2015.

Goossaert, Vincent, and David A. Palmer. *The Religious Question in Modern China*. Chicago: University of Chicago Press, 2011.

Ownby, David. "Redemptive Societies in the Twentieth Century." In *Modern Chinese Religion II: 1850–2015*, edited by Vincent Goossaert, Jan Kiely, and John Lagerwey, 685–727. Leiden: Brill, 2016.

Palmer, David A. "Chinese Redemptive Societies and Salvationist Religion: Historical Phenomenon or Sociological Category?" *Minsu quyi* 民俗曲藝, no. 172 (2011): 21–72.

Shao Yong 邵雍. *Zhongguo huidaomen* 中國會道門. Shanghai: Shanghai renmin chubanshe, 1997.

Wang Chien-chuan (Wang Jianchuan). "An Exploration of the Early History of the Tongshanshe (1912–1945)." *Chinese Studies in History* 44, nos. 1–2 (2010/11): 121–131.

CHAPTER 1

Giving Believers Back Their Voice: Agency and Heresy in Late Imperial China

Barend J. ter Haar

1 Preliminary Remarks

New religious groups and networks, terms I will attempt to define further below, are conventionally seen as a separate phenomenon in traditional and contemporary China, to be studied by social historians instead of historians of religion. In other words, they are perceived to be independent of mainstream Buddhist and Daoist traditions, and not studied by specialists in the latter fields. Reasons for this are manifold, but one is undoubtedly that their beliefs are deemed to be deviations from "real" Buddhism and Daoism and thus not very sophisticated. Moreover, because these groups are still largely prohibited today on the Chinese mainland and sometimes still actively persecuted, crucial fieldwork is practically impossible, making it difficult to get to know them really well. The situation in Hong Kong is much more open, although such groups as the Falun Gong 法輪功 still occupy a socially and politically sensitive position in local society. On Taiwan there is total freedom nowadays, although that also changes the social context in which these groups operate and makes the case less relevant for understanding the situation on the mainland.

The historiography of these groups and networks, including the above neglect by scholars specializing in China's "great traditions," is still influenced directly or indirectly by concepts such as heresy, heterodoxy, or "evil" as in "evil cults" (*xiejiao* 邪教). This type of "othering" vocabulary, which includes variants on the term "popular," takes away the agency of such groups and networks by adopting the state's outside and derogatory perspective as a point of departure. While the perspective of the state is relevant, since it shaped so much of our own point of view and heavily influenced the histories of these groups and networks, it is our task as scholars to give believers back their voice as much as is possible.

Now that we have finally abandoned the old label White Lotus Teachings (Bailianjiao 白蓮教), as well as the various associated stereotypes and

 | DOI:10.1163/9789004424166_003

problematic historiography, we can also explore more easily the many links of these labeled groups and networks with other religious groups and traditions.[1] Such a task would be worthy of a substantial monograph, but here I can only argue a few basic points. The core of this argument will be that these groups and networks attempted to regain religious agency for lay people, but were ultimately much closer to Buddhist and Daoist traditions than is commonly realized, whether the observers are late imperial state officials or modern academics. These groups and networks were examples of local creativity and an ongoing interest on the part of ordinary people in developing their own religious beliefs and practices. Their primary intention was not to diverge from mainstream religious culture, although sometimes this may have happened—whether they were aware of it or not. In this respect I diverge substantially from the standard work on these groups by Hubert Seiwert, which still treats them as an independent phenomenon, however sympathetic he may be in his analysis.[2]

An important aspect of most of these groups and networks was the production and transmission of their own religious texts and/or narrative and ritual materials, although the concrete place of these texts in different groups and networks diverged considerably. This was a major development in Chinese religious history, which I would date back to the second half of the sixteenth century. People had been publishing commented versions of Buddhist or Daoist scriptures, and they had been creating new scriptures in those traditions as well. Usually they maintained the format of a revelation by a divine being (e.g. the Buddha or an immortal) or claimed that the texts had been composed by such beings through spirit-writing. The figure of Luo Qing 羅清 (fl. ca. 1500–1520) is often placed at the beginning of the development of new religious groups and networks in the late imperial period. In some ways this is correct, for he served as a source of inspiration for some of them and he is a good example of someone with low social status outside a monastic context claiming the ability to explain the Buddhist teachings. In terms of format, his

1 Barend J. ter Haar, *The White Lotus Teachings in Chinese Religious History* (Leiden: Brill, 1992). For a Chinese language summary, see Paul Katz (Kang Bao 康豹), "Xifang xuejie yanjiu Zhongguo shequ zongjiao chuantong de zhuyao dongtai 西方學界研究中國社區宗教傳統的主要動態," *Wenshizhe* 文史哲, no. 310 (2009): 58–74. In addition, we can also get a better understanding of the mechanics of labelling in Junqing Wu, *Mandarins and Heretics: The Construction of "Heresy" in Chinese State Discourse* (Leiden: Brill, 2017).

2 Hubert Seiwert (with the help of Ma Xisha), *Popular Religious Movements and Heterodox Sects in Chinese History* (Leiden: Brill, 2003).

famous *Five Books in Six Volumes* 五部六冊 are primarily a collection of quotations from mostly Buddhist sources, provided with loose commentary by Luo Qing on how to practice or not practice the Buddhist way.[3] Luo does not claim to have a new message or mythology, but he innovates in not following the traditional format of commenting line by line. Instead his comments are loosely organized, as if they derive from oral lectures.

The new religious groups and networks that arose during the following centuries did not really follow this format of quotation and loose commentary. This is not to say that they or their adherents necessarily rejected more traditional Buddhist or Daoist texts, but they certainly created their own texts, with their own mythologies and even ritual practices, without the traditional claim of being a revelation by the Buddha or some Daoist divine entity. The practice of spirit-writing also took off during roughly the same period, but actual religious groups inspired by spirit-written texts seem to have appeared only in the late nineteenth century. These new texts and their interpretations were transmitted independently of the traditional ordained religious experts of the written word, such as Classicist (*ru* 儒) teachers (through the examination system) or Buddhist and Daoist monks and priests (through elaborate, state recognized ordination rituals). Often the leading figures in these new groups and networks were men, and sometimes women, of relatively low social backgrounds.

The most important of these new texts were the so-called Precious Scrolls (*baojuan* 寶卷), containing religious narratives, often even personal testimonies of faith, written in a mixture of rhymed passages and prose, suitable for oral performance.[4] Access to these texts did not necessarily imply literacy and even when people were literate, specific levels of literacy will have differed considerably. Whilst important, this article will not deal with issues of literacy. Instead I will use the term "textuality" to discuss the different degrees of access to and uses of texts. Although someone will need to be literate at one point in the chain of the creation and transmission of texts, much of the transmission process can take place orally, whether through literal repetition (rote learning) or by means of summaries and then further interpretation.

3 Barend J. ter Haar, "Patriarch Luo as a Writer and Reader: Speculating about the Creative Process behind the Five Books in Six Volumes," *Sungkyun Journal of East Asian Studies* 15, no. 1 (2015): 21–44.

4 Daniel L. Overmyer, *Precious Volumes: An Introduction to Chinese Sectarian Scriptures from the Sixteenth and Seventeenth Centuries* (Cambridge, MA: Harvard University Asia Center, 1999).

2 A Typology

When we compare some of the more prominent late Ming to mid-Qing new religious groups and networks which are traditionally labeled as heretical, we can create a typology which reveals interesting differences with respect to the coherence of these groups synchronically and diachronically. As it turns out, this also correlates with different intensities in using written texts. Moreover, the beliefs and practices, as well as the regional distribution of these groups and networks vary considerably. Especially in terms of their beliefs and practices, it makes little sense to discuss them as a single socio-religious phenomenon. Instead, they should be studied in conjunction with what we are accustomed to calling Buddhist and Daoist traditions. The present study still limits itself to those groups that are conventionally grouped together, in order to make some methodological points and in the hope that others will then continue and broaden the proposed analysis. The following table presents the small subset of different groups and networks that I will discuss in more detail below. Contrary to a common assumption, these groups do not necessarily share the belief in the Unborn Venerable Mother (Wusheng laomu 無生老母) that is often singled out as an essential characteristic of late imperial new religious groups, and most of them certainly do not have an acutely messianic or millenarian message. Indeed, these groups and networks differed considerably among each other in terms of actual beliefs and practices. Another important distinction is at the level of social organization. On the one hand, there were groups with strong horizontal connections between the different members of a local group, who would usually meet regularly and form integrated local groups. Alternatively, there were networks that primarily had vertical connections with a teacher and few connections between the other members (or pupils). In such networks, there was far less mutual control of the consistency of people's beliefs and practices, and we regularly see the phenomenon of individuals shopping around for additional religious and ritual lore. In both types of groups, texts might circulate, but their actual relevance and usage differed considerably, as I will explain below.

TABLE 1 Summary of late Ming-Qing new religious groups and networks[5]

	Group or network	Macro region	Type of texts	Comments
	Horizontally connected			
1	Non-Action Teachings 無為教	Lower Yangzi region, Fujian (including Taiwan), Jiangxi	selection of Buddhist quotations, short scriptures, liturgical texts	self-perception as Chan Buddhist, devotionalist worship of Amitābha and a strictly Buddhist liturgy, sense of supra-local identity and organized in independent vegetarian halls
2	Three-in-One Teachings 三一教	central coastal Fujian, Southeast Asia	broad range of liturgical texts and scriptures	strong inner cultivation (~Daoist) core, but self-perception as syncretic combination of Classicism, Buddhism and Daoism; strongly local identity and organized in independent local halls
3	Christianity 天主教	Nationwide	scripture and liturgical texts	received according to existing local religious models, sense of international identity and organized in underground churches, initially more public
4	Broad Yang Teachings 弘陽教	Northern China (esp. capital region, Hebei)	Precious Scrolls and liturgical texts	Buddhist inspired message, sense of shared supra-local identity

5 The summary is based on the literature quoted later in this essay. Seiwert, *Popular Religious Movements and Heterodox Sects in Chinese History*, is the most important secondary reference in a Western language.

TABLE 1 Summary of late Ming-Qing new religious groups and networks (*cont.*)

	Group or network	Macro region	Type of texts	Comments
	Horizontally connected			
5	Way of Yellow Heaven 黄天道	Northern China (Shanxi, Shaanxi)	Precious Scrolls	Daoist cultivation techniques and messianic soteriology, in a Buddhist institutional context
	Vertically connected			
6	Wang 王 family network	Northern China	Precious Scrolls (not transmitted downwards)	inner cultivation techniques; teachers possess scriptures with messianic soteriology, but no messianic message; largely vertical ties to the teacher and no separate (impersonal) institutions
7	Liu 劉 family network	Northern China		inner cultivation techniques; largely vertical ties to the teacher and no separate (impersonal) institutions
8	demonological messianic paradigm	China as a whole	poems and abstracts from the *Dragon Flower Sutra* 龍華經 (a Precious Scroll) as well as other scriptures	network always ad hoc, temporary and local, based on oral transmission and only partly on a written corpus

The above selection is largely based on the perceived prominence of these groups in the late imperial repertoire of new religious groups and networks, which is a function of the persecution record. As far as I am able to establish, the various criteria that we are interested in here did not play a role in these persecutions. Whether or not a group or network was persecuted depended mostly on contingent factors, such as their location in important nodes of the communication and transport networks (the Grand Canal in particular) and locations of military importance (such as the northern border). Based on this brief survey, we can already make some preliminary observations to be elaborated on in later sections.

One striking aspect of these groups and networks is that almost all of them, with the exception of Christianity, are limited to a single region or group of regions, which is usually characterized by a single language variant. This no doubt reflects the importance of the oral dimension of a religious group, which may no longer be apparent to us, but would have mattered a great deal in traditional China. All written texts would have needed to be accompanied by oral explanations, quite apart from the larger ritual contexts within which the use of these texts will be embedded. Religious practices generally differed according to local language variation, traditionally referred to as dialects.[6] We will find a similar correlation in the groups and networks discussed below. While this oral dimension is now largely lost to us, it is here that we find the strongest differences between the groups and networks under consideration.

Generally speaking, groups with a strong horizontal integration are much more prominent in southern China than in the north. The Non-Action Teachings as well as the Three-in-One Teachings appear to have survived over the course of the late imperial period, reappearing as well-established groups by the Republican period. Both were active exclusively in southern China. The Three-in-One Teachings remained limited to regions in which the Putian 莆田 (central Fujianese) language variant was spoken and only spread elsewhere (for instance South-East Asia) when speakers migrated. It always remained an ethnic or transnational religious culture. Interestingly, the Non-Action Teachings spread more widely, including into the Putian region where the Three-in-One Teachings flourished, though in the latter region, the Non-Action Teachings ultimately were unable to compete successfully.

6 In Barend J ter Haar, *Ritual and Mythology of the Chinese Triads: Creating an Identity* (Leiden: Brill, 1998), I discuss a similar case in which the same ritual practices and quasi-historical narratives were expressed differently according to the local languages of southern China. The same certainly appears to be true of temple cults and possible even of local Buddhist and Daoist ritual traditions.

The Non-Action Teachings became one of the few late imperial religious movements that were able to cross ethnic boundaries (specifically regions where Wu 吳, Fujianese, Gan 贛, and Hakka 客家 language variants were spoken), but it never moved into regions speaking Mandarin language variants and it never moved to South-East Asia, despite considerable migration of people from Southern Fujian. This may have reflected its origins in Northern Fujian and Southern Zhejiang, which were not areas of international migration at the time.[7] The only group that successfully crossed ethnic and language borders all over China was the imported tradition of Christianity, which was never tied to any specific ethnic identity from its arrival into China in the very late sixteenth century.[8] In the north, only the Broad Yang Teachings appears to have had a stronger horizontal integration that allowed it to survive over a longer time period until today, but it always remained limited to the eastern part of the Mandarin speaking north.

The relative absence of strong horizontal organizations in northern China is possibly the result of the weaker market economy and the resulting paucity of horizontal ties beyond local social units. But it could also be explained by the vagaries of Qing persecutions that appear to have been more severe in the north due to the occurrence of several religiously co-inspired rebellions, such as the Wang Lun 王倫 rebellion of 1774 and the Eight Trigram rebellion of 1813. Apart from the Broad Yang teachings, the obvious exception again is Christianity, where for instance the recent work of Henrietta Harrison has demonstrated that it was quite capable of surviving locally as an integrated coherent community in isolated places. All of these horizontally integrated groups, including Christianity, were characterized by an abundance of written texts that played an important role in liturgical practice and were available to all adherents. This was irrespective of the fact that many of them would not have been able to understand them fully.

Most teacher-pupil networks in our sample were northern, especially those with stronger vertical binding. By vertical integration I refer to the connections between a teacher and his pupils, with the teacher entirely in control of the religious lore and usually limiting its transmission downwards. In networks, differential degrees of access to the teacher's lore was a treasure that yielded status and income; mere possession of lore already provided

7 The Qingtian 青田 and neighboring Wenzhou 溫州 regions of Southern Zhejiang would be important migration regions in the twentieth century, for instance to Europe, but I have been unable to find traces of the movement outside of China.

8 It is of course possible that there existed regional differences within Chinese Christianity, causing divisions and making it difficult to cooperate cross-regionally. I will not explore this in this contribution.

ritual power to the pupils. In these networks this lore was ultimately based on written texts, but such texts were not shared and functioned mostly as a legitimating treasure. As far as we can tell on the basis of the archival evidence, ordinary members certainly did not have access to these resources and even teachers did not make much use of them. As a result, studying these networks through the contents of their written texts, rather than the actual lore that was being transmitted and the concrete ways in which it was being used, creates a significant distortion in our understanding of the networks as a socio-religious phenomenon.

These networks still differed quite fundamentally from the common hiring of ritual specialists, since the pupils in the network obtained the ability to directly influence their own fates with the lore that they had acquired. I see these networks as a form of ritual self-help with only a minor role for written texts. As such they were quite similar to other forms of ritual self-help such as exorcist amulets, small protective rituals, and so forth. In vertical networks, horizontal ties between pupils would be extremely limited, since it was not about collective religious action, but about obtaining ritual knowledge.

Thus, some form of texts was available in each of these groups and networks, but their role differed to such an extent that they should be treated as substantially different religious phenomena from a typological perspective. In horizontally oriented groups there was no ultimate control by a teacher over the religious lore of the group and all members could obtain the complete body of knowledge. A transfer of money was involved, but in the usual manner of gifts that accompany the establishment of social relations in late imperial China. All transfer of knowledge in traditional China, or for that matter in any society, involved some form of exchange, which we may label as a gift (as it would have been in traditional China), a payment (for instance to one's teacher), or tithes (out of which teaching may be funded).[9] In vertically oriented networks the teacher controlled the lore and the main aim was not transmission of a core text or a core religious narrative, but only of a small body of ritual with concrete benefits. It is only in our final example of a religious network that we find the transmission of lore that could be interpreted in a messianic or millenarian way, although this was not necessarily or even often the case. Even in this latter network, whatever texts were available remained in the background as a legitimizing treasure rather than a resource that was continually drawn upon.

A second observation that we can make on the basis of the above table is that the religious beliefs and practices of these groups differed considerably, indeed far more than is often assumed. In addition, as I will discuss in more detail further below, the same ideas might be contextualized very differently in

9 See also my discussion in *Ritual and Mythology of the Chinese Triads*, 420–424.

the various groups and networks. Knowledge that was potentially available on a textual level to the teachers through their possession of sacred books was by no means necessarily relevant on a lower level—nor is it clear to what extent the teachers themselves did very much with this knowledge. This is quite clear for messianic beliefs and the story of the myth of the Unborn Venerable Mother, which usually was not transmitted beyond the level of the teacher. It is impossible to deduce the beliefs of individual members from the overall body of religious lore available at some level in such a network. Therefore, we should always attempt to address the differing degrees of reception of beliefs and practices within the network as a whole. Although the Qing archival record is by no means perfect, it does allow some interesting conclusions in this respect.

In understanding late imperial religious groups and networks, the contribution by Thomas Dubois on the post-1976 situation in Cang 滄 County near Tianjin is especially salient, when he argues that participants in the groups and networks that he studied saw their relationships largely in terms of practical needs and benefits, and certainly not in doctrinal and/or mythological terms. DuBois stresses the local nature of new religious groups, even if they come in from elsewhere, since they are then interpreted in terms of local needs and the local availability (or absence) of other religious resources.[10] An example of this absence would be the relative weakness of Buddhist monastic institutions in northern China.[11] In other words, on a local level and in the eyes of most people, following certain teachers and joining certain groups usually did not primarily mean a doctrinal choice. Instead of making doctrinal choices, people "joined," or maybe better "followed" and "enlisted," because of the efficacy or charisma, i.e., the perceived personal attraction of a teacher, and/or a body of texts, and/or some kind of ritual lore. Such decisions were eminently individual and local, based on people's respective social and religious contexts, rather than a larger theological or political agenda.

In some ways, my analysis of horizontally integrated groups and vertically structured networks takes up to the binary typology proposed by Susan Naquin in her important 1985 article.[12] She divided the overall spectrum of persecuted groups in sutra recitation groups and meditational (in my terminology

10 Thomas DuBois, *The Sacred Village: Social Change and Religious Life in Rural North China* (Honolulu: University of Hawai'i Press, 2005), 187–195.

11 DuBois, *The Sacred Village*, 86–105. Barend J. ter Haar, "State and Samgha in the Qing Period: A New Look at Old Figures," in *The Middle Kingdom and the Dharma Wheel: Aspects of the Relationship Between the Buddhist Samgha and the State in Chinese History*, ed. Thomas Jülch (Brill: Leiden, 2016), 379–408.

12 Susan Naquin, "The Transmission of White Lotus Sectarianism in Late Imperial China," in *Popular Culture in Late Imperial China*, ed. David Johnson, Andrew T. Nathan, and Evelyn S. Rawski (Berkeley: University of California Press, 1985), 255–291.

"cultivational") groups, but still assumed a shared body of religious practices, ideas, and mythology. With the growth of our knowledge about these groups over the past decades, it is becoming clear that they involve very distinct types of beliefs and practices, each of which had a different geographical distribution and different contents. Even their internal social structures differed considerably. Furthermore, the actual religious lore or mythological narratives available at a lower level of vertically structured teacher-pupil networks in particular was quite limited. Thus, people joined the Non-Action Teachings to become lay Buddhists, with some expectation of concrete benefits as well as long term religious aims, but they joined the Broad Yang Teachings, as well as the Wang and Liu networks, largely with the purpose of finding some form of healing. As such, the differences with other Buddhist and Daoist forms of religious activity were very limited from a local perspective. An updated version of Naquin's typology would have to cover a much broader set of religious groups, networks, and individual teachers. Moreover, it would need to distinguish more clearly between different levels of command of narrative and ritual lore, as well as different forms of access to textuality and variations in internal structure.

A final observation that we can make on these groups, although not directly following from the table above, is that neither horizontal and more textual groups, nor vertical and more oral networks were frequently engaged in violent or rebellious activities. Since this was a major concern of the state, our sources were nonetheless largely produced in that context, creating a severe distortion of our knowledge of such groups and networks. Even when some of them did get involved in such activities, they were usually drawn into it by relative newcomers to their networks and by no means wholeheartedly. Indeed, the situation was not so different from the involvement in such activities of Buddhist monks and Daoist priests, or other kinds of local people with some kind of ritual and/or textual expertise. As I have already observed, the chief concern of people who joined these groups and networks was to improve their lives by direct contact with and possession of some form of narrative and/or merely ritual lore.

3 New Religious Groups

In the following subsections I will follow each of the above groups and networks in more detail, to elaborate on some of the points already summarized above. The most important of the new religious groups that appeared during the late Ming was the Non-Action Teachings that came into being sometime in the second half of the sixteenth century in the south of the Lower Yangzi region and the north of Fujian.[13] It certainly had some beliefs and practices in which they differed from the larger religious environment, such as their rejection of the separate worship of ancestors, a skeptical attitude towards statues and other external aids of worship, and the practice of fairly simple rituals by the adherents themselves. They practiced the Three Refuges and Five Precepts, just like any other activist lay Buddhist. In many ways, their practice could be described as going back to the basics of religious life, without depending on ritual experts outside of their group and without unnecessary frills—which would have been forms of attachment, although they do not explicitly make that point. They saw themselves as inheriting the mantle of Chan Buddhism, and practiced their own form of the Transmission Outside the Teachings. They promised that those who joined would be guaranteed registration in the Dragon Flower Assemblies of Maitreya, which seem to have been rather similar to the Pure Land of Amitābha, rather than messianic gatherings that take place in the imminent and concrete future. Indeed, Amitābha is mentioned far more frequently in their texts than Maitreya. In its early charismatic phase, individual teachers still mattered a great deal. Typically, they were of an ordinary social background, from the soldier and mythical patriarch Luo Qing 羅清 to the former pupil of a silver smith Ying Wenyu 應文宇 and the peddler Yao Ji'nan 姚繼南. Yao's grave became a pilgrimage destination for adherents and his descendants continued to serve as patriarchs well into the twentieth century.

The group developed a legitimation myth that claimed recognition by the Zhengde 正德 Emperor in the early sixteenth century, followed by a Proclamation in which the Kangxi 康熙 Emperor supposedly granted freedom of religious practice to their group. Local groups of this tradition sometimes actively pressured the local government to set free recently arrested members, though not always with the hoped-for positive effect. Nothing illustrates their own sense of agency more than these kinds of activities to defend their beliefs as rights granted and supported by the imperial state.

The group did not act against the state at any point, but ignored it as much as possible or tried to enlist it to its own advantage. One of the few violent incidents in which the movement was involved dates to 1748 and was an attempt by some local halls in northern Fujian to spring their leader free from prison.

---

13 I present a detailed analysis of this moment, its history, and its beliefs and practices in my *Practicing Scripture: A Lay Buddhist Movement in Late Imperial China* (Honolulu: University of Hawaiʻi Press, 2014).

He had been arrested because of his public proselytizing in the local streets, causing a local person to report him to the magistrate. A similar incident took place in 1847 when local members in southern Jiangxi cooperated with local Triad groups to free Triad members from prison. Not surprisingly, these attempts failed completely and many innocent members were caught up in the aftermath. In 1895, a local group in northern Fujian existing exclusively of disenfranchised males attacked a group of Western missionaries and their families, butchering most of them in a most brutal way. None of these three events expressed any aspect of the beliefs or practices of the movement, and in terms of social action they were quite untypical of the movement—though less so from the viewpoint of local protest and activism in general.[14] Apart from these three instances, there was no sustained repression of the movement. The local state took a very relaxed view of them as a larger movement, even in the aftermath of these three incidents. Prominent teachers were arrested now and then, most recently and rigorously in the 1950s and the 1960s by the communist state, more because of negative labeling than because of any intrinsic rebellious behavior.

Curiously, I found virtually no evidence of interaction between the Non-Action Teachings and Buddhist or Daoist monastic or priestly traditions, despite a relative abundance of sources on the movement. There is also little evidence of interaction with other new religious groups and what material we do have dates mostly from the early decades of the movement. They did not share in the then current attempts of combining Classicist (*ru*), Buddhist, and/or Daoist traditions, although at a certain stage they definitely absorbed some elements of inner cultivation that we usually categorize as Daoist. However, they did not make this kind of religious borrowing into a conscious activity, and therefore should not be considered syncretistic in orientation. The movement predominantly interpreted the lay Buddhist heritage of its time in creative new ways and saw itself as Chan Buddhist in nature.

A very different organization in terms of its beliefs was the Three-in-One Teachings. It remained largely limited to the region of Xinghua 興化 Prefecture, where it is still (or again) flourishing today.[15] It was founded in the second half of the sixteenth century by the local level literatus (*wenren* 文人) Lin Zhao'en 林兆恩 (1517–1598) and spread through the region very quickly. Even more

14 Compare the study of local protest by Ho-fung Hung, *Protest with Chinese Characteristics: Demonstrations, Riots, and Petitions in the Mid-Qing Dynasty* (New York: Columbia University Press, 2011).

15 Kenneth Dean, *Lord of the Three in One: The Spread of a Cult in Southeast China* (Princeton: Princeton University Press, 1998) is the authoritative study of this movement.

than other new religious groups and movements, it would always remain linked to a Putian identity, even when it migrated with them to Southeast Asia.[16] Unlike the Non-Action Teachings, its Qing history is largely undocumented by Chinese-language sources, making it hard to judge how accepted it was locally—although it probably had a high level of local acceptance that prevented it from being negatively noticed by the state, which explains the absence of an archival record. During the late Ming, the movement was very much part of the local network of socio-religious institutions, taking on a partially Classicist dimension, but propagating Buddhist as well as Daoist values and ideals. It was consciously culling from different sources and can therefore be called syncretic in its approach. At least during the Ming it was well-integrated into local society and cooperated with the state.[17]

A third organization that modern researchers do not did include in their category of problematic new religious groups and movements, while late imperial Chinese literati and the state certainly did, is that of Roman Catholic Christianity, later followed by Protestantism.[18] Recent research has shown how the early missionaries of the seventeenth century created communities that were capable of surviving and growing over extended periods of time, also in the absence of Western missionaries. Of course, their religious culture changed in various ways as compared with the Western original of its time—which was itself quite different from earlier as well as later Christianities (the plural is intended). For these local communities the practice of a variety of socio-religious rituals was crucial. In her recent work, Henrietta Harrison discusses the ways in which local Christianity in northern Shanxi in the seventeenth and eighteenth centuries was still quite similar to local religious life in general in its practice of funerary and protection rituals, ancestral sacrifice and so on. Similar arguments have been made by Erik Zürcher for late Ming Christianity, and Patrick Taveirne for Christian communities on the Han-Mongol border in the late nineteenth and early twentieth centuries.[19] A much more distinct

16 Dean, *Lord of the Three in One*, 134–135,179–183.

17 Unlike Christianity and the Non-Action Teachings (under its local appellations) the movement is not even mentioned in the relatively thorough persecution of 1748, see ter Haar, *Practicing Scripture*, 161–163.

18 Although the Chinese reception of Christianity produced distinct local variants, these were not sufficiently different until the early twentieth century that we need to summarize their contents for the average reader.

19 Henrietta Harrison, *The Missionary's Curse: And Other Tales from a Chinese Catholic Village* (Berkeley: University of California Press, 2013), esp. 25–40, 104–107, 201; Patrick Taveirne, *Han-Mongol Encounters and Missionary Endeavors: A History of Scheut in Ordos (Hetao), 1874–1911* (Leuven: Ferdinand Verbiest Foundation and Leuven University Press, 2004), 470–475, 479–482, including a summary of Zürcher's ideas.

Christian identity (in the sense of fitting more closely with what Western European academics would define as such) came into being in the nineteenth century, but not without producing tensions with established Christian communities.[20] From the early seventeenth century onwards, Christian groups might also be persecuted in the aftermath of more general persecutions of perceived heretical groups, or because of animosities among local Christians themselves.[21] On the whole, the movement was just as successful (or unsuccessful, which is a matter of perspective) as other new religious movements, so the traditional argument that Christian beliefs diverged too much from Chinese mainstream culture is not very convincing. Even the rejection of ancestor worship was shared with the Non-Action Teachings mentioned above and did not prevent people from joining at all. The main violent event inspired by Christian beliefs and practices was of course that of the Taiping Heavenly Kingdom of Great Peace 太平天國 (1851–1864). I have argued elsewhere that the specific millenarian roots of this movement are to be found partly in indigenous traditions, rather than exclusively in the Christian texts given to Hong Xiuquan 洪秀全 by Liang Fa 梁發 and the preaching which he had heard from Edwin Stevens.[22] Nonetheless, the Christian nature of the Heavenly Kingdom did not enhance the reputation of Christianity in the eyes of the imperial state.

None of the above three groups propagated an active messianic message, even though both the Non-Action Teachings and Christianity have some messianic elements as part of their historical baggage. In the case of the Non-Action Teachings there is no systematic mention of Maitreya in any of their religious texts over the four and a half centuries of their existence. We do find two isolated references to the three stages of the past, present, and future kalpa; as well as references to the belief that the Unborn Venerable Mother sent down the first two patriarchs (each reference mentioning a different patriarch). The dominant message of the movement is devotionalist, stressing Amitābha worship and rebirth in the Western Paradise, and selection for the Dragon

20 Harrison, *The Missionary's Curse*, 65–115.

21 Harrison, *The Missionary's Curse*, 39, 51–52.

22 Barend J. ter Haar, "China's Inner Demons: The Political Impact of the Demonological Paradigm," in *China's Great Proletarian Revolution: Master Narratives and Post-Mao Counternarratives*, ed. Woei Lien Chong (Lanham, MD: Rowman & Littlefield, 2002), 27–68; Rudolf G. Wagner, *Reenacting the Heavenly Vision: The Role of Religion in the Taiping Rebellion* (Berkeley: University of California, 1984); Robert P. Weller, *Resistance, Chaos and Control in China: Taiping Rebels, Taiwanese Ghosts and Tiananmen* (Basingstoke: Macmillan, 1994); Jonathan D. Spence, *God's Chinese Son: The Chinese Heavenly Kingdom of Hong Xiuquan* (London: Flamingo, 1997); and Thomas H. Reilly, *The Taiping Heavenly Kingdom: Rebellion and the Blasphemy of Empire* (Seattle: University of Washington Press, 2004) are other Western studies of the religious aspects of the rebellion.

Flower Assembly to be held by Maitreya in the very distant future. A lay Buddhist lifestyle is advocated which emphasizes a vegetarian diet, the rejection of alcoholic drinks, and simple rituals. In the Three-in-One Teachings, Lin Zhao'en himself is at one point identified with Maitreya, but more as a rhetorical example of the appearance of a great religious figure than anything more far-reaching. Christianity's early messianic origins and subsequent messianic transformations are well attested, but on the whole it was a devotional movement by the time it reached China.

Of the three movements, Christianity is actually the only one of the three that co-inspired a messianic event in Chinese history—to wit the Heavenly Kingdom of Great Peace. Finally, whatever messianic elements these three movements once had, they were very different from each other. Not surprisingly, there was little active interest on the part of the state in systemic persecution or repression of these three movements. When it did take place, it was usually in the context of a very localized incident, an outbreak of inchoate rumors, or in the aftermath of another group's uprising, when a broad variety of "suspicious" groups and figures would be rounded up in attempt to restore order by instilling fear of chaos. All three of the above movements produced a substantial number of new (or newly translated) texts and reprinted (or copied) old texts during the late Ming, and often went on to create more materials during the Qing period. Most likely only a minority of the adherents could actually read and even fewer properly write, but written texts occupied a central place in the rituals of all three movements.

A new religious movement with a clearly northern origin is the Broad Yang Teachings (Hongyangjiao 弘陽教). In this movement, the belief in the Unborn Venerable Mother is a crucial element of its religious mythology. The foundational narrative is that of Han Taihu 韓太湖 (1570–1598), who "discovered" the teachings after a long illness. The founder came from the far northeast of Ming China and the movement would always remain northern in orientation. He had practiced a lay Buddhist life style since his childhood, but when he barely survived a serious illness at fourteen and his mother also nearly died, he went on a long religious quest. His religious biography stresses that true belief cannot be bought with money, but must be based on opening up one's heart and discovering one's "original face" (*benlai mianmu* 本來面目). Such a statement makes his motivations quite similar to the search for religious basics that characterizes the contemporaneous Non-Action Teachings as well. It also sets the movement apart from the religious networks that will be discussed in the following section, in which a payment was demanded for the transfer of ritual lore. Thereupon, he started to teach throughout northern China and ultimately also in Beijing itself. Here he rapidly obtained a following among the dynastic nobility and court eunuchs—in other words elites that were associated with the imperial institution, who enjoyed more religious flexibility, rather than being limited in their outlook by the examination system with its dominant Neo-Confucian ideology.[23] The Broad Yang Teachings remained active mainly in the Shanxi, Hebei, Shandong, and later also the Manchurian regions.

The movement believed that mankind was made up of the sons and daughters of the Unborn Venerable Mother who had been banished to earth. Here they suffered terribly and needed to be saved by returning to their original source. The patriarch was sent by the Venerable Mother to rescue mankind, because the present-day Broad Yang period was about to end with an apocalypse and the White Yang period was about to begin. It was also believed that Confucius 孔子, Laozi 老子, and the exorcist deity Zhenwu 真武 had been sent to earth before, and that the patriarch was their youngest brother. Although this notion recalls Hong Xiuquan's idea that he was the younger brother of Jesus Christ, a direct connection seems unlikely. One should be a morally good person, and in the case of women, one's descendants should have the blood pond ritual performed (in the group's own version) in order to compensate for the karmic burden caused by the accumulated loss of blood through menstruation and giving birth.[24] Members also actively performed healing and funerary rituals for others, for relatively low fees. Faith-healing (using tea) and sutra recitation were important methods.[25] Clearly, from the perspective of the individual joining a network, whether for a short time as a customer or a longer term as an adherent was primarily about receiving practical benefits.

---

23 Ma Xisha 馬西沙 and Han Bingfang 韓秉方, *Zhongguo minjian zongjiaoshi* 中國民間宗教史 (Shanghai: Shanghai renmin chubanshe, 1992), 490–498, largely based on his internal religious biography and information in a late Qing local gazetteer. Sawada Mizuho 澤田瑞穗 blazed the way in studying this religious group already in the 1970s, "Kōyōkyō shidan 弘陽教試探," in *Zōho hōken no kenkyū* 增補寶卷の研究 (Tokyo: Kokusho kankōkai, 1975), 366–408. The local gazetteer of Guangping 廣平 from the late nineteenth century (quoted in Ma and Han, *Zhongguo minjian zongjiaoshi*, 495) records that a temple for him still existed as of 1841, when it was destroyed by a local official. He had a small biography in this gazetteer as well. Evidently, he had remained part of local memory over many centuries, despite his early death and founding a subsequently prohibited religious group.

24 Ma and Han, *Zhongguo minjian zongjiaoshi*, 505–518, treat the beliefs of this tradition.

25 Ma and Han, *Zhongguo minjian zongjiaoshi*, 516–518, 524–537. Also see the excellent studies by Song Jun 宋軍, *Qingdai Hongyangjiao yanjiu* 清代弘陽教研究 (Beijing: Shehui kexue wenxian chubanshe, 2002) and Qiu Lijuan 邱麗娟, "Qing Qianjiadao shiqi Hongyangjiao de yiliao chuanjiao 清乾嘉道時期紅陽教的醫療傳教," *Nanshi xuebao* 南師學報 37, no. 1 (2003): 17–35.

The recitation or reading of the movement's scriptures does not appear to be a central activity.[26]

At first sight, this may seem like the ultimate messianic movement and it therefore comes as something of a surprise that this was really an exceedingly peaceful and passive movement.[27] The only time that a Broad Yang-group was implicated in a messianic rebellion is the Eight Trigrams uprising of 1813. In this case the leader of the uprising, Lin Qing 林清, was originally a very successful healer, which will also have included faith-healing. One of his eunuch followers subsequently led a Broad Yang-group in an attack on the Imperial Palace, which succeeded in getting beyond the gates of the Forbidden City; however, the rebels were then rapidly defeated and killed, or first captured and then executed. The rest of the rebellion took place in Hua 滑 County, where there was no Broad Yang involvement.[28] Significantly, the messianic expectations of the Broad Yang Teachings were only actualized under the influence of Lin Qing's specific interpretations, which I discuss further below. Although their participation in the rebellion was marginal, it resulted in a devastating persecution of the Broad Yang Teachings and numerous other new religious groups over the following years. The group did not disappear, however, and can still be found today in Hebei province.[29]

The second major group in northern China with a considerable impact on local religious life in northern China of the late imperial period was the Way of Yellow Heaven (Huangtiandao 黄天道). Although it shared roughly the same Unborn Venerable Mother ideology as the Broad Yang Teachings, its beliefs were really quite different. The movement was founded in Wanquan 萬全 County in the north of modern Hebei, probably by a local soldier named Li Bin 李賓 (fl. 1553–1562/3).[30] In 1553 he encountered a charismatic teacher

26 There may be a bias here produced by the archival sources that focus on new networks, rather than routine practice.

27 Ma and Han, *Zhongguo minjian zongjiaoshi*, 538–548, list 32 Hongyang cases of which only seven precede the Eight Trigrams uprising of 1813 (actually taking place from 1746–1783, with one case following the panic of 1768 and four after the Wang Lun 王倫 uprising of 1774). As many as nineteen date from the years 1813–1819 (virtually none of them were involved in the 1813 rebellion), and four from 1818–1840, with two further undated cases.

28 Susan Naquin, *Millenarian Rebellion in China: The Eight Trigrams Rebellion of 1813* (New Haven: Yale University Press, 1976), 69–70, 170–171, 182–183; Ma and Han, *Zhongguo minjian zongjiaoshi*, 529–532, discuss events from a Chinese Marxist historian's point of view.

29 Ma and Han, *Zhongguo minjian zongjiaoshi*, 537.

30 Ma and Han, *Zhongguo minjian zongjiaoshi*, 363–368. The Teachings are also mentioned throughout Overmyer, *Precious Volumes*, e.g. pp. 190–191, 198–200, 343–351, although he does not provide a sustained discussion of the group as such. Ma and Han, *Zhongguo minjian zongjiaoshi*, 859–907, treat the network(s) around the *Dragon Flower Sutra* as an

and was given a technique of inner cultivation. The next year he reached the highest stage of cultivation and in 1558 he started to spread the teachings until his death a few years later. This was continued by his wife, who died in 1576. They were buried together in the local Azure Heaven Monastery (*Bitian si* 碧天寺), which functioned for over two centuries as their religious center and the goal of pilgrimages by their followers.[31] Although the tradition seems to have continued into the mid-twentieth century, we know little about their overall following on a local level.[32] The absence of sources may well be due to a general dearth of sources for this rather poor region. The Way of Yellow Heaven rarely attracted the attention of officials, allowing it to create extended local religious networks.[33]

In many ways, the Way of Yellow Heaven functioned like a Buddhist institution: the center of its teaching was a Buddhist monastery, the patriarchs had Buddhist sounding names (including the religious affiliation marker *pu* 普),

---

offshoot of the Way of Yellow Heaven. For a different analysis of that network as a teacher-pupil network see my discussion further below. After this article was completed, a new and extremely detailed case study of the movement came out, Cao Xinyu 曹新宇, *Zushi de zupu: Ming Qing bailianjiao shehui lishi diaocha zhiyi* 祖師的族譜—明清白蓮教社會歷史調查之一 (Taipei: Boyang, 2015). His research shows how the movement had deep roots in local society, despite the occasional persecution.

31 Ma and Han, *Zhongguo minjian zongjiaoshi,* 408–418. Local memory of Li Bin etc. did not disappear. In 1875, local people prayed for rain at his grave. When rain came, they erected a temple for Li Bin out of gratitude (Ma and Han, *Zhongguo minjian zongjiaoshi,* 424).

32 Ma and Han, *Zhongguo minjian zongjiaoshi*, 418–428, 433. Ma and Han, *Zhongguo minjian zongjiaoshi,* 469–487, discuss the influence exerted by the tradition, but much of their discussion takes for granted certain similarities in beliefs, rather than actually demonstrating them.

33 Ma and Han, *Zhongguo minjian zongjiaoshi,* 443–447, discuss political aspects of these teachings on the basis of their scriptures, but these were not what bothered officials (who did not know these texts before persecuting, and probably not afterwards either). Ma and Han argue that originally this new religious group, like most other Ming and Qing religious groups, did not harbor political (rebellious) thoughts, but only developed these later on. Their main evidence of such a change are memorials from 1743 and 1763, which testify to elements from the demonological messianic paradigm (the belief in a prince of the Zhao 趙, Zhu 朱, or Li 李 families coming to protect against apocalyptic disasters) in a "Way of Yellow Heaven" context. They do not provide further information on the kind of context and do not seem to be aware that these memorials are really talking about the same tradition (Ma and Han, *Zhongguo minjian zongjiaoshi,* 446–447). The list of texts confiscated in 1763 (Ma and Han, *Zhongguo minjian zongjiaoshi,* 487–488) indicates that the problematic texts referred to in the 1763 memorial were part of the religious "library" of the Azure Heaven Monastery, more specifically part of a series of protective amulets. This suggests that the texts in question were used as effective texts for ritual purposes by the resident Daoist priests, rather than as statements of beliefs. They therefore do not reflect the beliefs of the Way of Yellow Heaven as a whole.

and their texts used Buddhist sounding titles. Their pupils married and had children, but kept to the Three Refuges and Five Precepts just like any other lay Buddhist. At the same time, the Way of Yellow Heaven practiced a tradition of inner cultivation, with the ultimate aim of attaining immortality (conceived as being a Buddha), which we usually label as Daoist.[34] The movement conceived of the human body as homologous to the cosmos as a whole, but ultimately made of the same material (*qi* 氣, "stuff-energy"). Therefore, they saw obtaining the "one stuff-energy of the undivided origin prior to heaven" (*xiantian hunyuan yiqi* 先天混元一氣) as essential, to be achieved by obtaining the radiances of the sun and moon. The founder was called Puming 普明 (dispersing luminance) and his wife Puguang 普光 (dispersing radiance), and they were seen as personifications of the radiances of sun and moon.[35] The roots of these beliefs clearly are in the northern Golden Cinnabar 金丹 tradition (which combined religious beliefs that we are accustomed to labeling Buddhist and Daoist). Pudu 普度 (1255–1330), the apologist of the lay Buddhist White Lotus movement of the Southern Song and Yuan period, already had lambasted the "stupid people" practicing this kind of technique.[36] There was an awareness of elements from messianic traditions, such as the belief in the Unborn Venerable Mother and the idea that earthlings had once been banished from Heaven and now had to be rescued. However, there is no sense of messianic urgency and the banishment myth is not a central element of their beliefs.[37]

The Broad Yang Teachings and the Way of Yellow Heaven were the principal horizontally organized indigenous new religious groups active in northern China since the late Ming dynasty. Only in the Broad Yang Teachings did the

---

34 Ma and Han, *Zhongguo minjian zongjiaoshi*, 447–448, 461. The rule against lascivious feelings went quite well with the kind of cultivation techniques that they proposed, since excessive sexual contact would damage the preservation of essence/semen (*jing* 精).

35 Light and seeing are pervasive themes in Li Bin's personal religious biography, to wit: he had been blinded in one eye during battle (and had the alternative religious appellation Chan Teacher with the Tiger Eye), his teacher was a "perspicacious person" (*mingren* 明人) and the "inner pill" (*neidan* 内丹) which he succeeded in cultivating was called "radiance of the old mirror" (*gujingming* 古鏡明). The pagoda where he and his wife were buried was called after them, Pagoda of Luminance and Radiance (*mingguang ta* 明光塔). Ma and Han, *Zhongguo minjian zongjiaoshi,* 414–415 (biographical elements), 448–457 (core conceptions).

36 Ma and Han, *Zhongguo minjian zongjiaoshi,* 455–460, on the influence of Daoist inner alchemy. For Pudu's attack, see his *Lushan lianzong baojian* 廬山蓮宗寶鑑, *juan* 10 in *Yuandai Bailianjiao ziliao huibian* 元代白蓮教資料彙編, ed. Yang Ne 楊訥 (Beijing: Zhonghua shuju, 1989), 155. On its Daoist antecedents, see Isabelle Robinet, *Histoire du taoïsme des origines au XIV*^e^ *siècle* (Paris: Les Editions du Cerf, 1991), 171–172.

37 Overmyer, *Precious Volumes*, 190–191.

Unborn Venerable Mother narrative play an important role, but not as the basis for messianic activities. Again, textual production in these two movements was quite remarkable, testifying to a considerable degree of literacy at least among its leaders. Subsequent generations actively transmitted their texts as well, although more research is needed to see just how important access to writing really was. If we want to use modern labels, we might label the Broad Yang Teachings as lay Buddhist and the Way of Yellow Heaven as Buddho-Daoist or just Daoist. Local people probably just accessed these teachings as ways to shape their lives—irrespective of doctrinal concerns.

A striking commonality of at least four of the above movements is the importance of regionality, as befits the largely regional nature of culture in traditional China up to the highest social and educational levels. Except for Christianity, all four movements were geographically restricted to their regions of origins and all four knew different forms of memory connected to one or more graves that could be visited (in the case of the Non-Action Teachings, the Broad Yang Teachings, and the Way of Yellow Heaven) or an academy (in the case of the Three-in-One Teachings). Christianity too was shaped around the memory of a death, and for many centuries visiting the places in the Holy Land where Jesus had been born, lived, and died was an important part of one's devotion. The cult of saints in many ways replicated similar patterns on a more modest geographical scale, allowing people to express their Christian beliefs and practices through bodily practice and pilgrimage. The relationship of adherents in each of these religious groups to the textual core of their teachings differed considerably, although we do face here a lack of evidence in the cases of the Way of Yellow Heaven and the Three-in-One Teachings for much of their history. For both we possess an abundance of texts from the lifetimes of the founding fathers, but little information on their subsequent socio-religious history. The Three-in-One Teachings remained confined to Xinghua Prefecture and traveled with migrants from that region overseas, but we know very little of its history until the twentieth century. While the Way of Yellow Heaven had already largely vanished by that time, the Three-in-One Teachings has survived most of the vagaries of the twentieth century and has gained tremendous strength again today. The Non-Action Teachings and the Broad Yang Teachings continued to flourish, and texts remained important to the adherents throughout their histories.

4 Acquiring Ritual Power

Ritual activities were at the core of the religious activities of any religious group and network, including all of those discussed above. However, next to ritual these groups also created extensive narratives that were then also shared with the adherents, whether through texts and/or through the performance of rituals such as initiations based on texts. Moreover, rituals were not themselves esoteric knowledge, but part of a larger shared practice. In the networks to be discussed in this section, there were texts at the very top of the network, but there was a very restricted policy of access. Texts were a numinous resource that provided legitimation, rather than something to be shared.

Because of this restricted access, a hierarchy of knowledge was created that was vertical and not itself textual. As a result, the level of integration of these groupings of people was much more loose, suggesting that the term network describes their interactions much better than the term group. Nonetheless, there was still a crucial difference from ordinary ritual providers, who would not transmit any substantial knowledge at all, beyond the reassurance that the ritual would benefit the customers. In the networks to be discussed here, the conviction that one obtained valuable knowledge to practice oneself and for one's own benefit is central. In this respect, the networks were different from the much more restrictive networks of Daoist and Buddhist priests with their elaborate rituals for transmitting expertise of various sorts that was not distributed further, but retained as an esoteric body of knowledge in itself.

Two such vertically oriented teacher-pupil networks stand out in the history of late imperial China, both sometimes associated indirectly with violent events.[38] From an organizational perspective it is not surprising that upon closer investigation these networks were actually only rarely connected with such events, since their vertical structure produced rather weak connections between the members of the networks, making them unsuitable for successful rebellious action. One such long-lasting religious network was that of the Wang family, which started in the late sixteenth century and lasted into the early nineteenth century, despite recurrent persecutions.[39] Its founder Wang Sen 王森 (1542–1619) and his descendants lived in the sub-prefecture of Luan

38 For reasons of space I have left out the Dong 董 family, which is an even clearer example of ritual lore used for self-help.

39 Ma and Han, *Zhongguo minjian zongjiaoshi*, 549–652, 888–907 (this tradition is treated by Ma and Han as a separate tradition going back to the *Dragon Flower Sutra* [*Longhuajing* 龍華經], but actually the *Nine-Petaled Lotus Sutra* [*Jiulianjing* 九蓮經] and/or *August Extreme Sutra* [*Huangjijing* 皇極經] are much more relevant, and the groups usually trace themselves to the Wang family network); Susan Naquin, "Connections between Rebellions: Sect Family Networks in Qing China," *Modern China* 8, no. 3 (1982): 337–360; and "Two Descent Groups in Northern China: The Wangs of Yung-p'ing Prefecture, 1500–1800," in *Kinship Organization in Late Imperial China*, ed. Patricia N. Ebrey and James L. Watson (Berkeley: University of California Press, 1986), 210–244; Asai Motoi 淺井紀, *Min shin jidai minkan shūkyō kessha no kenkyū* 明清時代民間宗教結社の研究 (Tokyo: Kenbun shuppan, 1990), 343–380.

灤 close to the northern border. Wang Sen was not arrested for religious reasons, but because he got caught up in local conflicts, against a background of increasing border tensions. He propagated the burning of incense as a central devotional act. His network autonym was Great Vehicle Teachings (Dacheng jiao 大乘教).[40] They were extremely effective proselytizers, who structured their network into gatherings in which people received organizational titles. Such ranks were obtained in exchange for donations in silver or cash to the Wang family, whose leaders were seen as incarnations of Maitreya on earth through the generations. This was called "paying court and offering tribute" (*chaogong* 朝貢), not so much to create an actual organization, but as nodes in an exchange of religious charisma (the perception of divine power) for gifts.[41] Strictly speaking, however, theirs was still not a true messianic movement, since worship and tribute were all directed at an event in the distant future, rather than its immediate (passive or active) realization.

Some of the followers in the Wang Sen network got involved in a 1622 uprising in the sensitive Grand Canal region, but certainly not the movement as a whole. Local tensions caused by flooding and droughts, combined with the economic exactions for the war with the Manchus, were probably more important causes than messianic ideas.[42] The suppression of the rebellion took only

40 Ter Haar, *The White Lotus Teachings*, 228–234; Ma and Han, *Zhongguo minjian zongjiaoshi*, 614–616, discuss the importance of incense in their teachings based on the *Nine-Petaled Lotus Sutra*. A proclamation quoted in Asai Motoi, *Minshin jidai minkan shūkyō kessha no kenkyū*, 292, confirms the name "Smelling Incense" and adds another, "Transmission of the Single Character Cinnabar" (*yizidan* 一字丹). Ma and Han, *Zhongguo minjian zongjiaoshi*, 552–556, argue from later attempts of the tradition to claim Patriarch Luo that the Luo Teachings therefore also inspired Wang Sen. There is no evidence of this. In their attempts to link the teachings of Wang Sen to other new religious groups (pp. 552–560), the authors only create a further analytical conundrum, since none of these groups is messianic or millenarian. Hence they conclude rather paradoxically that the teachings are "rich in contents, yet without individuality" (p. 559).

41 Ma and Han, *Zhongguo minjian zongjiaoshi*, 561–570.

42 Analysis based on information given by Ma and Han, *Zhongguo minjian zongjiaoshi*, 569–570. The survival of the Wang family indicates that the family itself cannot have been too heavily involved. On the rebellion the standard work is Asai Motoi, *Minshin jidai minkan shūkyō kessha no kenkyū*. He sees the rising as a Maitreyist rebellion (pp. 287–288), but points out that actual evidence on this dimension is disappointingly small. Instead, notions of a change or restoration of the Heavenly Mandate receive much more central mention in the sources related to the uprising itself (rather than to the preceding religious groups). Nonetheless, Asai and other scholars still prefer to see the rebellion as a messianic event, probably because of the White Lotus label. He attributes the lack of information to disinterest among the persecuting bureaucrats (e.g., Asai Motoi, *Minshin jidai minkan shūkyō kessha no kenkyū*, 356–357). Given the richness of sources, I find this unconvincing.

a few months and in the end it was a minor event from a military (but not from a political) point of view. The family soon restarted its religious activities and flourished.[43] One branch later even collaborated with the Manchus, and its descendants no longer engaged in the ancestral religious teachings, but two other branches did. There was little cohesion over the following centuries, except the continuation of the family network of teachers.[44] This may be the result of persecutions, but also of the largely oral nature of transmission.

The Wang family patriarch always possessed texts, and over the following centuries the text that was confiscated over and over was the "Precious Scroll of the August Ultimate's Golden Cinnabar and Nine-Petaled Lotus [Path of] True Reliance to Take Refuge in the Truth and Return to the Home region" (*Huangji jindan jiulian zhengxin guizhen huanxiang baojuan* 皇極金丹九蓮正信歸真還鄉寶卷) (usually abbreviated as *Jiulianjing* or *Nine-Petaled Lotus Sutra*). Because this and other texts were generally not transmitted to pupils, but functioned as a legitimating treasure for the teachers, I treat this grouping as a network, rather than a well-integrated religious group.[45]

The oldest *Nine-Petaled Lotus Sutra* extant to date was printed in 1523 and therefore predates the Wang family network.[46] It stresses the importance of burning incense and teaches the Three Refuges and Five Precepts, entailing a strict vegetarian lifestyle. It sets out a messianic eschatology in three stages and mentions a mountain to which Amitābha was dispatched by the Unborn Father and Mother (*wusheng fumu* 無生父母) to save all their lost souls. By means of special cultivation techniques one had to make one's essence (*jing* 精), stuff-energy (*qi* 氣), and spirit (*shen* 神) coagulate inside the body, to produce the Golden which was then to be transported up through the body to the top of one's head or the Dark Gate (*xuanmen* 玄門). This would enable

43 Ma and Han, *Zhongguo minjian zongjiaoshi*, 574–576. Their discussion of the activities of devotional and messianic Buddhists in the Ming-Qing transitional period (pp. 574–594) is exciting, but cannot be used here without critical reanalysis of their sources.

44 Ma and Han, *Zhongguo minjian zongjiaoshi*, 595–596.

45 Naquin, "Transmission of White Lotus Sectarianism," 266–267, 271, seems to consider this precious scroll to belong to the texts used by "sutra recitation groups."

46 Ma and Han, *Zhongguo minjian zongjiaoshi*, 610–613 (but also see quotations pp. 888–907). We can leave aside the texts that Wang Haoxian 王好賢 got himself from Shandong, for even if Patriarch Luo's *Five Books in Six Volumes* 五部六冊 and the other text were among them (for which there is no evidence) there is no indication of any further influence. Naquin, "Transmission of White Lotus Sectarianism," 266–267, gives a list of dates when the text was confiscated, which is different from Ma and Han's, but does not specify any of the groups behind the text. On the scripture, see Overmyer, *Precious Volumes*, 136–177. There can be little doubt that the text antedates Wang Sen, contrary to Ma and Han, *Zhongguo minjian zongjiaoshi*, 622–623.

the practitioner to attain transcendence over life and death.[47] The messianic cosmology with a strong Pure Land coloring functions to legitimate a practice of internal cultivation, rather than serving as a script for messianic expectations or even messianic action. Even when we limit ourselves to this text—and as I argue below we should not—what we find here is a fusion of beliefs and practices that historically speaking could be labeled separately as Buddhist and Daoist, but had already been combined for several centuries.[48] The circulation of essence, stuff-energy and spirit inside the body was hardly a uniquely Wang family belief, but had venerable Daoist antecedents. Moreover, the same custom had already been attacked by Pudu in the early fourteenth century, this time as a distortion of Buddhist teachings.[49]

The actual teaching practices by members of the Wang family and their direct pupils differed considerably and did not involve propagating the *Nine-Petaled Lotus Sutra*. Typically, teachers retained their substantial texts as a private resource, but shared only mantras and simple ritual acts with their pupils, in addition to prescribing a vegetarian lifestyle. In exchange they requested small financial contributions.[50] We find the same pattern in other teacher-pupil networks of this period and none of this is unique to the Wang-family network. Typically, these were oral networks cemented by the transfer of a small body of esoteric knowledge and ritual practice, in exchange for recognition of the transmitter as one's teacher. In Chinese culture, a monetary gift creates a connection and is a common expression of gratitude. Similarly, Daoist priests will not be paid, but will instead participate in the banquets that accompany their rituals, as well as receiving gifts in kind (for instance the animals used in the rituals) and/or money that would be labeled a gift.[51] There is no indication of

---

47 Summarized from Ma and Han, *Zhongguo minjian zongjiaoshi*, 613–632, under consultation of Naquin, "Transmission of White Lotus Sectarianism," 266–267.

48 As I already pointed out for the Yellow Heaven Teachings above.

49 *Lushan lianzong baojian* 廬山蓮宗寶鑑, 141–142, 143–144, 156 (this last case is the closest to the practices of the Wang family).

50 Ma and Han, *Zhongguo minjian zongjiaoshi*, 593–610. Interpreting the evidence is not easy, because stereotypes and real information are mixed-up completely (e.g., the memorial from 1732 quoted in Asai, *Minshin jidai minkan shūkyō kessha no kenkyû*, 374, note 11; Ma and Han, *Zhongguo minjian zongjiaoshi*, 593, 638).

51 Ter Haar, *The Ritual and Mythology of the Chinese Triads*, 421–424, and Dean, *Lord of the Three in One*, 221–225, analyze the importance of donations. The exchange of money and gifts for religious lore has bemused many observers since the Qing period, although it is quite normal in Chinese as well as other cultural traditions (including our own). See Ma and Han, *Zhongguo minjian zongjiaoshi*, 990, for a statement (*passim* for evidence); Dian Murray, "Migration, Protection, and Racketeering: The Spread of the Tiandihui within China," in *Secret Societies Reconsidered: Perspectives on the Social History of Modern South China and Southeast Asia*, ed. David Ownby and Mary F. Somers Heidhues (Armonk, N.Y.:

institutionalized groups' meeting on a regular basis, and the stronger networks that sometimes appear result from individual charisma, rather than from any transmission of organizational expertise.

The second major family network of the Qing period was that of the Liu family, started by Liu Zuochen 劉佐臣 (fl. 1678–circa 1700) in Shandong province, and continued by his descendants until the persecutions that followed the Eight Trigrams rebellion of 1813. Throughout its existence, members of the network were arrested, executed, and banished, usually because they were caught up in the aftermath of other incidents and not because of messianic activities of their own.[52] One feature of this network is the way in which it constructed itself in terms of branches bearing the names of one of the eight trigrams.[53] Despite this usage, the different branches were not integrated strongly horizontally. There is some evidence of the use of networks for communicating messages and money, but not for systematic support.[54] In fact, there is some striking evidence that members of related networks actually did not support one another in times of need.[55]

Like the Wang family network, the Liu family possessed a set of scriptures, which were used as an esoteric source from which to teach, but not widely transmitted. Pupils paid contributions in cash and silver in exchange for receiving knowledge. The networks centered on the neighboring counties and prefectures of Shandong, Henan and Hebei. Local networks were in fact controlled by local teachers, with some of them founding their own family networks. Any overarching structure under the names of the Eight Trigrams was purely symbolic. Internal ranks were connected to different benefits after the expected arrival of a new age, rather than a permanent organizational structure. In the course of spreading their lore, the families of teachers on the higher level of the networks accumulated considerable wealth, with which they bought landed property and even Qing official titles.[56]

M.E. Sharpe, 1993), 177–189; Naquin, *Millenarian Rebellion*, 49–53, 280; Naquin, "The Transmission of White Lotus Sectarianism in Late Imperial China," 270–271, 282–285.

52 Ma and Han, *Zhongguo minjian zongjiaoshi*, 933–938, on the early stages of the Liu family tradition, and 946–968 on subsequent stages. Also Naquin, "Connections between Rebellions," 337–360.

53 Ma and Han, *Zhongguo minjian zongjiaoshi*, 942–946. The Nine Palaces (*jiugong* 九宮) are derived from the same basic notion, with the eight trigrams or squares arranged around a center, yielding the nine continents or nine palaces.

54 Blaine Gaustad, "Prophets and Pretenders: Inter-Sect Competition in Qianlong China," *Late Imperial China* 21, no. 1 (2000): 1–40, esp. 5–6.

55 Gaustad, "Prophets and Pretenders," 5–6.

56 Summarized from Ma and Han, *Zhongguo minjian zongjiaoshi*, 948–989.

Their central text was the *Five Saints [or: Maidens] Transmit the Way* (*wusheng [or: nü] chuandao* 五聖/女傳道), which uses less than 5000 characters and simple metaphors to present a fairly straightforward method for cultivating the inner pill and attaining long life, revealed by five bodhisattvas.[57] It is somewhat similar in message to the *Nine-Petaled Lotus Sutra*, except for the much less elaborate messianic cosmology and the lack of references to Buddhist practices. Archival sources confirm that the concrete message of these teachers did indeed focus on this kind of inner cultivation practice, sometimes supported by materials for oral usage. The archival sources indicate that one of the core practices was to worship the sun as a Saintly Emperor. One had to kowtow to the sun three times a day and sacrifice five times a year, in order to "eliminate disasters and pray for good fortune/happiness." When practiced for a long time, one could "heal illnesses and place needles for other people," in other words acupuncture—then a little esteemed medical approach that was despised by the much more prestigious Classicist Medicine (*ruyi* 儒醫).[58] Again, the early fourteenth-century apologist Pudu had already chided contemporaries for the practice of inhaling the radiance of the sun and moon when these have just risen, and for swallowing this radiance into one's stomach in order to let it bear fruit there.[59] Despite Pudu's remarks, the "method of transcending sun and moon" has venerable Daoist antecedents, going back many centuries to the Upper Purity (*shangqing* 上清) tradition.[60] Labeling it as "heretical" or "popular beliefs" ignores more interesting questions about the apparent descent of such age-old beliefs to a lower social (or educational) level, whilst losing fashion among the social elites that once created and practiced them.

There is little or no evidence that the tradition as a whole was messianic, but several features of the Eight Trigrams tradition confuse the issue here. First, some teachers taught an Eight Character Mantra with the words "the Home

57 Ma and Han, *Zhongguo minjian zongjiaoshi*, 990–997.

58 Summarizing from the evidence presented in Ma and Han, *Zhongguo minjian zongjiaoshi*, 997–1005. Also archival materials in Ma and Han, *Zhongguo minjian zongjiaoshi*, 952n1, 958n1, 965n3, 973n3), 979n1, 979n3, 984n1, 1002n1, 1004n1, with quotations from teachers and pupils on these ritual practices. Some teachers apparently equated the sun with Liu Zuochen, others identified him (his mythical form) as an incarnation of Maitreya. Specific identifications were not generally shared, it appears, but clearly Liu was thought to have divine characteristics.

59 *Lushan lianzong baojian* 廬山蓮宗寶鑑, 155. He does not label it in a very negative way, unlike some of his other attacks. See my "Whose Norm, Whose Heresy: The Case of the Song-Yuan White Lotus Movement." in *Häresien*, ed. Irene Pieper, Michael Schimmelpfennig, and Joost van Soosten (München: Wilhelm Fink Verlag, 2003), 67–93.

60 Isabelle Robinet, *Histoire du taoïsme des origines au XIVe siècle*, 171–172.

region of True Emptiness, the Unborn Father and Mother" (*zhenkong jiaxiang wusheng fumu* 真空家鄉無生父母), which originated in a messianic context (it fits very well, too, with the contents of the *Nine-Petaled Lotus Sutra*). The mantra, however, was transmitted as a ritual act and not necessarily as the prelude to obligatory messianic action. It expressed the practitioner's trust in the saving powers of the Unborn Father and Mother, much in the same way as other lay Buddhists recited the name of Amitābha or the Spell of Great Compassion 大悲咒 by Guanyin 觀音. No reference is made here to the story of the Unborn Venerable Mother.[61] Reciting the mantra was a performative act for practical benefits and not out of any messianic concern.[62] The Qing state used the presence of this mantra as a definitional characteristic of to-be-persecuted rebellious networks, and modern research has merely reversed the value judgment, but not the underlying analysis.

Secondly, some teachers also taught that Liu Zuochen was either an incarnation of Maitreya or Confucius. One of Liu's descendants was seen as "the son of the head of teaching who looked out for the kalpa."[63] This last title suggests that the underlying messianic expectation was a long-term one, rather similar to that of the Christian church, and certainly not something that would be realized in the short run. The only proper evidence is a group of texts confiscated in 1772 from two pupils in the network, which did include messianic

61 The notion of "returning to the origins" is quite basic in Chinese religious traditions. See for instance Overmyer, *Precious Volumes*, esp. 138, 145; on this notion in the *Nine-Petaled Lotus*.

62 Ma and Han, *Zhongguo minjian zongjiaoshi*, 949 (1744, a *jiazi* year; the teachers collected contributions, "for the expenses of going to Eastern Heaven and collecting gold dust" [以爲往西天取金沙費用]), 984 (1813, as part of a ritual aimed at practical benefits), 988 (1787, in a slogan that also lists the names of Tathāgata and Maitreya, but in a social context that makes clear that these particular and very poor teachers were mainly engaged in making a living), 1051 (1814), and 1056 (1811, explicitly because with it "one can hurry towards fortune and avert misfortune, and it can also rescue from poverty" [可以趨吉避凶，並可以救窮]). My interpretation of these data differs fundamentally from Ma and Han's (e.g., *Zhongguo minjian zongjiaoshi*, 1009–1011). Naquin, *Shantung Rebellion*, does not note it for the Wang Lun uprising (on which more below), which (or at least the core group of which) had become messianic in orientation several years before the actual rising. The treatment in Naquin, *Eight Trigrams*, 9–31, amalgamates information from rather different contexts into one story that is difficult to use once the notion that all of these contexts reflect one single phenomenon is dropped. However, Naquin, *Eight Trigrams*, 25–26, still confirms my judgment that to most adherents this mantra was a protective slogan.

63 Ma and Han, *Zhongguo minjian zongjiaoshi*, 958 (1782; also see the other quotations on their special abilities from 1772), and 979 (1813; also see the quotations on the special abilities of other trigram teachers from 1833 and 1816).

prophecies.[64] However, these prophecies played no role whatsoever in the actual teaching within this network. The owner of the texts even explicitly interpreted them in the light of the group's inner cultivation practices, rather than as a messianic message.[65]

The archival evidence concerning the Wang and Liu networks reveals quite clearly that most of the people involved only had access to and were interested in ritual lore that would bring them some form of good fortune and health. Identifications of teachers as a savior served to express the prestige of the teachers. They were quite rare in themselves and similar to claims made for instance by or about the late Ming teacher Lin Zhao'en of the Three-in-One Teachings, none of these figures would serve as leaders of or teachers in direct messianic events or violent rebellions.

In the Wang and Liu networks, the only persons who possessed substantial written texts were the teachers at the pinnacles of their respective networks, for whom these texts functioned as legitimating treasures rather than anything else. Reading or indirect access to texts therefore played virtually no role in these groups, beyond providing the owners of the ultimate texts at the pinnacle of the networks a form of prestige. The goal was to obtain simple ritual lore for personal usage, without shared practices and resulting in little or no horizontal cohesion that could have provided for long-term institutionalization. Teachers transmitted the lore, but did not become the object of grave cults and similar forms of spatially distributed reverence. Thus, these networks were much more fluid than the religious groups I discussed in the preceding section.

64 This is a re-analysis of the sources presented in Ma and Han, *Zhongguo minjian zongjiaoshi*, 952–961, 1017–1018. Most evidence presented by them to support the messianic nature of the Eight Trigrams tradition as a whole is external, or rests on the rather teleological state view in the 1772 case. They also present information from longer texts (*Zhongguo minjian zongjiaoshi*, 1007–1017) that are not necessarily from the particular tradition (in this instance the Eight Trigrams Teachings) in order to contextualize it, rather than going into the confessions themselves. The underlying assumption is that these texts and groups ultimately are one and the same religious phenomenon, a virtual White Lotus Teachings, although they do not use this term frequently.

65 Quoted in Ma and Han, *Zhongguo minjian zongjiaoshi*, 952–953. In my *The Ritual and Mythology of the Chinese Triads*, 10.2. in particular, I discuss how members in particular networks within which a particular body of lore was transmitted often did not understood what they learned and why they had to do it, but did it nonetheless.

5 Messianic Traditions and Ritual Self-Help

Messianic traditions per se were hardly a new phenomenon of the late imperial period. They had first come into being during the Han dynasty. Successive political movements, including some rather successful imperial dynasties such as the Tang and maybe even the very early Ming, made use of them for their legitimation. The belief in a savior was always feared by the ruling powers, but continued to draw political appeal as well because of their power and popularity (for many centuries up to the highest social and political level). Only after the initial phase of the Ming dynasty did messianic traditions come to be discredited as a form of legitimation and were more or less written out of the historical record of the foundation of the dynasty. This did not make these traditions go away, but they were no longer controlled and channeled by political action. On a local level, they flourished as before in a combination of oral and written transmission. We find an inactive form of these beliefs in the late imperial narratives of the Unborn Venerable Mother and/or the expectation of the imminent appearance of Maitreya, but in none of these narratives is the messianic expectation very acute.

This is different in the demonological messianic paradigm, which was informed by the overall demonological substrate of traditional Chinese religious culture. An individual ritual specialist invited figures, who were seen as rulers and/or generals, to come with their spirit armies from often quite specific places in the real world, in order to rescue the followers from a perceived apocalyptic threat. There was no need for a change of lifestyle. This type of practice sometimes led to violent events, but only very rarely. Most of the time, messianic or millenarian expectations remained peaceful, even within this particular paradigm, and it was often government action in combination with specific local circumstances which caused violent escalation.[66] Because China's demonological religious culture is set in the real-life world of local people, it was always difficult to distinguish what we would nowadays characterize as symbolic events from things happening in the "real" world. The whole point of exorcist ritual is that it is not symbolic, but concrete and real. Demons, barbarians, and humans, for instance, are seen to inhabit the same world. In our secular worldview we may choose to separate these two worlds or dimensions, but people inside the demonological paradigm did not. This lack of distinction was just as much a problem for the people involved, including the imperial state itself, for the demonological messianic expectations, including

66 This was even true of the Ma Chaozhu 馬朝柱 incident of 1747–1752. See ter Haar, *Ritual and Mythology of the Chinese Triads*, 236–253.

the advent of spirit armies to assist the participants, were so realistic that the state felt pressured to take preemptive action, and the participants thought that they were much stronger than they really were.

During the Qing, four rebellions in particular exhibited very clear religious ideas, although none of them was directly caused by the groups and networks briefly analyzed above. They are the Wang Lun rebellion of 1774, the so-called White Lotus rebellion of 1796–804, the Eight Trigrams rebellion of 1813, and the Heavenly Kingdom of Great Peace in 1851–1864. For reasons of space, I will only look at the example of the 1796–1804 rebellion as it is the one of which the socio-religious background has been studied the least, despite abundant documentation.[67] Since rebellions are unique events that are only documented retrospectively, it is difficult to assess the precise impact of their respective religious backgrounds. Similarly, all four events were very different in scope and scale, making them hard to compare amongst each other as well. What is clear is that each of these four events involved different parts of China and very different sets of beliefs. The Eight Trigrams rebellion is the only one that involved long-standing religious groups or networks. It has been studied extensively by Susan Naquin and others. Here I only discuss the specific case of the 1796–1804 rebellion, which at least on the surface also involved the long-standing transmission of messianic prophecies.

In the case of the so-called White Lotus rebellion of 1796–1804, the unstable socio-economic circumstances of the Shanxi-Sichuan-Hubei border regions in which the events took place are absolutely crucial, with a minor role for the stream of rumors of a messianic nature that circulated in the mid-1790s in these regions.[68] Ironically, it is attempts by the state to put down these rumors by arresting people spreading them which caused the socially unstable region to explode. The waves of arrests preceding, during, and following the events allow us to reconstruct some of the networks in which the rumors originally came into being. Take for instance the network that was traced back to a proselytizer named Yang Ji 楊集 and his pupil Fan Mingde 樊明德, whom Yang healed in 1774.[69] After being healed, Fan was given two scriptures, a prayer sheet,

67 On the Wang Lun rebellion, see for instance Naquin, *Shantung Rebellion*, 37–61, and Ma and Han, *Zhongguo minjian zongjiaoshi*, 1025–1036. On the Eight Trigrams rebellion, see for instance Naquin, *Eight Trigrams*, 72–83 and *passim*; Ma and Han, *Zhongguo minjian zongjiaoshi*, 1048–1091. On the Heavenly Kingdom of Great Peace there is an extended literature, referred to in note 22 above.

68 Wensheng Wang, *White Lotus Rebels and South China Pirates: Crisis and Reform in the Qing Empire* (Cambridge, Mass.: Harvard University Press, 2014).

69 My main source for the following discussion is Blaine Gaustad, "Religious Sectarianism and the State in Mid Qing China: Background to the White Lotus Uprising of 1796–1804,"

and oral instructions on ritual practice.[70] The first scripture was called "Text of the Undifferentiated Beginning to Transform by Illuminating" (*Hunyuan dianhua shu* 混元點化書), the second the "Greater and Smaller Sutra of Asking about the Way" (*Daxiao wendaojing* 大小問道經). He was to burn incense every night, silently recite his name, and then recite the "Sutra of Asking about the Way." In this way, he would be able to "obtain good fortune and destroy calamities, not fall into the underworld after his death, and be reborn as a good person time and time again" (*keyi hufu xiaozai, sihou buluo diyu, shishi zhuansheng haoren* 可以護福消災，死後不落地獄，世世轉生好人). Fan Mingde transmitted his lore further, and performed the healing of other people, but kept the "Text of the Undifferentiated Beginning to Transform by Illuminating" largely to himself. In exchange for transmitting smaller or larger bits of his lore he requested contributions in money. There is no mention of keeping a vegetarian lifestyle or any form of the cultivation of stuff-energy or *qi*, distinguishing this network in a fundamental way from the Wang and Liu family traditions.

In terms of actual practice, Fan Mingde's lore was perfectly innocuous and utilized by people in much the same way as that of the teachers from the Wang and Liu family networks, to support the transmission of a small body of ritual lore for self-help.[71] Indeed, in the eyes of local people he probably appeared as yet another travelling healer, not that different from a traveling doctor (*lingyi* 鈴醫) with a single pill for all ailments and some amulets, a Daoist priest or a fortuneteller who also possessed some amulets. At the same time, there can be little doubt that these texts were highly sensitive in their contents. The "Sutra of Asking about the Way" referred to the advent of the Dragon Flower Assembly, violent cosmic change and the fall of a dynasty. The "Text of the Undifferentiated Beginning to Transform by Illuminating" contained similar millenarian references (but no mention of the Dragon Flower Assembly), as well as stories about the advent of divine armies capable of defeating evil demonic creatures (i.e., those one might expect during the apocalypse). Although the lore that was available to Fan Mingde did have the potential of inspiring an active form of millenarian hope, when compared to the different

(PhD diss., University of California at Berkeley, 1994). He has published part of his findings in reworked form in Gaustad, "Prophets and Pretenders." I have also consulted Ma and Han, *Zhongguo minjian zongjiaoshi*, 1258–1311, and some primary materials (to verify my analysis, but the material is not quoted here for reasons of space).

70 This paragraph is based on Gaustad, "Religious Sectarianism and the State in Mid Qing China," 142–148, under consultation of Ma and Han, *Zhongguo minjian zongjiaoshi*, 1285–1293.

71 Gaustad, "Religious Sectarianism and the State in Mid Qing China," 149–150; Ma and Han, *Zhongguo minjian zongjiaoshi*, 1287.

narratives referred to with the preceding groups and networks, it still functioned in a context that was no different from other forms of ritual self-help. It seems to me that this limited usage context is extremely important in understanding why people joined such a network, viz., not in the expectation of any kind of apocalyptic and/or messianic event, but in the hope of obtaining a ritual cure for some kind of problem in their lives.

The pupils of Fan Mingde also transmitted a series of songs, which they had learned by heart and used in recruiting new pupils. The original name of the songs is unclear, but the pupils referred to them by their first words, "Most Great Person" (*shangdaren* 上大人), which apparently referred to Confucius as the first savior! The songs referred to the myth of the Unborn Venerable Mother and her banished children, the Cloud City, the three kalpas, as well as other elements of Qing messianic lore. They did not contain the references to apocalyptic disasters that were found in the other two texts, mentioned above.[72] Despite the evident messianic contents of these songs, they still functioned exclusively in the context of conventional healing and protection purposes, as powerful lore that enabled ritual self-help. Instead of thinking of the message as a model for concrete action, we should probably think of it as something akin to an underlying soteriology or mythology that most people most of the time would not be aware of. In the instable border regions, oral stories could easily become interpreted in a more apocalyptic manner, but all of this continued to serve as the background for selling protective mantras. As such it was not that different from other forms of demonological beliefs, in which people ascribe all kinds of attacks on their health to demonic activity and acquire protective amulets or have rituals performed to avert these dangers and hopefully be healed.

Over the years preceding the events of 1796–1804, these stories began to stress the advent of terrible apocalyptic disasters (such as military violence, floods, and storms) and the resulting need to obtain protection by reciting their mantras and following their saviors. What this concretely entailed remains unclear in the extant confessions, despite the considerable detail that has been preserved. The inquisition was always particularly interested in the reconstruction of networks of teachers and pupils, and therefore focused especially on the identification of the saviors who were to appear. These were identified as Maitreya and Zhu Ba 朱八 (Ba is part of the split version of Zhu or *muba* 木八, the family name of the Ming imperial house and therefore especially worrisome). Maitreya was thought to have been reborn in the

72 Ma and Han, *Zhongguo minjian zongjiaoshi*, 1286–1289.

Zhang 張 family on Shadowless Mountain (*wuyingshan* 無影山).[73] The appearance of the Zhu Ba figure and his alternative names Zhu Hongtao 朱紅桃 and Zhu Jiutao 朱九桃 in the rumors reflected the impact of southern demonological messianic traditions that were especially widespread in the late 1790s and early 1800s and would for instance feed into the mythology of the southern Chinese Triads. They were not yet present in the older teachings by Zhang Jindou 張進斗 or Fan Mingde.[74] Moreover, precisely in the years preceding the events of 1796–1804, many other elements from the original teachings appear to have been absent from the oral transmission, such as the Cloud City, the Unborn Venerable Mother, the Gongchang 弓長 Patriarch. Generally, there was a wide variety of prophecies in circulation, which created a sense of demonic threat and the perceived need to deal with these through the acquisition of protective mantras, but not through the preparation of any form of rebellious action. Even in combination with elements from the demonological messianic paradigm from the south, the network that the Qing inquisition traced back to Zhang Jindou, Fan Mingde and others was not destined to lead to messianic action. Many similar networks were never involved in actual violent activities and none of them were connected to the older religious groups and networks discussed above. What we see here is the diffusion of a largely oral culture, with teachings and practices that differed quite substantially according to each different charismatic teacher.

6 Concluding Observations

The preceding discussion is hardly a complete survey of new religious groups and networks in the late imperial period, but it does purport to be representative. I have tried to show that these various groupings do not necessarily form one single phenomenon from a socio-religious perspective, except if we persist in applying traditional labels such as the White Lotus Teachings or its modern quasi-academic derivatives such as "popular beliefs" (*minjian xinyang* 民間信仰) or "secret societies" (*mimi jieshe* 秘密結社, itself derived from pejorative nineteenth-century Western stereotypes about Jews and Free-Masons). I should add that the present selection of specific new religious groups and networks that I have used in this investigation is itself also still

73 Gaustad, "Religious Sectarianism and the State in Mid Qing China," 210, 212–213, 231–232, 238, 245, 257–258, 275–276 in particular.

74 Sources quoted in Gaustad, "Religious Sectarianism and the State in Mid Qing China," 202, 213, 231, 241–242.

prejudiced by this same historiography and its customary selection of socio-religious phenomena, a point that I return to further below.

In my analysis I have pointed out the specific geographical distribution of these various groups, because this point is often forgotten. In terms of their core regions, they did not really overlap spatially in the premodern period when they could function normally, suggesting that each group and network filled roughly the same kind of socio-religious need in their respective regions. I have not developed this point, but concentrated on two other aspects, namely differential access of adherents to textual lore and the nature of their access to ritual power. I have argued that we could imagine a scale of access to texts, independent of literacy—an issue that I have left out of consideration here. The adherents of new religious groups shared their religious knowledge as expressed in their sacred texts without fundamental restrictions on access, with all members potentially having the same basic lore. This category of religious practitioners might even be called "believers" in the Reformation sense of the word. The participants in new religious networks are perhaps best seen as customers, but the difference with being a customer of a regular Daoist priest or Buddhist monk would be that they actually obtained some ritual lore of their own. In these networks texts were available, but only used to validate the charisma of the higher-level teachers, without the latter sharing their overall soteriological narrative with the larger network. In some of these groups and networks there may have been potentially messianic narratives, but they never played a significant role. Indeed, the most important aspect of all of these groups (such as the Non-Action Teachings or Christianity) and networks (such as those of the Wang and Liu families) is their different degrees of access to religious narratives, lifestyles and ritual practices, rather than a messianic message about being rescued from the end of time.

We do find such narratives in one other type of network, which is even more diffuse than the family networks of the Wangs and Lius. Where these family networks still transmitted a fairly consistent and stable Buddho-Daoist message of inner cultivation directed at sharing in the energies of the larger cosmos, the even more fragmented demonological messianic networks did share a sense of end of time. However, even in these instances the primary function was to legitimate the transmission of simple ritual techniques to deal with this specific endtime. Rebellion intended to make this messianic expectation come true in the here and now was rarely part of it. This last type of network still used texts to legitimate the charisma of the ultimate teachers, but their texts were much shorter and less impressive. Their contents would be distributed in shorter oral form, losing many messianic and apocalyptic elements in the process. It would seem that these latter elements, which so worried the imperial state, were not the ritual core that mattered to most participants.

The actual socio-educational backgrounds of the members of new religious groups and participants in religious networks are difficult to ascertain. My own study of the Non-Action Teachings suggests that they could be urban or rural middle class, with some or even considerable education. It is probably the constant repression during the Qing in particular that kept their following restricted to non-elite groups and therefore hard to define more specifically in the absence of written sources. In some ways what we have here are the potential precursors to a reformation that could have been much more similar to the Protestant Reformation of the sixteenth century and after, had the political context been more amenable to it.

Another aspect of late imperial China that is often overlooked due to the tradition of analyzing these disparate groups and networks as a single coherent phenomenon, separate from mainstream Buddhism and Daoism, are the important historical connections with these traditions. I already mentioned that it makes more sense to see these groups and networks as local solutions to issues of faith (especially in the lay Buddhist case) and practice, but also of ritual power to address various life problems. Interestingly, some of these solutions drew on very old mainstream traditions that used to be elite Daoist or Buddhist practices, but which had stayed alive only on a local level. As a result, they appeared irregular and strange to the officials of the late Ming and Qing who were confronted with them. In many ways, however, these groups and networks were more in tune with ancient Chinese religious traditions than the Chan and Complete Perfection traditions that had come into being in the intervening centuries.

I should like to finish my discussion by drawing attention again to the problematic nature of my sample. Although the selection was determined by the conventional grouping of these various groups and networks in one single phenomenon of "heterodox sects," my analysis suggests that this is not a very fruitful approach. Instead, they should be understood as ever so many attempts to shape one's own religious life and ritual practice. In other words, they are attempts of local people to regain the religious agency that was largely denied to them in traditional Buddhist and Daoist ritual traditions; no doubt, this was also a major source of worry among the established religious institutions and the imperial state itself. Access to textual lore played a central role, but this access differed considerably and in my opinion fundamentally between the different groups and networks. They should be studied in the future as part of a much larger lay religious culture, together with "ordinary" lay Buddhist and lay Daoists, as well as religious groups and networks that are traditionally not understood as part of the same socio-religious phenomenon. Christianity and Islam would be cases in point, but I would propose including the late imperial spirit-writing and morality book movement here as well. All of these were local attempts by people of varying literate abilities and different socio-religious backgrounds to address fundamental religious as well as socio-political issues of their days. Texts played an increasingly important role in these activities, but sometimes more as objects of legitimation than for their actual message, and therefore people's different access to and varying ways of using texts should be a central topic of future study.

Bibliography

Asai Motoi 淺井紀. *Min shin jidai minkan shūkyō kessha no kenkyū* 明清時代民間宗教結社の研究. Tokyo: Kenbun shuppan, 1990.

Cao Xinyu 曹新宇. *Zushi de zupu: Ming Qing Bailianjiao shehui lishi diaocha zhiyi* 祖師的族譜—明清白蓮教社會歷史調查之一. Taipei: Boyang, 2015.

Dean, Kenneth. *Lord of the Three in One: The Spread of a Cult in Southeast China*. Princeton: Princeton University Press, 1998.

DuBois, Thomas. *The Sacred Village: Social Change and Religious Life in Rural North China*. Honolulu: University of Hawai'i Press, 2005.

Gaustad, Blaine. "Prophets and Pretenders: Inter-Sect Competition in Qianlong China." *Late Imperial China* 21, no. 1 (2000): 1–40.

Gaustad, Blaine. "Religious Sectarianism and the State in Mid Qing China: Background to the White Lotus Uprising of 1796–1804." PhD diss., University of California at Berkeley, 1994.

Harrison, Henrietta. *The Missionary's Curse: And Other Tales from a Chinese Catholic Village*. Berkeley: University of California Press, 2013.

Hung, Ho-fung. *Protest with Chinese Characteristics: Demonstrations, Riots, and Petitions in the Mid-Qing Dynasty*. New York: Columbia University Press, 2011.

Katz, Paul R. (Kang Bao 康豹). "Xifang xuejie yanjiu Zhongguo shequ zongjiao chuantong de zhuyao dongtai 西方學界研究中國社區宗教傳統的主要動態." *Wenshizhe* 文史哲, no. 310 (2009): 58–74.

Ma Xisha 馬西沙 and Han Bingfang 韓秉方. *Zhongguo minjian zongjiaoshi* 中國民間宗教史. Shanghai: Shanghai renmin chubanshe, 1992.

Murray, Dian. "Migration, Protection, and Racketeering: The Spread of the Tiandihui within China." In *Secret Societies Reconsidered: Perspectives on the Social History of Modern South China and Southeast Asia*, edited by David Ownby and Mary F. Somers Heidhues, 177–189. Armonk, N.Y.: Sharpe, 1993.

Naquin, Susan. *Millenarian Rebellion in China: The Eight Trigrams Rebellion of 1813*. New Haven: Yale University Press, 1976.

Naquin, Susan. "Connections between Rebellions: Sect Family Networks in Qing China," *Modern China* 8, no. 3 (1982): 337–360.

Naquin, Susan. "The Transmission of White Lotus Sectarianism in Late Imperial China." In *Popular Culture in Late Imperial China*, edited by David Johnson, Andrew T. Nathan, and Evelyn S. Rawski, 255–291. Berkeley: University of California Press, 1985.

Naquin, Susan. *Shantung Rebellion: The Wang Lun Uprising of 1774*. New Haven: Yale University Press, 1981.

Naquin, Susan. "Two Descent Groups in Northern China: The Wangs of Yung-p'ing Prefecture, 1500–1800." In *Kinship Organization in Late Imperial China*, edited by Patricia N. Ebrey and James L. Watson, 210–244. Berkeley: University of California Press, 1986.

Overmyer, Daniel L. *Precious Volumes: An Introduction to Chinese Sectarian Scriptures from the Sixteenth and Seventeenth Centuries*. Cambridge, MA: Harvard University Asia Center, 1999.

Qiu Lijuan 邱麗娟. "Qing Qianjiadao shiqi Hongyangjiao de yiliao chuanjiao 清乾嘉道時期紅陽教的醫療傳教." *Nanshi xuebao* 南師學報 37, no. 1 (2003): 17–35.

Reilly, Thomas H. *The Taiping Heavenly Kingdom: Rebellion and the Blasphemy of Empire*. Seattle: University of Washington Press, 2004.

Robinet, Isabelle. *Histoire du taoïsme des origines au XIVe siècle*. Paris: Les Editions du Cerf, 1991.

Sawada Mizuho 澤田瑞穂. "*Kōyōkyō shidan* 弘陽教試探." In *Zōho hōken no kenkyū* 増補寶卷の研究, 366–408. Tokyo: Kokusho kankōkai, 1975.

Seiwert, Hubert (with the help of Ma Xisha). *Popular Religious Movements and Heterodox Sects in Chinese History*. Leiden: Brill, 2003.

Song Jun 宋軍. *Qingdai Hongyangjiao yanjiu* 清代弘陽教研究. Beijing: Shehui kexue wenxian chubanshe, 2002.

Spence, Jonathan D. *God's Chinese Son: The Chinese Heavenly Kingdom of Hong Xiuquan*. London: Flamingo, 1997.

Taveirne, Patrick. *Han-Mongol Encounters and Missionary Endeavors: A History of Scheut in Ordos (Hetao), 1874–1911*. Leuven: Ferdinand Verbiest Foundation and Leuven University Press, 2004.

Ter Haar, Barend J. *The White Lotus Teachings in Chinese Religious History*. Leiden: Brill, 1992.

Ter Haar, Barend J. *Ritual and Mythology of the Chinese Triads: Creating an Identity*. Leiden: Brill, 1998.

Ter Haar, Barend J. "China's Inner Demons: The Political Impact of the Demonological Paradigm." In *China's Great Proletarian Revolution: Master Narratives and Post-Mao*

Counternarratives, edited by Woei Lien Chong, 27–68. Lanham, MD: Rowman & Littlefield, 2002.

Ter Haar, Barend J. "Whose Norm, Whose Heresy: The Case of the Song-Yuan White Lotus Movement." In *Häresien*, edited by Irene Pieper, Michael Schimmelpfennig, and Joost van Soosten, 67–93. München: Wilhelm Fink Verlag, 2003.

Ter Haar, Barend J. *Practicing Scripture: A Lay Buddhist Movement in Late Imperial China*. Honolulu: University of Hawai'i Press, 2014.

Ter Haar, Barend J. "Patriarch Luo as a Writer and Reader: Speculating about the Creative Process behind the Five Books in Six Volumes." *Sungkyun Journal of East Asian Studies* 15, no. 1 (2015): 21–44.

Ter Haar, Barend J. "State and Samgha in the Qing Period: A New Look at Old Figures." In *The Middle Kingdom and the Dharma Wheel: Aspects of the Relationship Between the Buddhist Samgha and the State in Chinese History*, edited by Thomas Jülch, 379–408. Leiden: Brill, 2016.

Wagner, Rudolf G. *Reenacting the Heavenly Vision: The Role of Religion in the Taiping Rebellion*. Berkeley: University of California, 1984.

Wang, Wensheng. *White Lotus Rebels and South China Pirates: Crisis and Reform in the Qing Empire*. Cambridge, Mass.: Harvard University Press, 2014.

Weller, Robert P. *Resistance, Chaos and Control in China: Taiping Rebels, Taiwanese Ghosts and Tiananmen*. Basingstoke: Macmillan, 1994.

Wu, Junqing. *Mandarins and Heretics: The Construction of "Heresy" in Chinese State Discourse*. Leiden: Brill, 2017.

Yang Ne 楊訥, ed. *Yuandai Bailianjiao ziliao huibian* 元代白蓮教資料彙編. Beijing: Zhonghua shuju, 1989.

CHAPTER 2

The Composition and Distribution of the Scriptures of the Tongshanshe 同善社, with a Focus on the *Ten Thousand Buddha Scripture* (1917–1949)

Wang Chien-chuan
Translated by David Ownby

1 Introduction

After the founding of the Republic of China in 1912, new state policies on religion led many religious groups to register with the government in the hopes of being recognized as such. Redemptive societies such as the Moral Study Society (Daode xueshe 道德學社), the Society for Goodness (Tongshanshe 同善社), and the Society for the Great Unity of World Religions (Shijie zongjiao datonghui 世界宗教大同會) were established as part of this trend, and became very active. The Tongshanshe grew out of the late Qing Way of Anterior Heaven (Xiantiandao 先天道), and advocated the unity of Confucianism, Buddhism, and Daoism. Their teachings emphasized the three great apocalyptic ages, or *kalpas*, and preached that the decadence of mankind prompted the heavens to send down disasters that would destroy humanity and that only those people who practiced the five ethical principles and the eight virtues would survive. The daily activities of the Tongshanshe focused on *The Ten Thousand Buddha Scripture* (*Wanfojing* 萬佛經) and inner alchemy (*neidan* 內丹) cultivation. The group's leader was Peng Huilong 彭迴龍 (1873–1950), who directed the group's activities throughout the country.

Research results over the past few decades have clearly illustrated that the Society for Goodness attracted a significant number of believers. Between 1917 and 1949, at least several million followers joined the organization, which makes it a well-known and sizeable religious group of the Republican period.[1] Past research on the society has addressed the group's history, rituals, and philanthropic activities, and has made numerous discoveries and filled in many

1 Wang Chien-chuan 王見川, "Tongshanshe zaoqi de tedian ji zai Yunnan de fazhan (1912–1937) 同善社早期的特點及在雲南的發展 (1912–1937)," *Minsu quyi* 民俗曲藝, no. 172 (2011): 128.

 | DOI:10.1163/9789004424166_004

blank spaces.[2] However, no one has at yet thoroughly studied Tongshanshe scriptures. Some work has indeed been done on spirit-writing texts connected to the Tongshanshe, such as the *Precious Notes from the Depths of Obscurity* (*Dongming baoji* 洞冥寶記), but such texts are not really Tongshanshe scriptures, and using them as a reflection of Tongshanshe teachings is problematic.[3] This essay takes the Tongshanshe text *The Ten Thousand Buddha Scripture* as its focus to discuss the following questions:

1. How were Tongshanshe scriptures composed?
2. How were Tongshanshe scriptures distributed?
3. Did the content of Tongshanshe scriptures change over the course of the evolution of the group?

2 Tongshanshe Scriptures and the Ten Thousand Buddha Scripture

In his *Research on the Great Way of Anterior Heaven System* (*Xiantian dadao xitong yanjiu* 先天大道系統研究), Lin Wanchuan 林萬傳, the well-known Taiwanese scholar of popular religion, noted that Republican-period texts served as the principal scriptures of the Tongshanshe, supplemented by earlier Xiantiandao or Buddhist, Daoist, and Confucian texts.[4] However, in his well-known volume, *The Society of Goodness* (*Tongshanshe*), Lu Zhongwei 陸仲偉, a mainland specialist on popular religious groups, mentions "texts written [by

2 Recent research on the Tongshanshe includes: Lu Zhongwei 陸仲偉, *Tongshanshe* 同善社 (Beijing: Shehui wenti yanjiu congshu bianji weiyuanhui, 2005); Wang Chien-chuan, "Tongshanshe zaoqi de tedian ji zai Yunnan de fazhan"; Wang Chien-chuan, "Mingshan shuju yu Tongshanshe: Jiantan *Xuanling Yuhuangjing* de liuchuan 明善書局與同善社：兼談《玄靈玉皇經》的流傳," *Mazu yu minjian xinyang: Yanjiu tongxun* 媽祖與民間信仰：研究通訊 1 (2012): 1–13.

3 Komukai Sakurako 小武海櫻子, "Tongshanshe de zongjiao shijieguan: Shixi *Dongming baoji* 同善社的宗教世界觀—試析《洞冥寶記》," in *Yanjiu xinshijie: Mazu yu Huaren minjian xinyang guoji yantaohui lunwenji* 研究新視界：媽祖與華人民間信仰國際研討會論文集, ed. Wang Chien-chuan 王見川 and Li Shiwei 李世偉 (Taipei: Boyang, 2014), 363–388.

4 Lin Wanchuan 林萬傳, *Xiantian dadao xitong yanjiu*先天大道系統研究 (Tainan: Tianju, 1986), 183–184, lists the following Xiantiandao scriptures: *Wenfa shuji* 聞法述記, *Zhongxue cantong* 中學參同, *Dongming baoji* 洞冥寶記, *Huixiang yulu* 回鄉語錄, *Huilong Shizun pudu yulu* 迴龍師尊普度語錄, *Xizi zhengyanlu* 惜字徵驗錄, *Pantao yanji* 蟠桃宴記, *Huanxiang zhizhi* 還鄉直指, *Pomi yulu* 破迷語錄, *Wulun dadao* 五倫大道, *Xiuzhen jiejing* 修真捷徑, *Liaodao milu* 了道秘錄, *Chushi biyao* 出世必要, and *Shugu laoren zhipo wushi da moguan* 述古老人指破五十大魔關.

the group] to spread the Way" (*bianzhuan chuandao dianji* 編撰傳道典籍).[5] On the basis of these two scholars' discussions of Tongshanshe scriptures, we can arrive at the following categorization of the Tongshanshe canon, which included:

1. Texts written by the group leader, such as *Records of Sayings of Master [Peng] Huilong who Saves the World* (*Huilong shizun pudu yulu* 迴龍師尊普度語錄) and *Tales of the Ancient Man who Identified and Destroyed Fifty Great Demons* (*Shugu laoren zhipo wushi damoguan* 述古老人指破五十大魔關).
2. Accounts composed by believers, such as *Accounts of Hearing the Dharma* (*Wenfa shuji* 聞法述記), *Records of Returning Home* (*Huixiang yulu* 回鄉語錄), or *Directions for Returning Home* (*Huanxiang zhizhi* 還鄉直指).
3. Spirit-writing texts and morality books linked to the Tongshanshe, such as *Precious Notes from the Depths of Obscurity*, *Record of the Banquet of the Peach of Immortality* (*Pantao yanji* 蟠桃宴記), and *The Great Way of the Five Cardinal Relationships* (*Wulun dadao* 五倫大道).
4. Tongshanshe documents and regulations, such as: *Regulations of the Tongshanshe* (*Tongshanshe zhangcheng* 同善社章程), *Collected Temple Rules* (*Fotang guize hebian* 佛堂規則合編), *Promulgation of the Patriarch's Lineage* (*Zupai jiexiao* 祖派揭曉), *Collection of Notifications of the Tongshanshe Headquarters* (*Tongshan zongshe chuandan huibian* 同善總社傳單彙編).
5. Morality books in wide circulation, such as the [*Yuan*] *Liaofan's Lessons for His Son* (*Liaofan xunzishu* 了凡訓子書).
6. Daoist *neidan* cultivation texts, such as *The True Teaching for Chanting the Way* (*Changdao zhenyan* 唱道真言), *Proof of the Golden Immortal* (*Jinxian lunzheng* 金仙論證), and *Scripture of the Life of Wisdom* (*Huimingjing* 慧命經).
7. Scriptures unique to the Tongshanshe, such as *The Scripture of the Completion of the Way* (*Liaodaojing* 了道經).

5 According to Lu Zhongwei's *Tongshanshe*, pp. 85–100, Tongshanshe scriptures included: *Liaodaojing* 了道經, *Huilong Shizun pudu yulu* 廻龍師尊普度語錄, *Tongshanshe zhangcheng* 同善社章程, *Fotang guize hebian* 佛堂規則合编, *Jiashennian fogui* 甲申年佛規, *Zupai xiuzheng buyi* 祖派修正補遺, *Zupai jiexiao* 祖派揭曉, *Tongshanshe chuandan huibian* 同善總社傳單彙編, *Wendao zhinan* 問道指南, *Xiuxing shiyao qianzhu* 修行十要簽注, *Huixiang yulu* 回鄉語錄, *Huanxiang zhizhi* 還鄉直指, *Pomi yulu*, 破迷語錄, *Xizi zhengyanlu* 惜字徵驗錄, *Changdao zhenyan* 唱道真言, *Jinxian lunzheng* 金仙論證, *Huimingjing* 慧命經, *Daomen yuyao* 道門語要, *Yufu zhizhi* 玉符直指, *Sanjiao qunji xingshilu* 三教群集醒世錄, *Liaofan xunzishu* 了凡訓子書, *Wugeng jiashu* 五更家書, and *Sanjiao hecan* 三教合參.

It is interesting that the only Tongshanshe scripture the two scholars mention is *The Scripture of the Completion of the Way*, which was composed only in 1932 after the group was suppressed, as a response to the changed political environment.[6] In that case, what texts did the Tongshanshe use before 1932? We find some clues in the *Collected Notifications of the Tongshanshe Headquarters* from the early Republican period:

1. In a text dated 1917 we find: "Practitioners should burn incense and light the lamp morning and night, should kneel and recite the *Perfected Scripture of the Ten Thousand Buddhas* (*Wanfo zhenjing* 萬佛真經) several times, and should silently pray to Heaven to save them from the coming apocalypse."[7]
   丁巳年（1917）…… 同仁尤宜早晚焚香點鐙，跪誦《萬佛真經》數遍，默禱蒼穹，挽回劫運。
2. In a text dated 1923 we find: "We long ago banned the circulation of tales of the miraculous feats of the gods of happiness and misfortune. How can it be that recently members from all over have been printing and circulating stories of strange events, for example a stele that has been discovered somewhere, or talismans and mantras revealed in some spirit-writing altar, or taken from *Lifeboat* [the title of a morality book], or from a text to avert disaster? In the past the Tongshanshe headquarters printed a combined version of the *Treatise of the Exalted One on Response and Retribution* (*Taishang ganyingpian* 太上感應篇), *Ledgers of Merit and Demerit of the God of Culture and Literature* (*Wenchang gongguoge* 文昌功過格), and the *Scripture of the Ten Thousand Buddhas to Avert the Apocalypse* (*Wanfo jiujiejing* 萬佛救劫經). These have been distributed to all groups and all members are to respectfully receive and recite them. The way to diminish catastrophes and avert the apocalypse is completely contained therein, which is why it is called the miraculous recipe to save [believers] from the apocalypse."[8]
   癸亥年(1923)……其他吉凶休咎神奇怪異之事……早已禁止傳說。詎近來各社社員間有印送怪異傳單，如某處發現之碑文，某壇乩書之符咒，以及救生船，避災文……總社前以《太上感應篇》《文昌功過

6 *Huilong Shizun pudu yulu* 迴龍師尊普度語錄 (Shanghai: Xuanhua, 1935), vol. 2, 21–22. The *Liaodaojing* used in this essay is the 1932 edition by the "Old Man from Longfengshan who told of ancient times" 龍鳳山述古老人, publisher unclear. Many thanks to Lu Zhongwei for providing me with this text.

7 *Tongshan zongshe chuandan huibian* 同善總社傳單彙編 (Beiping: Tianhua yinshuguan, n.d.), section *dingsi* 丁巳, p. 2.

8 *Tongshan zongshe chuandan huibian*, section *guihai* 癸亥, p. 9.

格》《萬佛救劫經》三種合刊，發行各社，原欲社員人人遵奉，持行誦讀，消災解劫之道，即備其中，此救劫妙方之所由名。

The *Treatise of the Exalted One on Response and Retribution* and *Ledgers of Merit and Demerit of the God of Culture and Literature* are popular morality books that preceded the founding of the Tongshanshe. Comparing this information with the texts cited above, it is clear that the *Perfected Scripture of the Ten Thousand Buddhas*, which the Tongshanshe members were supposed to recite morning and evening, must also have been called the *Scripture of the Ten Thousand Buddhas to Avert the Apocalypse*. This scripture is one that was used after the Tongshanshe was registered in 1917 and thus legally permitted to preach and proselytize.[9] Yang Jindong 楊覲東, leader of the Yunnan Tongshanshe, once mentioned his having "recited the *Ten Thousand Buddha Scripture* every morning" (每晨要唸《萬佛經》).[10] And the monk Xin'an 心庵頭陀 (Tang Guangxian 唐光先), a Tongshanshe activist from Yancheng 鹽城 in Jiangsu, urged his listeners as follows: To cultivate the great Way, you must first carry out one or two acts of philanthropy (*waigong* 外功), then practice meditation, and every day recite the *Ten Thousand Buddha Scripture* several times and finally follow the *Scriptures of the Three Sages* (*Sanshengjing* 三聖經, a collection of three morality books published together), after which one eventually enters the wonderful realm of cultivation.[11]

Given these clues, one wonders when the *Ten Thousand Buddha Scripture* became a Tongshanshe scripture, and who wrote it. Lin Wanchuan says that the *Ten Thousand Buddha Scripture* was proclaimed by the fifteenth patriarch of the Tongshanshe, Hu Huizhen 胡慧貞, the Buddha of the Merciful Sound 慈音佛.[12] Is this really the case? The text by the Tongshanshe leader, *Records of Sayings of Master [Peng] Huilong who Saves the World*, provides one answer:

> The Master said: Times being not peaceful, I have encouraged my followers to recite the *Ten Thousand Buddha Scripture*. But most of my followers did not obey me and did not carry out my suggestion. So they do not understand the importance and the origin of this scripture. In the spring of the *wuchen* year, I explained the origins of the *Ten Thousand Buddha*

9 On the topic of Tongshanshe's registration with the government, see Wang Chien-chuan 王見川, "Tongshanshe zaoqi de lishi (1912–1945) chutan 同善社早期的歷史 (1912–1945) 初探," *Minjian zongjiao* 民間宗教 1 (1995): 57–81. An English translation is available in Wang Jianchuan, "An Exploration of the Early History of the Tongshanshe (1912–1945)," *Chinese Studies in History* 44, nos. 1–2 (2010/11): 121–131.

10 Wang Chien-chuan, "Tongshanshe zaoqi de tedian," 144.

11 Xin'an toutuo 心庵頭陀, *Huixiang yulu* 回鄉語錄 (N.p.: 1931), 5.

12 Lin Wanchuan, *Xiantian dadao xitong yanjiu*, 162.

Scripture. Have you all forgotten? I will say it again: at the time, the gods were concerned about the imminent turning of the third kalpa, and those who wished to assist Maitreya took on human form and returned to earth to save the worthy. At this time, the heavenly master also sent many monsters, who also descended to earth. As they were on the point of leaving, they went to see the Buddha of the Merciful Sound to receive instructions. The Buddha of the Merciful Sound dispensed great mercy, fearing that the 96[00,000,000] imperial embryos would be harmed, and especially ordered the demons, saying: "When you descend into the world, do not harm the good men and believing women." The demons said, "How can we tell them apart?" The Buddha of the Merciful Sound replied, "Note those who recite the *Ten Thousand Buddha Scripture*." The demons assented. The Buddha of the Merciful Sound was still afraid that the demons would act chaotically on earth, harming the True Master of the Ten Thousand Souls, the Three Thousand Children of Buddha, and the 96[00,000,000] imperial embryos, so that they could not return to their origins, and he ordered them to sign their name to a document before going.

When I accepted the *daotong* [i.e., the leadership of the faith], the heavens commanded me to acquire this scripture. At this time I braved many difficulties and trials before arriving at Master Shandao's [i.e., Peng Huilong's master] place, where I first acquired the *Ten Thousand Buddha Scripture* from him. I then passed the scripture along to my disciples and in time it became popular everywhere. Everyone recited it and put its principles into practice as the only way to avoid the turning of the kalpa. Practicing inner and exterior cultivation, many succeeded in reaching the shore of the Way. However, should one encounter demons, what skill should believers use to resist them? The *Ten Thousand Buddha Scripture* works in this context as well. Reciting the *Ten Thousand Buddha Scripture* allows one to avoid the turning of the kalpa. One should know that the heavenly master in *The Commandments of the Ten Thousand Buddhas* [*Wanfoling*, a collection of incantations] is not Zhang Tianshi [Celestial Master Zhang, i.e., the founder of the Way of the Heavenly Masters in the latter Han dynasty], but instead the Martial Sage and Imperial Lord [Wusheng dijun, i.e., Guandi 關帝]. Still, various disasters are all revealed clearly in the *Ten Thousand Buddha Scripture*; one may avert most catastrophes, with the exception of the "catastrophe of plants killing humans." You should recognize the grimness of the forthcoming Way. Henceforth you must recite *The Commandments of the Ten Thousand Buddhas* daily, reciting it orally and believing it in your heart. You must cultivate this diligently morning and night, attentively cultivating *The Commandments of the Ten Thousand Buddhas*. I urge followers to recite the *Ten Thousand Buddha Scripture*, which will have lasting positive effects. Those who do not want to attain the truth and accomplish the Way, okay, but if you want to return to your roots and origins, you must practice the *Scriptures of the Three Sages*. Although I repeatedly ordered them do this, they ignored me as if I were just a chatty old man.[13]

師尊說曰:現在時勢不靖，吾嘗催諸大原人，虔誦《萬佛經》。奈諸大原人不聽吾話，是多未遵行者。由於不知此經之重要及其來歷。吾在戊辰春曾將《萬佛經》來由說明，諸子忘卻耶?吾再重申其說:當日諸天聖真仙佛為三期了道在急，各願協助彌勒佛分性下世收緣。有分性，有倒裝，現在全在人間。彼時天尊亦派諸大魔煞，一齊下界。臨行時，到慈音佛處請命。慈音佛大發慈悲，恐九六皇胎受其擾害，特囑諸大魔煞曰:爾等下界，對於善男信女，切莫傷他。諸大魔煞曰:何以分辨?慈音佛說曰:誦《萬佛經》者以為記。諸大魔煞於是唯唯。慈音佛又恐諸大魔煞下界胡為，擾亂萬靈真宰，三千佛子，九六皇胎，不得歸原。又令諸大魔煞各各簽押而去。

吾當日接受道統時，上天即命吾去取此經。彼時曾受了幾次槍林彈雨，艱苦備嚐……方達到山道師尊處，始將《萬佛經》求到手。吾即攜轉，傳與弟子，以期風行海內，人人風誦，各各躬行實踐，方可脫逃劫運。修持內外，庶幾同登道岸。不然遇到一般魔煞，拿什麼本領去抵擋!

至於《萬佛令》，亦復如斯。如願領《萬佛經》，只唸《萬佛經》，亦能免劫。須知《萬佛令》中之天師，非張天師，乃武聖帝君……但《萬佛經》之中諸劫俱易見，或可以得幸免，為草木傷人劫，這一條難獲免。各位要知道否。從茲要逐日唸此經，口誦心維《萬佛令》，要早晚煉……此時諸子趕緊用功，勤練《萬佛令》，勸同志誦《萬佛經》，久久自有無限好處。諸子不願登真成道則已，如欲返本還鄉，非實行遵從《三聖經》不可。吾一再叮嚀諸子，皆視為老生常談。

The "*wuchen*" year in the text is 1928, and the Buddha of the Merciful Sound is the title of Hu Huizhen, fifteenth patriarch of the Tongshanshe.[14] Peng Huilong's remarks are extremely important and provide considerable

13 *Huilong Shizun pudu yulu* 迴龍師尊普度語錄, vol. 1: 44–46.

14 Lin Wanchuan, *Xiantian dadao xitong yanjiu*, 162. According to Yang Jindong, *Zupai jiexiao* 祖派揭曉 (Shanghai: Mingshan, 1933), the fourteenth patriarch of the Tongshanshe was Li Wancheng 黎晚成, and the fifteenth was Yuan Shihe 袁世河. Hu Huizhen was one of Yuan Shihe's cadres and bore the title *zhengdao* 證道, the rough equivalent of "master" in Tongshanshe ranks.

information. First, reciting the *Ten Thousand Buddha Scripture* is the standard by which the Buddha of the Merciful Sound and the Damowang 大魔王 (Great Demon King) distinguish the saved from those that are not saved. Second, Peng Huilong received an order to retrieve the *Ten Thousand Buddha Scripture* from Master Shandao after becoming the leader of the Tongshanshe. Third, reciting and embracing the *Ten Thousand Buddha Scripture* and *The Commandments of the Ten Thousand Buddhas* is the way to avoid the apocalypse. Fourth, Peng Huilong had told his followers about the origins and importance of the *Ten Thousand Buddha Scripture* as early as 1928. Fifth, the heavenly master (chief deity) in the *Ten Thousand Buddha Scripture* is Guandi. Sixth, the *Scripture of the Three Sages* was taken as a scripture by the Tongshanshe. Viewed from this perspective, we have learned two important things: First, the *Ten Thousand Buddha Scripture* was a scripture that circulated in the Tongshanshe after the death of Hu Huizhen. The legend concerning the agreement between the Buddha of the Merciful Sound and the demon king was invented by the Tongshanshe leadership to strengthen its sacred character. Second, we learn about the importance of the *Scripture of the Three Sages* in the Tongshanshe.

Actually, as early as 1920, when the Tongshanshe leadership asked its cadres to spread the Way, they were asked to preach the *Scripture of the Three Sages* or other karmic maxims on a regular basis.[15] In 1927, the government crackdown on Tongshanshe frightened Tongshanshe followers, who believed that it meant that the apocalypse was nigh.[16] The Tongshanshe leadership immediately issued a proclamation from the Master to the effect that those practicing the teachings of the *Scripture of the Three Sages* could avoid the apocalypse.[17]

15 *Tongshan zongshe chuandan huibian*, section *gengshen* 庚申, 2.

16 Wang Chien-chuan, "Tongshanshe zaoqi de lishi," 66–67; Wang Chien-chuan, "Jindai Zhongguo de fuji, cishan yu 'mixin': Yi *Yinguang wenchao* wei kaocha xiansuo 近代中國的扶乩、慈善與「迷信」：以印光文鈔為考查線索," in *Xinyang, shijian yu wenhua tiaoshi: Disijie guoji Hanxue huiyi lunwenji* 信仰、實踐與文化調適：第四屆國際漢學會議論文集, ed. Kang Bao 康豹 (Paul Katz) and Liu Shufen 劉淑芬 (Taipei: Academia Sinica, 2013), 554–556.

17 See Appendix 1 at the end of this chapter, entitled "Fengxing *Sanshengjing* neng mian dajie zhi shuoming 奉行《三聖經》能免大劫之說明": "Yesterday I received via a third person a message from Lei Xingcheng's [Lei Xingcheng was one of Peng Huilong's most important disciples, and occupied a position in the Tongshanshe directly below Peng], which said that he had learned that actions had been taken against many Tongshanshe believers, and that he had seen such attacks with his own eyes. Hence I earnestly prayed to Yaotian [the Old Mother] to conceive of a way to protect sincere believers. If the men and women of the earth can carry out the *Sanshengjing*, remaining obedient to it throughout their life, then I will allow them to avoid the apocalypse." 昨轉奉雷興成先生教諭，啟者：前接各地函稱風潮四起，災難蘋來。原人社址竟有被其蹂躪者，是以

This illustrates the importance accorded to the *Scripture of the Three Sages* by the leadership of the Tongshanshe.

The Basic Elements of the Golden Rule (*Jinke jiyao* 金科輯要), a spirit-writing text produced by a Wenchang Dijun group in the late Qing period that emphasized the eight virtues (*bade* 八德) to be practiced to avert the apocalypse, was also seen as important by Tongshanshe leaders.[18] In the National Studies Academy 國學專修館 set up by the Tongshanshe, it was a rule that on the first and fifteenth of every lunar month there would be incense burned before the tablet of Confucius, and *The Basic Elements of the Golden Rule* would be recited. The reason the Tongshanshe leadership accorded such importance to this text was because of its emphasis on the eight virtues (filiality, brotherly love, loyalty, trustworthiness, propriety, integrity, honesty, a sense of shame), which were precisely the ethical values promoted by the Tongshanshe.[19] The same reason explains why the Tongshanshe selected the *Scripture of the Three Sages* as one of its basic texts.[20]

The crackdown on the Tongshanshe by the KMT government in 1927 forced the Tongshanshe either to change its name or to go underground.[21] But this was not a key moment in the history of the Tongshanshe. Instead 1932 was more important, because it was during that year that the Tongshanshe produced two new scriptures. The first was the *The Scripture of the Completion of the Way*. As we read in the *Records of Sayings of Master* [*Peng*] *Huilong who Saves the World*:

> As the third kalpa approached, my wish was to engage in universal salvation ... Thinking back on it, it had been five years since the crackdown. But such hardships were also a time for testing the faith of the followers ... And in the fall of 1932, the Old Mother revealed a [new regulation], and directly transmitted the *The Scripture of the Completion of the Way*. Heaven reestablished the three basic laws, and I expected my followers to apply the teachings diligently, completing others and completing themselves, together approaching the Dragon Flower Assembly. They should use this occasion to do careful reading of *The Scripture of the Completion*

懇祈瑤天設法保護。沐批：倘大地男女能遵《三聖經》，終身奉行者，准其免災。

18 *Tongshan zongshe chuandan huibian*, section *renxu* 壬戌: 4–5.

19 Wang Chien-chuan, "Cong 'bazi' dao 'bade': Jiantan bade zaoqi wenxian *Bazi jueyuan* 從「八字」到「八德」：兼談八德早期文獻《八字覺原》," in *Mazu yu minjian xinyang: Yanjiu tongxun* 4 (2013): 126–127.

20 See Appendix 1, at the end of this chapter.

21 Wang Chien-chuan, "Jindai Zhongguo de fuluan," 155.

> *of the Way*, and respect and practice *The Three Basic Buddhist Rules* [*Sanyuan fogui* 三元佛規, i.e., the guidelines to follow for Tongshanshe members], cultivating inner body and outer comportment.
>
> 時屆三期，緣開普度……憶自道務停擱，五易春秋。然停擱時間即考懲時間……壬申仲春，天示規章，直傳《了道真經》，重定三元條例，原期及門諸子，身體力行……成人成己，共赴龍華……爾生當乘時粹勵，熟讀《了道真經》，遵守續訂《三元佛規》，勤修內體，努辦外功。[22]

The Scripture of the Completion of the Way is also called the Scripture of the Three Teachings, Spoken by the Buddha, that Complete the Way (*Foshuo sanjiao liaodaojing* 佛說三教了道經).[23] According to the preface, the contents include the rules and regulations established by the Quiet and Unrestrained Buddha (Qingjing zizaifo 清靜自在佛), incantations, precious mandates recited to various gods, and scriptures. Having examined the entire scripture, two points are worthy of notice: 1. In the precious invocations, Guandi is referred to as the Eighteenth Heavenly Emperor (Shiba tianhuang 十八天皇) and the Mysterious and Numinous Lofty Emperor on High (Xuanling gaoshangdi 玄靈高上帝). 2. The scripture imitates the style of Buddhist scriptures, with the Master pronouncing the dharma, and recounts how the Peaceful Ancient Buddha Who is Carrying out the Transformations on Behalf of Heaven (Daitian xinghua qingjing gufo 代天行化清靜古佛) informs the believers how to escape the turning of the kalpa, the key to which is to implore everyone to follow the five cardinal relations and the eight virtues.

From this we see that the Tongshanshe consistently took the five cardinal relations and the eight virtues as scriptural content.[24] In addition, the Tongshanshe was relatively open to change, and evolved with the times. In the early 1930s, it was popular in religious circles in China to "take Guandi 關帝 as the Jade Emperor,"[25] and Guandi was called "the Eighteenth Heavenly Emperor."[26] In their scriptures, the Tongshanshe referred to Guandi as "the

---

22 *Huilong shizun pudu yulu*, vol. 2: 21–22.

23 Longfengshan Shugu Laoren version of the *The Scripture of the Completion of the Way.*

24 On the "eight virtues," see Wang Chien-chuan, "Cong 'bazi' dao 'bade'."

25 Translator's note: In religious circles in China the 1930s, stories circulated to the effect that Guandi, because of his interventions to avert the apocalypse, had been elevated to the position of the Jade Emperor (more specifically, the Eighteenth Jade Emperor), the supreme god in the pantheon of popular religion.

26 Wang Chien-chuan, "Cong 'Guandi' dao 'Yuhuang' tansuo 從「關帝」到「玉皇」探索," in *Jindai de Guandi xinyang yu jingdian: Jiantan qizai Xin, Ma de fazhan* 近代的關帝

Eighteenth Heavenly Emperor" and the "Mysterious and Numinous Lofty Emperor on High." Before long, in 1932 they proclaimed the *Scripture of the Mysterious and Numinous Jade Emperor* (*Xuanling Yuhuangjing* 玄靈玉皇經),[27] which was the second scripture produced by the group during this period. The Tongshanshe leadership considered this scripture to be extremely important, telling followers that it was as important as the *Ten Thousand Buddha Scripture*, another scripture that they should recite morning and night.[28] This practice of responding to new ideas in the larger religious community can be seen in the *Ten Thousand Buddha Scripture* as well.

3 Editions and Contents of the *Ten Thousand Buddha Scripture*

What changes in content do we find in the *Ten Thousand Buddha Scripture* that are reflective of the influence of the broader religious environment? For the sake of convenience, let's begin with a discussion of the different editions of the text.[29] According to what I have seen to date, there are at least the following editions:

1. 1923 edition, publisher Hongda Morality Bookstore 宏大善書.
2. 1925 edition, main deity, Limitless Dīpaṃkara Buddha (Wuji randengfo 無極燃燈佛), publisher Tang Jiyu 唐際虞, Taiping Street, Mengcheng 蒙城内太平街.
3. 1928 edition, main deity Quiet and Unrestrained Dīpaṃkara Buddha (Wuji qingjing zizai randengfo 無極清靜自在燃燈佛), publisher Tongshanshe of Xiangyun, Yunnan.
4. 1931 (fall) edition, publisher Tiyuan Lithographers 體元石印局.
5. 1957 edition, main deity Quiet and Unrestrained Limitless Dīpaṃkara Buddha Who Saves the Apocalypse (Qingjing zizai jiuzai jiunan wuji randengfo 清靜自在救災救難無極燃燈佛), photocopied from the Beiping Tianhuaguan edition, with additions.

信仰與經典：兼談其在新、馬的發展, ed. Wang Chien-chuan (Taipei: Boyang, 2010), 114–121.

27 Wang Chien-chuan, "Mingshan shuju," 7–8.

28 Wang Chien-chuan, "Mingshan shuju," 7–8.

29 I procured most of these editions of the *Ten Thousand Buddha Scripture* in the course of my research, with the exception of the 1925 and 1941 editions, which were kindly given to me by Professor Hou Chong 侯冲. The 1928 edition is included in Wang Chien-chuan et al., eds., *Zhongguo yuyan jiujieshu huibian* 中國預言救刼書彙編 (Taipei: Xinwenfeng, 2010), 390–434.

6. 1966 edition, main deity Quiet and Unrestrained Limitless Dīpaṃkara Buddha Who Saves the Apocalypse, publisher Taiwan Yonghe Believers Reedition.
7. 1978 edition, main deity Quiet and Unrestrained Limitless Dīpaṃkara Buddha Who Saves the Apocalypse, publisher Taipei City Believers Reedition.
8. Undated edition, main deity Quiet and Unrestrained Limitless Dīpaṃkara Buddha Who Saves the Apocalypse, publisher Taipei City Neihu Believers Reedition.

The 1925 edition[30] of the *Ten Thousand Buddha Scripture* was published prior to the suppression of the Tongshanshe, so its original appearance has been preserved. In consulting this edition, we learn that, according the preface, the original contents were as follows:

1. Cover: Scripture of the Ten Thousand Buddhas to Avert the Apocalypse;
2. With all my heart I take refuge in and honor the sixteen Buddhas including the Buddha Who Should Descend to the World, to avert the sixteen catastrophes, including among others the "five-hundred-thunderbolt catastrophe";
3. The special character of the *Ten Thousand Buddha Scripture*, according to the Buddha;
4. Worship the various gods and repent;
5. Disciples vow to practice the correct way, and avoid the sea of bitterness;
6. Believers ask for the heavens to extend grace, and request the Buddhas and bodhisattvas to emit their great vow to save all damaged souls;
7. Sentient beings encounter the final kalpa, and all must chant the various apocalypse-diverting scriptures morning and night, sincerely worship the gods, practice vegetarianism and refrain from killing, respect the Three Refuges and Five Precepts. When approaching disaster, pray to Buddha and silently recite the *Ten Thousand Buddha Scripture*, and the various devils will not invade;
8. Take a vow to avoid the final kalpa and avoid reincarnation;
9. With all my heart I take refuge in and honor Buddha Dīpaṃkara of the Non-Ultimate, Buddha Śākyamuni of the Great Ultimate, Buddha Maitreya of the August Ultimate.

---

30 The 1923 edition of *Wanfojing* has been collected and reprinted in *Jindai Zhongguo minjian zongjiao jingjuan wenxian* 近代中國民間宗教經卷文獻, ed. Wang Chien-chuan 王見川 and Fan Chun-wu 范純武 (Taipei: Xinwenfeng, 2015), vol. 3, 261–262. The 1925 edition was published by Tongshanshe, but has not been reprinted in modern collections, so the following discussion is based on this version. I would like to thank Chen Ling for her distance help in comparing the different versions of *Wanfojing*.

10. Concluding ritual: recite with reverence the name of Buddha Amitābha Who is the Grand Guardian of Celestial Prime.[31]

一、 首頁:《萬佛救劫經》。
二、 至心歸命禮:當來下世佛等十六佛,免脫五百雷霆劫等十六劫。
三、 《佛說萬佛經》特性。
四、 禮拜諸神懺悔。
五、 弟子誓行正道,脫苦海。
六、 信眾某哀懇上天開恩,討準諸佛菩薩,發洪願普渡一切眾殘靈(眾生)。
七、 生逢末劫,眾生要朝暮誦諸品救劫經,虔誠禮拜諸佛,持齋戒殺,謹守三皈五戒,臨難時拜佛,默念《萬佛經》,諸魔不侵。
八、 發誓願脫末劫,永不下生。
九、 至心歸命禮:南無無極燃燈佛、太極釋迦佛、皇極彌勒佛。
十、 結束:唸南無天元太保阿彌陀佛。

Looking at the contents, the *Scripture of the Ten Thousand Buddhas to Avert the Apocalypse* professes belief in the three kalpas, in the Three Refuges and Five Precepts, and in vegetarianism, all acts performed by various religious groups. At the same time, the language in the text that asks heaven's benevolence and makes vows shows evidence of Xiantiandao influence. As for vegetarianism, the *Scripture of the Ten Thousand Buddhas to Avert the Apocalypse* clearly was not composed while Peng Huilong was the leader, because the Tongshanshe did not advocate vegetarianism.[32] In other words, Peng Huilong accepted the importance accorded to the *Scripture of the Ten Thousand Buddhas to Avert the Apocalypse*, but overlooked contradictions between the contents of the text and his own teachings. We can also see that when the *Scripture of the Ten Thousand Buddhas to Avert the Apocalypse* became a Tongshanshe scripture an important value of the previous groups that had worshipped the *Ten Thousand Buddha Scripture* was obscured. In sum, we see no trace of Tongshanshe leader Peng Huilong in the 1925 edition of the *Ten Thousand Buddha Scripture*. However, when we get to the 1928 edition, not only has the name become the *Scripture of the Ten Thousand Buddhas to Avert the Apocalypse, with Additions by Master Huilong*,[33] but much has been added to the contents as well. These additions include:

1. Silent prayers to avoid disaster and find peace;
2. Precious incantations to the various gods, including "incantation to Shengdi [i.e., Guandi] to avert the catastrophe";

31 The 1925 edition of the *Ten Thousand Buddha Scripture*.

32 Lin Wanchuan, *Xiantian dadao xitong yanjiu*, 175.

33 *Huilong Shizun pudu yulu*, 21–22.

3. A vow: embrace the Tongshanshe with all your heart, helping mankind to return to his origins in heaven. Recite the three repentances, the ten repentances, the ten recompenses;
4. Recite the five great vows, kowtow to the Honor to Buddha Dīpaṃkara of the Non-Ultimate and other Buddhas, implore the old Buddha to extend his grace, so as to never be reincarnated again;
5. Respectfully present offerings to the assorted gods, recite the incantation of the peaceful gods.

一、 默禱，祈免劫平安。
二、 唸諸神呪、寶誥：其中包含〈聖帝救劫呪〉。
三、 發誓願：一心永歸統系，扶助收圓。唸三懺、十懺、十報。
四、 唸五大願，恭叩南無無極燃燈佛等，哀求古佛開恩、賞準永不下生。
五、 恭送諸佛，唸安神呪。

In the postface to *the Scripture of the Ten Thousand Buddhas to Avert the Apocalypse, with Additions by Master Huilong*, we learn that "because Master Huilong could not bear that the 96[00,000,000] imperial embryos fall into this disaster, he especially added five vows at the end of the scripture" (迴龍師尊不忍九六皇胎罹此浩劫，特於經末增入五願).[34] Actually, this remark has only general value. As is clear from what we said above, Peng Huilong's additions did not stop at "five vows," but included in addition "ten repentances" and "ten recompenses," which roughly doubled the length of the *Ten Thousand Buddha Scripture*. Among these additions, two points are worthy of notice. One is that in the "incantation to Shengdi to avert the catastrophe," Shengdi is called "Perspicacious Leader" (通明首相) and "Guandi." "Perspicacious leader" was the name of the position Guandi occupied before being promoted to that of Jade Emperor, and was a common way of referring to Guandi in late Qing times. At this point only the title "perspicacious leader" was used, and "Jade Emperor" had not yet appeared. Second, in the *Scripture of the Ten Thousand Buddhas to Avert the Apocalypse, with Additions by Master Huilong*, Honor to Buddha Dīpaṃkara of the Non-Ultimate (南無無極燃燈佛) was called Honor to Clear and Calm Sovereign Buddha Dīpaṃkara of the Non-Ultimate (南無無極清靜自在燃燈佛). Quiet and Unrestrained Buddha (Qingjing zizaifo 清靜自在佛) was one of the appellations of Peng Huilong.[35] Thus it is clear that the annotated version had already become a scripture that elevated Peng Huilong.

34 *Huilong Shizun zengding wanfo jiujiejing* 迴龍師尊增訂萬佛救劫經, in *Zhongguo yuyan jiujieshu huibian*, vol. 10: 432.

35 Yang Jindong, *Zupai jiexiao*, 8: "Mr. Jing'an said that in the seventh month of the *renzi* year, the Master received from heaven the title of Qingjing zizaifo, and his organization received the title of Hongxin" (「靜安先生云……壬子七月師尊接天盤，上蒼錫清靜自在佛，並頒天錫洪信號口……」).

In other words, in addition to its functions in averting the apocalypse, the 1928 edition of the *Ten Thousand Buddha Scripture* also served to promote the sacred character of Peng Huilong himself.

The 1931 edition of the *Ten Thousand Buddha Scripture* was also called *The Scripture of the Ten Thousand Buddhas to Avert the Apocalypse, with Additions by Master Huilong*. In terms of content, it largely followed the 1928 edition, and the three most important differences were the following: First, it is already impregnated with the "Guandi is the Jade Emperor" viewpoint. In the 1931 edition of *Ten Thousand Buddha Scripture*, Shengdi was called "Illustrious leader" and "Guandi" (關聖帝君昭明翊漢天尊) in the incantation to the Shengdi to avert the turning of the kalpa, but in the last chapter of the 1931 edition, Guandi was called Great Emperor of Central August [Heaven] (中皇大帝), which again indicates the influence that the notion that "Guandi is the Jade Emperor" had on this scripture. Second was the deification of Confucius. This edition of the *Ten Thousand Buddha Scripture* added twelve Buddha names at the very end. Among these is one where Confucius is granted a title, clearly indicating that Confucius had been added to the Tongshanshe pantheon. This title is similar to that used by the contemporary phoenix halls in southwestern China, although whether there is a direct connection would require more research.[36] The third is the addition of "the master's precious invocation" (*shizun baogao* 師尊寶誥). In this invocation we find that Peng Huilong is referred to as Celestial Worthy Who Saves the World and Rules the Dao, Highest Sage of the Non-Ultimate, Avatar of the Limitlessly Saving Clear and Calm Sovereign Dīpaṃkara, [residing?] at the Coiled Dragon's dwelling in front of Mt. Tianti (天梯山前迴龍宅畔無量度人清靜自在燃燈化身、無極上聖統道救世天尊), clearly yet another deification of Peng Huilong.[37]

In addition to the stand-alone editions of the *Ten Thousand Buddha Scripture*, in the 1930s and 1940s the Tongshanshe also published a few scriptures along the lines of "scriptures and incantations to avert the catastrophe," including *Ten Thousand Buddha Scripture* and *The Commandments of the Ten Thousand Buddhas*.[38] One of these "scriptures and incantations to avert the catastrophe" was printed and distributed by the Temple of Original Enlightenment (Xianjueci

---

36 See Wang Chien-chuan 王見川, "Popular Groups Promoting 'The Religion of Confucius' in the Chinese Southwest and Their Activities since the Nineteenth Century (1840–2013): An Observation Centered on Yunnan's Eryuan County and Environs," in *The Varieties of Confucian Experience: Documenting a Grassroots Revival of Tradition*, ed. Sébastien Billioud (Leiden: Brill, 2018), 90–121.

37 On this invocation, see also *Huilong Shizun pudu yulu*, vol. 1: 1.

38 There are three types of these incantations, two of which are in the author's possession and the other kindly donated by Professor Hou Chong.

先覺祠), where the titles Great Celestial Worthy, Jade August of Central Heaven (中天玉皇大天尊) and Mysterious and Numinous Lofty Emperor on High (玄靈高上帝) completely replaced Guansheng dijun 關聖帝君 in the Shengdi invocation section, and he was called the Eighteenth Heavenly Emperor. The text also included the entirety of the *Scripture of the Mysterious and Numinous Jade Emperor*, which again indicates that Tongshanshe leader Peng Huilong was aggressively promoting the notion that Guandi was the Jade Emperor.

There is also the 1941 edition, whose contents are even richer. There are more incantations, precious invocations to such gods as the Stove God, Emperor Wen, Lü Dongbin, and the Buddha of the Merciful Sound. *The Commandments of the Ten Thousand Buddhas* was also included. These commands are composed mostly of decrees of the heavenly master, with complementary scriptures that requested the three Dragon Flower assemblies to organize the [dispatch of the] Vajra World Saving Buddha (Jin'gang dushifo 金剛度世佛). The text insists that by reciting and cultivating these commands the final kalpa can be avoided. *The Commandments of the Ten Thousand Buddhas* was made up of some ninety characters, perfect for memorization and recitation.

By way of comparison, *The Commandments of the Ten Thousand Buddhas* in the *Ten Thousand Buddha Scripture* printed by the Xianjueci gave more weight to the Tianshi, and emphasized the importance of heavenly master decrees (*Tianshi chiling* 天師敕令). What should be noted is that this scripture called the Heavenly Master the "Sacred emperor heavenly master" (Shengdi Tianshi 聖帝天師), which corresponds to what we found in the 1935 version annotated by Peng Huilong: "the Tianshi in the *The Commandments of the Ten Thousand Buddhas* is not Zhang Tianshi, but rather Wusheng dijun [i.e., Guandi]" (《萬佛令》中之天師，非張天師，乃武聖帝君). It is clear that this scripture was composed after 1935.

As for the undated *Ten Thousand Buddha Scripture* printed by the Tianhua yinshuguan, it was called *The Ten Thousand Buddha Scripture Reader* (*Wanfojing duben* 萬佛經讀本) and in terms of content repeats the main scriptures of the *Ten Thousand Buddha Scripture* found in the 1928 incantations and scriptures to avert the catastrophe.[39] This edition put the original *Ten Thousand Buddha Scripture* at the very beginning, followed by *The Commandments of the Ten Thousand Buddhas*, and then the incantations to the various gods.

The most remarkable feature of this edition of the *Ten Thousand Buddha Scripture* was that the title Clear and Calm Sovereign Buddha Dīpaṃkara of the Non-Ultimate 清靜自在無極燃燈佛 was changed to Clear and Calm Sovereign Buddha Dīpaṃkara of the Non-Ultimate Who Saves from Calamities, Saves

39 Professor Hou Chong has a copy of this early edition.

from Difficulties, Saves the People from Floods and Fires 清靜自在救災救難救民水火無極燃燈佛. This change came from believers who, after reading the 1928 edition of the *Ten Thousand Buddha Scripture*, insisted that the Clear and Calm Sovereign Buddha Dīpaṃkara of the Non-Ultimate had saved them from disaster, hardship, flood, and fire. This unmistakably is an expression of the believers' worship of Peng Huilong. The contents of the *Ten Thousand Buddha Scripture* published after the war by Tongshanshe in Taiwan and Hong Kong are all based on this edition, with the addition of new god titles.

4 The *Ten Thousand Buddha Scripture*'s Publication and Distribution and the Tianhua Printing House

In comparison, the 1933 edition of the *Ten Thousand Buddha Scripture,* printed by Hongda Morality Bookstore,[40] is the simplest, consisting of a mere reprint of the original. We can divide the dozen or so editions of the *Ten Thousand Buddha Scripture* discussed above into three categories: 1. Those published by Tongshanshe branch offices or related groups; 2. those published by the Tongshanshe morality book press; 3. the Shanghai Hongda Morality Bookstore edition. Records indicate that the Shanghai Hongda Morality Bookstore grew out of the late Qing Shanghai Hongda paper company. Its manager was Jin Yousheng 金友生 from Zhenhai 鎮海. This bookstore had no connection to any religious group, and was instead a bookstore that specialized in publishing morality books.[41]

As for the *Ten Thousand Buddha Scripture* published by the Tongshanshe bookstores, these include the various editions of the *Ten Thousand Buddha Scripture* printed by the Shanghai Mingshan bookstore, the *Ten Thousand Buddha Scripture* and *The Ten Thousand Buddha Scripture Reader* printed by the Tianhua yinshuguan. According to my research, the Shanghai Mingshan Bookstore was founded by a Tongshanshe member in the winter of 1931, and the manager in the early period was Sun Mianzhi 孫勉之.[42] The Tianhua yinshuguan is little known and less studied.[43] In fact, the Tianhua

---

40 See the book image in appendix 2.

41 For more on the Hongda Bookstore, see Wang Chien-Chuan, "Morality Book Publishing and Popular Religion in Modern China: A Discussion Centered on Morality Book Publishers in Shanghai," in *Religious Publishing and Print Culture in Modern China, 1800–2012*, ed. Philip Clart and Gregory Adam Scott (Boston: De Gruyter, 2015), 233–264.

42 Wang Chien-chuan, "Mingshan shuju," 1–3， 11/12.

43 Wang Chien-chuan, "Mingshan shuju," 12 notes erroneously that the Tianhua yinshuguan seems to have closed in the wake of the 1927 crackdown on the Tongshanshe. As

yinshuguan was the first morality book bookstore set up after the founding of the Tongshanshe by the group itself, and its contribution to the distribution of Tongshanshe books and materials was very important. As to the origins of the Tongshanshe Tianhuaguan in Beijing (Beiping), a 1924 postface is revealing:

> When Jiangxi member Luo Bingwen was about to die, he summoned his younger brother Langshan and said: "There is one vow that I have not fulfilled, and I would like you to carry it out for me." Langshan assented, and subsequently printed the *Abstaining from Lustfulness* scripture and circulated it widely in response to Luo's wishes. In the third month of the *jiazi* year [i.e., 1924], Langshan requested that our printing company print 10,000 copies of this book. Once this was done, they asked me to write a preface recommending it. Shipin sincerely and respectfully proclaimed before the believers: "Your hopes are to become worthies, but since we have all been living in the dusty world for a long time, we are all the more lost in our desires, whence arises the lack of filiality, of brotherly love, of loyalty, of trustworthiness, or propriety, of integrity, of honesty, of a sense of shame. All good thoughts disappear for this reason. So I tell everyone—if we get rid of the causes of such disasters we can bring peace down from heaven. Such a contribution would be like when Yu calmed the floods in ancient times, an equally great salvation of humanity. If you want to purchase morality books to eliminate the causes of disaster and calamity, please come to our offices [i.e., the Tianhua shuguan)], where you will pay only one yuan of silver for one hundred copies (including postage, printed on the best paper)." From the director of the Tianhuaguan.
>
> 江西道友羅炳文之將歸空也，其介弟朗山在側，乃謂之曰:吾有願未償，子盍為我了之。朗山應之曰:諾。因以刊印戒淫文，廣為傳播為囑。甲子春三月，朗山委託本館代印是書萬冊。既竣，囑一言為介。時品掬誠敬告於諸道友之前，曰:士希賢……不孝不弟、不忠不信、不禮不義、不廉不恥，種種善念由此消……曉諭大眾。平禍水以召天和，其功當不在禹下……如向本館訂購，每百冊只收工料銀一元，係用毛太紙印，郵費在內。天華館主人敬識。[44]

The "Shipin" in the passage is Li Shipin 李時品. According to records, Li Shipin's *zi* was Mingshu 明庶, and he was from Ningyuan 寧遠 in Sichuan. He

the findings presented below show, the publisher continued to operate after 1927, so this should be corrected.

44 See appendix 3.

was born in 1886, and in 1913 studied at the Beijing Politics and Law School (Beijing zhengfa xuexiao 北京政法學校). He later worked in the [Auguste] Comte School in Beijing (Beijing Kongde xuexiao 北京孔德學校), and edited the *Confucian Journal* (Kongjiaobao 孔教報). He was a student of the well-known classical scholars Song Yuren 宋育仁 (1857–1931) and Liao Ping 廖平 (1852–1932), founded the Confucian Classics Lecture Society (Kongjing jiangxuehui 孔經講學會), and organized the Sichuan branch of the Confucian Religion Society (Kongjiaohui 孔教會).[45] He was one of the founders of the Tongshanshe in 1917.[46] In the above-cited postscript Li Shipin called himself the "director of the Tianhuaguan." Hence it is clear that Li Shipin was responsible for the Tianhuaguan printing house. As far as we know, the Tianhuaguan was already printing books by 1922 at the very latest. At the time it was called the Tianhuaguan Morality Books Division (天華館善書部), and was located in Beiping in the Andingmennei 安定門內 quarter, and it printed only the *Basic Elements of the Golden Rule* and materials for the Tongshanshe National Studies Academy, as well as some texts for outside individuals or groups.[47] According to preliminary statistics, the Tianhuaguan published at least the following scriptures and books:

1. *Collection of Notifications of the Tongshanshe Headquarters* (*Tongshan zongshe chuandan huibian* 同善總社傳單彙編, 1923);
2. *Guide to Seeking the Way* (*Wendao zhinan* 問道指南, 1924);
3. *Scripture of the Life of Wisdom* (*Huimingjing* 慧命經, 1925);
4. *Essential Elements of the Code of the Wheel, Approved by the Jade Emperor* (*Yuzhun lunke jiyao* 玉準輪科輯要, 1925);
5. *Simple Notes on Vows Published Together with Two Similar Texts* (*Shiyuan qianzhu deng sanzhong hekan* 誓願淺註等三種合刊, 1926);
6. *Emperor Wen and Ancestor Lü's Text against Lustfulness* (*Wendi Lüzu jieyinwen* 文帝呂祖戒淫文, 1927);
7. *Heavenly Rules and Saintly Regulations* (*Tianlü shengdian* 天律聖典, 1932);
8. *Essential Readings on the Way of Women* (*Kundao bidu* 坤道必讀, 1933).[48]

45 Zhongguo Kexueyuan jindaishi yanjiusuo, Zhonghua minguoshi zu 中國科學院近代史研究所中華民國史組, ed., *Zhonghua minguoshi ziliao conggao: Kongjiaohui ziliao* 中華民國史資料叢稿：孔教會資料 (Beijing: Zhonghua shuju, 1974), vol. 2 special edition, 79.

46 Wang Chien-chuan, "Tongshanshe zaoqi de lishi," 73.

47 Liaoyin Shanren 了因山人 and Guoyuan 果圓, eds., *Wendao zhinan* 問道指南 (Beiping: Tianhua, 1924), 1.

48 I have the complete editions of these scriptures, some of which are photocopies.

These publications can basically be divided into three categories: 1. books or scriptures that the Tongshanshe headquarters or local offices asked to have printed; 2. Master Peng Huilong's sayings and commands; 3. printing for other religious groups and individuals. Works like *The Collected Notifications of the Tongshanshe Headquarters* belong to the first category; the head of the Tianhuaguan is acting here as a believer, fulfilling his obligation to publish scriptures and texts for his own religion. By contrast, the Daoist text *Scripture of the Life of Wisdom* belongs to the second category. This scripture was published at the request of Master Peng Huilong, with the goal of providing believers with reference material for their Daoist cultivation practices. An example of the third category is *Essential Readings on the Way of Women*. The text was the combination of a number of spirit-writing collections.[49] Judging from the appearance of such elements as the special "mother" character, the reference to Lu Zhongyi 路中一, the seventeenth patriarch of the Yiguandao 一貫道 (Way of Pervasive Unity), known as Jingong 金公, and to "the old temples in Shandong" (Shandong laotang 山東老堂), this text was published at the request of an Yiguandao group. Because the Beiping Tianhuaguan performed well, a number of local Tianhuaguan were set up as well to print materials for the group, of which the Fanshui Tianhuaguan (汜水天華館) is a well-known example.[50]

Compared to other popular religious groups during the Republican period, the emergence and operation of the Tianhuaguan undoubtedly helped the Tongshanshe to distribute its scriptures and writings, and increased the group's influence and overall integration of believers. One could even say that for the Tongshanshe, one of whose religious characteristics was its belief in the written word, the Tianhua yinshuguan and the Mingshan Bookstore were the best platforms for society in general and for believers, both in open periods and in period of concealment. And the publication of Tongshanshe scriptures and texts by the Hongda Morality Bookstore explains even more clearly the openness and social nature of the Tongshanshe. Since Tongshanshe's scriptures and texts were publicly published and distributed via the Tianhuaguan, the Mingshan Bookstore, and the Hongda Morality Bookstore, they became morality books for a wider readership, and not simply the publications of one particular religion. These publications were not only the common property of all the people, but were commodities as well. As long as one had money, anybody could purchase them, reprint them, and read them! In this way, the scriptures and texts of the Tongshanshe were partially

49 See appendix 4.

50 Lu Zhongwei, *Tongshanshe*, 88.

removed from their sectarian context, thus becoming the first modern Chinese morality books with a life of their own.

5 Conclusion

In past discussions of modern Chinese popular religion, we have rarely talked about the scriptures these groups used. This is the case for the Moral Study Society, for the Yiguandao, the Wanguo daodehui 萬國道德會, and the Daoyuan 道院. And research on the Tongshanshe has been little different. I have sought to take another route in this essay by discussing the composition of scriptures, the evolution of their content, and their distribution.

My arguments have proven that in creating the Tongshanshe, Peng Huilong used a scriptural legacy from earlier groups—the *Ten Thousand Buddha Scripture*—as the Tongshanshe's principal scripture, and ordered his followers to recite it morning and night. In the original *Ten Thousand Buddha Scripture*, believers worshipped sixteen Buddhas, asked for relief from sixteen catastrophes, and recited a few vows. This text was a product of the late Qing Xiantiandao, and bore no imprint of Peng Huilong's Tongshanshe.

Big changes appear in the 1928 edition of the *Ten Thousand Buddha Scripture*. Not only was the title changed to *The Scripture of the Ten Thousand Buddhas to Avert the Apocalypse, with Additions by Master Huilong*, but in addition, five vows, ten prayers, and ten repentances were added. The key change was the title accorded to Peng Huilong that figured in the text—Clear and Calm Sovereign Buddha Dīpaṃkara of the Non-Ultimate replaced the original Buddha Dīpaṃkara of the Non-Ultimate—which made the *Ten Thousand Buddha Scripture* into a scripture that promoted the holiness of Peng Huilong. This change is perhaps related to the crackdown on the Tongshanshe in 1927, which frightened believers and required new measures to reintegrate them.

In the 1930s and 1940s, *The Commandments of the Ten Thousand Buddhas* was also added to *Ten Thousand Buddha Scripture*, as well as invocations to Wenchang 文昌, Lü Dongbin 呂洞賓, and various gods, along with new incantations, etc. Among these changes, not only was Guandi given new titles—Eighteenth Heavenly Emperor, Great Celestial Worthy, Jade August of Central Heaven, Mysterious and Numinous Lofty Emperor on High—but another related scripture, the *Scripture of the Mysterious and Numinous Jade Emperor*, was also published. These changes were the result of the influence of outside practices on the Tongshanshe, a response to mainstream religious thought. Subsequently, the Tongshanshe became a major participant in the movement to promote Guandi to the position of the Jade Emperor, and the

Scripture of the Mysterious and Numinous Jade Emperor was integrated into the *Ten Thousand Buddha Scripture* and became a Tongshanshe scripture.

The currently existing corpus of more than ten editions of the *Ten Thousand Buddha Scripture* illustrates that the scripture was distributed via three channels:

1. The Tongshanshe and its related, subsidiary organizations;
2. The morality book presses run by Tongshanshe members: Tianhua yinshuguan and Mingshan Bookstore;
3. General morality bookstores like Hongda Morality Bookstore.

Publishing and distribution covered the entire country and even the international arena. Especially after the crackdown on the Tongshanshe, the group also chose the traditional morality books *Scripture of the Three Sages* and *The Basic Elements of the Golden Rule* as scriptures for the group. The principal reason for this is that these scriptures conformed to the five cardinal relations and eight virtues, and thus served as behavioral standards for believers. In 1932, Peng Huilong created a new scripture known as the *Scripture of the Completion of the Way* which combined the five cardinal relations and the eight virtues with the Guandi as Jade Emperor belief. He commanded believers from all over to respect this scripture and cultivate according to its prescriptions, which would enable them to achieve the Way.

If the adoption of traditional morality books like the *Scripture of the Three Sages* and the *The Basic Elements of the Golden Rule* represents the "scripturalization" of morality books, then the printing and distribution of scriptures like the *Ten Thousand Buddha Scripture* and the *Scripture of the Mysterious and Numinous Jade Emperor* represents the transformation of scriptures into morality books. This is a special characteristic of the process of scriptural formation within the Tongshanshe.

Bibliography

Komukai Sakurako 小武海櫻子. "Tongshanshe de zongjiao shijieguan: Shixi *Dongming baoji* 同善社的宗教世界觀—試析《洞冥寶記》." In *Yanjiu xinshijie: Mazu yu Huaren minjian xinyang guoji yantaohui lunwenji* 研究新視界：媽祖與華人民間信仰國際研討會論文集, edited by Wang Chien-chuan 王見川 and Li Shiwei 李世偉, 363–388. Taipei: Boyang, 2014.

Liaoyin Shanren 了因山人 and Guoyuan 果圓, eds. *Wendao zhinan* 問道指南. Beiping: Tianhua, 1924.

Lin Wanchuan 林萬傳. *Xiantian dadao xitong yanjiu* 先天大道系統研究. Tainan: Tianju, 1986.

Lu Zhongwei 陸仲偉. *Tongshanshe* 同善社. Beijing: Shehui wenti yanjiu congshu bianji weiyuanhui, 2005.

Peng Huilong 彭迴龍. *Huilong shizun pudu yulu* 迴龍師尊普度語錄. Shanghai: Xuanhua, 1935.

Peng Huilong 彭迴龍. *Huilong Shizun zengding wanfo jiujiejing* 迴龍師尊增訂萬佛救劫經. In *Zhongguo yuyan jiujieshu huibian* 中國預言救劫書彙編, edited by Wang Chien-chuan 王見川, Fan Chun-wu 范純武, and Song Jun 宋軍, vol. 10. Taipei: Xinwenfeng, 2010.

Tongshan zongshe chuandan huibian 同善總社傳單彙編. Beiping: Tianhua yinshuguan, n.d.

Wanfojing 萬佛經. In *Jindai Zhongguo minjian zongjiao jingjuan wenxian* 近代中國民間宗教經卷文獻, edited by Wang Chien-chuan 王見川 and Fan Chun-wu 范純武, vol. 3. Taipei: Xinwenfeng, 2015.

Wang Chien-chuan 王見川. "Tongshanshe zaoqi de lishi (1912–1945) chutan 同善社早期的歷史 (1912–1945) 初探." *Minjian zongjiao* 民間宗教 1 (1995): 57–81.

Wang Chien-chuan 王見川. "Cong 'Guandi' dao 'Yuhuang' tansuo 從「關帝」到「玉皇」探索." In *Jindai de Guandi xinyang yu jingdian: Jiantan qizai Xin, Ma de fazhan* 近代的關帝信仰與經典：兼談其在新、馬的發展, edited by Wang Chien-chuan, 114–121.Taipei: Boyang, 2010.

Wang Chien-chuan 王見川. "Tongshanshe zaoqi de tedian ji zai Yunnan de fazhan (1912–1937) 同善社早期的特點及在雲南的發展 (1912–1937)." *Minsu quyi* 民俗曲藝, no. 172 (2011): 127–159.

Wang Chien-chuan 王見川. "Mingshan shuju yu Tongshanshe: Jiantan *Xuanling Yuhuangjing* de liuchuan 明善書局與同善社: 兼談《玄靈玉皇經》的流傳." *Mazu yu minjian xinyang: Yanjiu tongxun* 媽祖與民間信仰: 研究通訊 1 (2012): 1–13.

Wang Chien-chuan 王見川. "Cong 'bazi' dao 'bade': jiantan bade zaoqi wenxian *Bazi jueyuan* 從「八字」到「八德」: 兼談八德早期文獻《八字覺原》." *Mazu yu minjian xinyang: yanjiu tongxun* 媽祖與民間信仰：研究通訊 4 (2013): 126–137.

Wang Chien-chuan 王見川. "Jindai Zhongguo de fuji, cishan yu 'mixin': Yi *Yinguang wenchao* wei kaocha xiansuo 近代中國的扶乩，慈善與「迷信」: 以印光文鈔為考察線索." In *Xinyang, shijian yu wenhua tiaoshi: Disijie guoji Hanxue huiyi lunwenji* 信仰、實踐與文化調適: 第四屆國際漢學會議論文集, edited by Kang Bao 康豹 (Paul Katz) and Liu Shufen 劉淑芬, 531–568. Taipei: Academia Sinica, 2013.

Wang Chien-chuan 王見川. "Morality Book Publishing and Popular Religion in Modern China: A Discussion Centered on Morality Book Publishers in Shanghai." In *Religious Publishing and Print Culture in Modern China, 1800–2012*, edited by Philip Clart and Gregory Adam Scott, 233–264. Boston: De Gruyter, 2015.

Wang Chien-chuan 王見川. “Popular Groups Promoting ‘The Religion of Confucius’ in the Chinese Southwest and Their Activities since the Nineteenth Century (1840–2013): An Observation Centered on Yunnan’s Eryuan County and Environs.” In *The Varieties of Confucian Experience: Documenting a Grassroots Revival of Tradition*, edited by Sébastien Billioud, 90–121. Leiden: Brill, 2018.

Wang Chien-chuan 王見川 (Wang Jianchuan). “An Exploration of the Early History of the Tongshanshe (1912–1945).” *Chinese Studies in History* 44, nos. 1–2 (2010/11): 121–131.

Xin’an toutuo 心菴頭陀. *Huixiang yulu* 回鄉語錄. N.p., 1931.

Yang Jindong 楊覲東. *Zupai jiexiao* 祖派揭曉. Shanghai: Mingshan, 1933.

Zhongguo Kexueyuan jindaishi yanjiusuo, Zhonghua minguoshi zu 中國科學院近代史研究所中華民國史組, ed. *Zhonghua minguoshi ziliao conggao: Kongjiaohui ziliao* 中華民國史資料叢稿：孔教會資料. Vol. 2, special edition. Beijing: Zhonghua shuju, 1974.

Appendix 1

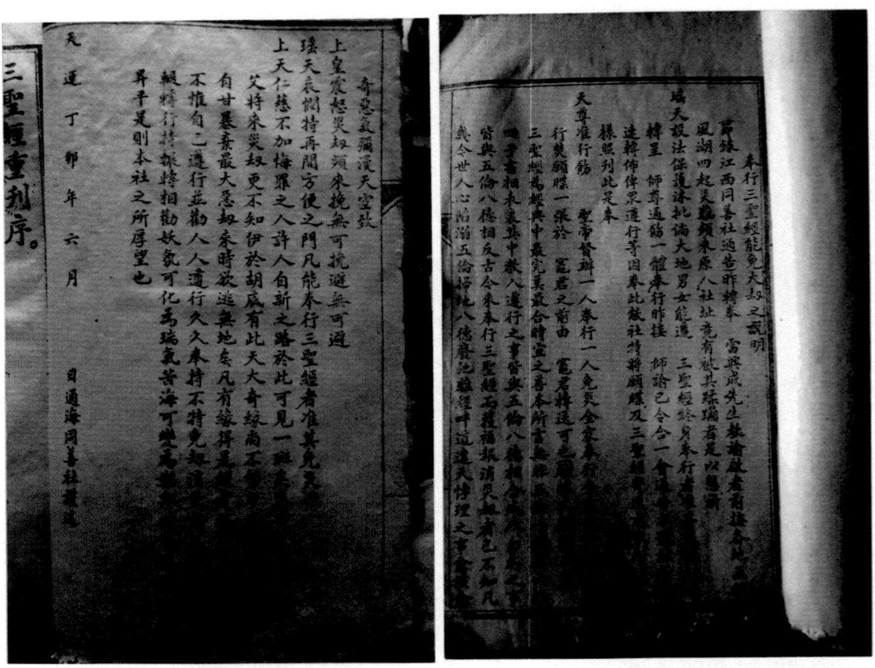

FIGURE 2.1 “Fengxing *Sanshengjing* neng mian dajie zhi shuoming 奉行《三聖經》能免大劫之說明” (1927)

Appendix 2

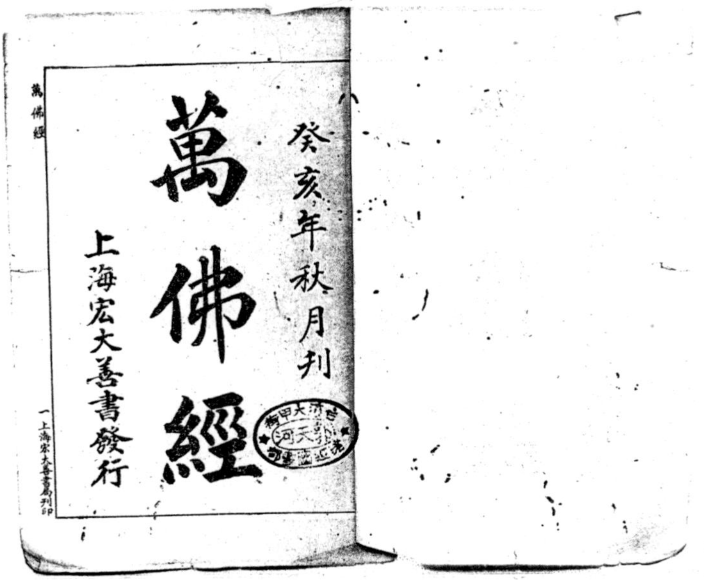

FIGURE 2.2 1923 edition of the *Ten Thousand Buddha Scripture,* printed by Hongda Morality Bookstore

Appendix 3

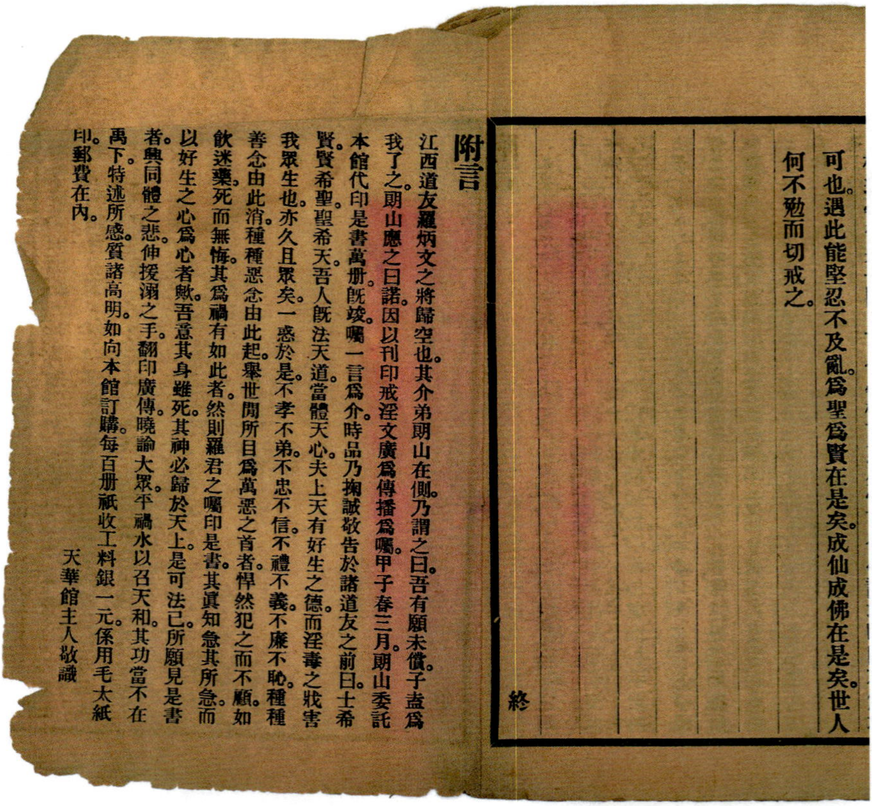

可也。遇此能堅忍不及亂。爲聖爲賢在是矣。成仙成佛在是矣。世人何不勉而切戒之。

終

附言

江西道友羅炳文之將歸空也。其介弟朗山在側。乃謂之曰。吾有願未償。子盍爲我了之。朗山應之曰諾。因以刊印戒淫文廣爲傳播爲囑。甲子春三月。朗山委託本館代印是書萬册。既竣。囑一言爲介。時品乃掬誠敬告於諸道友之前曰。士希賢。賢希聖。聖希天。吾人既法天道。當體天心。夫上天有好生之德。而淫毒之戕害我眾生也。亦久且眾矣。一惑於是。不孝不弟。不忠不信。不禮不義。不廉不恥。種種善念由此消。種種惡念由此起。舉世間所目爲萬惡之首者。悍然犯之而不顧。如飲迷藥。死而無悔。其爲禍有如此者。然則羅君之囑印是書。其眞知急其所急。而以好生之心爲心者歟。吾意其身雖死。其神必歸於天上。是可法已。所願見是書者。興同體之悲。伸援溺之手。翻印廣傳。曉諭大眾。平禍水以召天和。其功當不在禹下。特述所感。質諸高明。如向本館訂購。每百册祇收工料銀一元。係用毛太紙印。郵費在內。

天華館主人敬識

FIGURE 2.3 *Wendi Lüzu jieyinwen* 文帝呂祖戒淫文 (Beiping: Tianhua yinshuguan, 1927), final page

Appendix 4

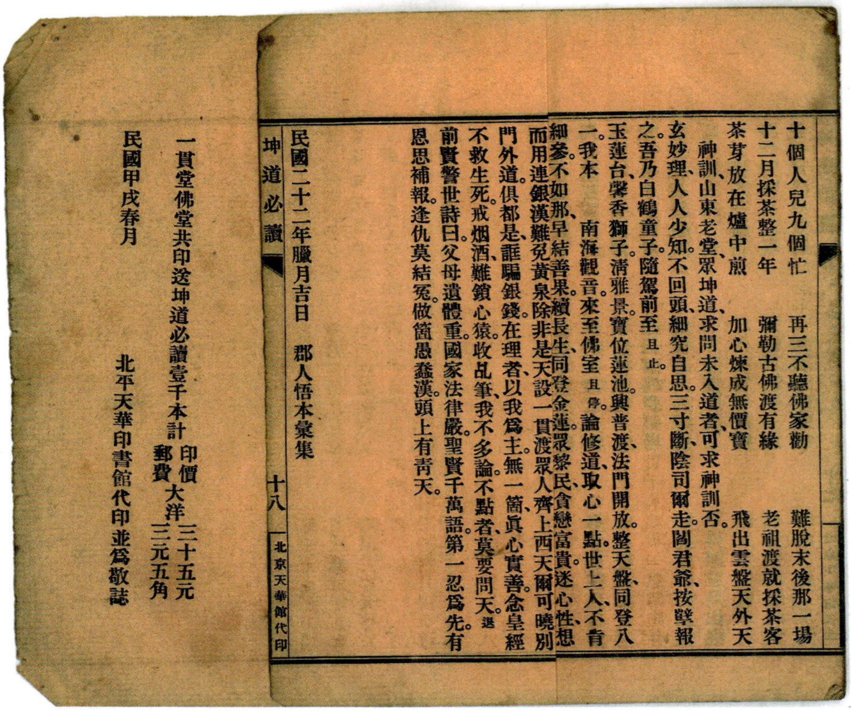

十個人兒九個忙　再三不聽佛家勸　難脫末後那一場
十二月採茶整一年　彌勒古佛渡有緣　老祖渡就採茶客
茶芽放在爐中煎　加心煉成無價寶　飛出雲盤天外天
神訓、山東老堂、眾坤道、求問未入道者、可求神訓否。
玄妙理、人人少知。不回頭、細究自思。三寸斷、陰司爾走。閻君爺、按孼報
之。吾乃白鶴童子。隨駕前至且止。
玉蓮台、馨香獅子。淸雅景。寶位蓮池。興普渡、法門開放。整天盤、同登八
一。我本　南海觀音。來至佛室且停。論修道、取心一點。世上人、不肯
細參。不如那、早結善果。續長生、同登金蓮。眾黎民、貪戀富貴。迷心性、想
而用連銀漢難免黃泉除非是天設一貫渡眾人齊上西天爾可曉別
門外道。俱都是、誆騙銀錢。在理者、以我爲主。無一箇、眞心實善。念皇經
不救生死。戒烟酒、難鎖心猿。收乱筆、我不多論。不點者、莫要問天。退
前賢警世詩曰。父母遺體重。國家法律嚴。聖賢千萬語。第一忍爲先。有
恩思補報。逢仇莫結冤。做箇愚蠢漢。頭上有靑天。

民國二十二年臘月吉日　郡人悟本彙集

坤道必讀　十八　北京天華館代印

一貫堂佛堂共印送坤道必讀壹千本計　印價大洋三十五元　郵費三元五角

民國甲戌春月　北平天華印書館代印並爲敬誌

FIGURE 2.4 *Kundao bidu* 坤道必讀 (Beiping: Tianhua yinshuguan, 1933), final page

CHAPTER 3

The Religious Texts of the Moral Studies Society: Print Publications, Photographs, and Visual Presentations

Fan Chun-wu
Translated by David Ownby

1 Preliminary Remarks

Modern Chinese redemptive societies are often seen as advocating the return to traditional culture and morality.[1] Groups such as Tongshanshe 同善社 (Society for Goodness), Kongjiaohui 孔教會 (Confucian Religion Society), Wanguo daodehui 萬國道德會 (Universal Morality Society), and Daode xueshe 道德學社 (Moral Study Society) did indeed take the propagation of traditional virtues, such as the three bonds *sangang* 三綱, the five cardinal relations *wulun* 五倫, and the eight virtues *bade* 八德, as their central mission, hoping to combat the increasing materialism of modern Chinese society and the more permissive Western views of the social value of traditional family and marriage. Thus, we can see the cultural and religious orientations of the redemptive societies from the perspective of the modern Western challenge, but at the risk of a certain over-simplification.

At the same time, it is easy to fall into the trap of seeing traditional and modern as purely antagonistic. Even as they preached traditional values, redemptive societies from the early Republican period had many basic differences with the popular groups of the Ming-Qing period discussed by Barend ter Haar, in terms of organizational form, philanthropic engagement, and general openness to a rapidly changing world.[2] For example, they all had similar ideas about the "great harmony" (*datong* 大同), which emerged from global trends in the early Republican period and were not simple reassertions of traditional

1 For the best studies of the concept of redemptive societies and the evolution of the field see Wang Chien-chuan 王見川, Kang Bao 康豹 (Paul Katz), and Zong Shuren 宗樹人 (David Palmer), "Daoyan: Jiushi tuanti yanjiu de huigu 導言：救世團體研究的回顧," *Minsu quyi* 民俗曲藝, no. 172 (June 2011): 13–14, and David Ownby, "Recent Chinese Scholarship on the History of 'Redemptive Societies'," *Chinese Studies in History* 44, no. 1–2 (2010/11): 3–9.

2 Wing-tsit Chan, *Religious Trends in Modern China* (New York: Columbia University Press, 1953), 167–185.

 | DOI:10.1163/9789004424166_005

religious discourse. The search for transcendent, universal values to promote morality and ethics, among others by the American missionary Gilbert Reid (1857–1927, one of founders of the Wanguo daodehui), and his embrace of evolutionary progress should also be understood in this way.

This essay examines this mixture of tradition and innovation by examining the Moral Study Society and its founder Duan Zhengyuan 段正元 (1864–1940). The development of the bureaucratic organization of the Moral Study Society is not altogether clear. Inner activities consisted of cultivation and prayer, and external activities included chiefly lectures and publishing. How did they intend to develop the group's influence? We will argue that the Moral Study Society explored a number of imaginative paths having to do with the printing of religious texts, the use of photographs, and visual presentations.

The Moral Study Society was a religious organization that spread its message of redemption above all by printing religious texts.[3] Duan Zhengyuan founded the Ethics and Morality Society (Renlun daodehui 人倫道德會) in Chengdu in 1912, and the Moral Study Society was established in Beijing in 1916. It achieved a certain success and branches were set up in many places. The relationships among Moral Study Society members seem not to have been particularly close; in existing documents concerning the group's expectations of its members, discussions concern solely members' rights and duties with regard to society literature. There was no clear hierarchical relationship between the center and the branches. According to information found in the 1923 publication, *The True Meaning of the Great Harmony* (*Datong zhendi* 大同真諦), the number of disciples and believers came to only 3,474 people.[4] Subsequently, development accelerated, and after 1930 branches sprang up one after the other. We lack definitive evidence concerning the ultimate number of followers, but many external sources reported that there were many hundreds of thousands. Looking solely at publications, print runs for Moral Study Society books were in the tens or hundreds of thousands, which lends credence to the idea that there were many members. What was the relationship between the Moral Study Society and the great number of religious publications that appeared during this period? This is the first question we will address.

---

3 In the circulation of its literature, the Moral Study Society was particularly attentive to sales and advertising. Detailed price lists were appended to the books, helping members to make their purchases. See Fan Chun-wu 范純武, "'Jingdian' de liubu yu duidie: Duan Zhengyuan Daode xueshe de shuji chuban shiye「經典」的流佈與堆疊：段正元道德學社的書籍出版事業," published in the conference proceedings of the international conference on "Jingdian, yishi yu minjian xinyang 經典、儀式與民間信仰," organized by Shanghai shifan daxue Dunhuangxue yanjiu suo 上海師範大學敦煌學研究所, October 25/26, 2014.

4 Duan Zhengyuan 段正元, *Datong zhendi* 大同真諦 (Beijing: Moral Study Society, 1923), 1.

One thing that distinguishes the religious publications from the early twentieth century from earlier scriptures was the use of many photographs, which became a broad trend. Books published by the Moral Study Society included Duan Zhengyuan's portrait photos. Many of these portrait photos have been preserved, which leads one to believe that Duan was especially fond of them. He was adept at using photographs to convey the meaning of his teachings, and had a deep understanding of the nature of photography. What role did photographs thus play in the religious activities of the Moral Study Society?

Frank Dikötter argues that modernity is a tool that can be appropriated by a variety of imaginations.[5] The process of acculturation creates vast changes in culture and material reality, which was particularly clear during China's Republican period. The radio brought traditional opera to the masses, vast amounts of imported products worked their way into the structure of daily life, and modern jails became new tools enforcing the order of traditional morality. We can see this kind of appropriation and penetration in the process of the Moral Study Society's development. In the context of modernity, the publication of new religious texts, the use of photography, and the creation of religious space in a visual sense contained many elements that were quite different from the scriptures and texts of traditional popular sects. The mass printing of religious texts, and their circulation in the broader world of book publishing, suggest the complete integration of religion and commercial publishing, which in turn suggests that the originally sacred and secret nature of scripture was gradually disappearing. At the same time, religious arguments spread more widely. A photograph was not only an image, but a trace of something real. The fact that the portrait photograph of the master of a religious group could be easily duplicated provided more avenues for believers to experience the sacred. Photographs of social aid, disaster relief, or religious assemblies (*fahui* 法會) stimulated the collective memories of followers. Religious texts under conditions of modernity came to possess more diverse imaginative and epistemological meanings, as our exploration of the Moral Study Society will illustrate.

5 Feng Ke 馮客 (Frank Dikötter), "Minguo shiqi de modeng wanyi, wenhua pincou yu richang shenghuo 民國時期的摩登玩意、文化拼湊與日常生活," in *Zhongguo de chengshi shenghuo* 中國的城市生活, ed. Li Xiaoti 李孝悌 (Taipei: Lianjing, 2005), 477–495.

2 The Moral Study Society: an "Imagined Community" Built on Printed Religious Texts

The culture of religious publishing in modern China is a field worthy of study. Modern printing, based on Western mechanized techniques, began to develop in the late nineteenth century and transformed the structure of religious publishing from its traditional woodblock based "old" books and scriptures to "new" books based on lithographic and typographic printing. New ways of printing brought the possibility of mass printing and distribution, which had several consequences. First, in the early Republican period, there was a clear demand for religious literature, and morality books, for example, became a very important type of modern publication, a medium through which flowed millenarian discourses and the ideas of various religious groups. Such changes and trends are made clear by the catalogues of Shanghai's Mingshan Bookshore 明善書局 (Illuminating Goodness Bookstore) and Hongda Morality Bookstore 宏大善書 (Great Bookstore). In the late Qing period, Shanghai's morality books were produced by the Yihuatang shanshuju 翼化堂善書局 (Morality Bookstore of Broad Transformation), and the Wenzhengtang shanshuju 文正堂善書局 (Morality Bookstore of Orthodox Culture). Popular morality book producers in Republican-period Shanghai included Hongda Morality Bookstore, Daode Bookstore 道德書局, Xiewenyi Printing House 謝文益印刷所, Dafeng Morality Book Distributors 大豐善書刊行所, and the Mingshan Bookstore, among others. Regular bookstores also printed and sold morality books, including famous stores like China Bookstore (Zhonghua shuju 中華書局), Jinzhang Bookstore (錦章書局), and Qianqingtang Bookstore (千頃堂書局).[6] One reason that religious texts were printed in great numbers was that under the chaotic conditions of militarist rule in the early Republic, morality books were a large and profitable market. The research of Philip Clart, Paul Katz, and Wang Chien-chuan has illustrated that these new methods of printing and sales had varying influences on the process of the production of religious literature by religious groups in the early Republic.[7] The development of religion in the early Republic

---

6 On Zhonghua shuju's publication of morality books, see Wang Chien-chuan, "Lufei Kui, Shengdetan yu Lingxuehui: Jiantan Minchu Shanghai de lingxue fengchao 陸費逵、盛德壇與靈學會：兼談民初上海的靈學風潮," published in the proceedings of the international conference on "Kexue yu wenhuade bianzou 科學與文化的變奏," organized by the History Department of Foguang University, Yilan, Taiwan, October 2–3, 2012.

7 Philip Clart, "New Technologies and the Production of Religious Texts in China, 19th to 21st Century," in *Modern Chinese Religion II, 1850–2015*, ed. Vincent Goossaert, Jan Kiely, and John Lagerwey, vol.1, 560–578 (Leiden: Brill, 2016); Wang Chien-chuan, "Morality Book Publishing and Popular Religion in Modern China: A Discussion Centered on Morality Book Publishers

was notably free and open, and much of this openness was supported by mass printing, based on the commercialization of religious literature.[8]

An important trend was for producers and distributors of religious literature to shift their targeted readership from group members to society at large, which meant that religious texts were no longer limited to believers. In addition, basic changes in printing technology obviously influenced the production and manufacture of religious literature. Yau Chi-on 游子安 has worked on the printing of morality books in the Qing, finding that some classic texts, such as *The True Scripture of Guandi's Awakening of the World* (*Guandi jueshi zhenjing* 關帝覺世真經), *The Ledgers of Merit and Demerit* (*Gongguoge* 功過格), and *The Treatise of the Exalted One on Response and Retribution* (*Taishang ganyingpian* 太上感應篇) circulated outside of the areas in which they were printed, and were constantly reprinted in new areas. In general, however, woodblock printing is inferior in both quality and quantity to machine letterpress printing. For a very long time, the Chinese publishing market was dominated by woodblock editions and by manuscripts, and religious literature was no exception. Quality woodblocks, when employed by qualified workers using high-quality paper, can yield more than ten thousand copies. Capital investment in woodblocks is not expensive, and yet the reason that the book market could develop rapidly in the Ming and Qing dynasties was basically because capital costs involved in paper-making were much less than in the Song and Yuan period, especially because of advances in the manufacture and production of bamboo paper.[9] Woodblock printing has its limitations in terms of quantity and layout, and after the "Gutenberg revolution" of the early Republican period, the new printing technology gradually replaced woodblocks, becoming the mainstream. Christopher A. Reed's research shows that in the period between 1876 and 1937, Western print technology gradually replaced Chinese woodblock printing, at the same time creating a modern print capitalism with Chinese characteristics. The developmental trend of the modern Chinese print technology, and the mechanization and modernization of publishing after 1895,

---

in Shanghai," in *Religious Publishing and Print Culture in Modern China: 1800–2012*, ed. Philip Clart and Gregory Adam Scott (Boston: De Gruyter, 2015), 233–264; and Paul R. Katz, "Illuminating Goodness: Some Preliminary Considerations of Religious Publishing in Modern China," in the same volume, 265–294.

8 See Philip Clart and Gregory Adam Scott, eds., *Religious Publishing and Print Culture in Modern China: 1800–2012* (Boston: De Gruyter, 2015).

9 On the production of bamboo paper, see Jacob Eyferth, *Eating Rice from Bamboo Roots: A Social History of a Community of Handicraft Papermakers from Rural Sichuan, 1920–2000* (Cambridge, Mass.: Harvard University Asia Center, 2009).

provided the technical basis for the circulation of all sorts of magazines, books, and information.[10]

To date, there has not been a great deal of research on the question of the use of new printing techniques in the production of religious literature. The simultaneous development of modern redemptive societies and print capitalism has also blurred the lines between them. Redemptive societies had their own publishing and distribution structures, and such practices more or less became a central feature of these religious organizations, since they published large amounts of sectarian scriptures or the writings of society masters. The Tongshanshe's Tianhua printing house 天華印書館, discussed by Wang Chien-chuan in the previous chapter, published inner alchemy *neidan* 內丹 texts, and Yiguandao's Chonghuatang 崇華堂 printing house in Tianjin and Shanghai also published scriptures.[11]

Although it became a trend for religious organizations to engage in printing, the purchase and upkeep of printing presses was problematic. The use of imported presses improved the capacity of Chinese print machines, and Shanghai became the center for copying the main techniques of Western print technology.[12] In the early twentieth century, advanced foreign print technology was absorbed as soon as it was imported, becoming a native industry on a national scale. Techniques such as letter-press printing, lithographic offset printing, stencil printing, stencil engraving, electroplated copper plates, photographic lithographs, and photogravure, among others, were introduced. In the 1920s, photogravure (photocopying) techniques were much better than the previously used offset printing; its printing effect was delicate and rich, with thick ink layers and large press runs, and it was used for books, pictures, and images printed in large quantities. Well-known companies such as the Commercial Press 商務印書館, Liangyou Printing 良友印刷, and Sanyi Printing 三一印刷 rushed to import similar machinery, which they used to print *Eastern Miscellany* (*Dongfang zazhi* 東方雜誌), *Friendly Pictorial* (*Liangyou huabao* 良友畫報), *Life* (*Shenghuo* 生活), and other pictorial journals. Print technology evolved quickly, which raised the threshold for capital accumulation in the production process and meant that there were not many specialized printing companies, and most printers were directly connected to publishing structures,

10 Christopher A. Reed, *Gutenberg in Shanghai: Chinese Print Capitalism, 1876–1937* (Honolulu: University of Hawai'i Press, 2004).

11 Wang Chien-chuan, "Morality Book Publishing and Popular Religion in Modern China"; Katz, "Illuminating Goodness: Some Preliminary Considerations of Religious Publishing in Modern China."

12 Reed, *Gutenberg in Shanghai*, 154.

or the two were combined.[13] Changes in print techniques brought a series of new practices, and Chinese publishers often integrated editing, printing, and distribution functions within a single company. We can see this phenomenon also in religious organizations in the early Republican period. In other words, religious organizations themselves managed the editing, publishing, printing, and distribution of religious literature.

The trend toward integration of religious organizations and print capitalism is quite clear in the 1920s and 1930s, and is visible in Buddhist and other groups as well. There is a close relationship between the reform of Buddhism in the early Republic and the establishment of printing and publishing channels and markets. Buddhist organizations that ran their own print shops included Yang Wenhui's 楊文會 (1837–1911) Jinling Scriptural Press (Jinling kejingchu 金陵刻經處) and the Great Transformation Society (Honghuashe 弘化社), run by Yinguang 印光 (1862–1940) and You Youwei 游有維 (1917–1990). Religious literature had traditionally been published via woodblock printing and copying, and these continued to occupy an important place in the 1920s, but traditional morality books and scriptures followed the progress of print techniques in the large Shanghai bookstores, and began moving toward exclusive use of letterpress or photogravure printing.

Among the various redemptive societies, the Moral Study Society appears to have been completely devoted to printing religious literature to achieve its objectives. Entrance into the group was comparatively easy, and regulations for group members particularly stressed that fees and expenses were to be paid on a monthly basis. Indeed, while the regulations said little or nothing about the nature of society teachings, they were very clear about what would happen were fees not paid. In other words, one entered the Moral Study Society by paying a certain fee, which also gave access to the printed materials of the society on a regular basis. In terms of publishing, the operations of the Moral Study Society were fairly elaborate. They had their own print division, the Beijing Moral Study Society printing house 北京道德學社印刷所, and they later set up the Dacheng Printing Company 大成印書社. This latter was situated in the Xidan 西單 area of Beijing, and chiefly published religious literature of the Moral Study Society. From late Qing times, Xidan, together with Wangfujing 王府井 and Dashilar 大柵欄, made up Beijing's three main flourishing urban quarters with a rich commercial and cultural life.

13 Han Congyao 韓從耀 and Zhao Yingxin 趙迎新, *Zhongguo yingxiangshi diliujuan, 1927–1937* 中國影像史第六卷, 1927–1937 (Beijing: Zhongguo sheying chubanshe, 2015), 120–121.

Outside of the Moral Study Society's main print operations in Beijing, local Moral Study Society branches also set up Dacheng Printing Companies and reading rooms. Some of these branches had their own printing capacities, while smaller ones were more like distribution offices, wholesaling or distributing materials produced by the head office in Beijing. Some of these branch offices were privately owned, even if they were called Moral Study Society, Dacheng Printing Company, or "reading room." The Moral Study Society organized many lecture activities to attract people, and in this context often organized free distribution or sales of books. For example, the Shanghai newspaper *Shenbao* 申報 printed the prices of the various Moral Study Society publications, some of which were offered at a discount during a certain period, but even more important, *Shenbao* provided information about the size of the print runs, which were calculated in the tens of thousands.[14] One thus might say that the Moral Study Society was an organization particularly devoted to the printing of religious literature.

When religion was integrated with printing, quantitative and qualitative changes occurred together. For example, as the printing of religious texts evolved with the improvement in technologies such as lithography and photogravure, this led to breakthroughs in the size of print runs. The appearance of the books changed as well. By contrast, the operations of religious organizations came more and more to resemble those of bookstores. For example, when the Moral Study Society attached a mail-order form for "how to buy our books" to the volume entitled *The Master's Selected Works* (*Shidao cuoyaolu* 師道撮要錄), it was acting in exactly the same manner as a commercial press. The instructions for book purchasing included:

1. Please pay in silver dollars at the stated price. There are separate rules for commissions.
2. Purchasers outside major cities without access to foreign exchange can pay with stamps worth one to fifteen cents, but once the amount exceeds five dollars, each dollar will be discounted 5 percent.
3. If purchased books are to be sent by the post, then the buyer must register with the post office and include a registration fee of five cents for each item purchased. Otherwise we will not be responsible for losses en route.
4. If a purchase has not arrived one month (two months for distant provinces) after the order has been sent, the purchaser should address himself to the local Moral Study Society branch, which will make enquiries (the Post Office will not make enquiries after six months).

14 *Shenbao* 申報, November 4, 1926, 11.

5. When sending money orders or postage stamps, wrap items carefully in oil paper or wax paper and send via registered mail so as to avoid water damage, loss, theft and other problems.

一、購費先惠現洋，不折不扣，代售另有章程。
二、外埠不通匯兌者，可用一分至一角五郵票代價；但過五元以上時，按超過之數，每元九五扣，作為補水。
三、所購書籍如欲郵遞確實，須向郵局掛號，但每件應由購書者加掛號費五分，否則中途有失，本社不負其責。
四、購書在發函後至遲一個月(遠省二個月)尚未收到回件，即宜知照本社清查(郵局定章過六個月不能代查)。
五、凡寄匯票、郵票務用油紙或蠟紙包封加蓋火漆戳記交郵局掛號，以免潮損及遺失、偷拆等弊。[15]

These five points address various questions about mailing religious literature, having to do with currency questions, non-reception, and when to ask for help. The first point having to do with commission sales is rather particular, especially concerning the details of policies on profit-sharing, account-checking, the calculation of discounts, and indemnification for losses. The "regulations concerning selling our society's literature on commission" suggests that there was considerable profit involved in the sale of this religious literature.

1. For those selling our books on commission, if they are in Beijing they need an appropriate guarantor, and if they are outside of Beijing then they need to first pay for the literature, after which the books will be sent.
2. Those selling on commission for the first time receive a 15 percent discount (as long as the amount is over 15 yuan), and subsequently, if sales proceed smoothly, they will receive a 20 percent discount.
3. Those selling on commission in Beijing should settle accounts on the tenth day of the month. If they are not in position to pay, then it will be the responsibility of the guarantor.

一、凡代售本社書籍者，在京須有妥實舖保。京外須先將書價郵費寄社，後發書。
二、初次代售按原價八五扣繳(但初次購書不滿十元者無折扣)以後能推廣如銷路，則按原價八扣藉資酬勞。
三、京內代售書款每月初十日清結一次；如將書售出價延不繳者，概由舖保照賠。[16]

These three points indicate that there was potential profit on commission sales, in that they received at least a 20 percent discount. And if ever they were

15 Wang Bingqian 汪秉乾, *Shidao cuoyaolu* 師道撮要錄 (Beijing: Daode yinshuasuo, 1925), 94.

16 Wang Bingqian, *Shidao cuoyaolu*, 94.

unable to pay, it fell to their Beijing guarantor to make up the losses. It is clear that the printing and circulation of religious literature occurred within the channels of the commercial book industry, and that the profits from commission sales expanded the influence of religion.

Morality bookstores and Buddhist bookstores in Shanghai employed the concept of the "merit economy," the idea that the printing of morality books or Buddhist texts could be moral or salvific acts, which supported the belief of the people who published these works in their efficacy in terms of good fortune and morality.[17] The Moral Study Society did not in fact emphasize the merit and virtue of buying books, but rather combined their ideas together with publishing and printing. They built their self-identity on the massive printing of religious texts.

3 The Importance and Function of the Use of Photographs in Religious Literature: the Example of the Moral Study Society's Publications of *Selected Texts of the Master and Further Collection of Past Teachings* 申集大成

In addition to innovations in terms of print runs and sales tactics, the new-style religious literature also saw important changes in layout and printing. One important change was the incorporation of portrait photographs of the master and members, as well as of religious assemblies and social activities in the printed pages of scriptures, for example, photographs of master Duan Zhengyuan, senior fellow (學長) Yang Sansheng 楊三生 (n.d.), and editor Wang Bingqian 汪秉乾 (1891–?) to the front matter of the Moral Study Society's 1925 edition of *Selected Texts of the Master*, accompanied by Wang's words of praise on the photograph. This is an early example of Moral Study Society literature that incorporated photographs. In the picture, master Duan Zhengyuan holds a feather fan, and he is seated before the altar. Wang Bingqian wears a marshal's uniform, decorated with many medals.[18]

Editor Wang Bingqian also has a considerable visual presence in the volume *Selected Texts of the Master*. Wang was born in 1891, in Zijiang 紫江, Guizhou 貴州, and was a graduate of the twelfth cohort of the Japanese Army War

17 Shi Ruige 史瑞戈 (Gregory Adam Scott), "Pingheng gongde yu liyi: Shanghai foxue shuju gufen youxian gongsi de jingli 平衡功德與利益—上海佛學書局股份有限公司的經歷," in *Gaibian Zhongguo zongjiao de wushi nian, 1898–1948* 改變中國宗教的五十年 1898–1948, ed. Kang Bao康豹 (Paul Katz) and Gao Wansang 高萬桑 (Vincent Goossaert) (Taipei: Zhongyang yanjiuyuan jindaishi yanjiusuo, 2015), 193–224.

18 Wang Bingqian, *Shidao cuoyaolu*, 1–3.

College. He originally served as a staff officer in the Hubei army. He participated as a representative in the 1925 reconstruction conference organized by Duan Qirui 段祺瑞 (1865–1936), and became a Major General in 1933. In 1940, he was the first commander of the advance team in the third theater, the Jiangsu-Zhejiang area. Early members of the Moral Study Society included many members of the civil and military elite of the Nationalist government. Wang Bingqian believed that the reason China's society was chaotic and her people unable to secure a living was because of a lack of values and the abandonment of traditional moral engagements. To realize the unification of the Republic and to bring all-under-heaven back to order, he added his own thoughts to the prefaces of Duan Zhengyuan's talks and books, and published them in small pamphlets, so that future readers could quickly grasp the important points of Duan's thought.

The printing techniques employed in *Selected Texts of the Master* were quite advanced for the time, or perhaps even ahead of the time. Widespread use of photogravure came into vogue in the 1920s, and this facilitated the gradual rise of the printing of all sorts of images. Generally speaking, the resolution of the photographs was poor, but the printed photographs in the *Selected Texts of the Master* were by contrast very good, as was the layout. Sometimes the layouts favored in the Beijing Moral Study Society's religious texts retained the old image of woodblock print texts to give the product a particular flair. The 1932 edition of *Further Collection of Past Teachings* was like this. It looked like an old edition, bound with silk thread, but included many high-resolution photographs on copperplate paper, and it was clear that photogravure techniques were employed. Later on, the *Origins of the Great Way* (*Dadao yuanliu* 大道源流), printed in quantities of hundreds of thousands, employed more modern layout and printing techniques.

Another important feature of the printing of religious texts was that, following advances in the techniques of printing photographs in the 1920s and 1930s, the addition of influential content by means of pictures and photographs became an important trend in all sorts of religious texts and publications.

The printing of photographs on regular paper required certain technical conditions. Around 1860 the copper plate method for printing photographs appeared. Photogravure was invented in 1880, allowing photographs to be printed directly into publications, providing the technical basis for the widespread diffusion of printed photographs. China began to import this technology in the 1920s, and the techniques spread quickly. Big cities such as Beijing, Shanghai, Nanjing, and Hangzhou all published pictorial magazines and picture books, reflecting the speed of the technology's spread.[19]

19 Han Congyao and Zhao Yingxin, *Zhongguo yingxiangshi diliujuan*, 107.

Pictures and photographs also appeared in religious literature because of these technical advances. To avoid state suppression, religious groups or sects in the Ming and Qing periods generally avoided including drawings of religious leaders or group members. In the early Republican period, state power over religion was reduced and religious activities were relatively open, and with the improvement in technology, it almost became *de rigueur* to print a photograph of the group founder on the title page of publications. In addition, photographs of the regular social activities of these religious groups, such as disaster relief, social work, as well as images of rituals and religious activities began to appear in the scriptures, publications, and transcripts of sermons and lectures. With their popularization, photographs came to play a role in the internal management of religious groups, appearing in printed pamphlets or on membership cards used by members to prove their identity.

After the Moral Study Society mastered the techniques and possibilities of photographs, they were used even more widely in all sorts of publications. In the society-published *Scripture of the Brocade Sack, a Special Gift of the Master's Way* (*Shidao teci jinnang jing* 師道特賜錦囊經), we find a photograph of master Duan Zhengyuan, wearing a robe and holding an insignia, followed by a detailed explanation of the publication of this scripture:

> Why did the master give us this brocade sack? Because we are living in an age where the Way is in difficulty. Karmic cycles have engulfed the powers that be, and the time has come to repay the lives of those murdered, the debts incurred. I worry over the fate of my followers as endtimes approach, that they may suffer from heaven's selection and perish in the apocalypse. Hence I have devised a way to save them, and specially made a present of this Way in a brocade sack, so that they may believe in it, keep to it, carry it out. They will pass through the endtimes and be saved at the appropriate moment.
>
> 此錦囊為何而賜？今因道難之期，因果循環當權，殺人償命，欠債還錢，大結帳時。恐有吾門弟子，歷劫惡緣未了，受天演淘汰，在劫難逃中，故設法挽救，特賜錦囊，信守奉行。將歷劫冤牽，登時解脫。[20]

Although this text bears the title of "scripture," it was originally published as a leaflet, and the photograph bore the message that its importance was that people apply it in their daily lives. But in order to help disciples apply the message in such a manner, the "brocade sack" was subsequently divided into separate sections and outlines. For example, the first brocade sack was called "know

20 *Shidao teci jinnang jing* 師道特賜錦囊經, undated pamphlet.

that grace will be repaid" (知恩必報). The second was "acknowledge sins and repent" (知過貞改). The third was "illumine the good and carry it out" (明善實行). The fourth was "do no evil" (諸惡不作). The fifth was "let goodness penetrate your soul" (福至心靈). Printed items like this pamphlet were easier to carry, and their simplified messages were easier to remember and recite, and thus assumed a greater role in the lives of believers.

There were many advantages to using printed photographs in religious literature, which could help readers originally not familiar with the organization to understand it. The Moral Study Society was not the only group to do this; other redemptive societies employed similar strategies. For example, in 1934, the Beiping Wanguo daodehui head office printed the *Records of Sincere Acts* (*Duxinglu* 篤行錄); the printing was outsourced to the China Printing Company (Zhonghua yinshuju 中華印書局), located outside the front gate of the city, on Yangmeizhu xiejie 楊梅竹斜街, in Beijing. Yangmeizhu xiejie was the center of publishing in Beijing, with seven bookstores located there: World Bookstore (Shijie shuju 世界書局), Fair and Honest Bookstore (Zhongzheng shuju 中正書局), Enlightened Bookstore (Kaiming shuju 開明書局), Broad Benefits Bookstore (Guangyi shuju 廣益書局), Global Bookstore (Huanqiu shuju 環球書局), The People's Bookstore (Dazhong shuju 大眾書局), and the China Printing Company. Wanguo daodehui was not as strongly organized around publishing as other redemptive societies, which is why the publishing and sales of this volume were outsourced. The price of this book was set at slightly more than one silver dollar. At the start of the book was a photogravure portrait of Wanguo daodehui leader Wang Fengyi 王鳳儀 (1864–1937).[21]

The Wanguo daodehui was established in 1921, in Shandong 山東, by Jiang Shoufeng 江壽峰 (1875–1926), a Confucian scholar from Licheng 歷城, Shandong, to militate for a return to morality in the wake of the reaction to the great massacres of the First World War. Kong Decheng 孔德成 (1920–2008) and Kang Youwei 康有為 (1858–1927) were appointed as leaders of the group, and following Kang's death, the Manchurian philanthropist Du Shaopeng 杜紹彭 (1878–1957) took his place. Du invited the Manchurian educational activist, Wang Fengyi (1864–1937), to enter the society, following which the group developed very quickly in Shenyang 瀋陽 and throughout Manchuria. It also had a headquarters in Beijing. Wang subsequently became the chief force behind the group's development, which under his guidance made significant contributions in building free schools for girls, operating kindergartens, and engaging in social relief. Wang Fengyi's particularity was to diagnose illness

21 Beiping Wanguo daode zonghui 北平萬國道德總會, ed., *Duxinglu* 篤行錄 (Beijing: Zhonghua yinshuju, 1934), 1.

through psychology, and not as the result of some injustice mysteriously transmitted over time. Wang frequently used his own life experience as proof when lecturing. His *Records of Sincere Acts* was compiled and edited by his son Wang Guohua 王國華 (n.d.); Wang's story was written in simple language, and the moral lessons were clear and moving. Perhaps to increase the reader's identification with Wang Fengyi, his brief biography and photograph appear at the front of the book. Beneath the photograph were "Wang Fengyi's portrait and brief biography" (王鳳儀先生肖像及略歷):

> Mr. Wang Fengyi, whose courtesy name was Shutong, was from Chaoyang county in Rehe province. For generations his family had lived to the south of the Chaoyang county seat, in a village facing Yunmeng mountain. The village was called Shulinzi, and it was 150 *li* from the county seat. When Wang was young, he kept cows for other people. When he became an adult, he was a hired laborer. Later, he returned home and farmed for himself. After the chaos of the Sino-Japanese war in 1894–1895, life in Wang's village was not peaceful, and he lectured in the local morality hall on morality books and other themes. He later traveled to Huaide, Dehui, and Anda, in Haicheng, to promote the idea of free schools for girls. In 1929 he joined the Wanguo daodehui. He continued preaching everywhere into his seventies.
>
> 王公鳳儀，印樹桐熱河朝陽縣人也。世居朝陽治城南，雲蒙山前。距城百五十里，村名樹林子。幼而為人牧牛，長而為人傭工。後自歸家業農。自清代甲午變亂，地方不靖，乃入宣講善堂，講善書格言。後到海城懷德、德惠、安達等處，提倡女子義學。於民國十八年加入萬國道德會。行年七十，仍到處講演勸化焉。[22]

Together with these words, the portrait photograph of Wang Fengyi seems to embody Wang's miraculous life. One feels that his eyes are full of wisdom. And like Duan Zhengyuan, he is dressed in a long robe, and is holding the insignia of the Wanguo daodehui before him. He looks every bit the wise man or gentry manager, his nature totally transformed in contrast with his peasant origins.

The use of portraiture by religious groups had already become widespread. In the 1920s and 1930s, well-known Buddhist masters like Taixu 太虛 (1890–1947), Yinguang, and Xuyun 虛雲 (1840–1959) were often pictured in Buddhist magazines and newspapers. In the case of redemptive societies, the portrait of master Zhang Tianran 張天然 (1889–1947) of the Way of Pervasive Unity

22 Beiping Wanguo daode zonghui, ed., *Duxinglu*, 1–5.

FIGURE 3.1
Wang Fengyi
SOURCE: DUXINGLU, 3.

(Yiguandao 一貫道), or that of the master of the Chinese Religion and Morality Society (Zhongjiao daoyihui 中教道義會), among others, could all be found at the beginning of the publications of their group.

If the photographs were joined together with text, the results could be different. The core of a religious group is made up of the master, rituals, sacred items, society titles, and organization. Among these, rituals and scriptures carry forward various symbolic systems, allowing believers to have various spiritual experiences. The existence of the master's photograph among these items provides believers with additional sacred symbols and religious significance. This is very clear when we take the Moral Study Society's *Further Collection of Past Teachings* as an example.[23]

23 See Fan Chun-wu 范純武, "Quanli, xiangxiang yu zaixian: Zhaoxiang dui jindai Zhongguo zongjiao tuanti chansheng de yingxiang 權力、想像與再現：照相對近代中國宗教團體產生的影響," *Minsu quyi* 民俗曲藝, no. 195 (March 2017): 247–306.

There are many photographs of Duan Zhengyuan in the 1932 publication of *Further Collection of Past Teachings*, at different ages and stages, revealing different poses, attitudes, and surroundings. Some pictures include his age, which varies from 45 to 54. There are also numerous photos of him in his 60s that do not mention his age. There are pictures of him standing and sitting, but most show him sitting in front of the altar. This is almost a photo album of Duan, and is rather rare. Duan himself had a special relationship to photographs, and attributed special meanings to each one. He believed that photographs revealed the clearest proofs of the great Way.

Further Collection of Past Teachings was composed in 1932, during the Battle of Shanghai, when Duan Zhengyuan was 69 years old. General He Yingqin 何應欽 (1890–1987) once invited Duan to a banquet and asked him to foresee how events would develop. Subsequently the situation became less tense, but Duan felt things were coming to an end, and that it was heaven's will that he not succeed. He further decided to use this series of events as a test for his disciples, to see if they were truly devoted in their commitment to carrying out the Way. The foreword to *Further Collection of Past Teachings* clearly explains the purpose of the book:

> Why did I compose this scripture? Because I understand the causes of past endtimes, and the difficulty of breaking the cycle. Today the world is achieving great harmony, which means breaking with the causes of endtimes and returning to the original sound [see below]. While in the past we could not return, today we are returning naturally. Hence I will gather explanations of karmic endings and returning to the origin into a book, whose proper name will be *Further Collection of Past Teachings*.
>
> 此經為何而述？因知道歷劫因緣，難了難歸。今日世界要成大同，打斷因緣歸元音。前不了歸者，今自然了，天然歸。故將了緣歸元說法，纂集一部，正名為《申集大成》。[24]

Duan Zhengyuan believed that fulfilling the true will of heaven required the unity of heaven and man. Collective prayers and intentions would bring forth signs from on high. At this particular time, the Way was not practiced, which meant that all people could do was to choose to pursue individual goodness in one's person, a state of mind illustrated by a number of photographs. The cameras that captured portraits in the early days were mostly large-format, fixed-focus lenses, and the images were quite sharp. There is one photo

24 Duan Zhengyuan 段正元, *Shenji dacheng* 申集大成 (Beijing: Moral Study Society, 1932), 1.

of Duan in a long robe, sitting on a bench, holding a cane, looking to the side. The inscription reads:

> With the Way, things are visible; without the Way they are hidden; residing in the Way, it is easy to await fate.
>
> Those who understand are not confused; those who are benevolent are not worried; they hide their tools and await the proper time.
>
> 有道則見，無道則隱，居易俟命。
> 智者不惑，仁者不憂.，藏器待時。[25]

FIGURE 3.2 Duan Zhengyuan
SOURCE: SHENJI DACHENG, SHANG CE, 15

25 Ibid., photograph section, 15. The first eight characters of each couplet are drawn from the *Analects*.

Duan clearly states that his attitude is one of withdrawing to await the heavenly mandate. Next to another upper-body photograph is the inscription:

> Cultivate your heart's territory, and without thinking, your entire being will be revealed;
> Cultivate your nature's heaven, abandon the myriad causes and your body will be at ease.

> 栽培心上地一念不生全體現，
> 涵養性中天萬緣放下自身閒。[26]

FIGURE 3.3 Duan Zhengyuan
SOURCE: SHENJI DACHENG, SHANG CE, 16

26 Ibid., photograph section, 16.

This is another example of Duan's taking his own appearance as the ultimate realization of the Way, in which all is revealed.

What is the function of the inscriptions added to photographs? Photographs on silver salt paper must be developed in the dark room to fix the colors. Different pictures can be attached to a panel and exposed for a second time to produce an image. This kind of combined technique had already appeared in the 1860s. In general, when portrait photos were inscribed, it was for friends of the person in the portrait, and rarely for the general public. But Duan Zhengyuan used such techniques a great deal, mainly because he saw photography as an important medium for the transmission of his teaching and thought. Looking at the many photographs that appear at the beginning of *Further Collection of Past Teachings* reveals that the words that accompany the pictures capture his core ideas.

On one photograph, a horizontal caption reads "the three-in-one, the myriad changes" (三位一體千變萬化), and on the right appear the words "quietly reside in your independence, exalt in the Way, cultivate the body, order the great family, keep whole the original sound in which men and the gods achieve long lives and fulfill their destinies" (閒居獨立樂道修身齊大家，保全元音中人神長生性命). On the left, we find "When you carry out the proper rituals in a timely fashion, you will also be adept at governing the country, bringing peace to the world, and harmonizing the various components of the universe" (正位時行兼善治國平天下，燮理宇宙間乾坤肅赫陰陽).[27]

These captions express several central concepts promoted by the Moral Study Society. The idea of the "three-in-one" refers to the three selves. The three selves are the body, the soul, and the great Way, that exist at three different levels. The body is the false self, the soul the true self, and the Way the great self. Everyone in the universe possesses the three selves, and if we can come to understand our three selves, then there will no longer be differences between our self and others, which means that there will no longer be personal opinions or class inequalities. With this understanding will arrive the world of great harmony. The idea of the three selves was the basis of Duan Zhengyuan's theory. In 1918 when he gave a speech opening a Moral Study Society altar, this was what he spoke about. The very beginning of the preface to the "Three Selves" states: "The great Way is a fact of nature, but requires a sage to lead it. Thus we promote the idea that the 'many return to the one'" (大道自然，而要必有聖人以導。故提倡「萬殊歸一」). The same sentence appears as the caption to one of the photos. The "three-in-one" is the main theme of *Further Collection of Past Teachings*. Many of the photos were taken at different times,

27 Ibid., photograph section, 9.

FIGURE 3.4 Duan Zhengyuan
SOURCE: SHENJI DACHENG, SHANG CE, 9

with Duan wearing different clothes; some appear to be double exposures or parallel mountings of different pictures. There are three or four of these "three selves" photographs. The caption beside one of them reads "Born in the dusty world, became a god in the joy of the three selves" (出塵在塵成仙佛在三我樂中). Moreover, there is one picture of the altar where we see three upper-body photos of Duan Zhengyuan taken from different angles, thus a three-self image hung above the center of the altar.[28]

The disciples clearly understood the importance of the relationship between the three-self theory and the master's photograph:

> The master's theory is based on the idea of the three selves, so today we use these three portrait photographs of the Master to represent the integration of his three selves, just as the three incarnations of the Way gave birth to the myriad things. As the myriad things are born, so do they return to their original unity, the unity that in turn gives birth to the Way. Hence morality is that which is most useful, and must be employed at all times.
>
> 師尊說法以三我為定宗，今將師尊肖影三片如師尊三我一體，如道之三生萬物，萬物以生，萬殊仍歸一本，本立而道生，道德從此為天下之至寶，時中之至用。[29]

Duan Zhengyuan was very attentive to the meaning attached to each posture, and illustrated the manifestations of the Way through changes in the appearance of his body.

Duan Zhengyuan's thought was full of technical terms borrowed from Confucian, Buddhist, and Daoist masters, in addition to notions that he created himself. An example mentioned above was the "preservation of the original sound" (*baoquan yuanyin* 保全元音). *Yin*/sound, usually means "vowel," or the basis of sound or noise. Duan Zhengyuan preached the importance of musical education, and used the idea of "original sound" as a symbol for the idea that all people of the world shared a common origin, to which they would return when they heard the sound. His term "great harmony-original sound" (*datong yuanyin* 大同元音) meant that if the world had no divisions of race, nationality, or religion, then there would be no conflict.[30] Those who understood this

28 Ibid., photograph section, 20.

29 *Duanfuzi* 段夫子 (Hangzhou: Moral Study Society, 1947), 12–16. My thanks to Professor Han Xing 韓星 of Renmin University for sharing this document with me.

30 Wang Bingqian, *Shidao cuoyaolu*, 33.

were called "original sound people (*yuanyinren* 元音人)." Thus, to help the world to return to its origins and to arrive at the great harmony, it was necessary to preserve the original sound.

There is another photograph with the caption "1932, eighth day of the first month, the true image of action and non-action, non-action and action, and nothing not accomplished" (壬申年新正初八，有為合無為，無為合有為，無所不為之真相), written in small characters. I mentioned above that it was in 1932 that Duan had decided to withdraw from the public scene. This photograph and its caption are meaningful in this sense, showing that his own body was the realization of the Way, and the reason why he wanted to retire was that even if he had accepted the mandate that heaven had extended to him, he still could not truly change the situation and deploy his influence, and this failure was also the Way of heaven. For Duan, the great Way was that through which everything was accomplished through non-action, which was clearly indicated in the caption of the photograph. Moreover, each sentence was phrased as follows. On the right:

> I will tell you that the main reason that the Master's great Way can be accomplished is because it is accomplished naturally. In his search for the Way, the Master, in his extreme sincerity, his willingness to accept instruction and seek out of the worthy, is like the Xuanyuan Yellow Emperor 軒轅 [traditional reign dates, 2697–2597 BCE], or like Zhang Liang 張良 [? –186 BCE].[31] In his ability to work hard with others, he is like Chengtang 成湯 [the first king of the Shang dynasty, 1675–1646 BCE] and Zhou Kings Wen 文王 [1152–1056 BCE] and Wu 武王 [? –1043 BCE]. Those who work with unflagging energy can enter the palace of the Way. The Master has done his utmost to help assist the Way, and never tires of helping others. The sincere achieve things of themselves, becoming persons of exemplary virtue. They accept heaven's way and accomplish their fate.
>
> 師道大成，申君自然曰:問道有軒轅、張良之至誠，可受教求賢。有成湯文武之聘請，可同謀盡功苦。勤勞數年如一日者可升堂。輾轉反側而來輔道，代勞始終無二者可入室。誠者自成，為大同師表，是奉天承命。

31 Translator's note: Zhang Liang was one of the "three heroes of the early Han period."

On the left side:

> According to the Exalted Vast Emperor, the great Way contains neither good nor evil, which are like the shadow that follows the form. The universe contains neither right nor wrong, but follows the natural endowment of things, and right and wrong are found therein. *Yin* and *yang* possess neither truth nor falseness, men and women are representatives of *yin* and *yang*, and truth and falseness are found between them. The world has neither order nor chaos, but government is up to the people, and gentlemen and petty people are found therein. Use the middle way to carry out the Way, accumulate the myriad teachings to make the great accomplishment.
>
> 太上鴻帝，天然曰:大道無善惡，如影隨形，善惡在其中。宇宙無是非，隨物稟賦，是非在其中。陰陽無真假，男女為代表，真假在其中。世無治亂，為政在人，君子小人在其中。用中行道，集萬教大成，是奉道承天。[32]

Duan Zhengyuan's idea of the great Way is based on passages from the *Treatise on Response and Retribution,* developed more systematically. In his talks he often mentioned the notion that the true reason for the chaos of the warlord period of the early Republic was that people had turned their backs on their hearts. Carrying out good works and social relief are not true solutions. When people's hearts have changed, this will have an impact on heaven's Way; signs will appear in heaven and changes will occur on earth. Man can do all things, which is also the realization of the Way of heaven. Duan Zhengyuan used many Confucian concepts and terms, while giving them new interpretations, and some of what he said must be understood within the wider context of his thought system. Adding inscriptions helped his audience to understand.

Further Collection of Past Teachings looks to be a comprehensive photographic record of Duan Zhengyuan's teaching of the Way. Among the pictures of Duan at various stages of his life, there are some from the early period that were taken in a photography studio, with outdoor scenery drawn in the background, or with table and chairs arranged. Many photographs were taken at the altar. Duan Zhengyuan attached great importance to the presentation of visual space. To make new adepts aware of the "beauty of the ancestral hall and the richness of the many buildings" (宗廟之美百官之富),[33] he was very

32 Duan Zhengyuan, *Shenji dacheng*, photograph section, 12.

33 Translator's note: This passage is taken from the Confucian *Analects*, 19.23.

FIGURE 3.5 Duan Zhengyuan
SOURCE: SHENJI DACHENG, SHANG CE, 12

particular about the appointment and arrangement of the temple settings, and there are many photographs of this sacred space, presented through the medium of printed religious texts.

John Berger once lamented the fact that in modern societies religion declined at the same time that photography developed, and wondered if capitalist culture has focused its telephoto lens on God.[34] With recent advances in research on visual culture, we have gradually come to understand the impact produced by visual materials on religious activities. Photographs are not mere

34 John Berger, *Understanding a Photograph* (New York: Aperture, 2013).

reproductions of the real world, and given that religious beliefs and spirituality contain many mysterious, abstract notions that are difficult to express in words, the use of photographs or images as visual materials can reveal these notions more easily, helping believers to understand them. Moreover, the ease of the mass production of photographs means that these religious images can readily be integrated into the daily lives of believers.[35]

4 Contemplating the Master's Image: the Relationship between Photographs and Quiet Sitting

"Spirit-photography" is a topic that has been at the forefront of recent discussions of the relationship between modern Chinese religion and photography, as seen in recent research by Wang Chien-chuan and Matthias Schumann.[36] At the time, images of gods or spirits were used to prove the actual existence of unimaginable worlds that science could not prove. Spirit-photography cannot be readily duplicated and its success rate is not high, and it eventually became merely a special branch of photography. In fact, the impact of photography on the various religious groups of the early Republican period was different, and requires further discussion.

As discussed above, Duan Zhengyuan greatly enjoyed using photographs to depict his appearance in different periods or phases of his life. Among the photographs in *Further Collection of Past Teachings* are some that may have been created through multiple exposures. Combinations of special photos became wonderful tools to explain how one became three, or three became the myriad.

An aspect of this that was even closer to the core of religious activities was Duan's incorporation of his own photograph into the rituals and *qigong*

35 Sarah Dunlop, "Visual Methods in the Study of Religion," available online at https://www.kent.ac.uk/religionmethods/documents/Visual%20approaches.pdf. On the theory of religion and visuality, see David Morgan, *Visual Piety: A History and Theory of Popular Religious Images* (Berkeley: University of California Press, 1998); and David Morgan, *The Sacred Gaze: Religious Visual Culture in Theory and Practice* (Berkeley: University of California Press, 2005).

36 See Wang Chien-chuan, "Jindai Zhongguo de fuluan, cishan yu 'mixin': Yi *Yinguang wenchao* wei kaocha zhongxin 近代中國的扶乩、慈善與「迷信」: 以印光文鈔為考查中心," published in the conference proceedings of the Disijie guoji Hanxue huiyi 第四屆國際漢學會議, June 20–22, 2012; and Wang Chien-chuan, "Lufei Kui, Shengdetan yu Lingxuehui: Jiantan Minchu Shanghai de lingxue fengchao 陸費逵、盛德壇與靈學會: 兼談民初上海的靈學風潮"; and Matthias Schumann, "Science and Spirit-Writing: The Shanghai Lingxuehui 靈學會 and the Changing Fate of Spiritualism in Republican China," in this volume.

practices of the Moral Study Society. According to the memoirs of Cao Juren 曹聚仁 (1900–1972), Moral Study Society members "had to fast and perform ablutions on the first and fifteenth of each lunar month, and bow before the jade photograph of the Master" (朔望兩日，必齋戒沐浴，向師尊的玉照行跪拜禮 [at this point Duan was still alive]). Clearly, the Master's photograph played a very important role in the daily activities of the group, and before practicing qigong, members focused on the photograph of Master Duan as part of quiet sitting. The third method explained in the *Scripture of the Way and the Law of the Original Beginning* (*Yuanshi daofajing* 元始道法經) discusses contemplating the Master's image, explaining that through contemplation of the photograph one could enter a state of quiet sitting. Duan Zhengyuan himself explained how contemplating the image of the Master in times of disaster or crisis could produce an effective response.[37]

The impression the Moral Study Society gave people was that it was a group that preached morality instead of a group that paid particular attention to quiet sitting or qigong.[38] In the documents we possess concerning the Moral Study Society, there are relatively few references to quiet sitting and *qigong* (although the *Transmission of the Heart of the Great Learning* [*Daxue xinchuan* 大學心傳] compiled by the disciples contains an introduction to a complete

37 "In the discussion of the third method, this scripture has a section on 'contemplating the Master's image,' which explains the benefits of the practice. Ever since I emerged from the mountains, whenever I have faced hardship, I have silently thought about the Master, who then came to save and protect me. For instance, last year I was in a small boat on the Yangzi River, and great waves suddenly appeared. What was worse was that we were in a rough part of the river, and even the deckhands were scared stiff. I said to myself that there was always hope even in the most desperate of times, and I said a silent prayer and saw my Master gesturing in the emptiness, after which the winds and the waves were calm and we continued our passage in safety." 此經第三法中有「觀師像」一語，論來觀師像有何好處？因吾自出山之後，凡遇危難之時，心中一默念吾師，即來救護，如上年在長江之中駕一葉小舟，突遇狂風巨浪，又在漩渦湍急之處，雖撐舵之船夫，亦驚惶失色。自謂萬無生望，經吾心中默禱，即見吾師在空中用手一指，立刻風平浪息，安然渡過。又如吾昔在大病之中，亦經吾師挽救，始能恢復原狀，此不過擇其要者，略述一二，至於小災小難之得救，更不可以數計。可見師愛弟子之心，無微不至。吾今以吾師愛吾之心，轉愛弟子，故教爾等臨大災大難之時，觀師像，默念此經，自然有感斯通，信者得救。倘至此時，而不能觀師像，則其平日對道之誠否，不問可知矣。Tianjin Daode yanjiushe 天津道德研究社, *Shizun wei Jinshe dianji shuofa* 師尊為津社奠基說法 (Tianjin: Moral Study Society, 1935), 36.

38 See Fan Chun-wu, "Confucian 'Religion' in the Early Republican Period: Historical Questions Concerning Duan Zhengyuan and the Morality Society," *Chinese Studies in History* 44, no. 1–2 (2010/11): 132–155; and Fan Chun-wu, "Minchu Ruxue de zongjiaohua: Duan Zhengyuan yu Daode xueshe de gean yanjiu 民初儒學的宗教化：段正元與道德學社的個案研究," *Minsu quyi* 民俗曲藝, no. 172 (June 2011): 161–203.

set of qigong techniques), Duan Zhengyuan never published a book or lectured exclusively on matters relating to qigong, so it appears that the Moral Study Society was not like Tongshanshe, which attracted members through healing and *qigong*. For example, the 1938 *Record of an Interview with the Moral Study Society* (*Daode xueshe fangwenji* 道德學社訪問記) was a small booklet introducing Moral Study Society activities to those outside the group, and no mention was made of qigong or quiet sitting. Nonetheless, improving health and curing illness through qigong were common means through which Duan Zhengyuan sought to cultivate the Way. Duan himself often said: "Since I have been practicing the Way, the qigong I have promoted is only for purposes of healing and extending life, which can also enhance wisdom. All dedicated Moral Study Society members who are committed to the Way, and who have been practicing diligently, have had good experiences with this" (吾自行道以來，所傳之功不惟怯病延年，並可增長智慧。考之南、北社中，凡能以道為己任，克盡功苦勤勞者，莫不有明效大驗).[39] In other words, for qigong to work it had to be practiced together with the totality of Duan's teachings, and only then would it be effective. Part of Duan's deification came from the fact that his qigong had helped some disciples recover from illness. This was the case for well-known political figures like Luo Jingxiang 羅景湘 (n.d.) and Wang Shizhen 王士珍 (1861–1930), who had asked Duan for help on this front, which had afforded Duan an opportunity to get close to the leadership of the Beiyang faction.[40]

Duan Zhengyuan divided his qigong into *xinggong* 性功 and *minggong* 命功. He believed that *xinggong* was the Way, which required complete attention and which had to be practiced in daily life. Duan taught people to "cultivate *ming* and *xing*, the Way and *qigong*" (性命雙修，道法並行). *Xinggong* was the Way, and *minggong* was *qigong*; *xinggong* involved daily ethical practice, *minggong* involved quiet sitting and "resting in wisdom."[41] In practice, this means that *xinggong* was the primary task, and *minggong* was secondary. The Moral Study Society had its own set of qigong beliefs and practices, combining

39 Ju Xi, ed., *Duan Zhengyuan yuyao*, 128. My thanks to Professor Cao Xinyu for photocopying these materials for me.

40 Fan Chun-wu, "Minchu Ruxue de zongjiaohua," 170–171.

41 Translator's note: "Coming to rest in wisdom (*zhizhi* 知止)" is from the *Great Learning*: "The Dao of Great Learning lies in making bright virtue brilliant; in making the people new; in coming to rest at the limit of the good. Only after wisdom comes to rest does one possess certainty …" (大學之道，在明明德，在親民，在止於至善。知止而后有定), http://www.indiana.edu/~p374/Daxue-Zhongyong.pdf, 11. Duan made the concept part of his qigong practice, a technique for controlling breath and concentration.

Confucian and Daoist cultivation techniques.[42] In *The True Meaning of the Great Harmony* we find a description of how *xinggong* and *minggong* are to be put into practice.[43]

Minggong appears to be complicated. In addition to the mantra that disciples received, Duan Zhengyuan often said that *minggong* methods were divided into three stages, which included 108 mantras and 360 *yinyang* 陰陽. In the *Draft History of the Master* (*Shizun lishi chugao* 師尊歷史初稿), Duan mentioned that he had received six methods from his master Long Yuanzu 龍元祖 (n.d.), who took them from the *Great Learning*: resting in wisdom (*zhizhi* 知止), certainty (*ding* 定), tranquility (*jing* 靜), security (*an* 安), contemplating alternatives (*lü* 慮), and comprehension (*de* 得).[44] Duan called his system the six-six-thirty-six, with three changes and nine transformations, and 108 mantras.[45] Master Duan's *qigong* made great use of technical terms drawn from traditional Confucian discussion of the condition of the mind. He boasted that his qigong was orderly, and that those who practiced would not fall into muddle-headedness as happened in other quiet sitting groups.[46]

Duan Zhengyuan demanded that people contemplate his photograph while meditating, which had a special purpose. In his *Master Yinshi's Quiet Sitting Method* (*Yinshizi jingzuofa* 因是子靜坐法), Jiang Weiqiao 蔣維喬 (1873–1958), one of the founders of modern-day *qigong*, had suggested that the "method for keeping mentally calm while observing the universe (*zhiguan famen* 止觀法門)" used what was called a "tethering causation (*xiyuanzhi* 繫緣止)" technique, which provided mental activities with an object, so that when people were meditating they could quickly put their thoughts aside.[47] Duan Zhengyuan also explained how contemplating the master's photograph could similarly help people achieve the meditative state more quickly.[48]

Through massive printing activities, Moral Study Society written materials were full of Duan Zhengyuan's photographs, so that if an adept wanted to use

---

42 Yang Fengqi 楊逢啟, "Yu Wuxi Wang Boying jun tan Daode xueshe gaikuang 與無錫汪伯英君談道德學社概況," *Yangshan banyuekan* 揚善半月刊 2, no. 20 (1935), 312.

43 In Ju Xi, ed., *Duan Zhengyuan yuyao*, 547.

44 Translator's note: Following Robert Eno's online translation, http://www.indiana.edu/~p374/Daxue-Zhongyong.pdf, 11.

45 In Duan's qigong, every level of technique had six mantras, and there were six levels, meaning a total of 36 mantras. There were also three changes and nine transformations in each level. See *Shizun lishi chugao* 師尊歷史初稿 (N.p.: n.d.), 10.

46 Ju Xi, ed., *Duan Zhengyuan yuyao*, 550.

47 Yan Hai 閻海, *Qigong jingxuan* 氣功精選 (Beijing: Renmin tiyu chubanshe, 1981; repr., Taiwan: Cimutang 慈母堂, n.d.), 69. Citation refers to the Taiwan edition.

48 Tianjin Daode yanjiushe 天津道德研究社, *Shizun wei Jinshe dianji shuofa* 師尊為津社奠基說法 (Tianjin: Moral Study Society, 1935), 65.

the image of the Master in the course of his cultivation, it would not be difficult to have one. In the above-mentioned *Further Collection of Past Teachings* there were also photographs with mudras, and on either side of them appear the following inscriptions:

> When meditating, one body naturally becomes three, putting *yin* and *yang* in order. People the world over enjoy harmony, freedom, equality and happiness.
>
> Abiding happily in my peacefulness, the myriad changes make their transition and the original sound returns to its primordial appearance as never-changing truth.
>
> 時中坐靜天然一體三位燮理肅赫陰陽，全世界人物享大同自由平等幸福。
>
> 常樂我淨而然千變萬化渡盡元音因緣，還本來面目成永生不滅無量真仁。[49]

Beside Duan Zhengyuan were two photographs in which he was performing mudras with both hands, in a posture that would be helpful to disciples attempting to cultivate.

In another of Duan's writings, the diary-like *Record of Daily Practice* (*Rixing jilu* 日行紀錄), there is a mention of a body of disciples making entreaties to the photograph of Duan Zhengyuan, which prompted Duan to explain the reason for the contemplation of the Master's photograph:

> Contemplating the Master's photograph concentrates the mind and accelerates spiritual processes. This brings you into contact with the spirit of the Master and the spirit of the Way, as the breath unites you with heaven and earth.
>
> 因觀師像，目注心想，再加神運，便與師一氣相貫，即與道氣相貫，天陽相接。[50]

In *The Record of Daily Progress* it is explained fairly clearly in a passage on the idea of "expressive communication" (*yiqi gantong* 一氣感通), meaning that the contemplator can become one with the Master and with the Way through

49 *Shenji dacheng*, photograph section, 17.

50 Duan Zhengyuan 段正元, *Rixing jilu* 日行紀錄 (Beijing: Moral Study Society, 1923/24), vol. 8, 1–2.

the concentration of his thoughts. What should be noted here is that the disciples asked for specially printed photographs in addition to those that were printed in religious literature, which were to be slightly bigger than normal photographs. Duan Zhengyuan constantly told his disciples that contemplating the Master's photo for a long period, and concentrating their spirit multiple times, would result in the realization of the heavenly Way, as well as relieving disasters.[51]

Looking at the Master's photograph also came to be seen as part of the group's ritual activities. The cover of *The Record of Daily Progress*, the volume that documents Duan Zhengyuan's activities, has a photo of a rather young Duan Zhengyuan teaching in front of the altar, and a citation from the Master that disciples are required to read and recite before cultivating:

> The Master's destiny has been to teach the Way. When the Way is exalted, dragons and tigers will be subdued; when virtue prevails, ghosts and spirits will be respectful. The ever sincere Master repeated that those hoping to exercise authority in carrying out the Master's Way must be prepared to receive the Master's direct and unvarnished teachings. For true disciples, no request will go unheard, no hardship will go unresolved, no happiness will be unobtainable.
>
> The Master's teachings proclaim the changes on behalf of heaven, rectify the Way and redeem the people's hearts, and remove heavenly and earthly disasters like wars, floods, epidemics, bandits, earthquakes—all natural and human disasters. The dusty world and the bitter sea will be transformed into a world of pure happiness. This is the joy of my Master and the joy of all peoples.
>
> It is the true nature of the Master to enable all things to return to their origin, and when looking at his photograph, the one is diffused to become the myriad things. Know that his heart contains great compassion, great intentions, great holiness and great mercy, hence all things are one with the will of the Master, who speaks and acts with the sincerity of the true man who creates the world of great harmony.
>
> 師尊命印，道高龍虎伏，德重鬼神欽。至誠尊師重道，請實行師道之職權，甘願受師直言無隱之教。真弟子有求必應，何災不可解，何福不可臻。

51 Ibid., 26–27.

> 師尊說法，代天宣化，挽回世道救正人心，消除天地否，刀兵、水火、瘟蝗、盜賊、地震、天災人患。紅塵苦海，化為極樂世界，吾師之幸也，天下人之幸也。
>
> 師尊真容，萬殊歸一本，觀其法相，一本散為萬殊。知其胸中包羅萬有之大悲大願，大聖大慈，故願與師同志願，為庸言庸行造大同世界之真人。[52]

In addition to emphasizing the feeling of the Master's Way and the Master's protection from disaster that was to be procured by reciting this passage while contemplating the Master's photograph, the idea was that the photograph would promote the common construction of the world of great harmony.

In the Moral Study Society, the photograph was a new religious text, not only an important symbol and marker of sacredness, but also a means for the disciples to cultivate themselves directly in their daily life.

5 Photographs and the Great Way: the Experience of Observation Constructed by Duan Zhengyuan

The first page of the 1939 volume *The Origin of the Great Way*, a pictorial record of the history of the Moral Study Society, has three different photographs of Duan Zhengyuan, explaining why he wore extravagant sable coats that others rarely wore:

> It is often said that that which is completed without anyone having done it is the work of heaven, that that which happens without anyone making it happen is fate. These three photographs are the same thing. The top photo is of me at age 55, preaching the Way, a photograph in which the disciples take me as their master. The photo on the bottom right is when I came to Beijing for the second time, to establish the Moral Study Society at the age of 52. On the bottom left is a photograph of me when I came to Beijing for the first time, at the age of 44. There are differences in these three pictures. The picture of me at age 44 is quite different, because when I decided to cultivate the Way, I took a vow that I would not wear silk and satin, but when I came to Beijing to meet people from the educational ministry, everybody said since I wasn't a monk, but wanted to preach the Way in society at large, then I had to follow the fashions. So I had no choice, and had to wear silk robes for the photograph. Once the photograph was done, I mailed it back to Sichuan. Later I

52 Ibid.

returned to Chengdu, where I established the Ethics and Morality Society, and three years later I returned to Beijing. I had lost track of the photograph, which was suddenly found in Chen Hanxiang's 陳翰香 papers, perfectly intact. I looked at the photograph and thought, "It's just like the Great Way, which accomplishes everything while doing nothing." When I thought about having it taken, my feeling was that the image had been formed in heaven, and then later, although it had been hidden [i.e., lost], it was discovered anew, creating the feeling that this tiny photograph had traveled from Beijing to Sichuan, and yet had come back across a distance of 10,000 *li* and a gap of more than twenty years, without being noticed or lost. It is clear that I am not an ordinary person. What I have accomplished will live throughout the ages. This is not an ordinary truth; even in darkness it is protected by heaven and earth, by gods and spirits. Truly, that which is completed without anyone have done it is the work of heaven, and that which happens without anyone making it happen is fate. Throughout time, in China and elsewhere, those gods and holy beings whose names and prestige have extended over a thousand generations, their images were all formed in heaven and materialized on earth, becoming true things in the world of men. Thus the 10,000 capabilities of heaven's will and the arrangement of human affairs come together in the same way.

常言莫之為而為者天也，莫之致而至者命也。即此三相，亦如是也。上一相是五十五三我說法，眾弟子尊我為師尊之相。下兩相，右是二次來京，成立道德學社，五十二之相；左是初來北京，四十四之相。觀此三相，雖前後懸殊。而四十四之相，變化莫測，因我修道時，發下宏誓大願，不穿綾羅綢緞，後到北京，遇學部人員，大眾云：既非出家人，又欲在世俗人情中辦事。要合時宜，我萬不得已，始穿錦衣狐裘，照成此相，當時照成，即寄回川，後轉成都，立人倫道德會，三年之久，復來北京。平日從未一見，突由陳翰香在字紙中發現，絲毫無毀損，我當審察，此相關乎大道，無為而有為。回思當照之時，自覺在天成象，故雖隱藏，而又發現，閱以人情說，小小相片，由北京至四川，往返萬餘里，相隔二十餘年，毫未注意，而亦未失落，足見非常之人，所成萬世不朽，非常之真容，暗中自有天地鬼神保護，正是莫之為而為者天也，莫之致而至者命也。古今中外，聖賢仙佛，能留名千載，馨香萬世者，皆在天成象，在地成形，在人成為實事，故天命之萬能，人事之安排，不亦而成也。[53]

53 Beijing Moral Study Society 北京道德學社, ed., *Dadao yuanliu* 大道源流 (Beijing: Moral Study Society, 1939), 1.

FIGURE 3.6 Duan Zhengyuan
SOURCE: DADAO YUANLIU

Duan Zhengyuan felt that there were profound differences between pictures of him at 44 and at 52, suggesting that different moods or different intentions can be seen through the photographs. He argued that the preservation of these photographs was the concrete expression of the fact that the Way could keep all things whole. If we savor Duan's language, we find that there is much in common with the opinion of contemporary theorists of photography, namely, that photography is a kind of immortal life.[54]

54 According to the leading theorists in the matter, Susan Sontag and John Berger, the most important difference between photography and other visual images is that photographs

Similar ideas clearly appear in the many pictures included in the 1932 *Further Collection of Past Teachings*. See the praise for one of the photographs of Duan at 60:

> Who was I on the day of my birth, on the first day of the fourth month in 1864? Here am I reborn after 60 years. People age but benevolence does not. Who am I after 60 years, formed and formless, formless and formed? Life is not erased. The non-me is me, I am the non-me; if I am truly non-me, who am I? By non-action nothing is left undone, by incapacity nothing is unable to be done. Outside I do not practice false benevolence and righteousness; inside I follow benevolence and righteousness. True virtue rests therein. Whether to acknowledge or reject me is clear from the first glance. Happiness resides in the Way, great virtue is life. The benevolent live long.
>
> 天元癸亥年四月一日，六十年前誰是我，花甲重生是我生。人老仁不老。六十年後我是誰，有形無形，無形有形，一生亦不滅。非我是我，是我非我，果非我，誰是我。無為無不為，無能無不能。外非行假仁義，內由仁義而行，真道德在其中。知我罪我，一望而知。樂哉道，大德曰生，仁者壽。[55]

The first day of the fourth month was Duan's birthday, and the above passage is his lament at 60. The Moral Study Society was ruled by the idea that the great Way was accomplished through non-activity. Does Duan's picture at age 60 indicate that he was seriously carrying out the great Way? Readers may judge from looking at the picture.

Duan Zhengyuan's understanding of photography and its impact was profound; one even might say that he developed photography and its functions to a new height. In the 1935 *Address at the Opening of the Tianjin Branch* (*Shizun wei Jinshe dianji shuofa* 師尊為津社奠基說法), Duan mentioned that he had fallen ill because of his ceaseless efforts to spread the Way, and his understandings of pictures taken after he was sick:

---

are not a description, an imitation or an interpretation of the subject, but instead are traces that the subject has left behind. See Zhang Guanghe 章光和, *Zhuzai Bate, Sangtage, Benyaming de zhaopianli* 住在巴特、桑塔格、本雅明的照片裡 (Nanning: Guangxi Shifan Daxue chubanshe, 2004), 78.

55 Duan Zhengyuan 段正元, *Shenji dacheng*, photograph section, 6.

> Today I will preach about my body. After a few decades, our flesh turns into clear wind and our bones turn to mud. Now I have passed 70, but my spirit is like that of a teenager. I can run around morning and night, I can work hard and do everything I want to. Why is this? Because I accepted my master's request, and in 1923–1924 devoted myself to saving the world, and worked myself into suffering and illness. Yet after a few months, I returned to my teenaged body. Last year in Beijing I was very ill, and for more than ten days neither ate nor drank. I wanted to take a photograph to mark the occasion, but who would have guessed it? When I looked at the photograph, not only did I not look sick, but again had my youthful appearance. As Śākyamuni said: If I don't save the people, who will save them? If I don't enter hell, who will enter?

> 今以吾現身說法，人生數十寒暑，即要肉化清風，骨化泥。吾今年逾古稀，精神仍如十餘歲之兒童，猶能朝夕奔忙，不辭勞苦，千事勞心，萬事勞形，何以要如此？因當年曾受師之托，在二甲交關之時，要捨身救世，故不得不如是，以致凡軀受傷，累成一身病；但吾只要幾個月，即可變成兒童身，加上年在北平大病，有十餘日，不進飲食，吾當想照一相，作為紀念，孰知一經照出，不但無病容，並且是一返老還童之相，由此可為證明。昔釋迦云:我不救眾生，誰救眾生；我不入地獄，誰入地獄？吾今亦然。[56]

Duan's reference to 1923–1924 was to the spread of rumors that the fifteenth day of the eighth lunar month in 1923 was to be the day of a great disaster, with changes in the heavens and a solar and lunar eclipse. This was only a few weeks after the great Tokyo earthquake, which had occurred on September 1 (the twenty-first day of the seventh month on the lunar calendar). The rumor spread widely and Tang Huanzhang 唐煥章 (n.d.), founder of the Society for the Great Unity of World Religions (Shijie zongjiao datonghui 世界宗教大同會), prepared a leaflet explaining to his followers how to survive the day.[57] Duan Zhengyuan had on many occasions explained to his disciples that such a thing would never occur. He used this photograph to link the effects of preaching the Way on disasters and his own health, yet this photograph, in which he

56 Tianjin Daode yanjiushe 天津道德研究社, *Shizun wei Jinshe dianji shuofa* 師尊為津社奠基說法 (Tianjin: Daode yanjiushe, 1935), 60.

57 See Wang Chien-chuan, "Shijie zongjiao datonghui chutan: Jiantan yu Jiang Xizhang de guanxi 世界宗教大同會初探：兼談與江希張的關係," *Taiwan zongjiao yanjiu tongxun* 台灣宗教研究通訊, no. 9 (2011): 107–139.

"returned to his youthful appearance," became a proof that he had sacrificed himself to avert disaster.[58]

I mentioned above that at the end of a talk or an activity in the Moral Study Society branches, those attending had to bow to a photograph of the master. Where did these photographs come from? Cameras began to proliferate in China in the 1920s and 1930s, and there were photographic studios in markets, stores, and parks. In Beijing's Dong'an market 東安市場, tea shops and photo studios were on the second floor.[59] The Moral Study Society, particularly interested in photography, set up a special photographic unit within the organization to take pictures of the master and to develop and distribute them.[60]

There were inscriptions on many of Duan Zhengyuan's photographs, some added onto the photos themselves after the images were developed, others on the sides of the photographs, and this style of photograph was much appreciated. We can say that Duan Zhengyuan truly opened the way for the use of photography in the religious field, which had a major impact on how photographs were used and viewed thereafter.[61]

6 The "Paradise Hall" and a Visualized Heaven

I mentioned above the rumor concerning the imminent disaster in 1923. Duan pronounced the rumor false, but felt that even if a disaster occurred, he could transform it through his teachings. During this same period, Duan focused most of his energy on the arrangement of the "Paradise" hall constructed within the Moral Study Society compound in Beijing. In the fourth month of that year, Duan Zhengyuan stopped activities aimed at recruiting disciples. From the middle of the seventh month of that year, Duan started every day by visiting various antique markets in Beijing, and spending a fair bit of money. There are many details in the first volume of *Record of Daily Practice*:

58 See, for example, Duan Zhengyuan 段正元, *Zhengyuan fayu* 正元法語, repr. in *Shidao quanshu* 師道全書 (Hongkong: Qiming shuju, 1940), 8: 53.

59 Feng Ke 馮客 (Frank Dikötter), "Minguo shiqi de moderg wanyi, wenhua pincou yu richang shenghuo," 482–484.

60 See the July 25, 1942 *Guiyuantang tongqi* 歸元堂通啟, July 25, 1942. This is a Beijing Moral Study Society internal communication.

61 The efficacy of contemplating the Master's image also appeared in sacred legends told in branch offices of the Moral Study Society. See, for example, *Youxue jilüe* 遊學紀略 (Beijing: Moral Study Society, 1946), 35.

7/19, went to Tianqiao, and bought pictures and other items in the Paradise hall I had set up;

7/20, went to the Dong'an market at 2:00 in the afternoon, and then to the Longfu temple to buy some antiques, which I placed in the Paradise hall.

7/21, got up at 7:00, and after my bath went to the Paradise hall to supervise the arrangement of objects. Stayed there until 2:00 when I came home to rest.

7/23, went to the Dongda temple where I bought a household shrine and 8 chairs in red peach wood, which cost more than 300 dollars.

7/24, got up at seven, and after my bath went to the Paradise hall to supervise the arrangement of objects. I got the household shrine installed to help deceased disciples, so that their souls would have a resting place. Went to Tianqiao at 1:00 and bought all sorts of lanterns, porcelain, and electric lights, which came to 100 dollars.

7/25, got up at 7:00, and after my bath there was heavy rain, but I still went to the Paradise hall to arrange things.

7/26, got up at 6:00 and went to the Paradise hall, where I set up the big mirror and arranged everything. Returned home to rest at 1:00. Looking at the arrangement of things, everything is connected and has its significance. Little things like this may look easy, but they are actually extremely difficult.

7/28, spent the past few days at the Paradise hall, because I figured that once I began preaching my transformation through music,[62] I would come less often and it would gradually come to look abandoned. I suddenly wanted to come in the middle of the night. Ever since the beginning of autumn things have revitalized. Now the Paradise hall doesn't look like a happy place. I think I'll spend another 3,000 dollars to buy some things and arrange them, so things will look nice.

七月十九記，往天橋一遊，所辦極樂天掛畫等物多件。……

七月二十日記　午後二點到東安市場，又到隆福寺買一切古物，安置在極樂天。……

七月二十一日記　七點起，盥洗畢，即到極樂天指揮陳列物品，至午後二點休息。……

七月二十三日記　至東大寺買神龕一座，紅花梨木椅子八張及一切物品，費洋三百餘元。……

62 Translator's note: This was Duan's adaptation of Confucian teachings regarding the uses of music.

> 七月二十四日記　　早七點起，盥洗畢即到極樂天，指揮陳列各物，將神龕安置，俾前有維持之弟子，靈魂有所依皈，作冥中護法。下午一點到天橋，買有各樣燈籠磁器電燈等物，共去一百元。……
>
> 七月二十五日記　早七點起，盥洗畢，天降大雨，吾仍到極樂天佈置一切。
>
> 二十六日記，早六點起至極樂天，安置大鏡，陳設一切物品，至午後一點休息。靜觀所列各物，均屬連絡映帶，各有意義；但此小事似乎極易，其實甚難。……
>
> 二十八日記　　我前幾日道極樂天，因想自開樂教以後，少到此地，漸形委靡不振之象，清夜忽然想來，我自立秋以後，凡事振興。今極樂天不成樂地，即想再以三千元，購置物品，陳列此處，以壯觀瞻。[63]

The above passages mentioned a large mirror set up in the Paradise hall. On the first day of the eighth month, all of the arrangement work stopped for a time:

> At 8:00 in the evening I brought all the many different lanterns to Paradise and they flickered in the mirror, reflecting one another, some big and some small. It was really as Śākyamuni said: observe the boundless universe.
>
> 晚八鐘，將極樂天五色電燈齊開，煥耀鏡中，層層相映，各有大小之差，真如釋迦云:照見三千大千世界。[64]

Religion often uses space to create a sense of the sacred. For example, Buddhism makes great use of the effects of optical illusions to erase the cognitive boundaries between the viewers and the viewed. There is a painted mirror palace in cave 31 of the Mogao 莫高 grotto in Dunhuang 敦煌. It is a space of infinitely increasing reproduction, where the sense of subjectivity of observers may disappear.[65] In the above example, Duan Zhengyuan used the multiple reflected images produced by the lanterns and the mirrors, and the arrangement of the beautiful antiques, to project an image of paradise on earth. The complexity of this earned Duan criticism from some disciples, to which

63 Duan Zhengyuan, *Rixing jilu*, vol. 1, 9–19.

64 Ibid., vol. 1, 23.

65 Eugene Y. Wang, "Oneiric Horizons and Dissolving Bodies: Buddhist Cave Shrine as Mirror Hall," *Art History* 27, no. 4 (2004): 494–521.

Duan responded. His efforts to exploit visual and spatial concepts surely exceeded that of other redemptive society leaders. The famous Peking University historian, Luo Rongqu 羅榮渠 (1927–1996), who had just graduated from Peking University in 1947, sighed with pleasure after visiting the Beijing Moral Study Society: "It really opened my eyes, it was like I was in the forbidden city" (一時令我大開眼界，疑是置身故宮之中).[66] One can see that this kind of visual challenge remained useful.

Photographs can be used as a visual display, often with a purpose. Duan Zhengyuan's photographs contain many pictures of him in a place like "paradise" (極樂天), in the magnificent hall, with everything covered in silk, the tables and chairs all exquisite and unique. Under the illumination of "colorful lanterns" (五色電燈), the Moral Study Society became a solemn world and a blissful religious space. Duan was clearly capable of mastering all kinds of modern communication tools and media. From the photos to the spatial arrangement of the Moral Study Society, the visual presentation became the best proof of the existence of heaven's Way.

7 Conclusion

More than once Duan noted that it seemed like there was a great phonograph or a great camera between heaven and earth, which made it possible to record the workings of the heavenly Way and cases of unclear retribution. At one point he noted that:

> As for preaching the Way, the *Treatise on Response and Retribution* says "Disaster and happiness do not occur arbitrarily. Retribution follows good and bad acts just as the shadow follows a body. Before scientific discoveries, there was no proof of this. Now science has invented photographic mirrors which can record a person's looks, be they beautiful or ugly. How marvelous this is! Recorders can preserve the happiness and anger of a person's voice without missing a thing. This proves the utility of the Way. When I preach in the temple today, not only those present can hear me, but if I broadcast it on the radio, then throughout the vast universe everyone can hear me. The human heart is the mechanism of the Way. Refrain from evil and pursue good and everything will follow the Way. The Way is empty, but people are practical and serious, which is what allows them to preach the Way. Cameras and recorders are material

66 Luo Rongqu 羅榮渠, *Beida suiyue* 北大歲月 (Beijing: Shangwu yinshuguan, 2006), 166–167.

objects with miraculous functions. The Way of heaven is invisible and yet comes to pass, good actions call forth good fortune, evil actions call forth disaster, which is also the proper process of nature."

再講道之究竟，《太上感應篇》曰：禍福無門，善惡之報，如影隨形。在科學發明以前，無所證實。今科學發明照像鏡，能照人容貌之妍蚩，畢妙畢肖；留音機能留人聲音之喜怒，纖微不漏，即可證明道之實用。我今在堂上講道，不但生等能聽，猶如將播音機打開，三千大千世界，凡有血氣、無血氣莫不聞聽。人心即是道之機關。存心諸惡不作，眾善奉行。不成道者，未之有也。道是虛的，在人事踏實認真，故曰人能弘道。照像鏡，留音機是有形之物，尚有如此妙用。天道無形而成化，作善降祥，作不善降殃，又是自然之禮。[67]

New things like movies and phonographs became manifestations of the Way, which is how the Way was able to exist.

Of course, at times when preaching, Duan might mention the view that Western machines were material objects, while the Way of China was metaphysical.[68] In 1928, when Duan had decided to take a rest because the great Way was stymied, he published *The Perfect Way* (*Yuandao* 圓道), in which he argued that the ego had provoked five revolutions and that the goal of the last revolution would be that all people would be one family. The book is full of revolutionary discourse. In 1948, disciples of the Beijing Moral Study Society published a book entitled *The World as One Family* (*Tianxia yijia* 天下一家), further elaborating on Duan's arguments.

If we expand the context surrounding the religious literature of redemptive societies in the early Republican period, the mass use of photographic reproductions made the visual experience of participation in religious life more direct. While mass printing of religious literature seems to diminish the originally sacred character of scripture, at the same time it expanded the reach of religious groups. As David Ownby notes in his chapter in this volume, the list of books in Tiandijiao (Teachings of the Heavenly Emperor 天帝教) leader Li Yujie's 李玉階 (1901–1994) library included Duan Zhengyuan's works. Duan Zhengyuan made many contributions to the modernization of the printing, sales, and distribution of religious texts, integrating religion and printing, preaching and photographs, displays, all of which have become a basic pattern employed by religious groups today.

67 Duan Zhengyuan 段正元, *Dingchou fayu* 丁丑法語 (Beijing: Moral Study Society, 1937), 60.

68 See, for example, Moral Study Society 道德學社, ed., *Shidao quanshu* 師道全書, 9: 37.

Bibliography

Beijing Moral Study Society 北京道德學社, ed. *Dadao yuanliu* 大道源流. Beijing: Moral Study Society, 1939.

Beiping Wanguo daode zonghui 北平萬國道德總會, ed. *Duxinglu* 篤行錄. Beijing: Zhonghua yinshuju, 1934.

Berger, John. *Understanding a Photograph*. New York: Aperture, 2013.

Chan, Wing-tsit. *Religious Trends in Modern China*. New York: Columbia University Press, 1953.

Clart, Philip. "New Technologies and the Production of Religious Texts in China, 19th–21st Century." In *Modern Chinese Religion II, 1850–2015*, edited by Vincent Goossaert, Jan Kiely, and John Lagerwey, vol. 1, 560–578. Leiden: Brill, 2016.

Clart, Philip, and Gregory Adam Scott, eds. *Religious Publishing and Print Culture in Modern China: 1800–2012*. Boston: De Gruyter, 2015.

Duan Zhengyuan 段正元. *Datong zhendi* 大同真諦. Beijing: Moral Study Society, 1923.

Duan Zhengyuan 段正元. *Dingchou fayu* 丁丑法語. Beijing: Moral Study Society, 1937.

Duan Zhengyuan 段正元. *Rixing jilu* 日行紀錄. Beijing: Moral Study Society, 1923/24.

Duan Zhengyuan 段正元. *Shenji dacheng* 申集大成. Beijing: Moral Study Society, 1932.

Duan Zhengyuan 段正元. *Zhengyuan fayu* 正元法語. Reprinted in *Shidao quanshu* 師道全書. Hongkong: Qiming shuju, 1940.

Duanfuzi 段夫子. Hangzhou: Moral Study Society, 1947.

Dunlop, Sarah. "Visual Methods in the Study of Religion." Available online at https://www.kent.ac.uk/religionmethods/documents/Visual%20approaches.pdf.

Eyferth, Jacob. *Eating Rice from Bamboo Roots: A Social History of a Community of Handicraft Papermakers from Rural Sichuan, 1920–2000*. Cambridge, Mass.: Harvard University Asia Center, 2009.

Fan Chun-wu 范純武. "Confucian 'Religion' in the Early Republican Period: Historical Questions Concerning Duan Zhengyuan and the Morality Society." *Chinese Studies in History* 44, no. 1–2 (2010/11): 132–155.

Fan Chun-wu 范純武. "Feiluan, xiuzhen yu banshan: Zheng Guanying yu Shanghai de zongjiao shijie 飛鸞、修真與辦善—鄭觀應與上海的宗教世界." In *Cong chengshi kan Zhongguo de xiandaixing* 從城市看中國的現代性, edited by Wu Renshu 巫仁恕, Lin Meili 林美莉, and Kang Bao 康豹 (Paul Katz), 247–274. Taipei: Zhongyang yanjiuyuan jindaishi yanjiusuo, 2010.

Fan Chun-wu 范純武. "'Jingdian' de liubu yu duidie: Duan Zhengyuan Daode xueshe de shuji chuban shiye 「經典」的流佈與堆疊:段正元道德學社的書籍出版事業." In the conference proceedings of the international conference on "Jingdian, yishi yu minjian xinyang 經典、儀式與民間信仰," organized by Shanghai shifan daxue Dunhuangxue yanjiu suo 上海師範大學敦煌學研究所, October 25/26, 2014.

Fan Chun-wu 范純武. "Minchu Ruxue de zongjiaohua: Duan Zhengyuan yu Daode xueshe de gean yanjiu 民初儒學的宗教化:段正元與道德學社的個案研究." *Minsu quyi* 民俗曲藝, no. 172 (June 2011): 161–203.

Fan Chun-wu 范純武. "Quanli, xiangxiang yu zaixian: Zhaoxiang dui jindai Zhongguo zongjiao tuanti chansheng de yingxiang 權力、想像與再現:照相對近代中國宗教團體產生的影響." *Minsu quyi* 民俗曲藝, no. 195 (March 2017): 247–306.

Fan Chun-wu 范純武. "Sheying yu shushi: Qingmo Minchu de lao zhaopian, mingxinpian, yu tigan lishi 攝影與敘史:清末民初的老照片、明信片與體感歷史." In *Tuxiang, dianying yu lishi* 圖像、電影與歷史, edited by Li Jixiang 李紀祥, 73–94. Yilan: Foguang renwen shehui xueyuan, 2006.

Feng Ke 馮客 (Frank Dikötter). "Minguo shiqi de modeng wanyi, wenhua pincou yu richang shenghuo 民國時期的摩登玩意、文化拼湊與日常生活." In *Zhongguo de chengshi shenghuo* 中國的城市生活, edited by Li Xiaoti 李孝悌, 477–495. Taipei: Lianjing, 2005.

Giddens, Anthony. *The Consequences of Modernity*. Stanford: Stanford University Press, 1990.

Guiyuantang tongqi 歸元堂通啟. Beijing Moral Study Society internal communication.

Han Congyao 韓從耀 and Zhao Yingxin 趙迎新. *Zhongguo yingxiangshi diliujuan, 1927–1937* 中國影像史第六卷, 1927–1937. Beijing: Zhongguo sheying chubanshe, 2015.

Jameson, Frederick. *A Singular Modernity: Essay on the Ontology of the Present*. London: Verso, 2012.

Ju Xi 鞠曦, ed. *Duan Zhengyuan yuyao* 段正元語要. Jilin: Jilin wenshi chubanshe, 2003.

Katz, Paul R. "Illuminating Goodness: Some Preliminary Considerations of Religious Publishing in Modern China." In *Religious Publishing and Print Culture in Modern China: 1800–2012*, edited by Philip Clart and Gregory Adam Scott, 265–294. Boston: De Gruyter, 2015.

Lee, Leo Ou-fan. *Shanghai Modern: The Flowering of a New Urban Culture in China, 1930–1945*. Cambridge, MA: Harvard University Press, 1999.

Lee, Leo Ou-fan. (Li Oufan 李歐梵). "WanQing wenhua, wenxue yu xiandaixing 晚清文化、文學與現代性." In *Zhongguo xiandai wenxue yu xiandai xing shijiang* 中國現代文學與現代性十講, edited by Li Oufan, 1–19. Shanghai: Fudan daxue chubanshe, 2002.

Liu Xun 劉迅. "Xiulian yu jiuguo: Minchu Shanghai Daojiao neidan, chengshi xinzhong de xiuxing, yinshua wenhua yu tuanti 修煉與救國：民初上海道教內丹、城市信眾的修行、印刷文化與團體." In *Cong chengshi kan Zhongguo de xiandaixing* 從城市看中國的現代性, edited by Wu Renshu 巫仁恕, Lin Meili 林美莉, and Kang Bao 康豹 (Paul Katz), 221–246. Taipei: Zhongyang yanjiuyuan jindaishi yanjiusuo, 2010.

Luo Rongqu 羅榮渠. *Beida suiyue* 北大歲月. Beijing: Shangwu yinshuguan, 2006.

Moral Study Society 道德學社, ed. *Shidao quanshu* 師道全書. Hong Kong: Qiming shuju, 1940 reprint.

Morgan, David. *The Sacred Gaze: Religious Visual Culture in Theory and Practice*. Berkeley: University of California Press, 2005.

Morgan, David. *Visual Piety: A History and Theory of Popular Religious Images*. Berkeley: University of California Press, 1998.

Ownby, David. "Recent Chinese Scholarship on the History of Redemptive Societies." *Chinese Studies in History* 44, no. 1–2 (2010/11): 3–9.

Reed, Christopher A. *Gutenberg in Shanghai: Chinese Print Capitalism, 1876–1937*. Honolulu: University of Hawai'i Press, 2004.

Shenbao 申報.

Shi Ruige 史瑞戈 (Gregory Adam Scott). "Pingheng gongde yu liyi: Shanghai foxue shuju gufen youxian gongsi de jingli 平衡功德與利益—上海佛學書局股份有限公司的經歷." In *Gaibian Zhongguo zongjiao de wushi nian, 1898–1948* 改變中國宗教的五十年 1898–1948, edited by Kang Bao 康豹 (Paul Katz) and Gao Wansang 高萬桑 (Vincent Goossaert), 193–224. Taipei: Zhongyang yanjiuyuan jindaishi yanjiusuo, 2015.

Shidao teci jinnang jing 師道特賜錦囊經. Undated pamphlet.

Shizun guli jiyao 師尊故里紀要. N.p.: 1944.

Shizun lishi chugao 師尊歷史初稿. N.p.: n.d.

Tianjin Daode yanjiushe 天津道德研究社. *Shizun wei Jinshe dianji shuofa* 師尊為津社奠基說法. Tianjin: Moral Study Society, 1935.

Wang Bingqian 汪秉乾. *Shidao cuoyaolu* 師道撮要錄. Beijing: Daode yinshuasuo, 1925.

Wang Chien-chuan 王見川. "Jindai Zhongguo de fuji, cishan yu 'mixin': Yi *Yinguang wenchao* wei kaocha xiansuo 近代中國的扶乩，慈善與「迷信」：以印光文鈔為考察線索." In *Xinyang, shijian yu wenhua tiaoshi: Disijie guoji Hanxue huiyi lunwenji* 信仰，實踐與文化調適：第四屆國際漢學會議論文集, edited by Kang Bao 康豹 (Paul R. Katz) and Liu Shufen 劉淑芬, 531–568. Taipei: Academia Sinica, 2013.

Wang Chien-chuan 王見川. "Lufei Kui, Shengdetan yu Lingxuehui: Jiantan Minchu Shanghai de lingxue fengchao 陸費逵、盛德壇與靈學會：兼談民初上海的靈學風潮." Published in the proceedings of the international conference on Kexue yu wenhua de bianzou 科學與文化的變奏, organized by the History Department of Foguang University, Yilan, Taiwan, October 2/3, 2012.

Wang Chien-chuan 王見川. "Morality Book Publishing and Popular Religion in Modern China: A Discussion Centered on Morality Book Publishers in Shanghai." In *Religious Publishing and Print Culture in Modern China, 1800–2012*, edited by Philip Clart and Gregory Adam Scott, 233–264. Boston: De Gruyter, 2015.

Wang Chien-chuan 王見川. "Shijie zongjiao datonghui chutan: Jiantan yu Jiang Xizhang de guanxi 世界宗教大同會初探: 兼談與江希張的關係." *Taiwan zongjiao yanjiu tongxun* 台灣宗教研究通訊, no. 9 (2011): 107–139.

Wang Chien-chuan 王見川, Kang Bao 康豹 (Paul Katz), and Zong Shuren 宗樹人 (David Palmer). "Daoyan: Jiushi tuanti yanjiu de huigu 導言: 救世團體研究的回顧." *Minsu quyi* 民俗曲藝, no. 172 (June 2011): 13–14.

Wang, Eugene Y. "Oneiric Horizons and Dissolving Bodies: Buddhist Cave Shrine as Mirror Hall." *Art History* 27, no. 4 (2004): 494–521.

Xiong Yuezhi 熊月之. "Zhang Yuan yu wanQing Shanghai shehui 張園與晚清上海社會." Available online at http://www.aisixiang.com/data/13010.html.

Yan Hai 閻海. *Qigong jingxuan* 氣功精選. Beijing: Renmin tiyu chubanshe, 1981. Taiwan reprint by Cimutang 慈母堂, n.d.

Yang Fengqi 楊逢啟. "Yu Wuxi Wang Boying jun tan Daode xueshe gaikuang 與無錫汪伯英君談道德學社概況." *Yangshan banyuekan* 揚善半月刊 2, no. 20 (1935): 312–333.

Youxue jilüe 遊學紀略. Beijing Moral Study Society, 1946.

Zhang Guanghe 章光和. *Zhuzai Bate, Sangtage, Benyaming de zhaopianli* 住在巴特、桑塔格、本雅明的照片裡. Nanning: Guangxi Shifan Daxue chubanshe, 2004.

CHAPTER 4

Science and Spirit-Writing: The Shanghai Lingxuehui 靈學會 and the Changing Fate of Spiritualism in Republican China

Matthias Schumann

1 Introduction[1]

The early Republican period was a time of "scientism," when many Chinese intellectuals such as Chen Duxiu 陳獨秀 (1879–1942) advocated the application of the fairly new concept of science (*kexue* 科學) in all spheres of life.[2] As a consequence, science became a key concept and a major source of legitimacy for a variety of groups and individuals. This was particularly the case for religious actors, who were threatened by an emerging discourse of "anti-superstition," which criticized certain practices, and sometimes religion in total, as irrational and as a hindrance to national progress.[3] As the chapter by David Ownby in this volume shows, redemptive societies therefore at times attempted to cloak their religious ideas in a scientific discourse. Some religious actors even tried to reform their beliefs and practices along scientific lines, leading to attempts to combine science with, for example, Daoist inner alchemy.[4]

---

1 Research for this article was facilitated by a three-year doctoral scholarship from the German Research Foundation (DFG) awarded to me by the Cluster of Excellence "Asia and Europe in a Global Context" at the University of Heidelberg for which I am very grateful. For useful feedback and suggestions on earlier drafts of this article I would like to thank Joachim Kurtz, Rudolf G. Wagner, Daniel Hausmann, as well as the editors.

2 The classic reference to scientism in China remains D.W.Y. Kwok, *Scientism in Chinese Thought, 1900–1950* (New Haven: Yale University Press, 1965). Kwok defines scientism "as that view which places all reality within a natural order and deems all aspects of this order, be they biological, social, physical, or psychological, to be knowable only by the methods of science." (p. 21) For a recent treatment of scientism in China see Grace Yen Shen, "Scientism in the Twentieth Century," in *Modern Chinese Religion II, 1850–2015*, ed. Vincent Goossaert, Jan Kiely, and John Lagerwey (Leiden: Brill, 2016), 91–137.

3 Cf. Vincent Goossaert, "1898: The End of Religion in China?," *The Journal of Asian Studies* 65, no. 2 (2006): 307–335.

4 See, for example, Erik J. Hammerstrom, "Science and Buddhist Modernism in Early 20th Century China: The Life and Works of Wang Xiaoxu 王小徐," *Journal of Chinese Religions* 39 (2011): 1–32, and Xun Liu, *Daoist Modern: Innovation, Lay Practice and the Community*

 | DOI:10.1163/9789004424166_006

After WWI there emerged a particular noteworthy reform attempt, shedding light on contemporary scientific discourses as well as on the reconfiguration of religious practices during that time. Drawing on a global debate about science, matter, and spirit, a number of prominent individuals and organizations called for the establishment of a scientific spiritualism (*lingxue* 靈學). Chinese spiritualists appropriated the concept of science to legitimate the investigation of spiritualist topics such as life after death. In particular, they tried to present the Chinese practice of spirit-writing (*fuji* 扶乩) as part of a global spiritualist movement. To this end, both the practice as well as the functions of spirit-writing were reformed in light of spreading scientific discourses. This reform process, however, was not straightforward. The relation between science and spirit-writing was constantly negotiated against the background of the historically formed understanding of the practice, sometimes resulting in contestation and conflict.

Spiritualism in China was part of a global new spirituality,[5] which emerged in Europe and the US at the end of the nineteenth century and sought to redefine the relation between matter and spirit. Even though advocates of this global movement were united in their critique of "materialism," this new spirituality did not have a fixed meaning but was shaped by particular actors in specific historical contexts. What set it apart from prior spiritual traditions within religion and philosophy, however, was its active engagement with science.[6] Movements such as Theosophy, New Thought, psychical research, and spiritualism all presented themselves as alternatives to scientific materialism,[7] but also adopted scientific concepts and practices to establish institutions that were modeled on the emerging academic profession. As a consequence, they

of Inner Alchemy in Republican Shanghai (Cambridge: Harvard University Asian Center/ Harvard University Press, 2009), especially chap. 3.

5 In this article I define spirituality as a worldview that emphasizes non-material forces or entities in human life and the cosmos at large, whether these are called mind, psyche, or spirit.

6 This new spirituality was thus markedly different from, for example, Christian spirituality, which, in Pauline terminology, can be understood as referring to the spiritual influence of the Holy Spirit and is neither bound to a scientific worldview nor necessarily opposed to the material. See Arthur Holder, "Introduction," in *The Blackwell Companion to Christian Spirituality*, ed. Arthur Holder (Malden: Blackwell Publishing, 2005), 1–3.

7 On these disciplines see, for example, Beryl Satter, *Each Mind a Kingdom: American Women, Sexual Purity, and the New Thought Movement, 1875–1920* (Berkeley et al.: University of California Press, 1999); Roger Luckhurst, *The Invention of Telepathy, 1870–1901* (New York: Oxford University Press, 2002); Alex Owen, *The Place of Enchantment: British Occultism and the Culture of the Modern* (Chicago: University of Chicago Press, 2007); Olav Hammer, *Claiming Knowledge: Strategies of Epistemology from Theosophy to the New Age* (Leiden: Brill, 2001); and Heather Wolffram, *The Stepchildren of Science: Psychical Research and Parapsychology in Germany, c. 1870–1939* (Amsterdam: Rodopi, 2009).

offered scientific legitimacy, while allowing for the acknowledgement of spiritual entities or even the belief in supernatural beings. It was exactly this role that made the new spirituality attractive in China as well.

One of the most prominent spiritualist organizations in Republican China was the Shanghai Spiritualist Society (Lingxuehui, from here on LXH). Founded in late 1917, it sought to scientifically prove the existence of the soul and supernatural beings through a reformed practice of spirit-writing.[8] In late imperial China, spirit-writing had been a prominent part of elite literary culture as well as a popular divinatory practice, providing medical prescriptions and other information related to personal welfare. It had also been used to compose book-length writings—especially "morality books" (*shanshu* 善書) and religious scriptures—which were completed in sessions stretching over several days and often called for a "moral transformation" (*jiaohua* 教化) to avert disasters and personal misfortune. These functions of spirit-writing continued into the Republican period when many redemptive societies were formed around the practice.[9] While the LXH shared the moral emphasis of other spirit-writing organizations, it dedicated itself to the promotion of spiritualism (*lingxue*), or the investigation of spiritual forces and entities. The Society adopted new organizational models to establish a "spiritual science" and reform spirit-writing in accordance with the scientistic tendencies of the Republican period.

The growing cultural authority of science had a sizeable influence on the practice of spirit-writing within the LXH. The Society circumscribed the topics to be discussed at the altar and downplayed a previous interest in personal welfare. In their spirit-written texts, which were ascribed to different deities, they instead engaged with spiritualist concepts and practices such as spirit-photography[10] to argue for the empirical existence of a spiritual energy (*ling* 靈) that could survive physical death. The writings produced at the society thus clearly show the imprint of the Republican context and illustrate the

---

8 Spirit-writing in China (also *fuluan* 扶鸞, lit. "wielding the phoenix") refers to a specific form of communication with supernatural beings. Practitioners place a wooden tool, the *ji* 乩 (usually shaped like the letter T or Y), supported by either one or two bystanders, above a tray of sand. Following prayers and the burning of incense, deities and other beings are thought to descend into the tool and, through an interaction with the inner spiritual forces of those wielding the tool, write characters in the sand.

9 See Matthias Schumann, "Redemptive Societies," in *Handbook on Religion in China*, ed. Stephan Feuchtwang (Cheltenham: Edward Elgar Publishing, forthcoming).

10 This practice involves the production of blurry shapes on photographs through double exposure, which were then interpreted as the souls of deceased relatives or eminent persons. It was first used by the American William H. Mumler (1832–1884) in 1862. Bridget Bennett, *Transatlantic Spiritualism and Nineteenth-Century American Literature* (New York: Palgrave Macmillan, 2007), 25.

reconfiguration that many religious practices underwent during this period. Spiritualist concepts and techniques were used to attract new members and to defend the legitimacy of spirit-writing against a critical public, consisting mostly of secular intellectuals such as Chen Duxiu. Its prominent membership and creative adaptation of globally circulating concepts led to a brief flowering of spiritualism within China during the late 1910s and early 1920s and prompted some redemptive societies to pick up spiritualism as a legitimizing concept. Yet the case of the Society also shows the intricacies involved in reforming religious practices along scientific lines. In the course of establishing their spiritualist science, they needed to balance reforms with the interests of the wider public and the functions usually attributed to this practice. In 1920, many of its members temporarily turned their back on the Society after it had completely prohibited private inquiries at the altar in an intensified process of scientific institutionalization. The LXH was only able to survive once it reset its course in early 1921. It once more provided space for the personal interests of its members while preserving its appeal to science and spiritualism. At the same time, it redirected its activities in the direction most redemptive societies had chosen in the first place, emphasizing philanthropy and religious self-cultivation. The case of Chinese spiritualism therefore sheds light on the opportunities and limitations which the concept of science presented for redemptive societies—and religious actors more generally—in Republican China.

2 Science and the New Spirituality

The popularization of science was vital for the development of a new spirituality in North America and Europe in the nineteenth century. Spiritualism, the most prominent current of this new spirituality, was a broad movement based on the conviction that communication between the material and the spirit world was possible.[11] The birth of spiritualism is usually dated to the year 1848 when the two sisters Margaret (1833–1893) and Kate (1837–1892) Fox reported an exchange with a spirit in their house in Rochester, New York, an incident that, due to the specific method of communication, became known as the "Rochester Rappings." From this initial episode, séances with spirits turned into a veritable fashion, which spread from the United States to almost every

11 Bennett, *Transatlantic Spiritualism*, 5. On the history and ideas of spiritualism see also Tatiana Kontou and Sarah Willburn, eds., *The Ashgate Companion to Nineteenth-Century Spiritualism and the Occult* (Farnham and Burlington: Ashgate, 2012).

European country.[12] One of the principal reasons for the popularity of spiritualism was its refashioning of the supernatural in a scientific manner through the use of new technology and the invention of an elaborate spiritualist vocabulary. Photography and "scientific apparatuses" were used to document "spirit materializations" and the assumed workings of a "psychic force." Emphasis on spiritualist "experimentation" and the personal experience of séances struck a chord within European societies that remained deeply religious while becoming aware of the authority of science.[13] Indeed, new discoveries in the realm of electricity or radioactivity led some to believe that science would soon be able to explain disputed spiritual phenomena like telepathy or the relation between mind and matter more generally.[14] In this context, some members of the scientific profession became vocal proponents of the new spirituality. From the mid-nineteenth century onward, scientists such as William Crookes (1832–1919) or Alfred Russel Wallace (1823–1913) participated in séances with the dead and were deeply impressed by the empirical nature of these phenomena.[15]

The scientific approach to spiritual phenomena found its most vivid expression in the founding of the Society for Psychical Research in London in 1882. Many of its members, who included illustrious figures such as the British physicist Sir Oliver Lodge (1851–1940), were troubled over materialist tendencies in science and wanted to provide a scientific venue for the investigation of spiritual phenomena.[16] They tried to widen the confines of science because they were convinced that phenomena such as telepathy or clairvoyance were valid

---

12 Spiritualism became particularly popular in France, but it garnered an audience in Germany and Russia as well. See Lynn Luise Sharp, *Secular Spirituality: Reincarnation and Spiritism in Nineteenth Century France* (Lanham, MD et al.: Lexington Books, 2006); Michael Hochgeschwender, "The Religion of the Modern Man: 19th Century Spiritualism in the US and Germany," in *Religion in the United States*, ed. Jeanne Cortiel et al. (Heidelberg: Universitätsverlag Winter, 2011), 3–23; and Ilya Vinitsky, *Ghostly Paradoxes: Modern Spiritualism and Russian Culture in the Age of Realism* (Toronto et al.: University of Toronto Press, 2009).

13 Roger Luckhurst, "Religion, Psychical Research, Spiritualism, and the Occult," in *The Oxford Handbook of Modernisms*, ed. Peter Brooker et al. (Oxford: Oxford University Press, 2010), 429–433, and John J. Cerullo, *The Secularization of the Soul: Psychical Research in Modern Britain* (Philadelphia: Institute for the Study of Human Issues, 1982), 18–37.

14 Sherrie Lynne Lyons, *Species, Serpents, Spirits, and Skulls: Science at the Margins in the Victorian Age* (Albany: State University of New York Press, 2009), 13. See also William Barrett, *Psychical Research* (New York: Henry Holt and Company, and London: Williams and Norgate, n.d.), 11–12.

15 Lyons, *Species, Serpents, Spirits, and Skulls*, 87–109, 111–145.

16 On the history of the Society for Psychical Research see Cerullo, *The Secularization of the Soul*, and Janet Oppenheim, *The Other World: Spiritualism and Psychical Research in England, 1850–1914* (Cambridge: Cambridge University Press, 1985).

expressions of human mental capabilities rather than "mystical superstitions."[17] Psychical research became a global movement in its own right and inspired branches in many countries, among them the United States. In difference from spiritualists, many members of the Society for Psychical Research retained a more skeptical attitude towards the existence of the human soul after death. They claimed adherence to a strict scientific methodology and criticized spiritualists for being overly credulous.[18] Yet, lines between spiritualism and psychical research were porous and both sought to present themselves as anti-materialist and scientific.[19]

The emergence of spiritualist movements in Europe and North America soon caught the attention of contemporaries in Asia. In Japan, after the Meiji restoration state reformers regulated the religious sphere and targeted the practices of healers and spirit-mediums, which they perceived as superstitious.[20] Psychical research and spiritualism filled a void for people willing to probe the mental side of human life at a time when practices like faith-healing and new religions in general were subject to growing state repression.[21] Techniques of spirit-communication and hypnosis introduced from Europe and North America seemed sufficiently "modern" and rational to be embraced by a cosmopolitan clientele, which conducted spiritualist "experiments" in the

---

17 Barrett, *Psychical Research*, 14.

18 William James (1842–1910), who was an important figure in the British as well as the American Society for Psychical Research, thus remained critical of a belief in the spirits of deceased individuals (although he believed in "mental telepathy"). Part of the reason for this may be that he considered many spiritualist mediums, in particular those producing "materializations" of spirits, as fraudulent and distasteful. See Marcus Ford, "William James's Psychical Research and Its Philosophical Implications," *Transactions of the Charles S. Peirce Society* 34, no. 3 (1998): 605–626; and Robert D. Richardson, *William James: In the Maelstrom of American Modernism, A Biography* (Boston & New York: Mariner Books, 2007), 259–260.

19 The Society for Psychical Research adopted a presidential system, including a council for the election of suitable members and associates, for which women were also eligible, and they established a library and held regular meetings. They saw themselves as "men of undisputed scientific culture" aiming to provide "scientific evidence" regarding disputed phenomena such as telepathy or hypnotism. Anon., "Objects of the Society," *Proceedings of the Society for Psychical Research* 1 (1882): 3–4; and Henry Sidgwick, "Proceedings of the Society for Psychical Research," *Proceedings of the Society for Psychical Research* 1 (1882): 7–12.

20 Gerald Figal, *Civilization and Monsters: Spirits of Modernity in Meiji Japan* (Durham and London: Duke University Press, 1999), 77–152.

21 Jason Ānanda Josephson, *The Invention of Religion in Japan* (Chicago and London: University of Chicago Press, 2012), 238–244.

newly spreading salon culture.[22] In addition, they could be linked to an existing tradition of self-cultivation, which still enjoyed great popularity.[23]

In China, we can observe a similar dynamic. Practices and concepts of the new spirituality could be linked to an existing tradition of self-cultivation, but due to their popularity in Europe and the US they also seemed legitimate enough to be applied in the sphere of politics and medicine. Thus, in the 1890s, Tan Sitong 譚嗣同 (1865–1898) combined established philosophical and new scientific concepts to argue for the potential value of "mental powers" (*xinli* 心力) in strengthening the Chinese state.[24] In his footsteps, there emerged a whole discourse on the power of the mind and its application in politics.[25] A belief in the political value of mental powers in turn facilitated the spread of psychic organizations which mostly focused on the propagation and application of hypnotism (*cuimianshu* 催眠術). Japan served as an important mediator in the transmission of these discourses. Many Chinese exchange students participated in Japanese hypnotism groups and started to establish their own organizations.[26] They emphasized the importance of the mind in

22 Helen Hardacre, "Asano Wasaburō and Japanese Spiritualism in Early Twentieth-Century Japan," in *Japan's Competing Modernities: Issues in Culture and Democracy, 1900–1930*, ed. Sharon A. Minichiello (Honolulu: University of Hawai'i Press, 1998), 133–153.

23 For example, Japanese practitioners in the latter half of the nineteenth century began to integrate theories about hypnotism with practices taken especially from Buddhism. Shini'ichi Yoshinaga, "The Birth of Japanese Mind Cure Methods," in *Religion and Psychotherapy in Modern Japan*, ed. Christopher Harding et al. (London and New York: Routledge, 2015), 76–102.

24 Ingo Schäfer, "Natural Philosophy, Physics and Metaphysics in the Discourse of Tan Sitong: The Concepts of *Qi* and *Yitai*," in *New Terms for New Ideas: Western Knowledge and Lexical Change in Late Imperial China*, ed. Michael Lackner et al. (Leiden: Brill, 2001), 261. Tan drew a number of his ideas from John Fryer's (1839–1928) *A Method for Healing the Mind and Avoiding Sickness* (*Zhixin mianbing fa* 治心免病法). This book was an amended translation of Henry Wood's (1834–1909) *Ideal Suggestion through Mental Photography*, which posited that there was a higher spiritual consciousness that was superior to the material plane and needed to be developed and enhanced to better human life. Woods was part of the American New Thought Movement, which shows the influence, if only indirectly, of the new spirituality in the Chinese cultural sphere at the time. See Schäfer, "Natural Philosophy, Physics and Metaphysics in the Discourse of Tan Sitong," 261; and Fu Lanya 傅蘭雅 (John Fryer), trans., *Zhixin mianbing fa* 治心免病法 (Shanghai: Shanghai Gezhi shushi, 1896).

25 Joyce C.H. Liu, "Psychic Force and its Betrayals: Re-treating Tan Sitong's Translation of Psyche," in *Modern China and the West: Translation and Cultural Mediation*, ed. Peng Hsiao-yen and Isabelle Rabut (Leiden: Brill, 2014), 153–181.

26 The most notable among these was the Chinese Institute of Mentalism (Zhongguo xinling yanjiuhui 中國心靈研究會), which was founded in 1911 by Chinese exchange students

human life and tried to apply mental powers to the sphere of medicine and individual well-being, thereby building on an existing tradition of meditation. While self-cultivation practices did not face the same political pressure as in Japan, a similar logic was at play here. Psychical research and hypnotism promised some of the same effects as existing techniques of meditation while also offering scientific legitimacy. Psychical researchers aimed to set up scientific institutions and established research institutes, journals, and study programs. They therefore enabled practitioners to circumvent the religious sphere, which was in public discourse sometimes conflated with the newly coined concept of "superstition." While psychical researchers were often critical of religion and spirit-writing, they provided many concepts and theories for the larger public interested in spiritualism.

Another important mediator linking the global interest in a new spirituality with the Chinese context was the high ranking official Wu Tingfang 伍廷芳 (1842–1922). Wu had served twice as minister to the United States and during that period had become interested in psychical research, spiritualism, and later in Theosophy.[27] Wu had engaged in what he called the study of the soul (*linghunxue* 靈魂學) since the late 1900s and gave a number of talks about the topic in China after the founding of the Republic.[28] The currents of Theosophy and spiritualism offered him a legitimate venue to articulate his belief in the existence of the human soul and his interest in self-cultivation. His efforts were also key to the popularization of the new technique of spirit-photography in China.[29] During his many talks on spiritualism, he displayed several images

---

in Tokyo (after they had founded a Chinese Psychic Club [Zhongguo xinling julebu 中國心靈俱樂部] already in 1909) and devoted itself to the introduction and implementation of psychical research (*xinlingxue* 心靈學/ *xinling yanjiu* 心靈研究) and hypnotism in Japan and China. Anon., "Zhongguo xinling yanjiuhui lüeshi 中國心靈研究會略史," *Xinling* 心靈 1, no. 4 (1916): 58.

27 Wu became acquainted with Theosophy and spirit-photography during his two stays in the United States, which lasted from 1896–1902 and from 1907–1910, respectively. He joined the Theosophical Society in New York at some point after 1900 and eventually founded the first Chinese branch in Shanghai. Hu Xuecheng 胡學丞, "Wu Tingfang de tongshenxue yu lingxue shengya 伍廷芳的通神學與靈學生涯," *Zhengda shicui* 政大史粹, no. 22 (2012): 8.

28 In a talk that he gave in 1918, he claimed that he had been pursuing the topic for more than ten years. See Wu Tingfang, "Xuanjiang linghunxue 宣講靈魂學," in *Wu Tingfang ji* 伍廷芳集, 2 vols, ed. Ding Xianjun 丁賢俊 and Yu Zuofeng 喻作鳳 (Beijing: Zhonghua shuju, 1993), 854.

29 Wu's photographs were published by Di Baoxian 狄葆賢 (1872–1941), a well-known literatus and poet, in the *Xiaoshuo shibao* 小說時報 in 1911. See Zheng Yayin 鄭雅尹, "Qingmo Minchu de 'gui' yu 'zhaoxiangshu': Di Baoxian *Pingdeng Ge biji* zhong de xiandaixing

which he explained as the photographic representation of human *qi* 氣.[30] He served as a major inspiration for later spiritualists who experimented with this new technique.[31] Indeed, the links between his belief in the human soul, his practice of self-cultivation as well as his interest in new technologies are representative of the larger spiritualist sphere in Republican China. Wu's activities also illustrate the opportunities which presented themselves to spiritualists during and after WWI. The new spirituality proved particularly attractive after the war, which many intellectuals ascribed to excessive tendencies of materialism and militarism in Europe.[32] Spiritual alternatives, many believed, could restore human morality and counter materialist tendencies by proving scientifically that human life transcended mere physical existence.

3 The Founding of the Lingxuehui

The circumstances leading to the founding of the LXH reflect the above tendencies, especially the growing popularity of spiritualism and psychical research in early Republican China. In addition, social networks based on workplace and native-place affiliations played an important role. The founding of the organization as well as the establishment of their spirit-writing altar, the Altar of Flourishing Virtue (Shengde tan 盛德壇), are inextricably bound to the Yang 楊 family from Wuxi 無錫 in Jiangsu 江蘇 province. The family members who were important for the later founding of the LXH were Yang Guangxi 楊光熙 (n.d.) and his two sons, Yang Jianxing 楊踐形 (Ruilin 瑞臨, 1891–1965) and Yang Zhenru 楊真如 (n.d.).[33] All three of them already had experience with spirit-writing before becoming the main practitioners of the Society.

meiying 清末民初的「鬼」與「照相術」—狄葆賢《平等閣筆記》中的現代性魅影," *Qinghua zhongwen xuebao* 清華中文學報, no. 13 (2015): 241–242.

30 Hu, "Wu Tingfang de tongshenxue yu lingxue shengya," 21.

31 In his later years he wrote a number of books on the topic of spiritualism (*lingxue*), but they were unfortunately lost when his office burnt down. Ding and Yu, *Wu Tingfang ji*, 13.

32 See Matthias Schumann. "Protecting the Weak or Weeding Out the Unfit? Disaster Relief, Animal Protection and the Changing Evaluation of Social Darwinism in Japan and China," in *Protecting the Weak in East Asia: Framing, Mobilisation and Institutionalisation*, ed. Iwo Amelung et al. (Abingdon and New York: Routledge, 2018), 26–27.

33 It was Zheng Guo 鄭國 who discovered that Yang Ruilin, as he is called in the sources of the LXH, was none other than Yang Jianxing, the famous scholar of *qigong* 氣功 and the *Yijing* 易經. See Zheng Guo, "Shanghai Lingxuehui yanjiu: Jian lun Minchu zhishijie dui kexue de renzhi jinbu 上海靈學會研究：兼論民初知識界對科學的認知進步" (PhD. diss., Beijing, Guoji guanxi xueyuan, 2007), 40. See also Yang Jianxing, *Xueduo*

Yang Guangxi had served as a low-level official in different locations at the end of the Qing dynasty. He first encountered a spirit-writing altar in 1893 while he was serving in Wuchang 武昌.[34] Upon obtaining spirit-writing instruments in 1902, he set up his own altar and operated it with his elder brother. Two years later he established a more regular altar to practice spirit-writing in his spare time, first in Wenzhou 温州 and later in Shaoxing 紹興.[35] After the founding of the Republic, Yang went to work in Lufei Kui's 陸費逵 (1886–1941) China Bookstore (Zhonghua shuju 中華書局) in Shanghai.[36] It was at this company that the LXH was eventually established, in the process of which we observe not only a fascination with spirit-writing, but also an engagement with the new spirituality in China.

One can argue that the LXH might not have been founded were it not for new spiritualist concepts and practices which provided a fresh perspective on spirit-writing. One of the main inspirations that drew the later members of the LXH to the study of spiritualism was Wu Tingfang. Yang Guangxi recalled in one writing that before the LXH was founded he had "mentioned the spirit-photographs of Doctor Wu [Tingfang] and the principles of spirit-writing" (談及伍博士鬼影片各事。並及扶乩之理) in a conversation with Yu Fu 俞復 (1856–1943), who also worked at China Bookstore, and other acquaintances in the autumn of 1917.[37] At this point, some of the later members had already come in touch with the new spirituality and were seeking to link spirit-writing with this new body of knowledge. Yang Jianxing, the son of Yang Guangxi, had learned spirit-writing with his father and uncle while young and served as their assistant. He later also taught spirit-writing to his younger brother Zhenru. Spirit-writing sparked in Jianxing a more general interest in spiritual topics, so that in 1916 he began to study "mental philosophy (*jingshen zhexue* 精神哲學) and the principles of the soul (*linghun yuanli* 靈魂原理)" as well as the "practices of hypnosis and telepathy" (催眠通腦諸術).[38] According to his own account, he received the materials for his studies from the lay Buddhist and book collector Ding Fubao 丁福保 (1874–1952) as well as from Wang Chongyou 王寵佑 (1879–1958), a famous scholar who had studied mining and

---

she yixue congshu 學鐸社易學叢書 (Taipei: Xiangda tushu youxian gongsi, 2010). His younger brother Zhenru later also published books on the *Yijing*.

34 Yang Ruilin 楊瑞麟 (Jianxing), "Fuji xueshuo 扶乩學說," *Lingxue congzhi* 1, no. 1 (1918): 4.

35 Yang Guangxi 楊光熙, "Shengde tan yuanqi 盛德壇緣起," *Lingxue congzhi* 1, no. 1 (1918): 5–6.

36 On Lufei Kui and the China Bookstore see Christopher A. Reed, *Gutenberg in Shanghai: Chinese Print Capitalism, 1876–1937* (Vancouver: UBC Press, 2004), 225–240.

37 Yang Guangxi, "Shengde tan yuanqi," 5.

38 Yang Ruilin (Jianxing), "Fuji xueshuo," 2.

geology in Europe and the USA and at that time sold books of European and American spiritualist societies.[39] Together with his brother Zhenru he even joined the Chinese Society for the Study of the Mind (Zhongguo jingshen xuehui 中國精神學會). We have little information about this society, but it seems to have been part of a growing number of organizations focusing on hypnotism.[40] Maybe it was at this organization that Jianxing learned about hypnosis and telepathy in the first place. Be this as it may, after he had become acquainted with psychical practices, he again started to practice spirit-writing and was amazed by the spiritual phenomena witnessed at the altar. He gained a profound belief in the credibility and importance of spirit-writing activities and even quit his job at a school to pursue his spiritual quest.[41] Yang's engagement thus points to the growing popularity of the new spirituality in the early Republican period and its potential to rub off on spirit-writing.

Finally, in October 1917 the establishment of the LXH took shape. As mentioned above, in the autumn Yang Guangxi discussed spirit-writing with acquaintances who remained skeptical and wanted to view the practice by themselves. Together they went to an already existing altar in Shanghai,[42] which convinced those attending of the credibility of the phenomenon.[43] Hence, they started to collect the necessary materials to set up their own altar. Just at that time, the Chinese Society for the Study of the Mind decided to establish a branch office in Shanghai and sent Yang Jianxing and Zhenru from

---

39 Yang Jianxing, *Xueduo she yixue congshu*, 5.

40 In the *Shenbao*, Wang Chien-chuan has found an organization of this name which was led by a certain Yao Guifen 姚桂芬. However, he does not provide further information. See Wang, "Lufei Kui yu 'Shengde tan,' 'Lingxuehui': Jiantan Minchu Shanghai de lingxue fengchao 陸費逵與「盛德壇」、「靈學會」：兼談民初上海的靈學風潮," in *Lishi, yishu yu Taiwan renwen luncong (3): 'renwu' zhuanji* 歷史、藝術與臺灣人文論叢 (3):「人物」專輯, ed. Liu Wenxing 劉文星, Xiao Baifang 蕭百方, and Wang Chien-chuan 王見川 (Taipei: Boyang wenhua shiye youxian gongsi, 2013), 81.

41 Yang Ruilin (Jianxing), "Fuji xueshuo," 2.

42 This was the Jisheng tan 濟生壇 (Altar for Saving Life). The character *ji* also refers to the popular deity Jigong 濟公, who served as the main patron of the Chinese Life Saving Society (Zhongguo jisheng hui), founded in 1916 in Shanghai on the basis of a pre-existing local spirit-writing cult. See Wang Chien-chuan 王見川, "Qingmo Minchu Zhongguo de Jigong xinyang yu fuji tuanti: Jian tan Zhongguo Jisheng hui de youlai 清末民初中國的濟公信仰與扶乩團體：兼談中國濟生會的由來," *Minsu quyi* 民俗曲藝, no. 162 (2008): 139–169. Despite the similar name, however, the altar did not belong to the Society. Based on the differing locations of the above altar and the headquarters of the Chinese Life Saving Society, Wang Chien-chuan has established that the altar to which the members went was simply another local spirit-writing cult that venerated the same deity and sought after the Society's fame. See Wang, "Lufei Kui yu 'Shengde tan,' 'Lingxuehui,'" 69.

43 Yang Ruilin (Jianxing), "Fuji xueshuo," 3.

Wuxi.[44] Once they reached Shanghai, however, Yang Guangxi ordered his two sons to set up a spirit-writing altar together with Yu Fu and Lufei Kui who had by then developed a profound interest in the practice.[45] Accordingly, they abandoned the plan to establish a branch office for the society and set up the Altar of Flourishing Virtue instead, where they initiated their first session of spirit-writing on October 3, 1917. Through the incoming spirit-writing messages Yang Jianxing received the order to found a journal (namely the *Lingxue congzhi* 靈學叢誌 or the *Spiritualist Magazine*) and to establish a society for the study of spiritualism, i.e., the LXH.[46]

In the following years, the LXH grew in size and attracted considerable attention due to its prominent members. Zheng Guo has shown that the early membership of the LXH depended mostly on native-place and workplace affiliations. Almost all of the early participants such as Ding Fubao, Lufei Kui, or Wu Zhihui 吳稚暉 (1865–1953) originally came from Wuxi or worked at Lufei's Bookstore.[47] What also seems remarkable is that many of its members had received a modern education and were active in different social reform pursuits. Thus, Ding Fubao had studied medicine in Japan to improve health care in China, while Lufei Kui had come in touch with scientific knowledge early in his youth and later devoted himself to educational reform. The same holds true for many of their illustrious supporters such as the famous translator Yan Fu 嚴復 (1854–1921).[48] The individual reasons for joining the LXH can only be hinted at here, but many of its members deplored a moral decline in society and were convinced that scientific proof of the existence of supernatural beings would provide a source for the moral rectification of humanity. It was to facilitate a reorientation of human life, a shift from a this-worldly egocentric focus to a consideration of the moral workings of the cosmos. For the LXH, engaging with spiritual phenomena was therefore not only a scientific matter,

44 Yang Guangxi, "Shengde tan yuanqi," 5–6.

45 Yang Jianxing, *Xueduo she yixue congshu*, 5. In his account, Jianxing merely mentions that he went to Shanghai with his younger brother Zhenru where they awaited their father Yang Guangxi at the China Bookstore. Yang Ruilin (Jianxing), "Fuji xueshuo," 3.

46 Yang Ruilin (Jianxing), "Fuji xueshuo," 3. Unfortunately, we do not know exactly when the LXH was founded. However, Lufei writes in one account that after the altar had existed for two months the devotees decided to establish a society (*xuehui* 學會) to make the divine messages known more widely. This would imply that the LXH was established around December 1917. Lufei Kui 陸費逵, "*Lingxue congzhi* yuanqi 靈學叢誌緣起," *Lingxue congzhi* 1, no. 1 (1918): 3.

47 Zheng, "Shanghai Lingxuehui yanjiu," 60–80.

48 For more on his connection to the LXH and his views on science see Huang Ko-wu 黃克武, *Wei shi zhi an: Yan Fu yu jindai Zhongguo de wenhua zhuanxing* 惟適之安：嚴復與近代中國的文化轉型 (Beijing: Shehui kexue wenxian chubanshe, 2012), 134–169.

but part of larger moral concerns connected to the alleged spread of materialism in society. Spirit-writing was practiced by many religious groups in early Republican Shanghai which featured the same emphasis on moral reform, including redemptive societies.[49] However, it seems that the scientific agenda of the LXH gave it an edge over other groups when it came to attracting these modernizing elites, at least initially. The LXH offered a venue to combine science and social reform while satisfying a widely shared curiosity concerning spiritual phenomena and practices such as spirit-writing.

4 Models and Meanings of Chinese Spiritualism (*lingxue*)

The LXH attempted to establish a new spiritual science by adopting the model of psychic organizations such as the Society for Psychical Research. One article that is especially illuminating regarding the role the LXH envisioned for itself was written by an anonymous member of the society and is contained in the fifth issue of the *Spiritualist Magazine*. As the author states at the beginning, it is an abridged and modified version of a Japanese translation of the article "Are there Objective Apparitions?", written by Sir Alfred Russel Wallace for the journal *Arena* in 1891.[50] The anonymous author's explicit aim was to introduce the research and publications of their English and American[51] counterparts to China.

> For years, the members of the American and English Societies for Psychical Research have pursued this study [of psychical research] and the different types of evidence and examples they have collected are numerous. They rely on them to obtain knowledge about human life and human nature. If one is not crazy or idiotic, one cannot but be interested [in this]. The reports of these societies are bundled in huge editions. The examples documented in them the scholars have either seen with their own eyes, subjected to a close investigation, or obtained a definite confirmation for them. In no way do they allow for fictitious or false things to

49 One example would be the aforementioned Chinese Life Saving Society (see fn. 42).

50 Alfred Russel Wallace, "Are There Objective Apparitions?" *Arena* 3, no. 13 (1891): 129–146 (http://people.wku.edu/charles.smith/wallace/S430.htm). The Japanese translation had been attached to the translation of Sir Oliver Lodge's *The Survival of Man* (1909) by Takahashi Gorō 高橋五朗 (1856–1935), a Meiji-period translator. See Sir Oliver Lodge, *Shigo no seizon* 死後の生存, trans. Takahashi Gorō (Tokyo: Genkōsha, 1917).

51 The American Society for Psychical Research had been founded in 1884 under the leadership of William James.

> mingle in. Moreover, in case they have only the slightest doubt concerning a matter, they invest much time and effort to investigate its true form and study its causes and effects. […] From this the benefit of psychical research (*lingxue*) is obvious.
>
> 英美靈學會員。研究斯學有年。種種證例。蒐集極多。藉以獲關於人生性命之學識。苟非瘋癡。未有不感興味者也。該會報告書纍纍巨冊。所載實例。均研究家目擊之事。或經嚴密之考察。或得確實之證明。決不容虛僞之事。攙雜其間。不特此也。每對于稍有疑義之事。輒費甚大之時間勞力。調查其真相。研究其因果。... 於是靈學益彰著矣。[52]

Here the respectable and scientific nature of the Society for Psychical Research is stressed, which aimed to validate similar activities in China as well. Wallace and Lodge are (correctly) introduced as being "experts in natural studies and evolutionary theory" as well as "leading authorities in science."[53] What is striking, moreover, is that the Society is actually translated into Chinese as Lingxuehui.[54] At least to a certain degree, the members of the LXH saw their organization as mirroring the English and American Societies. The prominence of the Society for Psychical Research in this article thus attests to the global importance of the latter as an institution engaging with psychical topics but emanating scientific authority.

These new institutional models point to the transformation of spirit-writing by organizations such as the LXH. In the late imperial period, spirit-writing was usually practiced at small lineage altars or semi-public spirit-writing associations, which, despite substantial elite-involvement, retained an unofficial status due to the technically illegal status of spirit-writing.[55] The LXH, on the other hand, similar to its English counterpart, was a public organization, which had a specified purpose, advertised in the big newspapers of the day,

---

52 Anon., "You gui lun zhi zhengming 有鬼論之證明," *Lingxue congzhi* 1, no. 5 (1918): 2.

53 Anon., "You gui lun zhi zhengming," 1.

54 It seems likely that the author adopted the translation of the Society for Psychical Research from Yan Fu who similarly translated it as Lingxuehui in a letter that was published in the third issue of the *LXCZ*. See Yan Fu, "Yan Jidao xiansheng zhi Hou Yishi shu 嚴幾道先生致侯疑始書," *Lingxue congzhi* 1, no. 3 (1918): 2.

55 See Richard J. Smith, *Fortune-Tellers and Philosophers: Divination in Traditional Chinese Society* (Boulder: Westview Press, 1991), 221–233, and Fan Chun-wu 范純武, *Qingmo minjian cishan shiye yu luantang yundong* 清末民間慈善事業與鸞堂運動 (Taipei: Boyang wenhua youxian gongsi, 2015).

and was open to anyone able to muster the relatively hefty membership fees.[56] New is also their focus on science, which they shared with the Society for Psychical Research and which is visible in the documents through which the members intended to define their scientific project. Most illuminating here is the first general statement of the regulations for the Altar of Flourishing Virtue, which bespeaks the member's dedication to "the thorough study of science to profoundly open up [human] nature and the soul" (研窮學術、濬發性靈).[57] Similar statements are found in the constitution of the LXH: "This society has the aim of stimulating and enlightening [human] nature and the soul (*xingling*) and studying scientific principles" (本會以啟瀹性靈、研究學理、為宗旨).[58] The Society used a fresh emphasis on scientific language to engage with human life, both before and after physical death. While the great majority of the publications of the LXH did not touch upon science but rather discussed the moral workings of the universe or the existential basis of spirits, Fan Chun-wu has pointed out that even such a systematic treatment of life after death and the existence of the soul was something quite novel in Chinese spirit-writing.[59] Yet, these rather general allusions to science also invite questions as to the specific meaning of *lingxue* and its relation to global discourses of spiritualism and psychical research.

First of all, *lingxue* means the study of *ling*, or spiritual energy, as I will translate it. It is through this term that we have to understand the new concept of spiritualism. Quite fundamentally, in Chinese religious discourse *ling* was closely bound to conceptions of life after death, visible in the term for soul, *linghun*. *Ling* could be used as a synonym for the human soul, and souls traveling to heavenly spheres to encounter supernatural beings might be designated as *ling*. This reading of *ling* as bound to the human soul was very much alive

56 The constitution of the LXH lists different forms of membership, with varying fees, ranging between 10 and 50 *yuan* per year. These were considerable sums at the time. In one of his articles on the LXH, Huang Ko-wu writes that at that time the monthly income of a merchant ranged between 30 and 50 *yuan*, while that of a worker was only about 15 *yuan*. Huang Ko-wu 黃克武, "Minguo chunian Shanghai de lingxue yanjiu: yi 'Shanghai Lingxuehui' wei li 民國初年上海的靈學研究：以「上海靈學會」為例," *Jindaishi yanjiusuo jikan* 近代史研究所集刊, no. 55 (March 2007): 131.

57 "Shengde tan tangui 盛德壇壇規," *Lingxue congzhi* 1, no. 1 (1918): 1.

58 Lingxuehui 靈學會, "Lingxuehui jianzhang 靈學會簡章," *Lingxue congzhi* 1, no. 1 (1918): no pages, article 1.

59 Fan Chun-wu 范純武, "Kexue lingji: Diexian yu Minchu lingxue sichao xia fuji de 'xin' neihan 科學靈乩：碟仙與民初靈學思潮下扶乩的「新」內涵," in *Wenhua yu kexue de bianzou: Jindai Zhongguo jiushi tuanti, xinyang wenhua de fazhang yu weilai* 文化與科學的變奏：近代中國救世團體、信仰文化的發展與未來, ed. Foguang Daxue (collection of conference papers, Foguang daxue, 2012), 209–210.

within the LXH. The members believed that the soul could survive physical death and that it was closely related to, or even consisted of, spiritual energy.[60] This close link also explains why the study of the human soul is mentioned above as one of the main objectives of their spiritualist society: no spirit without *ling*. If this spiritual energy was exhausted, they believed, then the human spirit would become blurry and vanish, after which it would again enter the process of transmigration. Existence thus followed a pattern of the "congealing" and "dispersal" (*ju* 聚 and *san* 散) of spiritual energy.[61] However, echoing widely held beliefs,[62] many members of the LXH argued that humans could cultivate their spiritual energy to aspire to divine existence after death, which would allow them to persist longer than regular human spirits.[63] Moreover, in this cultivated form, *ling* constituted a thread, linking humans to spirits and deities, as both embodied this energy, and allowing communication between them through spirit-writing. According to this logic, the practice depended on a resonance between the human and divine spheres based on the principle of "stimulus and response" (*ganying* 感應). This concept, which is closely related to theories of retribution, entails that the different ontological realms of heaven, men, and earth are connected and that actions in one realm will have resonances in the other realms.[64] Spiritual energy was one medium (another would be *qi*) on the basis of which this resonance was thought to function.[65] The LXH thus understood *ling* as a spiritual energy, which was constitutive

60 See Ding Fubao 丁福保, "Wo lixiang zhong zhi gui shuo 我理想中之鬼說," *Lingxue congzhi* 1, no. 1 (1918): 15–18.

61 Ding, "Wo lixiang zhong zhi gui shuo," 16–17. This phrase echoes the famous statement in the Chapter "Knowledge Wandering North" ("Zhi bei you 知北遊") of the *Zhuangzi* 莊子: "Man's life is a coming-together of breath. If it comes together, there is life; if it scatters, there is death." Burton Watson, trans., *The Complete Works of Zhuangzi* (New York: Columbia University Press, 2013), 177.

62 Vincent Goossaert and David A. Palmer, *The Religious Question in Modern China* (Chicago & London: University of Chicago Press, 2011), 21.

63 Ding Fubao argued that one could gain special powers through self-cultivation. Ding, "Wo lixiang zhong zhi gui shuo," 17–18.

64 The concept was coined by scholars of the Buddhist Tiantai 天台 School to describe benign reactions from Buddhas or Bodhisattvas towards practitioners, which depended on the accumulation of positive karma through good deeds. Beverley Foulks McGuire, *Living Karma: The Religious Practices of Ouyi Zhixu* (New York: Columbia University Press, 2014), 6–7.

65 Hence, Yang Jianxing ascribed communication with deities to the principle of "stimulus and response" of human and divine spiritual energy. Yang Jianxing (Ruilin), "Fuji xueshuo," 2. *Ling* is therefore often translated as "spiritual (or magical) efficacy." See Adam Yuet Chau, *Miraculous Response: Doing Popular Religion in Contemporary China* (Stanford, CA: Stanford University Press, 2006), 2.

of human and divine existence, but which could also be cultivated to elevate one's status during life and after death. Due to the close connection to conceptions of the soul, Chinese spiritualism shows many similarities to the beliefs of European and American spiritualists who sought out human spirits in their séances.

The term *ling*, however, underwent a significant reconfiguration during the late nineteenth and early twentieth century due to the introduction of new concepts and practices stemming from disciplines such as psychology and psychical research. In 1889, for example, Yan Yongjing 顏永京 (1839–1898) chose the term *Xinlingxue* 心靈學 to translate the book *Mental Philosophy* by Joseph Haven (1816–1874). At this time, the original connotation of psychology as the "the study of the soul" was still very much palpable, which might have led Yan to choose *xinlingxue* instead of the later standard term *xinlixue* 心理學.[66] In the early twentieth century, the term further featured in Japanese psychical research which, as we saw above, was deeply intertwined with Chinese spiritualist discourses. According to Nancy Stalker, the term *ling* (Jap.: *rei*), which she translates as "spirit," became popular in Japan in the 1910s as more and more religious organizations engaged with the spiritual world instead of focusing on self-cultivation.[67] During this time, psychic organizations like the Taireidō 太霊道 (The Way of the Great Spirit) also embraced the term as it appeared less suspicious after the prohibition of hypnotism in 1908.[68] During the early Republican period these sources were also received in China, and *ling* gained new connotations from psychical research.[69] In 1918, for example, a translation of an article by the famous Japanese psychologist and psychical researcher Fukurai Tomokichi 福来友吉 (1869–1952) was published in the journal

66 Finding the appropriate vocabulary to translate novel terminology was a troublesome task. Different from Yan, the Japanese translators of the book had chosen *shinrigaku* 心理学 already fourteen years earlier. Still, Yan's definition of *xinlingxue* in his preface makes it very clear that he was referring to psychology, or mental philosophy, and not to psychical research. Cf. Yang Xinhui 楊鑫輝, ed., *Xinlixue tongshi* 心理學通史 (Ji'nan: Shandong jiaoyu chubanshe, 1999) 2: 105–112.

67 Nancy K. Stalker, *Prophet Motive: Deguchi Onisaburô, Oomoto, and the Rise of New Religions in Imperial Japan* (Honolulu: University of Hawai'i Press, 2008), 76.

68 Yoshinaga Shin'ichi 吉永進一, "Tairei to kokka: Taireidô ni okeru no kokkakan no imi 太霊と国家: 太霊道における国家観の意味," *Jintai kagaku* 人体科学 17, no. 1 (2008): 41–42.

69 In 1933, the book company of the Chinese Institute of Mentalism published a book by Amagishi Koji 天岸居士 (n.d.), which introduced and criticized theories about the *tairei*, or Great Spirit, put forward by Tanaka. The book gives an impression of the ideas associated with the concept. See Amagishi Koji 天岸居士, ed., *Tailingdao* 太靈道 (Shanghai: Xinling kexue shuju, 1933).

Xuesheng 學生 (The Student), in which he writes that "[p]sychical researchers go beyond the material forces and study the existence of the functions of the psyche" (心靈研究者。乃於物質力以外。以研究靈的作用之存在者也).[70] In his essay, Fukurai used the terms *ling* and *xinling* (spirit/psyche) interchangeably, which indicates the close connection between the two. Chinese psychical researchers similarly employed the terms *ling* and *xinling* as designations for the human psyche and used them to explain the application as well as the functions of hypnotism.[71] The usage of the term *ling* thus also points to some of the more substantial differences between psychical researchers and spiritualists in China (and elsewhere). Psychical researchers used the term *ling* in its new and more secular meaning as "psyche" which was by then translated as *xinling*. The spirit-writing organizations, on the other hand, understood the term more in a spiritual or religious sense. For them, *lingxue* meant the study of the soul or spiritual energy. Due to these differing ontological assumptions, it is necessary to distinguish between spiritualism and psychical research in the Chinese context. Nevertheless, Chinese spiritualists profited from a cross-fertilization between the two disciplines and from the scientific legitimacy ascribed to discourses about *ling* or *xinling*.

The term *ling*, one can argue, constituted a bridge toward the new spirituality and the scientific concepts and practices associated with it. The LXH retained an understanding of life after death that was congruent with established theories such as "stimulus and response." Yet, by pointing to the ideas and activities of international psychic and spiritualist organizations, they argued for potential ways of scientifically explaining spiritual phenomena such as the existence of the soul. Thus, Yan Fu claimed in one of his letters to the members of the LXH that the experiments of the Society for Psychical Research about telepathy or hypnosis "proved that human life is spiritual and that it is certainly not exhausted by the physical body" (證明人生靈明。必不與形體同盡).[72] To counter alleged trends of materialism in society, the LXH invoked recent scientific concepts, which seemingly undermined a strictly materialist view of the cosmos. For example, in one article ascribed to the deity Lü Dongbin 呂洞賓, the concept of ether (*yituo* 以脫) is mentioned. The article argues that by cultivating themselves, spirits and deities "become benevolence (*ren* 仁), they become ether" (為仁。為以脫).[73] This statement seems to echo

70 Fukurai Tomokichi 福来友吉, "Xinling yanjiu zhi jiazhi 心靈研究之價值," *Xuesheng* 學生 5, no. 11 (1918): 43–55.

71 See, for example, Yu Pingke 余萍客, *Cuimianshu hanshou jiangyi* 催眠術函授講義, 3 vols. (Shanghai: Zhongguo xinling yanjiuhui, 1931), 2: 46.

72 Yan Fu, "Yan Jidao xiansheng zhi Hou Yishi shu," 2.

73 "Lü Zushi mixin lun 呂祖師迷信論," *Lingxue congzhi* 1, no. 2 (1918): 24.

Tan Sitong's *Exposition of Benevolence* (*Renxue* 仁學) in which he also linked ether with benevolence.[74] The use of the concept of ether is noteworthy in this context. Although it was never experimentally proven and remained subject to debate, it still turned into a well-established concept in physics. It therefore became very popular especially among psychical researchers to explain phenomena such as telepathy, but it was also used by staunch critics of spiritualism, both in China as well as in Europe.[75] For the spiritualists, concepts such as ether seemed to provide explanations for spiritual phenomena such as spirit-writing. The article ascribed to Lü Dongbin thus argues that concepts such as ether, electricity, and X-rays have the potential to explain the "principles of communication between spirits and humans" (鬼人[...]交通之理).[76] Quite possibly, it was assumed that these forces could serve as media for the transmission of spiritual energy. Other articles mention hypnotism, which was similarly invoked to indicate the scientific potential of spirit-writing.[77] While these concepts were never developed in a systematic fashion, Chinese spiritualists quoted recent scientific concepts to argue for a spiritualist view of human life and to enhance the legitimacy of spirit-writing.

One final aspect of note was the attempt of spiritualists in China and Europe to establish scientific institutions. The establishment of the LXH itself reflects this development as it had only been founded once the altar had been opened and the scientific ambitions of the participants ripened. Most vital for their scientific approach, however, and most noteworthy in the context of the present volume, was their journal, the *Spiritualist Magazine* (*Lingxue congzhi*). It was published by China Bookstore and contained writings produced through spirit-writing or penned by members. By founding a journal, the LXH followed general trends in the religious sphere. Numerous redemptive societies set up their

74 Tan Sitong argued that ether permeates everything in the universe. For him it was a moral concept and in its applied form he likened it to benevolence (*ren*) or universal love (*jian'ai* 兼愛). Much of his knowledge on ether he seems to have learned from John Fryer's translation of Henry Wood's *A Method for Healing the Mind and Avoiding Sickness*, in which the concept also plays a prominent role. See David Wright, "Tan Sitong and the Ether Reconsidered," *Bulletin of the School of Oriental and African Studies, University of London* 57, no. 3 (1994): 551–575.

75 One prominent example is the chemist Wang Xinggong 王星拱 (1887–1949) who attacked psychical research, and the LXH in particular, in a number of writings. See, for example, his answer to a letter sent to the *New Youth*. Mo Deng 莫等, "Guixiang zhi yanjiu 鬼相之研究," *Xin qingnian* 新青年 5, no. 6 (1918): 619–620.

76 "Lü Zushi mixin lun," 24.

77 Hou Yishi 侯疑始 (Yi 毅), "Ji shen you Qiong Yuan shi 記神游瓊苑事," *Lingxue congzhi* 1, no. 4 (1918): 9–12.

own periodicals and made use of new mass media to circulate their religious views among either the general public or initiated members.[78] The *Spiritualist Magazine* was freely sold and, according to some estimations, initially had a circulation in the thousands.[79] Among other types of writings, the journal contained "essays" (*lunshuo* 論說) that breathed life into the investigation of the "principles of humans and spirits as well as life and death" (人鬼生死之理) to which the LXH and its publications were devoted.[80] While relatively few articles addressed scientific issues in a straightforward manner, the agenda of the journal set the LXH apart from other spirit-writing organizations and redemptive societies. Additionally, in the 1920s they published their spirit-written messages in a new journal, the *Essence of Spiritualism* (*Lingxue jinghua* 靈學精華),[81] while the Shengde yinshuaji 盛德印刷機, a printing company founded by the LXH, published a series on spiritualism (*lingxue*). Through the above, the LXH shared in a global tendency to establish scientific institutions devoted to the investigation of disputed spiritual phenomena. Even though the LXH never engaged in systematic "research," *lingxue*, in distinction to former spirit-writing activities, therefore referred to a more institutionalized study of spiritual energy and, more concretely, of the human soul, spirits, and deities in which it was embodied.

5 The Reform of Spirit-Writing and the Empirical Proof of Supernatural Beings

Theories and institutional models appropriated from global spiritualist discourses were vital in sparking an interest in spirit-writing among the educated clientele of the LXH. However, even more important than the explanations of spiritual phenomena was the actual practice. In the context of spiritualism, spirit-writing retained its role as a medium for supernatural beings, but it

78 For an overview of religious publishing during that period, see Paul R. Katz, "Illuminating Goodness: Some Preliminary Considerations of Religious Publishing in Modern China," in *Religious Publishing and Print Culture in Modern China, 1800–2012*, ed. Philip Clart and Gregory Adam Scott (Boston: De Gruyter, 2015), 265–294.

79 Huang Ko-wu, "Minguo chunian Shanghai de lingxue yanjiu," 113–114.

80 Anon., "Huishu zhi xie 惠書誌謝," *Shenbao*, July 4, 1918.

81 See Yang Zhenru 楊真如, *Jingshen qidao* 精神祈禱 (Shanghai: Shanghai Lingxuehui, 1926), 2, for a reference to this journal. Unfortunately, I have not yet been able to locate any issue of this journal. However, one article by a contemporary redemptive society mentions that it was a monthly publication. See Anon., "Lingxue jinghua lu 靈學精華錄," *Jiushi xinbao* 救世新報, October 25, 1927: 1.

came to serve a new purpose: It was reconceptualized as a form of "spiritualist experimentation" able to provide empirical proof of the existence of spirits. As part of this reconceptualization, the LXH sought to emphasize its own role as scientific reformers of spirit-writing.

Due to the influence of new spiritualist and psychic models, the LXH perceived itself as a novel spirit-writing organization dissociated from other non-scientific practitioners past and present. They were aware of existing Chinese works dealing with the supernatural, but these Chinese examples did not count as scientific evidence, in distinction to Western spiritualist writings (and their own). In reviewing different types of spiritual phenomena introduced by Alfred Russel Wallace in the article mentioned above, the anonymous translator offers the following evaluation of previous Chinese spirit-writing accounts:

> [The spiritualist phenomena introduced by Wallace] are like [the phenomena] in the *Liaozhai zhiyi*, the *Yuewei caotang biji*,[82] and other books. They have been seen numerous times and are nothing new. The facts [within these books, however,] have in the majority been derived mostly from hearsay to which strained interpretations were added. In the opinion of the writer and his readers, these do not go beyond mere topics for leisure talk. The foreigners, on the other hand, have subjected all of these examples to a close investigation and [thus] obtained definite confirmation. [Moreover], regarding the slightest doubtful aspects they have invested much time and effort to investigate their true form and study their causes and effects. This is because these men have long possessed the knowledge and ability of studying science.
>
> 篇中所舉實例五項。除靈魂照相。爲吾國昔日未有傳聞外。其餘四者。如聊齋志異閱微草堂筆記等書。散見不鮮。其事實大概得之傳聞者居多。而間或加以附會。在作者和讀者之意。皆不過視爲茶餘酒闌之談助而已。而外人對於此等實例。均經嚴密之考察。得確實之證明。於稍有疑義之處。輒費甚大之時間勞力。調查其真相。研究其因果。蓋彼人皆夙具有研究科學之識力。[83]

82 These are both works from the Qing period dealing with supernatural beings and occurrences and containing numerous references to spirit-writing. See Judith T. Zeitlin, *Historian of the Strange: Pu Songling and the Chinese Classical Tale* (Stanford, Calif.: Stanford University Press, 1993), and Leo Tak-Hung Chan, "Narrative as Argument: The *Yuewei caotang biji* and the Late Eighteenth-Century Elite Discourse on the Supernatural," *Harvard Journal of Asiatic Studies* 53, no. 1 (1993): 25–62.

83 Anon., "You gui lun zhi zhengming", 10.

In this remarkable passage the anonymous author lays claim to a new scientific approach. When dealing with spiritual phenomena such as spirit-writing, the task is not only to record but to investigate and confirm spiritual phenomena in a scientific way, however vaguely defined. This testifies to the changed epistemic context and explains why the LXH made almost no use of existing spirit-writing messages when it comes to showing the scientific nature of the practice, despite the many continuities in their understanding of spiritual energy. On the contrary, the LXH strove to dissociate itself from earlier spirit-writing groups. This they tried to accomplish through the scientific reform of spirit-writing.

To serve its new role as a technique of "experimentation," spirit-writing could not remain unchanged. It needed to accord with the model of the Society for Psychical Research and be different from the "hearsay" and the "leisure talk" of old. To achieve this goal, the LXH sought to clearly circumscribe the topics discussed at the altar, prohibiting questions about what the Society called "prosperity and misfortune" (*xiujiu* 休咎). The constitution warned all those interested in matters of a more personal nature: "With [...] worldly matters [the Society] categorically does not engage" (...世事。概不與聞).[84] Some members such as Lufei Kui were even more outspoken, rejecting the use of spirit-writing for the composition of poetry or personal inquiries as unscientific:

> Spirit-writing altars have flourished for a long time, but their influence on human life has been extremely marginal. For what reason? It is because former spirit-writing altars merely inquired about [personal] prosperity and misfortune or about diseases. Even the best among them merely [produced] poetry. An altar like ours that inquires about scientific principles and investigates the problems of human life is especially rare.
>
> 乩壇之興久矣。而影響于人生者至微。果何故耶。蓋以向來乩壇。不過叩問休咎。問疾病。上焉者亦僅詩文酬唱而已。如吾壇之叩問學理。研究人生問題者。殊不多覯。[85]

Lufei saw the Altar of Flourishing Virtue as representing a new step in the history of spirit-writing due to its emphasis on "scientific principles." But what did these "principles" refer to?

The Society initially only vaguely circumscribed their scholarly pursuits, but it generally intended to engage with the existence of the soul and spiritual

84 Lingxuehui, "Lingxuehui jianzhang," 1.

85 Lufei, "*Lingxue congzhi* yuanqi," 3.

aspects of human life in a manner comparable to contemporary spiritualism and in accordance with their understanding of *lingxue* as spelled out above. In his account of the founding of the Altar of Flourishing Virtue, Yang Guangxi accordingly recalls how the participants at the altar inquired about topics such as "spirits and deities, the heavenly bodies, religion" (鬼神星球宗教), "the survival of the soul" (靈魂不滅), "phonetics" (*yinyunxue* 音韻學), "the explanation of labyrinths and the expounding of scientific principles" (解釋迷津。闡發學理).[86] The LXH thus restricted the content of spirit-writing to topics of social or scholarly value. As can be seen from the quote above, this reform of spirit-writing was seen as an asset through which the Society set itself apart from other practitioners.

Due to the reformed setting in which it was practiced, many members of the LXH first became convinced of the existence of supernatural beings through the experience of spirit-writing. Lufei Kui recounts that he came to believe in deities and spirits only after he himself had participated in spirit-writing. He witnessed the descent and the actions of the supernatural beings at the Altar of Flourishing Virtue.

> [T]he sages, worthies, immortals and Buddhas, deities and earth spirits all attended the shrine one after the other. One hundred and eighty mentioned [their] names[87] and 46 poems were written down. Their [specific] identities were revealed in the meaning of the poems. Furthermore, their handwriting was not identical.
>
> 聖賢仙佛神祇。相率臨壇。題名者百八十人。題詩四十六章。詩義各見身份。且字跡亦各不同。[88]

As the spirit-writing practitioners were usually the same (i.e., Yang Jianxing and Yang Zhenru), the observable individual character of the deities' messages served to prove their reality. Spirit-writing, so the practitioners argued, more or less empirically demonstrates the existence of spirits and the human soul. The experience of spirit-writing therefore had a very tangible effect on the beliefs of the members. Lufei recalls how he formerly had "never believed in theories about spirits and deities" (素不信鬼神之說) and even "refuted Buddhism and Daoism and smashed superstition" (闢佛老。破迷信), while now firmly

86 Yang Guangxi, "Shengde tan yuanqi," 6.
87 Deities often introduced themselves by name.
88 Lufei, "*Lingxue congzhi* yuanqi," 1.

believing in the veracity of spirit-writing.[89] Yang Guangxi underwent a similar "conversion experience" upon encountering spirit-writing.[90] This empirical dimension even trumped a theoretical understanding of supernatural beings. Thus Hua Xiangzhi 華襄治 (n.d.), who had edited several textbooks on chemistry and algebra for China Bookstore,[91] stressed that "[e]ven though the conditions of spirits and deities are not yet profoundly known to the world, theories about the soul, on the other hand, have already been generally acknowledged" (夫鬼神之情狀。雖未為世界所深知。而靈魂之學說。則已為世界所公認).[92]

The experimental and empirical aspect was even stronger in the case of spirit-photography (or "soul photography" in the words of the LXH, *linghun zhaoxiang* 靈魂照像/靈魂照相). Quite possibly due to the example of Wu Tingfang, the members were eager to experiment with the practice. After initial attempts met the reluctance of the deities, a comprehensive account of these spirit-photography activities was written by Yu Fu and published in the sixth issue of the *Spiritualist Magazine*. He recalls that at a meeting Ding Fubao had revealed to him and an acquainted photographer the practice of spirit-photography, handing around some photographs that he had previously acquired. This sparked the interest of Yu who convinced his photographer friend to come to the LXH and try the practice. So, on September 11, 1918, after they had received the permission of the deity Master Changsheng 常勝子 to take his picture, the photographer set up his camera opposite the spirit tablet of the deity (*shenzuo* 神座) at the altar, only leaving incense and an electric light burning. Master Changsheng had reminded them that success or failure all came down to their "sincerity" (*cheng* 誠), thus alluding to the moral nature of divine communication and the principle of "stimulus and response." In the end all went well and the photographer returned the next day to present a slightly blurry picture of the deity (see fig. 4.1).[93] This image was only one among many which the members produced over a period of several months. For example, Yang Tingdong 楊廷棟 (1879–1950), a famous translator, who

89 Lufei: "*Lingxue congzhi* yuanqi," 1.

90 Yang Guangxi, "Shengde tan yuanqi," 4.

91 Huang Ko-wu, "Lingxue yu jindai Zhongguo de zhishi zhuanxing: Minchu zhishi fenzi dui kexue, zongjiao yu mixin de zai sikao 靈學與近代中國的知識轉型：民初知識 分子對科學、宗教與迷信的再思考," *Sixiang shi* 思想史, no. 2 (2014): 138.

92 Hua Xiangzhi 華襄治, "*Lingxue congzhi* fakanci 靈學叢誌發刊辭," *Lingxue congzhi* 1, no. 1 (1918): 3–4.

93 See Yu Fu 俞復, "Shengde tan shi zhao xian ling ji 盛德壇試照仙靈記," *Lingxue congzhi* 1, no. 6 (1918): 2–4. Image taken from Lingxuehui 靈學會, ed., *Xianling zhaoxiang, fu guiling zhaoxiang* 仙靈照相、附鬼靈照相 (Shanghai: Zhonghua shuju, 1921). Master Changsheng is said to be one Sima Qian 司馬潛 from the Yuan dynasty (1280–1368).

FIGURE 4.1
Changshengzi xiang 常勝子像, in Lingxuehui, ed., Xianling zhaoxiang
SHANGHAI MUNICIPAL LIBRARY

was also involved with the LXH, received permission to take a picture of his deceased father.[94] Apart from the oft-repeated demand of sincerity, the technical procedures did not depart significantly from the preparations for a regular portrait. However, as it linked the engagement with the supernatural realm with a technology only recently introduced to China,[95] spirit-photography enjoyed considerable popularity among the members who repeatedly inquired with the deities for permission to produce photographs. Visitors addressed the Society as well, calling for more spirit-photography sessions.[96] The members' interest in photography echoes the prominent role that this technical device

94 Yang Tingdong 楊廷棟, "Linghun zhaoxiang ji 靈魂照像記," *Lingxue congzhi* 1, no. 7 (1918): 6.

95 The daguerreotype camera was first used on Chinese soil in the 1840s and photography became an important part of elite leisure culture in the closing decades of the Qing dynasty. See Terry Bennett, *History of Photography in China: Chinese Photographers, 1844–1879* (London: Bernard Quaritch Ltd, 2013), 2–30. See also the chapter by Fan Chun-wu in this volume.

96 Yang Tingdong, "Linghun zhaoxiang ji," 5.

played within redemptive societies (see the chapter by Fan Chun-wu in this volume) and indicates the growing importance of new technologies in the religious sphere during this time more generally.

Apart from the curiosity and the personal motivations figuring in the above accounts, spirit-photography heightened the Society's scientific appeal. At the beginning, Yu Fu was concerned about the photographs, which seemingly "contradict the conventions of science" (違乎科學之常例). Some of the photos had even been taken with the light extinguished, which went against the "principles of optics" (光學之原理). After overcoming his initial reservations, Yu Fu assumed that it might have been the "spiritual aura" (*lingguang* 靈光) of the deities which appeared on the photos. However, even though he continued to see the pictures as "impossible to explain" (*moming* 莫名), he soon came to believe in the reality and the scientific value of these images. This was due to the almost experimental setting in which they had been taken. Several of the images had been developed at the altar, with him watching closely. He himself had adjusted the light and opened the lenses. Therefore, he vouched with his moral integrity and his reputation for the accuracy of his account. Accordingly, he was certain that the images would eventually be explained and "would have a profound impact on the future of science" (關於未來學理影響極大).[97] Indeed, his article bespeaks a strong belief in the ability of science to eventually explain all phenomena within the universe but also in the legitimacy of spirit-photography. Even doubts concerning the workings of spirit-photography did not lead Yu Fu to question its scientific nature or the principles of science more generally. Instead, the "experimental" setting in which they photographs were produced seemed to bolster the scientific credibility of the LXH.

Due to their tangible nature, spirit-photographs served another important purpose: material proof of spirits and deities. The LXH saw spirit-writing, and especially spirit-photography, as material confirmation of the existence of spirits and deities. While the spiritualists were not unanimous in their attitude towards the materiality of supernatural beings, one article ascribed to Lü Dongbin argues that deities and spirits "indeed have a material substance, but [that] it cannot be beheld by using the power of sight" (實有其質。但非目力之所能得耳).[98] Spirit-photography, however, was able to bring out this material dimension of supernatural beings. The same point was made in the anonymous article about Wallace and the Society for Psychical Research. In the original article, Wallace had used the case of spirit-photography to rebuke theorists of psychical research who ascribed all spiritual phenomena to "mental factors," since the production of images involved changes made to a material

97 Yu, "Shengde tan shi zhao xian ling ji," 2–4.

98 "Lü Zushi mixin lun," 24.

object. However, he deliberately left open the question whether spirits were the agents in these instances.[99] The anonymous author shared in this critique, but he also saw the spirit-photographs of the Society for Psychical Research as providing definite proof for the existence of spirits.

> The examples of spirit-photography are too many to enumerate. That these examples prove the existence of the soul (*linghun*) is definitely true. The reasons for this are twofold: First, they have indeed been derived from experimentation. Second, they were obtained according to the experimentation of experienced specialists. It is not only that, they can further prove that the soul really has a material [dimension] and that it does not stem from hallucination. Because if it were a hallucination, it would not have a material [dimension] and could not be absorbed by a photo camera and leave its [material] form.
>
> 靈魂照相之實例。不勝枚舉。此事證明靈魂之存在。尤爲確實。其理由有二。確由實驗而來。一也。係老練專門家實驗所得。二也。不寧惟是。且可證明靈魂之確有其物。而非由于幻覺。蓋幻覺則無物。決不能攝入照相器而留其形態也。[100]

Apart from the invocation of the scientific authority and the experimental approach of the Society for Psychical Research, this quote attests to the importance the LXH accorded to material proof despite their emphasis on spiritual forces. Spirit-photography was presented as being caused by spirits and served at the same time as evidence for the existence of spirits. Wallace had been more cautious and saw these occurrences only as proving the objectivity of what he called phantasms, "a term that does not necessarily imply *materiality*."[101] The anonymous author, on the other hand, was making a much stronger claim, which is already indicated by his translating the title as "A Confirmation of Theories about the Existence of Spirits."[102] For the members of the LXH, spirit-photography, similar to spirit-writing, provided conclusive proof of supernatural life and the existence of the human soul.[103] Several slogans preceding Yu Fu's article about spirit-photography article were even more outspoken, calling the LXH "pioneers in communicating between the

99 Wallace, "Are There Objective Apparitions?", 131.
100 Anon., "You gui lun zhi zhengming," 10.
101 Wallace, "Are There Objective Apparitions?", 146. Italics in the original.
102 Takahashi Gorō had instead chosen a literal translation of Wallace's title.
103 Yang Tingdong, "Linghun zhaoxiang ji," 8.

two spheres" (兩界溝通之先導) of the living and the dead, and referring to spirit-photographs as "the future of the scientific revolution" (科學革命之未來).[104]

In general, the scientific reform of spirit-writing and practices such as spirit-photography served as an important source of legitimacy in the period after WWI, when many contemporaries grew doubtful over a materialist understanding of human life, yet also held a deep-seated belief in the authority of science. These practices brought science and spiritualism together. They bolstered the scientific claim of the spiritualists due to their technical, empirically observable, and reproducible nature. Proving the existence of deities and spirits was no end in itself however. It entailed a belief in retribution and punishment after death that was supposed to lead people to change their ways in this life already. Yang Tingdong thus argued that "[i]f all the people of the world had hands on witnessed the reality of the photographs of the soul and thus really believed in the theory that the soul does not vanish" (親見靈魂照像之事實。而確認靈魂不滅之理論), it would lead to a general reform of the populace.[105] Spiritualism was seen as a forceful answer to tendencies of materialism and amorality that the members of the LXH deplored.[106] Indeed, the *Spiritualist Magazine* was—not despite but because of its emphasis on science—also published for the benefit of "moral transformation" (*jiaohua*) and thus continued the former mission of morality books.[107] What seemed new was the scientific legitimacy that spiritualism provided, which made the instructions received at the altar even more compelling. Other, non-spiritualist, altars were unable to provide this legitimacy, wherefore the LXH proved attractive to many Shanghai residents who sought a venue to engage with the supernatural, and not only to them.

Maybe the best indication of how well this spiritualist project was initially received is that the concept of *lingxue* was soon adopted by other newly

104 Yu, "Shengde tan shi zhao xian ling ji," 2.

105 Yang Tingdong, "Linghun zhaoxiang ji,", 7.

106 In an instructive piece called "The Soul and Education" ("Linghun yu jiaoyu 靈魂與教育"), published in 1918 in the journal *Zhonghua jiaoyujie* 中華教育界 (*China's Educational Sphere*) and in the *Spiritualist Magazine*, Lufei Kui therefore argued for a "spiritual education" (*jingshen jiaoyu* 精神教育), one of whose sources was religion and the belief in the soul. This spiritual education would fill people with hope for a future life and lead to a moral reform of the populace. See Lufei Kui, "Linghun yu jiaoyu 靈魂與教育," in *Lufei Kui wenxuan* 陸費逵文選, ed. Yu Guolin 俞國林 (Beijing: Zhonghua shuju, 2011), 194–199, and "Linghun yu jiaoyu," *Lingxue congzhi* 1, no. 1 (1918): 8–15. See also Wang, "Lufei Kui yu 'Shengde tan,' 'Lingxuehui'," for an instructive comparison of the differing versions published in the two journals.

107 Anon., "Jieshao xin kan."

established spirit-writing organizations. Following the LXH, a number of redemptive societies founded shortly after WWI, such as the Daoyuan 道院 (School of the Dao) and the Wushanshe 悟善社 (Society for Enlightenment and Goodness) joined the spiritualist cause. The Daoyuan aimed at synthesizing the five main religions to promote a universal morality, but also devoted itself to "the study of philosophy and spiritualism" (哲學靈學之研究).[108] The journals published by the Daoyuan therefore featured a number of articles that dealt with science or scientific theories.[109] The Wushanshe focused mainly on the implementation and propagation of philanthropic work, but its most important journal, the *Lingxue yaozhi* 靈學要誌 (Essential Magazine of Spiritualism), was also established "to provide studies by scholars of spiritualism and philosophy" (供靈哲學家之研究).[110] Moreover, the members of the Wushanshe conceded that their redemptive activities depended on the scientific proof of supernatural beings provided by the LXH. Indeed, a spirit-written message transmitted before the founding of the Wushanshe in 1919, and ascribed to its leading deity, Lü Dongbin, ordered the devotees to consult the magazine of the LXH and establish a press in a similar fashion, thus attesting to the influential model of the Society.[111] More concretely, the Wushanshe presented itself as part of a community of organizations united in their quest to spread morality and benevolence through the study of spiritualism (*lingxue*).[112] While allusions to science in the writings of these organizations remained rather vague, they attest to the popularity of the new spirituality in China and to the legitimacy associated with spiritualist concepts and institutions.

108 Wang Daocheng 王道成, ed., *Daoci wenxuan* 道慈文選 (Beijing, n.d.), 68.

109 See Shuzhong 樹中, "Fuji de xueli shuoming 扶乩的學理說明," *Daode zazhi* 道德雜誌 1, no. 1 (1921): 13–16, for an example directly related to spiritualism and psychical research. Additionally, the Daoyuan officially encompassed a Spiritualist Society (Lingxuehui), intended "to investigate spiritualism and philosophic principles" and a special scientific organization in Ji'nan 濟南, the Society for the Study of Spiritualism (Lingxue yanjiuhui 靈學研究會). See Anon., *Daoyuan yuangang: Yuanze, banshi xize* 道院院綱：院則、辦事細則 (n.p., n.d.), 2. Whether and to what degree these organizations actually operated is, however, hard to ascertain.

110 See Anon., "Wushanshe guanggao 悟善社廣告," *Lingxue yaozhi* 靈學要誌 1, no. 1 (1920), no page.

111 Wushanshe 悟善社, "*Lingxue yaozhi* yuanqi 靈學要誌緣起," *Lingxue yaozhi* 1, no. 1 (1920): 1–2.

112 They also considered the Tongshanshe 同善社 to be part of this community. See Anon., "Jishi 記事," *Lingxue yaozhi* 1, no. 2 (1921): 18.

6 The Limits of Scientism and the Redemptive Turn of the LXH

As seen above, the establishment of a scientific spiritualism initially appealed to many members, secured the LXH broad media coverage, and even inspired redemptive societies. Yet, the scientific reform of spirit-writing and the restriction of the content of the transmitted messages also posed a danger. If the practice was too institutionalized, the Society ran the risk of alienating those participants who sought out spirit-writing altars for quite personal reasons such as reuniting with deceased relatives or learning about their future.

Indeed, in the beginning the LXH had tried to take these interests into account. Thus, on Saturdays the LXH had invited visitors to the altar and allowed questions about personal welfare (*xiujiu*) and medical issues.[113] Even personal inquiries by members not connected to "scientific principles" had been tolerated to a certain degree. Most prominently, when his publishing company, China Bookstore, ran into serious economic and financial troubles in late 1917,[114] Lufei Kui had been able to seek divine guidance and over several sessions received detailed advice, demanding a complete overhaul of his company's organization.[115] However, starting from mid-1918, due to an uneasiness over continuing inquiries about "prosperity and misfortune," the Society intensified its institutionalization process and tried to specify the scientific nature of its spirit-writing activities.

In the context of this institutionalization process, the content of legitimate spirit-written messages was further restricted. As mentioned above, the "scientific principles" to which legitimate inquiries by members of the LXH were to be limited, had remained rather vague. In a message transmitted on June 6, 1918, the Immortal Mingyue 明月 explained the content of "scientific principles" in more detail. It seems likely that this was a direct response to the continued discussion of personal matters at the altar.

> Scientific principles: All those inquiring about scientific principles are restricted [to questions] about the models of the soul, spirits and

113 Lingxuehui, "Lingxuehui jianzhang," no pages, article 9.

114 Reed, *Gutenberg in Shanghai*, 235–236.

115 See "Han Zhu Wen Shi si gong Zhonghua shuju panci 韓朱文史四公中華書局判詞," *Lingxue congzhi* 1, no. 1 (1918): 5; "Sheng Xian Zhonghua shuju panci 生仙中華書局判詞," *Lingxue congzhi* 1, no. 1: 5; "Fude Zunshen Zhonghua shuju panci 福德尊神中華書局判詞," *Lingxue congzhi* 1, no. 1: 6; "Fude Zunshen Zhonghua shuju panci," *Lingxue congzhi* 1, no. 1: 8–9; "Yuying Zhenren Zhonghua shuju panci 玉英眞人中華書局判詞," *Lingxue congzhi* 1, no. 1: 6; and "Yuding Zhenren Zhonghua shuju panci 玉鼎眞人中華書局判詞," *Lingxue congzhi* 1, no. 1: 7–8.

> deities, philosophy, morality (*daode*), and personal conduct. Everything apart from these five [topics] belongs to the worldly and the practical [sphere] and will not be answered. Among [these topics] the soul generally encompasses human and [non-human] beings, living and not living. [The category of] spirits and deities encompasses the cause for the creation of heaven and earth and the virtue of the deities and the earthly spirits. Philosophy generally encompasses the final cause of the universe and the ethical principles of the divine way (*shendao*).
>
> 學理凡叩問學理者。以關於靈魂、鬼神、哲理、道德、處身、諸法爲限。五者之外。屬於世間業識者。不應。内靈魂。以人類、物類、有生、無生、均賅。鬼神。以天地造化之原、神明祇鬼之德、均賅。哲理。以宇宙一原神道綸倫、均賅。[116]

The LXH thus tried to confine the topics discussed at the altar to issues involving either the scientific discussion of the existence of supernatural beings or the moral worldview such an existence would justify. No longer tolerated were questions about "all worldly and practical matters such as material interests, money making, politics, and law" (一切世間業職。如功利、生財、政治、法律之項).[117] This certainly included inquiries about business prospects such as those posed by Lufei.

The revision of the guidelines for the altar by the Immortal set off a longer debate about the confines of spiritualism (*lingxue*) and its relation to spirit-writing, which went on over the following months. In general, there was unanimity about the general scientific course adopted by the Society, but the specific contours needed to be negotiated. Several messages lamented the lack of dedication to the project of spiritualism among the members.[118] One message criticized in harsh tones that the members had not been sufficiently engaged in "scholarship" (*xueye* 學業), instead some had allegedly used the LXH to make money.[119] This might have been an allegation against those such as Lufei Kui who had inquired about business affairs. Another deity ordered the members not to inquire about "prosperity and misfortune," medical prescriptions, and "not to respond to technologies for amusement" (不答遊技).[120]

116 "Zhengzhen tan Mingyue Xianzi xiuzheng tangui san ze 正鎮壇明月仙子修正壇規三則," *Lingxue congzhi* 1, no. 4 (1918): 1.

117 "Zhengzhen tan Mingyue Xianzi xiuzheng tangui san ze," 2.

118 See, for example, Anon., "Jizai 記載," *Lingxue congzhi* 1, no. 7 (1918): 19.

119 Anon., "Jizai 記載," *Lingxue congzhi* 1, no. 10 (1918): 8.

120 Anon., "Jizai 記載," *Lingxue congzhi* 1, no. 10 (1918): 11. See also Wang Chien-chuan, "Jindai Zhongguo de fuji, cishan yu 'mixin': Yi *Yinguang wenchao* wei kaocha xiansuo 近代中

Even the therapeutic use of spirit-writing was thus restricted. Instead, the members were to focus on the role of spirits in the world, the principles of the netherworld, and the "soul-philosophy of East and West."[121] The members had chosen to take the scientific path and now had to stick with it.

The harsh remarks by the deities have to be seen in the context of a growing interest in spirit-writing within Republican society and the backlash by critical intellectuals which resulted therefrom. Contemporary observers had credited the Society with sparking an upsurge in spirit-writing and spiritualist activities.[122] Yet, these other spirit-writing altars, the messages of the LXH bemoaned, used the name of the Society without adhering to its aims.[123] Not all engagement with supernatural beings was thus seen positively. One spirit-written message therefore pointed out that the only solution was to dissociate oneself from "superstitious" altars through a strengthened scientific approach.[124] This message also hints at the anti-superstition discourse of the time, which began to take aim at spirit-writing. Starting from mid-1918, the LXH had become the target of criticism of a number of well-known intellectuals and scientists like Chen Duxiu, Lu Xun 魯迅 (1881–1936), and Chen Daqi 陳大齊 (1886–1983).[125] They derided spirit-writing as superstitious and rebutted the Society's appeal to the concept of science. As a result, the LXH strove to set itself apart even more from other non-spiritualist spirit-writing altars. Even though not all members were altogether pleased,[126] the divine voices therefore

---

國的扶乩，慈善與「迷信」：以印光文鈔為考察線索," in *Xinyang, shijian yu wenhua tiaoshi: Disijie guoji Hanxue huiyi lunwenji* 信仰，實踐與文化調適：第四屆國際漢學會議論文集, ed. Kang Bao 康豹 (Paul R. Katz) and Liu Shufen 劉淑芬 (Taipei: Academia Sinica, 2013), 548–549.

121 Anon., "Jizai," *Lingxue congzhi* 1, no. 10: 11.

122 Contemporaries attested a growing interest in spirit-writing and a growing number of societies associated with this practice in the late 1910s and early 1920s. See, for example, Richard Wilhelm, *Die Seele Chinas* (reprint: Wiesbaden: Marixverlag, 2009), 313–314.

123 One divine message mentioned that the high deities, among them Lü Dongbin, were worried about the growing number of spirit-writing altars which followed in the lead of the LXH. Anon, "Jizai", *Lingxue congzhi* 1, no. 10: 9.

124 Anon., "Jizai," *Lingxue congzhi* 1, no. 10: 11.

125 See Huang Ko-wu, "Lingxue yu jindai Zhongguo de zhishi zhuanxing", 121–197, and Zheng, "Shanghai Lingxuehui yanjiu," chap. 5.

126 Yu Fu in particular responded to the criticism of the deities. He was the editor of the *Spiritualist Magazine* and might have felt especially spoken to. He pointed to his own pedigree in smashing superstition while he was younger to indicate his sincerity. In addition, he asserted that medical prescriptions and personal inquiries had long been prohibited, certainly having the altar regulations in mind. For his answer see Anon., "Jizai," *Lingxue congzhi* 1, no. 10: 11–12. Being the editor of the journal of the LXH, Yu Fu's word carried substantial weight and eventually forced the voices of the deities to soften their criticism

insisted on a restrictive approach towards the topics of spirit-writing intended to secure the scientific standing of the Society. And this was, eventually, the direction into which the LXH moved over the years of 1919 and 1920. Following the restriction of spirit-writing quoted above, we see no questions pertaining to economic or personal interests documented in the issues of the *Spiritualist Magazine*.

The renegotiation of spiritualism also had a substantial impact on the practice of spirit-photography. Indeed, the admonition "not to respond to technologies for amusement" mentioned above referred exactly to this practice. Despite the pervasive interest in spirit-photography, the deities eventually advised against the practice and prohibited the members from experimenting with it. It was on October 29, 1918, that the members of the LXH took spirit-photographs for the eighteenth and last time.[127] One reason to stop spirit-photography was that the spread of the technique, which the LXH ascribed to its own role as one of the pioneers in the field, had brought many imitators to the scene. One message pointed out that many "misuse the name of the LXH to gain profit from it. They have already produced many photos, which [claim] to be images of the eight immortals, but are really absurd and laughable. Most of them are like paintings and clearly do not have the appearance of photographs" (假托靈學會名。從中取利。已出多張。竟有八仙之像。荒謬可笑。大部如繪圖。並非影形).[128] They charged these altars with fakery and with undermining trust in the practices of the LXH. Prohibiting the practice was therefore similarly part of their attempt to set themselves apart from "imposters" and unscientific altars. Plus, once supernatural beings had been proven, as the LXH claimed, the technique was not really needed anymore. Images of deceased relatives only amounted to a personal affair and had no greater social value.

Whether or not it was understandable from the viewpoint of the scientific mission of the Society, this institutionalization process had a devastating effect on the financial resources and the membership of the LXH. Many members and visitors, similar to the case of European spiritualism, were excited about the access to the divine for very personal reasons. Spirit-writing offered

---

of the members. Nevertheless, the divine messages insisted on the adoption of the "scientific path."

127 See Anon., "Jizai," *Lingxue congzhi* 1, no. 10: 16, and Yang Tingdong, "Linghun zhaoxiang ji," 8. See also Wang Hongchao 王宏超, "Shenjie lingguang: Shanghai Shengde tan zhi linghun zhaoxiang huodong 神界靈光：上海盛德壇之靈魂照相活動," *Shanghai wenhua* 上海文化, no. 6 (2016): 67–76.

128 Anon., "Jizai," *Lingxue congzhi* 1, no. 10: 11. Ironically, similar charges of fakery were leveled against the LXH.

knowledge about one's future and the fate of one's deceased relatives. For many, personal questions were a much more pressing concern than "scientific principles," however much they valued the scientific setting of the LXH. In one article in the newspaper *Shenbao* 申報, we learn that more than one hundred people sought answers to questions of individual prosperity and misfortune (*xiujiu*) at a later public sprit-writing meeting of the LXH, while only three or four inquired about questions of science.[129] Hence, even after the renewed prohibitions of personal inquiries had been issued, visitors kept coming to the LXH to inquire about personal questions. Now, however, they had to be turned down.[130] After the restriction of spirit-writing and the harsh admonishments by the deities, even the members themselves were at a loss about what to ask. As one spirit-written message from the beginning of 1919 pointed out:

> [T]his year, the altar has been opened one whole month, and still there have been very few questions [towards the deities] regarding complicated scientific principles (*xueli*). No interest has emerged.
>
> 於疑難學理。今年開沙已匝一月。而所問無幾。興趣無從發生。[131]

The restriction of spirit-writing thus went counter to the interests of many visitors and members. Due to this lack of interest, the LXH was in turn unable to produce sufficient "essays" (*lunshuo*) for the publication of the *Spiritualist Magazine*, which in turn drove away even more supporters. The prohibition of spirit-photography further accelerated this development. The members had been highly enthusiastic about the practice. Not only Yang Tingdong but also many visitors linked up with the LXH to procure images of their deceased relatives.[132] Considering that the LXH depended on membership fees and donations, which were demanded for services such as spirit-writing inquiries and photographs, and faced the competition of other spirit-writing altars, these restrictions certainly posed an obstacle to the recruitment of new members.

The LXH struggled to come to terms with the implications of this institutionalization process (and the public critique leveled at them). Some members such as Ding Fubao departed the Society for good, others such as Lufei Kui at least temporarily. Those members who continued to drive the

---

129 Anon., "Xinwen shiyi 新聞拾遺," *Shenbao*, May 28, 1921.

130 Anon., "Jizai," *Lingxue congzhi* 1, no. 7: 19.

131 Anon., "Jizai," *Lingxue congzhi* 2, no. 1 (1919): 7.

132 Yang Tingdong, "Linghun zhaoxiang ji," 8.

institutionalization process began to assemble at a new Western Altar (Xi tan 西壇),[133] which was set up on the properties of Silas Aaron Hardoon (1851–1931, Chin. Hatong 哈同).[134] Here, however, few spirit-written messages were forthcoming. At the end of 1920, the Society finally ran out of funds, wherefore their journal had to be canceled temporarily. The dire straits came to an end only in early 1921 when the leadership and membership of the Society changed again (important members such as Lufei Kui returned) and the Society adapted its principles to once again redefine its understanding of spiritualism but also to broaden its aims and activities.[135] In the winter of 1921, the reorganized Society published the first quarterly issue of the reinvigorated *Spiritualist Magazine*, which provides insight into the strategies adopted to counter the former troubles of the Society and into the reasons for these changes. The issue includes a completely new constitution (*jianzhang* 簡章). Here, five "undertakings" (*shiye*) are mentioned: "research" (*yanjiu* 研究), "social work" (*shehui shiye* 社會事業), "self-cultivation" (*xiuyang* 修養), "religion," and "connecting with the spiritual" (*lingtong* 靈通). They also explicitly mention "philanthropy" as a new part of their social outreach.[136] That is to say, the Society changed from a narrow focus on "scientific principles" to substantially widen its activities to include self-cultivation, philanthropy, and religion.

In the following years, these organizational changes were filled with life. First of all, the Society lifted many of the above-mentioned restrictions. In a message transmitted April 30, 1921, the deity Master Changsheng came forward and volunteered to answer questions "about prosperity and misfortune" as long as they would not touch upon the "working of heaven" (*tianji* 天機) or the principles of "the netherworld" (*mingmo* 冥漠).[137] While the deity warned that the former regulations were still in place and may not be violated, the above represents a striking departure from the path the LXH took after mid-1918.

---

133 The date of establishment is not clear, but it was up and running by end of March 1919. See Anon., "Jizai," *Lingxue congzhi* 2, no. 1. (1919): 8. The original altar was accordingly referred to as Eastern Altar from then on.

134 Hardoon was a well-known Jewish businessman and philanthropist (who had traded in opium until at least 1918), who provided shelter to many illustrious figures in his famous Aili 愛儷 Garden. Chiara Betta, "Silar Aaron Hardoon and Cross-Cultural Adaptation in Shanghai," in *The Jews of China, Vol. 1: Historical and Comparative Perspectives*, ed. Jonathan Goldstein (London & New York: Routledge, 1999), 216–229.

135 See Anon., "Xinyou nian san yue zhi shi'er yue zhi zong shou ge huiyuan jijin tebie juan ji huifei xiangjin 辛酉年三月至十二月止總收各會員基金特別捐及會費香金," *Lingxue congzhi* 1, 2nd ser., no. 1 (1921): 1–2, for a list of the members of the reorganized Society.

136 Lingxuehui, "Lingxuehui jianzhang," 1–4.

137 "Changshengzi zhun pan xiujiu 常勝子准判休咎," *Lingxue congzhi* 1, 2nd ser., no. 1 (1921): 1.

In 1922, even the practice of spirit-photography was taken up again, reflecting the members' decision to lay greater emphasis on their connection with the spiritual sphere.[138] While this cannot be treated in detail, it seems that early members such as Lufei, Yang Guangxi, and Yang Zhenru, who were all part of the reorganized Society, were reestablishing control over the operation of the LXH. Under their leadership the Society reacted to its previous difficulties by again making its practice of spirit-writing more flexible to the demands of their constituency. The above message by the deity Master Changsheng clearly indicates that at least some of the measures were intended specifically to attract new members. Even though the Society preserved its appeal to spiritualism,[139] this reorientation indicates that a scientific spirit-writing, if it was too institutionalized, failed to satisfy the interests of many potential participants.

More substantially, the LXH ventured into new directions, conducting philanthropic activities and staging grand religious rituals. It thereby followed the direction of redemptive societies such as the Daoyuan and the Wushanshe. In the philanthropic sphere, the Society aspired to the prominent role of the Daoyuan and its philanthropic sub-branch, the World Red Swastika Society (Shijie Hongwanzihui 世界紅卍字會). Similar to the latter, they founded a relief corps (*jiujidui* 救濟隊) that distributed help within disaster regions after collecting donations from members and through newspaper advertisements. Although the LXH remained confined to Shanghai, specific relief operations would take them to other provinces as well.[140] Other philanthropic projects of the LXH included opening a "store for the issuing of interest free loans" (*mianli daibenchu* 免利貸本處)[141] and, at least starting from 1924, the Society also managed several "compulsory primary schools" (*yiwu xiaoxue* 義務小學) that were attached to it.[142]

At the same time, the LXH began to stage public rituals to acquire a more prominent position within Shanghai's religious sphere. In his book *Jingshen qidao* 精神祈禱 (Spirit Praying) from 1926, Yang Zhenru recalls how the LXH conducted collective prayers in 1923 and 1924 that were called Assemblies for

138 Anon., "Lingxuehui zhi sitian yu tuanbai 靈學會之祀天與團拜," *Shenbao*, February 6, 1922.

139 In the same issue, they put forth a new program for the study of spiritualism. Lingxuehui, "Lingxue yanjiu fa 靈學研究法," *Lingxue congzhi* 1, 2nd ser., no. 1 (1921): 1–3.

140 For their relief activities see, for example, Anon., "Lingxuehui xinyang chazhentuan baogao 靈學會信陽查賑團之報告," *Shenbao*, April 10, 1926, and Anon., "Henan guanshen dianxie Lingxuehui shizhen 河南官紳電謝靈學會施賑," *Shenbao*, May 17, 1926.

141 Anon., "Cishan xiaoxi 慈善消息," *Shenbao*, April 16, 1924.

142 One article in the *Shenbao* mentions that in July 1924 the first graduation ceremony was held for students of these schools. Possibly, therefore, the schools, or at least one of them, had already opened in 1923. Anon., "Biye li zhi畢業禮誌," *Shenbao*, July 20, 1924.

Spirit Praying (Jingshen qidao dahui 精神祈禱大會). These assemblies were specifically convened to counter the warfare that was raging in the two provinces Jiangsu and Zhejiang 浙江 at the time, but they were supposed to put down all kinds of disasters. Yang Zhenru explained that, due to the logic of "stimulus and response," all disasters were caused by the "wicked behavior" (*wangxing* 妄行) of humans. However, disaster could be prevented through public acts of repentance such as communal prayers and the unification of "the five teachings of Confucianism, Buddhism, Christianity, Islam, and Daoism."[143] The members had received the order for staging these assemblies at one of their altars with the specific form and date given. According to Yang, they were big events with many members of the elite paying tribute.[144] Instead of truly bringing relief, however, conditions in the region worsened during the year of 1925. The LXH, therefore, wanted to continue its communal activities and petitioned the deities for further orders. In response, they received the method for Spirit Praying (*jingshen qidao*). Yang's book was then later published to propagate the new method, which was essentially a meditation technique following in the line of the many methods of "quiet sitting" (*jingzuo* 靜坐) popular during the time (see the chapter by David Ownby in this volume). The divine messages also indicated that the assemblies were only a prelude and that a Society for Spiritual Prayer should be established. The members drafted a constitution, which was approved through spirit-writing, and the Society held its first prayer according to the new method in April 1925.[145]

These organizational changes were accompanied by a partial change in leadership. At the time of its establishment the strong Wuxi network featured most prominently with Lufei Kui, Yang Guangxi, Ding Fubao, and other local figures leading the society. These individuals do not feature as prominently anymore in the sources published after 1922. In the mid-1920s the LXH was instead led by a board of directors chaired by Wang Yiting 王一亭 (1867–1938).[146] Wang was an accomplished businessman, a famous painter, and a well-connected philanthropist. He was also a practicing Buddhist and involved in

143 Yang Zhenru, *Jingshen qidao*, 3/16. See also an article by the Shanghai Jesus Church (Shanghai Yesu Jiaohui 上海耶穌教會), which planned a similar sounding conference and decided to publish a disclaimer, quoting the original advertisement of the LXH in the course. Anon., "Shanghai Yesu jiaohui bu yuwen Lingxuehui wu jiao qidao dahui 上海耶穌教會不與聞靈學會五教祈禱大會," *Xinghua* 興華 20, no. 36 (1923): 29.

144 Yang Zhenru, *Jingshen qidao*, 1–2.

145 Yang Zhenru, *Jingshen qidao*, 1–2.

146 Anon., "Cishan xiaoxi 慈善消息," *Shenbao*, April 16, 1924. The board was staffed by other local entrepreneurs and philanthropists.

many redemptive societies in Shanghai.[147] His networking certainly played a vital role in the implementation of the above-mentioned philanthropic projects, but they may have also contributed to the Society's reorientation along the lines of other redemptive societies.

7 Conclusion

The LXH was one among a number of actors in the Republican period who employed the concept of science to legitimate their activities in a changing social and epistemic context. In particular, they adopted ideas and practices from a global new spirituality, which criticized a "scientific materialism" while adopting the model of academic science. The LXH took up new practices such as spirit-photography, which offered a new perspective on spirit-writing and supernatural existence. In their spirit-written texts, they engaged with new scientific concepts that were compatible with their understanding of human life and reconfigured spirit-writing as a form of "spiritualist" experimentation able to "prove" supernatural life. Despite the larger moral mission of the organization, of which their scientific approach was a part and at which I have only hinted here, this presents a striking reconstruction of spirit-writing. This reconstruction, in turn, played an important role in attracting educated members of the elite such as Lufei Kui or Yu Fu and indicates more generally the authority vested in the new concept of science during the Republican period. At the same time, the deliberate attempt to propagate a scientific approach to the spiritual world also sheds new light on the relationship between science, religion, and secularism in the late 1910s. While the LXH initially avoided the term religion and focused instead on philosophy and morality, their spiritual science must also be seen as a response to secularizing tendencies in Chinese society which aimed to eradicate the belief in supernatural beings.

However, the difficulties the Society faced in 1919 and 1920 also indicate some of the intricacies in legitimating practices such as spirit-writing through an appeal to science. Certainly, many members welcomed the scientific approach of the LXH and some only joined due to the scientific reconceptualization of spirit-writing. At the same time, many of them had been engaged in spirit-writing before entering the Society and brought their own expectations as to the benefits of the practice. Their interests had to be balanced with the scientific reform of spirit-writing. The strengthened institutionalization

147 On his religious activities, see Paul R. Katz, *Religion in China and Its Modern Fate* (Waltham, Mass.: Brandeis University Press, 2014), 109–154.

process, which the LXH initiated after mid-1918, failed to take these interests into account and repelled many members. Interestingly, with its strictures on spiritualist practice, the LXH almost shared the fate of the Society for Psychical Research. While membership figures of the British Society had peaked in 1920, they dropped by half ten years later. In the preceding decade numerous rival organizations had been established, charging that the Society's insistence on proper scientific standards limited its access to spontaneous spiritual phenomena.[148] In both China and Britain, the personal experience of spiritual phenomena could potentially come into conflict with the restrictive influence of scientific models.

The LXH, however, reacted more successfully than the Society for Psychical Research. After 1921, its members put forth a more flexible understanding of spiritualism, but also connected to the spheres of self-cultivation, philanthropy, and religion, which similarly promised legitimacy. This was actually the approach redemptive societies such as the Daoyuan and the Wushanshe had been taking all along. They appealed to the concept of spiritualism and also institutionalized spirit-writing, even to the point of prohibiting questions about matters of personal welfare, but never enforced them strictly.[149] In addition, they did not narrow down the content of spirit-writing messages as severely, but allowed a broad range of questions related to philanthropy, health, self-cultivation, and even the revelation of religious scriptures. One can argue that through its reorganization in the 1920s the LXH redirected itself towards the religious and philanthropic agenda of many redemptive societies. This redirection proved highly successful. Not only was the LXH able to open additional altars,[150] but they once more attracted a large network of members and supporters. As one report in the *Shenbao* tells us, more than seven hundred onlookers watched a spirit-writing session of the LXH on May 18, 1921![151] Interest in spirit-writing in Shanghai thus continued unabated, only its relation to spiritualism had to be renegotiated.

Following the reorientation of the LXH, and the public criticism that accompanied it, Chinese spiritualism (*lingxue*) lost some of its appeal within

148 Elizabeth R. Valentine, "Spooks and Spoofs: Relations between Psychical Research and Academic Psychology in Britain in the Inter-War Period," *History of the Human Sciences* 25, no. 2 (2012): 71–73.

149 Compare "Fuyou Dijun biaoming Wushanshe yu qita shen tan you bie wen 孚佑帝君表明悟善社與其他神壇有別文," *Lingxue yaozhi* 1, no. 7 (1921): 21–24, for a spirit-written message transmitted at the Wushanshe, which warns against emphasizing personal welfare over philanthropy.

150 They eventually operated four altars in different parts of Shanghai.

151 Anon., "Xinwen shiyi 新聞拾遺," *Shenbao*, May 19, 1921.

society, and allusions to spiritualism by Chinese actors decreased over the 1920s. This development reflected shifts in the larger social and political context of Republican China in which redemptive societies were embedded. Following an intensified critique of superstition during the late 1910s, and the anti-superstition campaigns of the Guomindang 國民黨, many organizations formed around spirit-writing chose to emphasize religion, "national learning" (*guoxue* 國學), or philanthropy. The LXH's engagement with philanthropic practices was in line with this development and enabled it to operate well into the 1940s. Nevertheless, spirit-writing organizations, and even the LXH itself, continued to invoke science to enhance their legitimacy. There were even isolated attempts to link science and spirit-writing in a manner comparable to spiritualism (*lingxue*).[152] Yet, none of these attempts was able to match the clamor that spiritualism caused in the late 1910s. The period around the end of WWI presented a unique opportunity to link science and spirit-writing and profit from the legitimacy ascribed to a global spirituality that was opposed to materialism and militarism.

Bibliography

Primary Sources

"Changshengzi zhun pan xiujiu 常勝子准判休咎." *Lingxue congzhi* 靈學叢誌 1, 2nd ser., no. 1 (1921): 1–2.

"Fude Zunshen Zhonghua shuju panci 福德尊神中華書局判詞." *Lingxue congzhi* 1, no. 1 (1918): 6, 8–9.

"Fuyou Dijun biaoming Wushanshe yu qita shen tan you bie wen 孚佑帝君表明悟善社與其他神壇有別文." *Lingxue yaozhi* 靈學要誌 1, no. 7 (1921): 21–24.

"Han Zhu Wen Shi si gong Zhonghua shuju panci 韓朱文史四公中華書局判詞." *Lingxue congzhi* 1, no. 1 (1918): 5.

"Lü Zushi mixin lun 呂祖師迷信論." *Lingxue congzhi* 1, no. 2 (1918): 23–26.

"Mingyue Xianzi xianling sheying ji tanqin panci 明月仙子仙靈攝影及彈琴判詞." *Lingxue congzhi* 1, no. 4 (1918): 4.

"Sheng Xian Zhonghua shuju panci 生仙中華書局判詞." *Lingxue congzhi* 1, no. 1 (1918): 5.

"Xu Banhou xiansheng linghun sheying 徐班侯先生靈魂攝影." *Lingxue congzhi* 1, no. 2 (1918): n.p.

"Yuying Zhenren Zhonghua shuju panci 玉英眞人中華書局判詞." *Lingxue congzhi* 1, no. 1 (1918): 6.

152 See Fan Chun-wu, "Kexue lingji," 215–222.

"Yuding Zhenren Zhonghua shuju panci 玉鼎眞人中華書局判詞." *Lingxue congzhi* 1, no. 1 (1918): 7–8.

"Zhengzhen tan Mingyue Xianzi xiuzheng tangui san ze 正鎭壇明月仙子修正壇規三則." *Lingxue congzhi* 1, no. 4 (1918): 2–3.

Amagishi Koji 天岸居士, ed. *Tailingdao* 太靈道. Shanghai: Xinling kexue shuju, 1933.

Anonymous. "Biye li zhi 畢業禮誌." *Shenbao*, July 20, 1924.

Anonymous. "Cishan xiaoxi 慈善消息." *Shenbao*, April 16, 1924.

Anonymous. *Daoyuan shuoming shu* 道院說明書. n.p., n.d.

Anonymous. *Daoyuan yuangang: Yuanze, banshi xize* 道院院綱：院則、辦事細則. n.p., n.d.

Anonymous. "Henan guanshen dianxie Lingxuehui shizhen 河南官紳電謝靈學會施賑." *Shenbao*, May 17, 1926.

Anonymous. "Huishu zhi xie 惠書誌謝." *Shenbao*, July 4, 1918.

Anonymous. "Jieshao xin kan 介紹新刊." *Shenbao*, April 10, 1918.

Anonymous. "Jishi 記事." *Lingxue yaozhi* 1, no. 2 (1921): 1–28.

Anonymous. "Jizai 記載." *Lingxue congzhi* 1, no. 2 (1918): 1–40.

Anonymous. "Jizai 記載." *Lingxue congzhi* 1, no. 7 (1918): 1–20.

Anonymous. "Jizai 記載." *Lingxue congzhi* 1, no. 10 (1918): 1–18.

Anonymous. "Jizai 記載." *Lingxue congzhi* 2, no. 1 (1919): 1–8.

Anonymous. "Lingxuehui xinyang chazhentuan zhi baogao 靈學會信陽查賑團之報告." *Shenbao*, April 10, 1926.

Anonymous. "Lingxuehui zhi sitian yu tuanbai 靈學會之祀天與團拜." *Shenbao*, February 6, 1922.

Anonymous. "Lingxue jinghua lu 靈學精華錄." *Jiushi xinbao* 救世新報, October 25, 1927: 1.

Anonymous. "Lingxue yanjiu fa 靈學研究法." *Lingxue congzhi* 1, 2nd ser., no. 1 (1921): 1–3.

Anonymous. "Shanghai Yesu jiaohui bu yuwen Lingxuehui wu jiao qidao dahui 上海耶穌教會不與聞靈學會五教祈禱大會." *Xinghua* 興華 20, no. 36 (1923): 29.

Anonymous. "Wushanshe guanggao 悟善社廣告." *Lingxue yaozhi* 1, no. 1 (1920): n.p.

Anonymous. "Xinwen shiyi 新聞拾遺." *Shenbao*, May 19, 1921.

Anonymous. "Xinwen shiyi 新聞拾遺." *Shenbao*, May 28, 1921.

Anonymous. "You gui lun zhi zhengming 有鬼論之證明." *Lingxue congzhi* 1, no. 5 (1918): 1–10.

Anonymous. "Zhongguo xinling yanjiuhui lüeshi 中國心靈研究會略史." *Xinling* 心靈 1, no. 4 (1916): 58.

Bao Fangzhou 鮑芳洲. *Cuimianshu* 催眠術. Shanghai: Zhongguo jingshen yanjiuhui, n.d., n.p.

Barrett, William. *Psychical Research*. New York: Henry Holt and Company, and London: Williams and Norgate, [preface 1911].

Ding Fubao 丁福保. "Wo lixiang zhong zhi gui shuo 我理想中之鬼說." *Lingxue congzhi* 1, no. 1 (1918): 15–18.

Fu Lanya 傅蘭雅 (John Fryer), trans. *Zhixin mianbing fa* 治心免病法. Shanghai: Shanghai Gezhi shushi, 1896.

Fukurai Tomokichi 福来友吉. "Xinling yanjiu zhi jiazhi 心靈研究之價值." *Xuesheng* 學生 5, no. 11 (1918): 43–55.

Hou Yishi 侯疑始 [Yi 毅]. "Ji shen you Qiong Yuan shi 記神游瓊苑事." *Lingxue congzhi* 1, no. 4 (1918): 9–12.

Hua Xiangzhi 華襄治. "*Lingxue congzhi* fakanci 靈學叢誌發刊辭." *Lingxue congzhi* 1, no. 1 (1918): 3–4.

Lingxuehui 靈學會, ed. *Xianling zhaoxiang, fu guiling zhaoxiang* 仙靈照相、附鬼靈照相. Shanghai: Zhonghua shuju, 1921.

Lingxuehui 靈學會, ed. "Lingxuehui jianzhang 靈學會簡章." *Lingxue congzhi* 1, no. 1 (1918): n.p.

Lingxuehui 靈學會, ed. "Shengde tan tangui 盛德壇壇規." *Lingxue congzhi* 1, no. 1 (1918): 1–8.

Lingxuehui 靈學會, ed. "Xinyou nian san yue zhi shi'er yue zhi zong shou ge huiyuan jijin tebie juan ji huifei xiangjin 辛酉年三月至十二月止總收各會員基金特別捐及會費香金." *Lingxue congzhi* 1, 2nd ser., no. 1 (1921): 1–2.

Lodge, Sir Oliver. *Shigo no seizon* 死後の生存. Translated by Takahashi Gorō 高橋五朗. Tokyo: Genkōsha, 1917.

Lufei Kui 陸費逵. "*Lingxue congzhi* yuanqi 靈學叢誌緣起." *Lingxue congzhi* 1, no. 1 (1918): 1–3.

Lufei Kui 陸費逵. "Linghun yu jiaoyu 靈魂與教育." *Lingxue congzhi* 1, no. 1 (1918): 8–15.

Lufei Kui 陸費逵. "Linghun yu jiaoyu 靈魂與教育." In *Lufei Kui wenxuan* 陸費逵文選, edited by Yu Guolin 俞國林, 194–199. Beijing: Zhonghua shuju, 2011.

Mo Deng 莫等. "Guixiang zhi yanjiu 鬼相之研究." *Xin qingnian* 新青年 5, no. 6 (1918): 616–624.

Shuzhong 樹中. "Fuji de xueli shuoming 扶乩的學理說明." *Daode zazhi* 道德雜誌 1, no. 1 (1921): 13–16.

Sidgwick, Henry. "Proceedings of the Society for Psychical Research." *Proceedings of the Society for Psychical Research* 1 (1882): 7–12.

[Society for Psychical Research]. "Objects of the Society." *Proceedings of the Society for Psychical Research* 1 (1882): 3–6.

Wallace, Alfred Russel. "Are There Objective Apparitions?" *Arena* 3, no. 13 (1891): 129–146.

Wang Daocheng 王道成, ed. *Daoci wenxuan* 道慈文選. Beijing, n.d.

Wilhelm, Richard. *Die Seele Chinas*. Reprint, Wiesbaden: Marixverlag, 2009.

Wu Tingfang. "Xuanjiang linghunxue 宣講靈魂學." In *Wu Tingfang ji* 伍廷芳集, edited by Ding Xianjun 丁賢俊 and Yu Zuofeng 喻作鳳, 854–855. 2 vols. Beijing: Zhonghua shuju, 1993.

Wushanshe 悟善社. "*Lingxue yaozhi* yuanqi 靈學要誌緣起." *Lingxue yaozhi* 1, no. 1 (1920): 1–2.

Yan Fu 嚴復. "Yan Jidao xiansheng zhi Hou Yishi shu 嚴幾道先生致侯疑始書." *Lingxue congzhi* 1, no. 3 (1918): 1–4.

Yang Guangxi 楊光熙. "Shengde tan yuanqi 盛德壇緣起." *Lingxue congzhi* 1, no. 1 (1918), 4–6.

Yang Jianxing 楊踐形. *Xueduo she yixue congshu* 學鐸社易學叢書. Taipei: Xiangda tushu youxian gongsi, 2010.

Yang Ruilin 楊瑞麟 [Jianxing]. "Fuji xueshuo 扶乩學說." *Lingxue congzhi* 1, no. 1 (1918), 1–10.

Yang Tingdong 楊廷棟. "Linghun zhaoxiang ji 靈魂照像記." *Lingxue congzhi* 1, no. 7 (1918), 5–8.

Yang Zhenru 楊真如. *Jingshen qidao* 精神祈禱. Shanghai: Shanghai Lingxuehui, 1926.

Yu Fu 俞復. "Shengde tan shi zhao xian ling ji 盛德壇試照仙靈記." *Lingxue congzhi* 1, no. 6 (1918), 2–4.

Yu Pingke 余萍客. *Cuimianshu hanshou jiangyi* 催眠術函授講義. 3 vols. Shanghai: Zhongguo xinling yanjiuhui, 1931.

Secondary Sources

Bennett, Bridget. *Transatlantic Spiritualism and Nineteenth-Century American Literature.* New York: Palgrave Macmillan, 2007.

Bennett, Terry. *History of Photography in China: Chinese Photographers, 1844–1879*. London: Bernard Quaritch Ltd, 2013.

Betta, Chiara. "Silar Aaron Hardoon and Cross-Cultural Adaptation in Shanghai." In *The Jews of China, Vol. 1: Historical and Comparative Perspectives*, edited by Jonathan Goldstein, 216–229. London & New York: Routledge, 1999.

Cerullo, John J. *The Secularization of the Soul: Psychical Research in Modern Britain*. Philadelphia: Institute for the Study of Human Issues, 1982.

Chan, Leo Tak-Hung. "Narrative as Argument: The *Yuewei caotang biji* and the Late Eighteenth-Century Elite Discourse on the Supernatural." *Harvard Journal of Asiatic Studies* 53, no. 1 (1993): 25–62.

Chau, Adam Yuet. *Miraculous Response: Doing Popular Religion in Contemporary China*. Stanford, CA: Stanford University Press, 2006.

Ding Xianjun 丁賢俊 and Yu Zuofeng 喻作鳳, ed. *Wu Tingfang ji* 伍廷芳集. 2 vols. Beijing: Zhonghua shuju, 1993.

Fan Chun-wu 范純武. "Kexue lingji: Diexian yu Minchu lingxue sichao xia fuji de 'xin' neihan 科學靈乩：碟仙與民初靈學思潮下扶乩的「新」內涵." In *Wenhua yu kexue de bianzou: Jindai Zhongguo jiushi tuanti, xinyang wenhua de fazhang yu weilai* 文化與科學的變奏：近代中國救世團體、信仰文化的發展與未來, edited by Foguang Daxue (collection of conference papers), 203–223. Foguang daxue, 2012.

Fan Chun-wu 范純武. *Qingmo minjian cishan shiye yu luantang yundong* 清末民間慈善事業與鸞堂運動. Taipei: Boyang wenhua youxian gongsi, 2015.

Figal, Gerald. *Civilization and Monsters: Spirits of Modernity in Meiji Japan*. Durham: Duke University Press, 1999.

Ford, Marcus. "William James's Psychical Research and Its Philosophical Implications." *Transactions of the Charles S. Peirce Society* 34, no. 3 (Summer 1998): 605–626.

Goossaert, Vincent. "1898: The End of Religion in China?" *The Journal of Asian Studies* 65, no. 2 (May 2006): 307–335.

Goossaert, Vincent, and David A. Palmer. *The Religious Question in Modern China*. Chicago: University of Chicago Press, 2011.

Hammer, Olav. *Claiming Knowledge: Strategies of Epistemology from Theosophy to the New Age*. Leiden: Brill, 2001.

Hammerstrom, Erik J. "Science and Buddhist Modernism in Early 20th Century China: The Life and Works of Wang Xiaoxu 王小徐." *Journal of Chinese Religions* 39 (2011): 1–32.

Hardacre, Helen. "Asano Wasaburō and Japanese Spiritualism in Early Twentieth-Century Japan." In *Japan's Competing Modernities: Issues in Culture and Democracy, 1900–1930*, edited by Sharon A. Minichiello, 133–153. Honolulu: University of Hawai'i Press, 1998.

Hochgeschwender, Michael. "The Religion of the Modern Man: 19th Century Spiritualism in the US and Germany." In *Religion in the United States*, edited by Jeanne Cortiel, Kornelia Freitag, Christine Gebhardt, and Michael Wala, 3–23. Heidelberg: Universitätsverlag Winter, 2011.

Holder, Arthur. "Introduction." In *The Blackwell Companion to Christian Spirituality*, edited by Arthur Holder, 1–11. Malden: Blackwell Publishing, 2005.

Hu Xuecheng 胡學丞. "Wu Tingfang de tongshenxue yu lingxue shengya 伍廷芳的通神學與靈學生涯." *Zhengda shicui* 政大史粹, no. 22 (2012): 1–22.

Huang Ko-wu 黄克武. "Lingxue yu jindai Zhongguo de zhishi zhuanxing: Minchu zhishi fenzi dui kexue, zongjiao yu mixin de zai sikao 靈學與近代中國的知識轉型:民初知識分子對科學、宗教與迷信的再思考." *Sixiang shi* 思想史, no. 2 (2014): 121–196.

Huang Ko-wu 黄克武. "Minguo chunian Shanghai de lingxue yanjiu: yi 'Shanghai Lingxuehui' wei li 民國初年上海的靈學研究:以「上海靈學會」為例." *Jindaishi yanjiusuo jikan* 近代史研究所集刊, no. 55 (March 2007): 99–136.

Huang Ko-wu 黄克武. *Wei shi zhi an: Yan Fu yu jindai Zhongguo de wenhua zhuanxing* 惟適之安:嚴復與近代中國的文化轉型. Beijing: Shehui kexue wenxian chubanshe, 2012.

Josephson, Jason Ānanda. *The Invention of Religion in Japan*. Chicago and London: University of Chicago Press, 2012.

Katz, Paul R. "Illuminating Goodness: Some Preliminary Considerations of Religious Publishing in Modern China." In *Religious Publishing and Print Culture in Modern China: 1800–2012*, edited by Philip Clart and Gregory Adam Scott, 265–294. Boston: De Gruyter, 2015.

Katz, Paul R. *Religion in China and Its Modern Fate*. Waltham, Mass.: Brandeis University Press, 2014.

Kontou, Tatiana and Sarah Willburn, ed. *The Ashgate Companion to Nineteenth-Century Spiritualism and the Occult*. Farnham and Burlington: Ashgate, 2012.

Kwok, D.W.Y. *Scientism in Chinese Thought, 1900–1950*. New Haven: Yale University Press, 1965.

Liu, Joyce C.H. "Psychic Force and its Betrayals: Re-treating Tan Sitong's Translation of Psyche." In *Modern China and the West: Translation and Cultural Mediation*, edited by Peng Hsiao-yen and Isabelle Rabut, 153–181. Leiden: Brill, 2014.

Liu Xun. *Daoist Modern: Innovation, Lay Practice and the Community of Inner Alchemy in Republican Shanghai*. Cambridge: Harvard University Asian Center/Harvard University Press, 2009.

Luckhurst, Roger. *The Invention of Telepathy, 1870–1901*. New York: Oxford University Press, 2002.

Luckhurst, Roger. "Religion, Psychical Research, Spiritualism, and the Occult." In *The Oxford Handbook of Modernisms*, edited by Peter Brooker, Andrzej Gasiorek, Deborah Longworth, and Andrew Thacker, 429–444. Oxford: Oxford University Press, 2010.

Lyons, Sherrie Lynne. *Species, Serpents, Spirits, and Skulls: Science at the Margins in the Victorian Age*. Albany: State University of New York Press, 2009.

McGuire, Beverley Foulks. *Living Karma: The Religious Practices of Ouyi Zhixu*. New York: Columbia University Press, 2014.

Oppenheim, Janet. *The Other World: Spiritualism and Psychical Research in England, 1850–1914*. Cambridge: Cambridge University Press, 1985.

Owen, Alex. *The Place of Enchantment: British Occultism and the Culture of the Modern*. Chicago: University of Chicago Press, 2007.

Reed, Christopher A. *Gutenberg in Shanghai: Chinese Print Capitalism, 1876–1937*. Vancouver: UBC Press, 2004.

Richardson, Robert D. *William James: In the Maelstrom of American Modernism, A Biography*. Boston: Mariner Books, 2007.

Satter, Beryl. *Each Mind a Kingdom: American Women, Sexual Purity, and the New Thought Movement, 1875–1920*. Berkeley: University of California Press, 1999.

Schäfer, Ingo. "Natural Philosophy, Physics and Metaphysics in the Discourse of Tan Sitong: The Concepts of *Qi* and *Yitai*." In *New Terms for New Ideas: Western Knowledge and Lexical Change in Late Imperial China*, edited by Michael Lackner, Iwo Amelung, and Joachim Kurtz, 257–269. Leiden: Brill, 2001.

Schumann, Matthias. "Protecting the Weak or Weeding Out the Unfit? Disaster Relief, Animal Protection and the Changing Evaluation of Social Darwinism in Japan and China." In *Protecting the Weak in East Asia: Framing, Mobilisation and Institutionalisation*, edited by Iwo Amelung et al., 21–51. Abingdon and New York: Routledge, 2018.

Schumann, Matthias. "Redemptive Societies." In *Handbook on Religion in China*, edited by Stephan Feuchtwang. Cheltenham: Edward Elgar Publishing, forthcoming.

Sharp, Lynn Luise. *Secular Spirituality: Reincarnation and Spiritism in Nineteenth Century France*. Lanham, MD: Lexington Books, 2006.

Shen, Grace Yen. "Scientism in the Twentieth Century." In *Modern Chinese Religion II, 1850–2015*, edited by Vincent Goossaert, Jan Kiely, and John Lagerwey, 91–137. Leiden: Brill, 2016.

Smith, Richard J. *Fortune-Tellers and Philosophers: Divination in Traditional Chinese Society*. Boulder: Westview Press, 1991.

Stalker, Nancy K. *Prophet Motive: Deguchi Onisaburô, Oomoto, and the Rise of New Religions in Imperial Japan*. Honolulu: University of Hawai'i Press, 2008.

Valentine, Elizabeth R. "Spooks and Spoofs: Relations between Psychical Research and Academic Psychology in Britain in the Inter-War Period." *History of the Human Sciences* 2, no. 25 (2012): 67–90.

Vinitsky, Ilya. *Ghostly Paradoxes: Modern Spiritualism and Russian Culture in the Age of Realism*. Toronto: University of Toronto Press, 2009.

Wang Chien-chuan 王見川. "Lufei Kui yu 'Shengde tan,' 'Lingxuehui': Jiantan Minchu Shanghai de lingxue fengchao 陸費逵與「盛德壇」、「靈學會」: 兼談民初上海的靈學風潮." In *Lishi, yishu yu Taiwan renwen luncong (3): 'renwu' zhuanji* 歷史、藝術與臺灣人文論叢 (3):「人物」專輯, edited by Liu Wenxing 劉文星, Xiao Baifang 蕭百方, and Wang Chien-chuan, 65–86. Taipei: Boyang wenhua shiye youxian gongsi, 2013.

Wang Chien-chuan 王見川. "Jindai Zhongguo de fuji, cishan yu 'mixin': Yi *Yinguang wenchao* wei kaocha xiansuo 近代中國的扶乩，慈善與「迷信」:以印光文鈔為考察線索." In *Xinyang, shijian yu wenhua tiaoshi: Disijie guoji Hanxue huiyi lunwenji* 信仰，實踐與文化調適:第四屆國際漢學會議論文集, edited by Kang Bao 康豹 (Paul R. Katz) and Liu Shufen 劉淑芬, 531–568. Taipei: Academia Sinica, 2013.

Wang Chien-chuan 王見川. "Qingmo Minchu Zhongguo de Jigong xinyang yu fuji tuanti: Jiantan Zhongguo Jisheng hui de youlai 清末民初中國的濟公信仰與扶乩團體:兼談中國濟生會的由來." *Minsu quyi* 民俗曲藝, no. 162 (2008): 139–169.

Wang Hongchao 王宏超. "Shenjie lingguang: Shanghai Shengde tan zhi linghun zhaoxiang huodong 神界靈光:上海盛德壇之靈魂照相活動." *Shanghai wenhua* 上海文化, no. 6 (2016): 67–76.

Watson, Burton, trans. *The Complete Works of Zhuangzi*. New York: Columbia University Press, 2013.

Wolffram, Heather. *The Stepchildren of Science: Psychical Research and Parapsychology in Germany, c. 1870–1939*. Amsterdam: Rodopi, 2009.

Wright, David. "Tan Sitong and the Ether Reconsidered." *Bulletin of the School of Oriental and African Studies, University of London* 57, no. 3 (1994): 551–575.

Yang Xinhui 楊鑫輝, ed. *Xinlixue tongshi* 心理學通史. Ji'nan: Shandong jiaoyu chubanshe, 1999.

Yoshinaga Shin'ichi 吉永進一. "Tairei to kokka: Taireidô ni okeru no kokkakan no imi 太霊と国家：太霊道における国家観の意味." *Jintai kagaku* 人体科学 17, no. 1 (2008): 35–51.

Yoshinaga Shin'ichi 吉永進一. "The Birth of Japanese Mind Cure Methods." In *Religion and Psychotherapy in Modern Japan*, edited by Christopher Harding, Iwata Fumiaki, and Yoshinaga Shin'ichi, 76–102. London: Routledge, 2015.

Zeitlin, Judith T. *Historian of the Strange: Pu Songling and the Chinese Classical Tale*. Stanford, Calif.: Stanford University Press, 1993.

Zheng Guo 鄭國. "Shanghai Lingxuehui yanjiu: Jian lun Minchu zhishijie dui kexue de renzhi jinbu 上海靈學會研究：兼論民初知識界對科學的認知進步." PhD. diss., Beijing, Guoji guanxi xueyuan, 2007.

Zheng Yayin 鄭雅尹. "Qingmo Minchu de 'gui' yu 'zhaoxiangshu': Di Baoxian *Pingdeng Ge biji* zhong de xiandaixing meiying 清末民初的「鬼」與「照相術」—狄葆賢《平等閣筆記》中的現代性魅影." *Qinghua zhongwen xuebao* 清華中文學報, no. 13 (June 2015): 229–281.

CHAPTER 5

Text and Context: A Tale of Two Masters

David Ownby

1 Introduction

This is the story of two redemptive society leaders, the texts they penned, the worlds they inhabited. The first is Xiao Changming 蕭昌明 (1897–1943),[1] a self-described god descended from heaven to save the world, who inhabited the body of a rural Sichuanese peasant born in 1897. Xiao founded a redemptive society, the Tiandejiao (天德教, Teachings of the Heavenly Virtue), in Hunan province in the 1920s and had some success in building the group into a nation-wide organization in the 1930s. His foundational text, *The Compass of Life* (人生指南), was published in 1930, and consisted of Xiao's personal glosses on the twenty Chinese characters that he considered central to classical Chinese culture and moral practice. Xiao died (or willfully returned to heaven) on Huangshan 黄山 in 1943, despairing of his inability to save the world from imminent catastrophe of war and destruction. The second is Li Yujie 李玉階 (1901–1994),[2] born to a Confucian gentleman farmer and his wife in Suzhou and educated in Shanghai at the Zhongguo gongxue (中國公學), well known as a "revolutionary" institution. Li was a student leader during the Shanghai May Fourth Movement and joined the Guomindang later the same year. He subsequently became a technocrat, working in the Ministry of Finance first under T.V. Soong 宋子文 (1894–1971) and later under H.H. Kung 孔祥

1 For an introduction to Xiao Changming in English, see Holmes Welch and Chün-Fang Yü, "The Tradition of Innovation: A Chinese New Religion" *Numen* 27, no. 2 (1980): 222–246.

2 On Li Yujie, see Liu Wenxing 劉文星, *Li Yujie xiansheng nianpu changbian* 李玉階先生年譜長編 (Nantou: Tiandijiao jiaoshi bianzuan weiyuanhui, 2001); and Tiandijiao Jiyuan jiaoshi weiyuanhui 天帝教極院教史委員會, ed., *Tiandijiao jianshi* 天帝教簡史 (Taipei: Dijiao, 2005). English-language treatments of Li Yujie and the Tiandijiao include David Palmer, "Dao and Nation: Li Yujie—May Fourth Activist, Daoist Cultivator, and Redemptive Society Patriarch in Mainland China and Taiwan," in *Daoism in the Twentieth Century: Between Eternity and Modernity*, ed. David A. Palmer and Liu Xun (Berkeley: University of California Press, 2012), 173–195; Lee Fongmao, "Transmission and Innovation: The Modernization of Daoist Inner Alchemy in Postwar Taiwan," in *Daoism in the Twentieth Century*, 196–227; and David Ownby, "Sainthood, Science, and Politics: The Life of Li Yujie," in *Making Saints in Modern China*, ed. David Ownby, Vincent Goossaert, and Ji Zhe (New York: Oxford University Press, 2017), 241–271.

 | DOI:10.1163/9789004424166_007

熙 (1881–1967). Li met Xiao Changming in Nanjing in 1930, and immediately became his disciple. He helped Xiao set up the Shanghai branch of his redemptive society in 1934 and, on Xiao's urging, left with his family for Xi'an in 1935 in order to spread the Way in China's poor and backward Northwest (he kept his government job, nonetheless, thanks to H.H. Kung's finagling). In 1937, a few days before the Japanese invasion of North China, Li quit his job and settled on nearby Huashan 華山, the famed Daoist mountain, with his wife and four sons, again at the behest of Tiandejiao gods. He remained on Huashan until the end of the war in 1945, among other things deploying his spiritual powers to prevent Japanese armies from crossing the Yellow River at Tongguan 潼關; had they crossed, the route to Chongqing and the probable demise of the Nationalist government would have been clear.

When Xiao Changming returned to heaven, the Tiandejiao gods chose Li Yujie to replace him (a choice disputed by some of Xiao's followers). Even before Xiao's death, Li had already been at work on a new scripture that was to address certain troubling aspects of Xiao's teachings which, like those of many redemptive periods of the time, carried over certain deities, discourses, and practices associated with the "White Lotus"[3] tradition, even as the same groups claimed to embrace Western religions and modern science and to follow the government's anti-superstition policies on religion. Li composed this text through collaboration with his disciple Huang Zhenxia 黃震遐 (1909–1974), his then sixteen-year old son Li Ziyi 李子弋 (1926–2016), and with the gods of the Tiandejiao tradition. The contents of this modernizing scripture were conveyed via spirit-writing, the characters appearing on a piece of yellow cloth in the rustic Tiandejiao "temple" next to Li's home on Huashan, and were transcribed by Li's son. The contents of the volume, originally entitled *A New Religious-Philosophical System* (新宗教哲學體系) and published in Xi'an in 1944 (and subsequently renamed *The Ultimate Realm* [新境界]) are remarkable for their efforts to develop a new scientific vocabulary (perhaps drawing on quantum mechanics, which I suspect Huang Zhenxia, an impressive auto-didact, might have studied) to describe the origins and functions of the universe, the earth, and man. The text also applies this new vocabulary and framework to religious phenomena: spiritual healing, spirit-writing, the physical benefits of virtuous behavior.

3 I am well aware of the problems surrounding the use of the term "White Lotus" in describing any historical iteration of what we are calling "redemptive societies" in this volume, and I do not use this term in my work. I use it here because Huang Zhenxia, a major character is the drama described in this chapter, chose "White Lotus" as a derogatory description of the teachings of Xiao Changming.

Xiao's name does not appear in *The Ultimate Realm* (although Li does make one reference to his "master") and none of Xiao's writings are cited. This was not necessarily a betrayal. Li continued to consider Xiao his master even as he became the leader of the redemptive society, which he renamed Tianrenjiao 天人教 (Teachings of Heaven and Man), and portraits of Xiao are found in Tiandijiao 天帝教 churches today in Taiwan and Los Angeles.[4] But he intended *The Ultimate Realm* to be a new foundational public text for their shared tradition, a text that would be consistent with modern, scientific values, as well as loyal to Chinese religious culture—indeed, to China's culture in general.

In the longer biography of Li Yujie that I am currently completing, I dwell considerably on the social, cultural, and political contexts surrounding Xiao and Li. As religious leaders, both Xiao and Li were necessarily social and political actors. Both interacted with many important figures in the Guomindang and in other elite circles (including Communists). Li, especially, seems to have been a gifted social butterfly.

Even while living in "isolation" on Huashan, he maintained frequent ties with such military figures as Hu Zongnan 胡宗南 (1896–1962) and Jiang Weiguo 蔣緯國 (1916–1997); civil and military personnel constantly climbed Huashan to speak with him, and he came down frequently to seek them out. Li later became a journalist on Taiwan in the 1950s, serving as the owner-editor of the *Independent Evening News* (*Zili wanbao* 自立晚報) between 1951 and 1965. In this very different context, Li became an activist for freedom of the press (although he originally became a journalist in the hopes of using the newspaper as a platform to spread his religious views), going so far as to abandon his GMD membership in protest of a new press law passed in 1958. He finally founded the Tiandijiao in 1980. Legalization followed the rescinding of martial law in 1987, and Li died in 1994. His long life, his decades-long implication in redemptive societies, the copious documentation made available by his followers, and the fact that he was something other than a guru for much of his life, allow me to put meat on the bones of redemptive society history in a way that is more difficult with most groups.

In the context of the present essay and in keeping with this volume's theme, however, I will concentrate mostly on texts, examining the way in which Xiao and Li shaped their message with an eye toward attracting followers. In Xiao's

4 Li changed the name of Xiao's original Tiandejiao ("Teachings of Heavenly Virtue") to Tianrenjiao ("Teachings of Heaven and Man") when he assumed leadership of the tradition in 1943. When he revived the group on Taiwan in the late 1970s he called it Tiandijiao ("Teachings of the Heavenly Emperor" or "Lord of the Universe Church" in the English translation used by the group). Li insisted that this was the original name of the group.

case, we have Tiandejiao texts that target the general public as well as texts delivered to converts and insiders. The difference is instructive, because the message conveyed to insiders is a familiar if "heterodox" doctrine drawing on "White Lotus" themes, while the public message seeks to assure readers (and the government) that Xiao is a man of science who eschews superstition, even as he claims great powers of spiritual healing. Li Yujie and Huang Zhenxia's efforts to modernize Xiao's teachings by removing "White Lotus" elements (Huang employs precisely this term in repeated criticisms directed at Xiao's teachings) and "scientizing" Tiandejiao doctrine are even more revealing of the tensions and ambiguities at the heart of many redemptive societies' beliefs and practices. That their efforts "failed"—in the sense that their new scripture, *The Ultimate Realm*, did not succeed in marrying modern science to traditional Chinese popular religion in an intellectually or emotionally satisfying manner—takes nothing away from the importance and the drama of the effort to reconcile the discourses of popular Chinese religion with those of the modern world.

At the same time, my impression from having done fieldwork in Taiwan with current practitioners of Li Yujie's Tiandijiao is that the important changes Li and Huang carried out at the textual level mask a broader continuity in terms of the appeal and the practice of the teachings. The appeal of Tiandijiao teachings for contemporary practitioners is a combination of access to healing powers (or more broadly, to supernormal powers), and to an experience of spirituality not offered by modern secular life, mediated through the presence of the master and the shared life of the faith community. Of course, I have not done fieldwork with Xiao Changming's pre-WWII followers, but the texts Xiao penned during this period suggest that these elements were the key to his success as well. This in turn suggests that in these cases, the foundational public texts may have less to do with religious practice as lived by adepts, and more with how the group situates itself vis-à-vis the broader political and social culture. As Fan Chun-wu's essay in this volume illustrates, production and circulation of texts were at the very center of the experience of most if not all of Republican-period redemptive societies. Masters had to produce texts, and these texts had to circulate publicly. Thus, the text must place the master and his teachings within the broader culture, establishing a brand that signals to authorities, to the broader public, and to practitioners (actual or potential) who the master is and what he has to say.

The very different social identities of the two masters examined in this essay introduced a surprising factor of discontinuity into the Tiandejiao-Tiandijiao "tradition." As a modern, educated intellectual, Li Yujie felt the need to "modernize" part of Xiao Changming's teachings. Yet this modernization was only "paper-deep," and for practitioners served as proof that they were not "backward" or "superstitious," and that their faith was relevant to the contemporary and future worlds.

2 Xiao Changming Builds a Textual Persona

Until the 1920s, Xiao Changming seems not to have produced written texts. According to his biographers,[5] he spent his early years healing, preaching, and cultivating on various sacred mountains in Sichuan and Hunan, having left home at a very young age to launch his salvational mission.[6] There are hints in his biographies that preliminary versions of his eventual "twenty characters" teachings (still an important part of today's Tiandijiao practice) formed at least part of his oral repertoire during this period; one biographer notes that in 1907 at the age of 13, while Xiao was meditating on Qingchengshan 青城山, the famous Daoist mountain close to Chengdu, he added six new characters (德廉忍公覺讓) to his original four (忠孝仁慈).[7]

It is not hard to imagine that a precocious teen-ager who preached the healing power of traditional morality, and accompanied such teachings with real-time demonstrations of his own healing abilities, might attract a following. Another redemptive society of roughly the same period, the Wanguo daodehui 萬國道德會 (Universal Morality Society), was launched in no small measure through the buzz created by the "Confucian child prodigy," Jiang Xizhang 江希張 (1907–2004) , who composed commentaries on the Confucian classics before reaching the age of ten.[8] In China, as elsewhere, youth have long been associated with purity of character and intention. If such youth are unusually literate or erudite to boot, this can only add to their status, particularly in a culture like China's which places great value on the written word. Mastery of

---

5 There are two biographies of Xiao, both written by followers in a highly hagiographical style. Pan Shuren 潘樹仁, *Lihai shengge: Xiao Dazongshi Changming chuanqi yisheng* 歷海笙歌：蕭大宗師昌明傳奇一生 (Hong Kong: Boxue, 2007); and Lu Yuding 盧禹鼎, *Xiao Changming dazongshi zhuan* 蕭昌明大宗師傳 (Taipei: printed by the author, 1973).

6 Scholars have connected Xiao's teachings with the Xiantiandao 先天道 tradition. See for example Vincent Goossaert and David A. Palmer, *The Religious Question in Modern China* (Chicago: University of Chicago Press, 2011), 100. Xiao does not self-identify as belonging to that tradition, and his biographers, who accept his self-presentation as a god descended from heaven, are not inclined to seek out the sources of his vision.

7 See Pan, *Lihai shengge*, 135.

8 For an English-language overview of the Wanguo daodehui, see Goossaert and Palmer, *The Religious Question in Modern China*, 93–97. Melissa Inouye of the University of Auckland is currently preparing a book-length study of the group.

such traditions surely qualified as one aspect of charisma, a key element in the construction of a successful redemptive society.

By the 1920s, Xiao was ready to put brush to paper and circulate his teachings in printed form. The production of written scriptures had of course long been part of Chinese religious culture, even in the late imperial "sectarian" tradition where "precious scrolls" occasionally served as evidence in police pursuit of "heterodox rebels."[9] The Republican period saw an explosion of such scriptures, including stand-alone texts that might be seen as the continuation of the "precious scroll" tradition, as well as religious journals (full of articles on various aspects of religion), flyers, leaflets, etc. This development was made possible both by the freer political conditions of post-dynastic China, as well as by advances in technology and communications; many groups (including Xiao's Tiandejiao) set up their own printing presses to print their own texts as well as other relevant or profitable materials, as indicated in several chapters of this volume. The huge influence of print culture on journalism, literature, politics, and popular culture from late Qing times forward has been explored by many scholars; the impact was surely just as important in religion.[10] No redemptive society leader worth his salt (to say nothing of a god descended from heaven) could afford not to join the competition, and Xiao Changming seems to have been no less ambitious than other leaders.[11]

Scriptures were also an important aspect of the organization of a redemptive society, which Xiao undertook at the same time he began writing. He first established the Society for the Promotion of Religious Unity (Zongjiao datong cujinshe 宗教大同促進社) in Changsha in 1921. The name of the organization was later changed to the Society for the Study of Religion and Philosophy (Zongjiao zhexue yanjiushe 宗教哲學研究社), perhaps in 1927. Xiao eventually established several Oriental Institutes of Spiritual Healing (Dongfang jingshen liaoyangyuan 東方精神療養院) to complement the Tiandejiao and the Society for the Study of Religion and Philosophy—which over time

9 On "precious scrolls," see among others Daniel L. Overmyer, *Precious Volumes: An Introduction to Chinese Sectarian Scriptures from the Sixteenth and Seventeenth Centuries* (Cambridge, MA: Harvard University Asia Center, 1999); on questions of heterodoxy, see among others Barend J. ter Haar, *The White Lotus Teachings in Chinese Religious History* (Leiden: Brill, 1992).

10 See Philip Clart and Gregory Adam Scott, eds., *Religious Publishing and Print Culture in Modern China: 1800–2012* (Boston: De Gruyter, 2015).

11 The "market" for these teachings and skills in the early Republican period has been brilliantly explored by Vincent Goossaert, "Daoists in the Modern Chinese Self-Cultivation Market: The Case of Beijing, 1850–1949," in *Daoism in the Twentieth Century: Between Eternity and Modernity*, ed. David A. Palmer and Xun Liu (Berkeley: University of California Press, 2012), 123–153.

expanded to number 46 branches in Jiangsu, Hunan, Hubei, Anhui, Zhejiang, Hebei, Jiangxi, Guangdong, Shanxi, Sichuan, and Shaanxi. All of these were the "public" (對外) face of the religion, known as Tiandejiao from the outset. Some sources credit Xiao with more than one million followers by 1923.[12]

Reading through the texts produced by Xiao and his followers during this period, we can discern at least part of the strategy deployed to attempt to attract followers and to "build a brand" in an environment that was competitive and to some degree state-regulated.[13] Some texts are clear advertisements, based particularly on Xiao's claims to powers of spiritual healing. Others—while still trying to attract followers—meet a potentially skeptical public half-way, assuming the posture of a doubting Thomas and providing answers to questions the group fears might serve as stumbling blocks. Still other texts were produced for society insiders and are full of information that is only hinted at in other texts. We begin our analysis, however, with another kind of text, one that I have dubbed the "foundational public text," written to convince the authorities and the general public that the master who composed the text has the moral and intellectual qualities necessary to merit respect and perhaps devotion.

Xiao's foundational public text is the already mentioned *The Compass of Life*. It is not Xiao's earliest publication nor, to my mind, the most interesting, but it is the scripture most identified by followers as his master work, and has been reprinted several times since its initial publication in 1930. The text consists of brief explanations and commentaries on the twenty characters Xiao considers as constituting the core of Chinese tradition—or perhaps Chinese civilization and spirituality. The characters are *zhong* (忠, loyalty), *shu* (恕, reciprocity or forgiveness), *lian* (廉, frugality or honesty, in the sense of something's being "unadorned"), *ming* (明, intelligence, transparency), *de* (德, virtue, magnanimity), *zheng* (正, uprightness), *yi* (義, righteousness), *xin* (信, trustworthiness), *ren* (忍, patience, forbearance, the capacity to endure), *gong* (公, impartiality), *bo* (博, breadth, inclusiveness), *xiao* (孝, filial piety), *ren* (仁, kindness, benevolence, empathy), *ci* (慈, mercifulness), *jue* (覺, enlightenment, the quality of being awakened), *jie* (節, restraint, modesty, temperance), *jian* (儉, thrift), *zhen* (真, genuineness), *li* (禮, propriety), and *he* (和, harmony or balance). I imagine that the text is a reworked version of oral presentations

---

12 Welch and Yü, "The Tradition of Innovation," 223.

13 Xiao's textual activities went far beyond the handful of texts analyzed here, and I make no claim that my discussion does justice to the full corpus of Xiao's writings. For an extremely valuable introduction to that corpus, see Liu Wenxing 劉文星, "*Decangjing* shumu tiyao 《德藏經》書目提要," available online at http://www.tienti.tw/node/1197.

Xiao had been giving for some years, although if that is indeed the case, the oral quality of the original talks has been largely erased in the reworking. The language of the text is quite formal, to the point that I am not sure if it would have been comprehensible to a general audience if read aloud. The formality of the scripture is surely part of what is expected of a foundational public text; it speaks to the writer's seriousness of purpose, the equivalent of an American political candidate's flag pin and three-piece suit.

As for the content of Xiao's text, each character is presented in a brief essay of some 250 to 750 characters. The essays often begin with the etymology of the character, and locate part of the profound meaning of the character in its composition. For example, Xiao points out that the character *zheng* (uprightness) is made up of the characters *yi* (一, one) and *zhi* (止, to stop), meaning that one stops once one has reached a state of oneness. This sort of analysis is of course a favorite Chinese pastime, and Xiao makes no pretense of being scholarly or original.

Following the etymology, the essays go on to elaborate on the meaning of the characters, generally by quoting classic works and adding exegetical comments. To continue with the example of the commentary on the character *zheng*, Xiao begins by quoting the *Great Learning* (大學) to the effect that *zheng* is the basis of a number of other virtues (several of which are included in Xiao's list of twenty): "A ruler rests in benevolence, a government official in respect, a child in filial piety, a father in mercy, a citizen in trust. Relations between the state and the people rest in confidence. At the basis of all of these lies one thing: uprightness" (為人君止於仁，為人臣止於敬，為人子止於孝，為人父止於慈，與國人交止於信，皆止於一也，即所以為正也).[14] He continues with another quote from the *Great Learning*, noting that uprightness is impossible for those whose hearts are full of anger, fear, evil, or anxiety. Xiao concludes on the basis of these two quotes that the ruler must himself be upright in order to make his government officials upright, which in turn will render mankind, and eventually all things, equally upright.

Just when the reader starts to think that Xiao might be making a subtle political statement, he pivots to make roughly the same point on a personal rather than a governmental level by noting that the basis of the Confucian

14 Hsiao, Chang Ming (Xiao Changming), *The Compass of Life*, trans. Chung Hing Sin, Marv Goldberg, and Jim Hollander (New Hyde Park, NY: Religion and Philosophy Research Society, 1999), 17–20. This is a bilingual edition, and I have modified the translation in accordance with my understanding of the original Chinese text. All further references are to this edition.

admonition to "cultivate oneself, order one's family, govern the country and bring order to the world" (修身，齊家，治國，平天下) is also uprightness, here defined as being without selfishness or wicked intentions. A person who embraces uprightness should also practice decorum, Xiao insists, and cites the example of Confucius who refused to sit on a mat that was improperly positioned or to eat food that was improperly served.

Xiao notes nonetheless that in the "last days" we are living in prior to the turning of the kalpa (末劫), the upright are often cheated and denounced. This is because, as part of the coming endtimes, creatures from the "four types of birth and six realms of transmigration" (四生六道) have been reincarnated as human beings. Over the past several hundred years, Xiao continues, the heavy presence of these creatures has threatened the primacy of uprightness and driven the righteous into seclusion.

Yet all is not lost. If we begin with personal cultivation, Xiao argues, we can transform our essential, upright *qi* (精正之氣) into original upright *qi* (原正之氣), and our original upright *qi* into indestructible upright *qi* (剛正之氣). Indestructible upright *qi* can face down heterodox demonic *qi* (邪魔之氣) and bring mankind back from the brink. Xiao makes the same point several times in a variety of ways, finally noting that if man cultivates uprightness sufficiently, he will become a god, who is one with the void and with the Way. Xiao admits that the logic behind this process is not immediately obvious, but identifies it with his healing method, which requires no medicine but functions according to "feeling and response" (感應), a concept basic to Chinese religion and which Xiao adapted to the purposes of his spiritual healing, as explained in more detail below. Xiao ends on a less optimistic note, however, suggesting that while salvation of the world is possible, there are many false teachers abroad whose teachings are not upright. The key is to examine the teacher's heart, testing him for sincerity and uprightness. Obviously, Xiao believes that he will pass the text, but does not say so explicitly. Bragging in a foundational public text is not upright, it would seem.

Xiao's gloss on *zheng* stands as a fairly good summary of the overall message of *The Compass of Life*, and indeed of Xiao's teachings as a whole, combining references to ancient virtues with self-cultivation, spiritual healing, and references to deviance and the apocalypse. However, most of Xiao's explanations for his twenty characters are more anodyne than that for *zheng*, and reading his gloss on *zheng* in isolation makes *The Compass of Life* seem more powerful and coherent than it in fact is. Xiao's gloss on the character *zhong*, "loyalty," for example, is more typical of the general tone of the volume (his discussion of "filial piety" is similarly predictable):

> The Chinese characters "center" and "heart" combine to form the character *zhong* (loyalty or faithfulness). Thereby, *zhong* means "to do your utmost to keep your heart unbiased" upon making a decision. During the imperial period, the official who spoke out directly against the ruler's errors was a *zhong* and straightforward official. The official who did not hesitate to sacrifice himself in times of national calamity was a *zhong* and virtuous official. Officials like these acted to preserve the lives of the people and institutions of the country, and did not think in terms of their own interests. Our Tiandejiao uses *zhong* as the first character of our doctrine. People must exhaust their loyalty toward the country, toward family, toward friends and toward all manner of things before they can genuinely consider themselves human beings.
>
> I have observed that plants and trees are *zhong* to the four seasons, and that animals are *zhong* to their offspring. Heaven and earth are vast, but remain *zhong* to climate. The sun and the moon are bright, but are *zhong* to day and night. It is only man, cunning and full of guile, who cannot exhaust his authentic heart/mind in his dealings with friends and worldly affairs. Alas, man is beyond comparison to heaven and earth, the sun and the moon, yet how can he be inferior to plants, trees, and animals?
>
> 中心為忠，中者，盡其忠正之心之謂也。當君主時代，君有過則犯顏值諫，是謂忠直之臣。國有事則殺戮不辭，是謂忠節之臣。斯二者，無非保全民生，顧全國體，而不以個人之利害為利害也。今吾德教以忠字為首，蓋人必忠於國，忠於家，忠於朋友，忠於事事物物，而後可以謂之人也。
>
> 吾觀草木之類，忠於四時，禽獸之類，忠於卵育。天地之大，忠於氣候，日月之明，忠於晝夜。惟人最奸巧，最詭詐，交朋待友，處世接物，不能盡其中正之心。噫，人固非天地日月所可以比，而何草木禽獸之不如也。[15]

Most of *The Compass of Life* sounds just such conventional themes, as one would perhaps expect of a foundational public text. True, there are mentions of Christian and Islamic virtues in *The Compass of Life*, but these references function essentially as gestures that allow Xiao to present himself as modern and ecumenical; mentions of science are similarly cursory.

In terms of overall structure, the essays on the twenty characters appear to have been written independently. There are discursive links between some expositions, less because Xiao sought to put together a coherent text and more

15 Xiao, *Compass*, 1.

because there is a certain amount of inevitable repetition in discussions of basic moral values and orientations.

Consequently, the volume as a whole displays little thematic or narrative development, although it is not incoherent. *The Compass of Life* is quite impersonal, as well, and reveals little if anything about Xiao's background or personality (although "charismatic" photographs are included in more recent editions of the scripture, as were portrait photos of Duan Zhengyuan and other redemptive society leaders, as discussed in Fan Chun-wu's chapter in the present volume). Nor are supernormal powers discussed in any detail in this text beyond scattered references to the healing power of traditional culture. For people already drawn to Xiao and his teachings, the text is presumably meant to supplement Xiao's self-presentation as a healer by placing his powers and his charisma within a familiar, if threatened (by modernity), universe of spiritual discourse, and to identify Xiao, their master, as someone important enough to publish a book of his teachings. It was surely hoped that those readers who encountered Xiao for the first time through *The Compass of Life* would be intrigued enough to explore further. The wide popularity of redemptive societies during this period suggests there was considerable hunger for comfortable, familiar messages grounded in the sort of discourses denounced by May Fourth radicals, even if the eventual Communist victory has convinced many that the radicals won. The very blandness of much of *The Compass of Life* may have been an important selling point; "comfort food" is rarely adventurous or spicy.

As a foundational public text, *The Compass of Life* aimed to project an authoritative and philosophical voice, a voice somewhat disengaged from the huckstering pursuit of new members (as well as from claims that might seem too outlandish). Other public texts address the audience more directly and make claims that are clearly designed for the purposes of recruitment. Two such texts deal with Xiao's claims to great powers of spiritual healing, which may have been more appealing to new converts than Xiao's mastery of traditional culture.

The first text is "Explanation of Spiritual Healing" (精神治療解說), published in 1929.[16] This short text repeats many of the themes already discussed in the context of *The Compass of Life*, but in a more direct, coherent fashion, which is only natural since Xiao is discussing a single topic. Once again, Xiao's language and discourse are wholly rooted in familiar cosmologies of ancient

16 See Qin Shude 秦淑德, *Decangjing: Tiande lüzang, yibulü* 德藏經： 天德律藏，一部律 (Tainan: Tiandeshengjiao, 1986). The text in question is in volume 2, entitled "Xiuchi zhinan 修持指南," 14a–18b.

China: "The Way is the beginning of heaven and earth, and heaven and earth reside in the Way so as to give birth to mankind. Heaven functions according to yin-yang and the five elements, which transform to become the ten thousand things, while the earth becomes manifest to host the ten thousand things" (夫道為天地之始，天地載道一生人，天地以陰陽五行，化生萬物，地乃成像，而載萬物). The primary narrative developed in this text is one describing the decline from original innocence and health. Primitive man lived in caves, had few desires, and as a result was healthy and long-lived. Later on, the sage kings taught primitive man the bases of civilization, including herbal medicine. But with the development of civilization man lost his original purity. "We admire only material things, and are blinded by material desires" (專尚物質，為物慾所蔽) for physical pleasure, profit, luxury. As a result, man has lost his original balance, and with it, his health.

Xiao's solution was, unsurprisingly, his twenty-characters teachings, which embody the upright *qi* of heaven and earth. "There is no illness that this cannot cure, no person that this cannot transform" (以此治病，無病不瘳，以此化人，無人不化). Xiao claims to have been approached by more than 100,000 people over the past few years for health reasons, and to have helped more than half of them. Promoting the twenty-characters teaching, he insists, will allow him "to heal man's body and mind, and to reverse the trends of the times. When morality flourishes times will be harmonious; when ritual and integrity are sufficient the country will be well managed and families orderly. The twenty characters are the mother of the sacred, the foundation of the gods" (治人身心，挽回世運，道德興而時和世泰，利益足則國治家齊。廿字為聖賢之母，佛仙之基). The text is studded with references to traditional Chinese sources and medical figures, as well as with less frequent references to Jesus and Mohammad.

A second, very similar text, entitled "Simple Explanation of Spiritual Healing" (精神療養淺解), was published four years later in 1933 and repeats many of the same themes.[17] The text was written not by Xiao himself but by She Zixian 佘子誠, one of Xiao's close disciples known particularly for his medical knowledge. The text—which circulated with other Tiandijiao materials even if it was not written by the master himself—adds new information drawn from biomedical discussions of disease and healing, pointedly suggesting that Xiao and his society were aware of modern developments. A passage from the first section of the document entitled "Principles of the organization of the human body" (人體組織之原理) sets the tone:

17 See Qin Shude, *Decangjing*, volume 2, 22a–33a.

> From a scientific point of view, the reason that people can exist in the world is seen to be nothing other than elements and cells that receive material nourishment and thus are born and exist. From this point of view, the emphasis is on the formed [in contrast to the "formless"] and the material, but a purely material explanation cannot explain human existence.
>
> 一個人在這地面上何以能生存，在科學上講起來，不外元素細胞，得物質滋養以生存。此是重在有形質的方面，僅此物質一方面，一個人決不能生存。

The text goes on to supplement the biomedical view of human life with a discussion of *qi* 氣, *shen* 神, and *jing* 精, drawn from traditional Chinese medical discourse and Daoist *neidan* 內丹 practice: without *qi* our lungs cannot breathe; without *shen* "a person's body has no master and loses consciousness, seeing nothing, hearing nothing, tasting nothing" (全體無主宰，失了知覺，目無見，耳無聞，食不知味); without *jing* the movement of the various body systems is compromised. The author subsequently repeats notions we have already encountered concerning the power of desire to produce dangerous imbalances. He further acknowledges the explanatory power of modern germ theory, but insists nonetheless that:

> Our method of healing does not use medicine, which views and heals man as if he were a completely corporal, material being. The reason for this is that the organization of the human body is not solely, as science says, a matter of material elements, but is instead a function of spiritual miracles. Living in this environment, if we treat illness with purely material means, taking the [material] body as the object of healing, ignoring all important elements, this will not work, and is the same as waiting to die. Our method of spiritual healing completes what has been missing in all past healing methods. Our method is particularly efficacious for those chronic diseases that medicines and other remedies have a hard time curing.
>
> 這個治病的方法，不是用藥品，把人做一個完全肉體的物質去治病，因為人體的組織，不僅是由科學上所謂元素物質而成，是由精神靈妙的動作，生活在這大空氣的當中。如果有病但知用物質之末，把肉體做本位來治療，將一切為主要的成分丟開，是不能收效的，惟有待死而已。這個精神治療的方法，是補向來一切的缺點，尤其對於藥石所難奏效的慢性病，收效甚速。

Healing is accomplished through "emotional connection" (*gantongli* 感通力), She continues in a core explanatory passage (elaborating on the principle of *ganying* evoked by Xiao in *The Compass of Life*):

> If person A has a certain spiritual notion with regard to person B, the function of emotional connection will necessarily influence the brain to emit a reaction that will be transmitted by wave power, thus reaching B. The heart is the mechanism that controls this emission, and intention is what governs the transmission of wave energy. It is exactly like a transmitter which, without electricity, cannot emit and thus cannot transmit wave energy. The human body possesses electricity—everyone knows that—this is why how people transmit energy. Of course, B must be open to the idea of receiving energy from A. This kind of spiritual healing is not like hypnosis. In our method of spiritual healing, as long as the recipient is completely sincere, and truly believes with no doubt, then the healing will work.
>
> 如甲對乙起一個精神的觀念，這感通的作用，必直接影響於腦的分子，發生反應。這精神的發射出來，必隨這分子的波動力傳播，可及於乙。這司發射的機關就是心，這隨波動力傳播的就是意，就如現在的播音機一樣，缺了電氣，他就發射不出來，也就不可能隨空中的波動力傳播了。人的身體上有電，這是大家所公認的。他能以發射傳播，就是這個道理。但甲方來播送這種觀念，而乙方拒抗不受，也是不能感通的，就同有了播音機播送出來，沒有收音機來收，一樣的無效。所以人與人的感通，必得雙方有誠意的觀念。與催眠術不同。只要受者具有十分誠意，確信無疑，就可發生效驗。

At the very end of this text, the purpose of which is to illustrate that he is a master of both Western and Chinese theories of illness and healing, she returns to a discussion of the character *zheng* (uprightness), which recalls his master's discussion in *The Compass of Life*:

> The way of cultivating the heart lies squarely in *zheng*/uprightness. To rectify one's heart, one must first make his intentions sincere. To make his intentions sincere, he must first extend his knowledge. Extending knowledge requires investigating things. The way of investigating things is to comprehend the origin of heaven, earth, and the ten thousand things ... The heart, moreover, must rest in uprightness. As it is said: if the heart is upright, then the *qi* is nourished; if the *qi* is nourished, then balance is

> achieved; if balance is achieved, then there is no illness. This is how we heal ourselves. This is how we heal others. This is called spiritual healing.
>
> 修心之道，就在正而已矣。欲正其心者，必先誠其意，欲誠其意者，必先致其知。致知在格物。這格物的道理，就是要明悉天地萬物的始源……這個心又非放在正中不可。所謂心正則氣養，氣養則和，和則無病矣。以此自治，以此治人，是謂精神治療。

In sum, these spiritual healing texts seek to establish links between Master Xiao's philosophical pronouncements and his claims to healing powers. The object of the texts is to suggest that Xiao's healing methods are not only compatible with modern science but in many instances superior to it: modern science heals only disease; Xiao's methods heal the entire body—indeed the social and national bodies. Of course, the specific methods Xiao employs to heal disease are not outlined, and discussion is confined to their operating principles and their connection to Xiao's larger philosophical vision. The goal of the text is to attract members, not to give away the store.[18]

Similar themes appear in *Questions and Answers Concerning the Society for the Promotion of Religious Unity* (宗教大同促進社問答, hereafter *Q&A*), a somewhat different public text that is addressed to prospective members who may also be skeptical about some of Xiao's claims. The form of this text is loosely based on Western catechisms and has been widely used by many Chinese religious groups in the modern period, although Xiao's text does not address believers, but prospective believers. The text was published in

---

18 As for Xiao's precise measures of spiritual healing, Li Yujie's wife, Guo Chunhua 過純華, recalled her initiation into the Tiandejiao, in the process of which Xiao Changming had the initiates kneel down and receive a formless miracle drug (無形靈丹妙藥) in the palm of their outstretched hands. He subsequently wrote the characters for "golden light" (金光) in cinnabar on their palms as well, and ordered the initiates to lick the cinnabar off their hands and rub them together, after which the golden light would be absorbed by the "third eye" (性竅) found between the eyebrows. Xiao then had the initiates extend their three central fingers so as to receive a "formless golden needle" (無形金針), after which everyone sat down and recited the twenty characters. Xiao explained that the golden light and the golden needle were part of spiritual healing and that he had taught them this "expedient method" (方便法門) so that they could save the world. Elsewhere, Guo associated these powers with what she called "palm light" (掌光). On yet another occasion, Xiao transmitted to her methods for reversing unjust punishment and relieving karma (解冤釋業), and for saving those in hell (渡幽濟冥). See Liu Zhishan 劉至善, "Tianren qigong lishi yan'ge 天人炁功歷史沿革," available online at http://www.tienti.tw/node/993.

1926 when Xiao's redemptive society went by the name of the Society for the Promotion of Religious Unity.[19]

Although *Q&A* begins with a general introduction to Xiao's teachings, emphasizing the need for the unity of all religions (a theme very common in most redemptive societies but less emphasized, if still present, in Xiao's *The Compass of Life*), the body of the text is composed of 53 questions and answers addressing various aspects of Xiao's teaching and practice. Almost half of the questions—26 out of 53—challenge Xiao's claims to possess healing powers. This suggests that Xiao saw such claims as central to his teachings, as well as a possible stumbling block to the audience he was trying to reach, presumably including educated people like Li Yujie. The questions—which I assume Xiao or his assistants thought up—are often extremely direct. Examples include: "Aren't the twenty characters just a way of living? How can they cure illness" (二十字不過為做人之法，為什麼可以治病呢)? "In the modern scientific era, everything has a material base. Yet your society preaches empty nonsense. Isn't absurd to want to cure people in such a way" (現時科學時代， 皆以物質為本，而貴社空空洞洞，與人治病，豈不荒謬歟)? "When did your society's healing methods originate? By whom were they handed down" (貴社之治病方法始於何時，又為何人所傳)? "How did your society's founder come up with the idea of healing without medicine" (貴社創始人，何以感想到不藥治病)? "What fees are required to join and learn to heal illness? How long must one practice" (皈依學診病，要多少贊敬，要練習多少時間呢)? Clearly, whoever composed *Q&A* sought to anticipate doubters' questions.

The answers are often less direct and straightforward than the questions, at least from the point of view of a non-practitioner. To a question asking for a scientific explanation of the healing power of Xiao's twenty characters, the answer is: "Our healing is based precisely in science. Modern science relies entirely on evidence, and our society provides this proof, openly" (我們治病，正是為科學而發生。現在科學，無不講求證據。吾社以此證明，而發揚光大吾社也). Instead of explaining how spiritual healing works, Xiao says, in effect, "Watch me heal, then judge for yourself," which is something less than an explanation. Responding to another question regarding the scientific basis of his healing practices, Xiao's answer relativizes science rather than "scientizing" his practices:

> Modern scientists manufacture airplanes, weapons, poison gas, and death rays. These have all been invented via research. We heal illness through the use of [yellow] cloth and the ash of yellow paper. This is also the fruit

19 The text is available online at http://tainde.blogspot.ca/2008/08/004_8536.html.

> of research … Bamboo is the raw material out of which yellow paper is made; bamboo stems are woven together in parallel fashion, and take liquid nourishment from the earth and transmit it through the nodes to make leaves. Its flavor is sweet, its *qi* cool, its function relieves "heat poison." Burning the petition made of the paper extracts its original essence which then enters into the bloodstream to cool overheated blood.
>
> Cotton is the original material out of which cloth is made. Cotton takes its nourishment from the soil which it converts into cotton blossoms through its special biological traits. Its nature is warm and its essence light. Using it in the place of medicine, it warms the cold to make it humid, releasing neutralizing *qi* and expanding the veins. In our organization, spirit is our formless method, and as for "formed" things we employ cloth and paper in the place of medicine.… In modern Germany people use cotton seed pills to cure all sorts of illnesses and as an aid in fasting. If imported materials can heal illness and aid in fasting, then why can't Chinese materials do the same? We have been curing illnesses in this way for more than thirty years. There is proof everywhere. Just ask those around you.
>
> 現在科學家造飛機、大砲、毒瓦斯、死光等，皆從研究而發明。我們以布與黃表灰治病，亦從研究而來。茲將黃表與布之性能略一言之。黃表之原料為竹，竹莖為平行纖維組合而成，引地中養液，從茹層通過結節，上達枝葉。其味甘，其氣清涼，功能平虛熱，用表化灰取其原性，可以入脈清解血熱也。
>
> 又大布之原料為棉花之絮，棉由土中攝取養料，以特殊生理化為棉絨。其性溫煖，其體輕揚，用之代藥，溫寒化濕，俾中和之氣，足以充達脈絡。本社治病，無形之法以精神，有形之藥用布表代，此乃創始人所研究精神與物質并用之治病法。近代德國人士，用棉子丸，以治一切雜症，或用以辟穀。舶來品能治病、辟穀，豈中國貨而不可哉？我們以之治病，已逾三十年矣，處處皆有證明，處處皆有證據，先生問諸過來人便知。

The authors of *Q&A* are clearly aware of the politically sensitive nature of Xiao's undertaking. They repeatedly deny that his teachings—even those dealing with healing via the twenty characters—are superstitious, and insist on their scientific basis. They note that the teachings are in accord with the law. They insist that Xiao does not ask for money for healing, "as many other groups do." They defend his society from charges of being "too Buddhist," insisting on the ecumenical and universal nature of his teachings (although many of Xiao's religious references are indeed to Buddhism). The skepticism expressed in many of the questions in Xiao's catechism suggests that Xiao and his lieutenants were aware that modern science constituted a challenge to these traditions, but they chose to attempt to co-opt or circumvent scientific challenges to claims of spiritual healing powers in a grand synthesis that promised health and wholeness to sincere disciples and their families.

In the scriptures we have examined to this point, Xiao Changming has played his cards pretty close to his chest. By contrast, *The Master of the Single Pre-Heavenly Qi Discusses the Scriptures* (一炁宗主經談, hereafter, *Master*) is a very different kettle of fish.[20] This text is a transcription of lectures given by Xiao Changming to his eighteen true lords (i.e., his eighteen most loyal and capable lieutenants) during a 100-day long retreat in Shanghai in 1934. The retreat followed the very successful and highly mediatized establishment of the Shanghai branch of Xiao's Society for the Study of Religion and Philosophy. Indeed, the opening of the Shanghai branch, attended by Shanghai mayor Wu Tiecheng 吳鐵城 (1888–1953), Guomindang luminaries like Pan Gongzhan 潘公展 (1895–1975), and Shanghai cultural and business heavy-weights like Wang Yiting 王一亭 (1867–1938), and Wang Xiaolai 王曉籟 (1886–1967), reminds us that textual production was only one way for a redemptive society leader to build his persona, and perhaps not the fastest or most effective. In any event, Xiao's lectures at this retreat were transcribed by one of the 18 true lords, and eventually published as *Master*. If it is not clear to what extent this scripture circulated at the time, Li Yujie was in attendance, meaning that he was considered an insider worthy of the "secret" knowledge imparted during these talks—indeed, as one of Xiao's closest disciples since taking him as master in 1930, Li may well have already known everything Xiao revealed during the retreat.

What was revealed had little to do with Xiao's basic vision, which remains basically unchanged vis-à-vis the more public texts just discussed. His professed goal remains that of saving the world from imminent disaster, which "is not like saving someone from flood or fire, which requires merely a single intervention. My twenty characters are the right medicine, the right doctor. With this we can save heaven and earth and create sages, worthies, immortals, and buddhas, and thereby save mankind" (非如救火水，只救一時也，我教之廿字，即良藥良醫，可救天地，而造成聖賢仙佛，以此救人).[21] Yet as his reference to the "creation of sacred gods" suggests, what is different about the

20 Wang Diqing 王笛卿, *Decangjing: Yiqi zongzhu tanjing* 德藏經：一炁宗主談經 (Tainan: Zhongguo jingshen liaoyang yanjiuhui 中國精神療養研究會, 1985).

21 Wang Diqing, *Decangjing: Yiqi zongzhu tanjing*, vol. 1, 6b.

Master text is that Xiao largely discards the somewhat secular pose assumed in his other writings, and imbeds his teachings in a landscape very familiar to anyone versed in Chinese popular religion. Xiao's following remarks about "superstition" are quite revealing of his attitude toward secularism and toward government policy: "In today's society, when someone talks about the gods, this is often considered superstition. What I am talking about is not superstition. Superstition refers to something where there is no way to prove its validity. When I talk about the gods, I am talking about myself" (今社會上談到神字，即認為迷信，吾言則為非迷信，所云迷信者，因無法證據也，所言神者，即我也).[22]

First let us look at Xiao's vocabulary and language. The 1985 edition of *Master* comes in three volumes. The titles of the volumes are "Primal Chaos 混元章," "Heaven and Man are One 天人合一章," and "Entering the Dusty World 入塵章." The chapters of the "Primal Chaos" volume are: "Primal Chaos," "Leaving the Dragon Flower [Assembly] for the First Time 龍華初別章," "Cutting Open [the Primal Chaos] 分闢章," "The Establishment of the Five Religions 五教鼎立章," "Correct Enlightenment 正覺章," and "Opening the Mystery 啟玄章." The chapters of the other volumes are similar. Throughout *Master*, the language employed is what one would expect, given the volume and chapter headings. There is much discussion of cosmology and the origin of the universe:

> Primordial *qi* 炁 is the true-yang *qi* 真陽之氣 of the former heavens. Prior to the creation of heaven and earth, the *qi* of the primordial chaos was true-yang *qi*. This *qi* contained the formless mysteries of heaven, earth, yin and yang, with true-yang predominating and true-yin present in lesser proportions, representing *qian* 乾 [male principle] and *kun* 坤 [female principle]. When form and substance evolved, earth, water, fire and wind were contained within [this *qi*] … all of which evolved out of primordial *qi*.
>
> 炁者，先天真陽之氣也，未有天地以前，混沌時之氣乃真陽，此炁含有天地陰陽無形奧妙，真陽居下，上者乃乾，下者乃坤，有形有象，更有地水火風藏之期間……俱從一炁所生。[23]

22 Wang Diqing, *Decangjing: Yiqi zongzhu tanjing*, vol. 1, 7a.

23 Wang Diqing, *Decangjing: Yiqi zongzhu tanjing*, vol. 1, 18b.

Another example:

> The *sanyuan* are the formless *wuxing*, the limitless *wuji*, and the ultimate *taiji*. The formless is vast and dark, the limitless has form, and the ultimate is in the middle. Since the Yellow Emperor defeated Chiyou, the *sanyuan* engaged in mutual destruction, out of which were born yin and yang and the five elements. Out these constraints developed the human planning for clothing, food, and shelter, as well as basic envies and desires. Thus the strong abused the weak and at some point morality was no longer practiced.
>
> 三元者，乃無形、無極、太極是也。無形渺冥，無極有形，中為太極。自軒轅戰勝蚩尤，尚互相殘殺。因陰陽判，五行分，受其拘束。為謀衣食住，而生貪嗔痴者，於是以強凌弱，漸無道德。[24]

To me, such statements read like variations on themes in basic Chinese cosmology; I have no idea if Xiao is attempting to innovate. What seems important in this context is that these statements are much more abstruse, more willfully mysterious than what we generally find in the more public texts discussed above, although there is admittedly some overlap.

Master also contains a good deal of poetry, which is not found in the other texts discussed above. All chapters begin with several lines of verse, which are (generally) explained in the following chapter. For example, the "[Heavenly] Palaces Save the World from the Kalpa 分殿挽劫章" chapter in volume 2 begins with four lines of seven-character rhyming verse: "81 halls and 72 palaces; my desire is that all the worthies establish great merit; we will save the living beings and restore their original nature; and will together reach the opposite shore where our joy will be without end" (八十一殿七二宮，我願諸尊立大功，挽回眾生復本性，同登彼岸樂無窮). In addition, while most of *Master* is written in fairly straightforward prose, half-way between classical and modern, the text is also punctuated with poems and spoken texts of a variety of forms and styles. Many of these are spoken passages by various gods, including Xiao Changming in a variety of personae, in four-character, five-character, or seven-character verse, sometimes rhyming, sometimes not. Some of these are identified as Buddhist hymns (讚) or gatha (偈/頌), others as songs (歌), others as sermons (言法).

---

24 Wang Diqing, *Decangjing: Yiqi zongzhu tanjing*, vol. 1, 22b.

These spoken passages grow organically out of the major motif of the book, which is the meeting of gods in heaven to discuss interventions to save the world from the imminent turning of the kalpa. Many of the meetings are called Dragon Flower Assemblies (龍華會) and are attended by a bewildering variety of gods—including but not limited to those of the White Lotus sectarian tradition. Much of the discussion is predictably bureaucratic, as gods throw their weight around and order other gods to carry out certain tasks, or praise other gods for a job well done. Other discussions are more explanatory: the origin and decline of the universe, and of virtue, are expounded upon many times, often in verse. The discussions and debates are extremely lengthy and repetitive, and littered with the names and descriptions of the gods, their palaces, their assistants. A representative passage might be the following, which is only the beginning of a narrative that goes on for several pages in the same vein:

> The Qiande Dharma King Buddha received the order from the Formless Ancient Buddha and the Unborn Holy Mother to lead the Dragon Flower Assembly. The Dīpaṃkara (Lamp-lighting) Buddha helped him. The Qiande Dharma King Buddha sat on the Golden Dharma Light throne, and, emitting a limitless golden light … together with 488 Heavenly Dragon God Generals, chanted [as follows] …
>
> 乾德法王佛，承受無形古佛無生聖母之命，為龍華會之主。然燈佛輔之，乾德法王佛即於金光法座之上，用無量無邊之金光，四百八十八部天龍神將……而作偈曰……[25]

One important purpose of the repetition of such narratives is the illustration of Xiao Changming's role as a fellow god; indeed the entire third volume, "Entering the Dusty World 入塵章," is given over to this autobiographical theme (which appears elsewhere in *Master* as well), and recounts Xiao's multiple descents to earth, his returns to heaven, his discussions with the gods, his encounters with the gods' representatives on earth, and his interventions to save mankind. This unambiguous claim to be a god descended from the heavens does not appear in Xiao's texts discussed above. In those public texts, Xiao is hardly modest, and makes claims to possess great healing powers, but we find no clear claim to divinity beyond very general assertions concerning the abstract unity of heaven and man. One suspects that such claims might have sounded "superstitious" in the social and political context in which Xiao was

25 Wang Diqing, *Decangjing: Yiqi zongzhu tanjing*, vol. 1, 43a.

attempting to build his society, even if the notion that man can become a sage or even a god through cultivation is hardly a radical notion in popular Chinese religious culture.

A final element that appears in *Master* but not in the other texts already discussed is clear evidence of Xiao's association with the "old mother" and with "White Lotus" sectarian tradition. The central role of the Unborn Holy Mother is one indication;[26] current Tiandijiao practitioners, who have inherited the same god, consider the name to be a variation of the more common Unborn Venerable Mother (無生老母), a deity worshipped by other redemptive societies, including Yiguandao 一貫道. The Unborn Holy Mother is far from the only god in Xiao's text—and it is not clear that she is the most important god—but other elements often associated with the far from unitary "sectarian tradition" appear as well. We find for example the image of the primordial "seed people" (先天種子) who fell from heaven to earth and are now in need of salvation.[27] Elsewhere they are referred to as the 92 million original souls to be saved,[28] language that is repeated in the texts of other redemptive societies and spirit-writing groups.[29] The familiar apocalyptic schema involving three kalpas (三期浩劫) and associated gods appears frequently in *Master*,[30] although the names of the kalpas seem to be somewhat new: the first kalpa is the "dragon drought kalpa" (龍旱劫), associated with the god Patriarch of the Way of Vast Harmony (Hongjun Daozu 鴻鈞道祖, identified as the master of Taishang Laojun 太上老君, Yuanshi Tianzun 元始天尊, and Tongtian Jiaozhu 通天教主, and hence originally part of the Daoist tradition); the second kalpa is the "red sheep kalpa" (紅羊劫) (obviously a variation on the more common "red sun kalpa" [紅陽劫]), associated with the Lamp-lighting Patriarch 燃燈道祖; and the third kalpa is the Yankang kalpa (延康劫, *yankang* appears to be a Daoist term meaning "kalpa"), and the associated deity is the Maitreya Buddha 彌勒佛 (it does not appear that Xiao is claiming to be the Maitreya himself). The general idea of the kalpa is mentioned in the public texts discussed above, but technical details and the names of the gods associated with the kalpas

26 Cao Xinyu informed me in a personal communication that this deity is fairly widespread in Sichuan.

27 Wang Diqing, *Decangjing: Yiqi zongzhu tanjing*, vol. 2, 1a; see also vol. 2, 14b.

28 Wang Diqing, *Decangjing: Yiqi zongzhu tanjing*, vol. 2, 24b.

29 For two quick online examples see http://www.holyheart.com.tw/holybooks/mainroad/b18lightup/bligupcont21.htm http://www.qztao.url.tw/ymqp/ymqp20.htm.

30 See for example Wang Diqing, *Decangjing: Yiqi zongzhu tanjing*, vol. 2, 13b.

are not provided. The "Cloud City"[31] (雲城) is evoked as an image of paradise: "Now the Yankang kalpa is approaching, and we must organize the great Cloud City meeting so as to save the original seed people. The good will be saved, and the bad destroyed. With the deployment of this great method we will transform the 92 [million] original souls" (今延康已臨，同組雲城大會，度濟原來種子，有善皆度，無善皆滅，從此法門大開，化回九二原靈).[32]

In other words, in addition to whatever else he was teaching, Xiao Changming imparted to his eighteen true lords a version of the White Lotus sectarian message, a message considered heterodox both by the late imperial dynasties and by the Guomindang government. Nothing in the text allows us to gauge what might have been the reaction of the true lords, many of whom were GMD members, government officials, or military figures. Xiao offers no apologies for "heterodoxy" in his lectures, no attempts to modernize or scientize or otherwise whitewash White Lotus discourse. As already mentioned, such high-level disciples may well have already heard the message, rendering "apologies" unnecessary, although the apparent disconnect between their private and public lives still strikes the modern reader as curious.

And perhaps all they heard was a fiery, devoted preacher, as suggested in the following passage from Master: "When people talk about the Dao, they talk about it in a passive way, but in fact that Dao is a positive thing … and as a positive force … if one man puts it into practice, millions will follow" (人言道乃消極，而道乃積極之事……積極者……一人行之，千百萬人效之).[33]

3 Li Yujie's *Ultimate Realm*

It is not clear when or if Li Yujie, May Fourth activist, GMD member, and high-ranking civil servant, became troubled by the White Lotus elements in his master's teachings. Throughout his life, Li seemed largely untroubled by contradictions. As noted above, Li became a fervent disciple of Xiao Changming after their first meeting in 1930. Even if he did not learn of these elements until the Shanghai retreat in 1934—which seems to me unlikely—he continued to follow Xiao's counsel, abandoning Shanghai for Xi'an in 1935, and spending the

31 Wang Diqing, *Decangjing: Yiqi zongzhu tanjing*, vol. 3, 7a; the same language can be found in Susan Naquin, *Millenarian Rebellion in China: The Eight Trigrams Uprising of 1813* (New Haven: Yale University Press, 1976), 13–14.

32 Wang Diqing, *Decangjing: Yiqi zongzhu tanjing*, vol. 2, 24b.

33 Wang Diqing, *Decangjing: Yiqi zongzhu tanjing*, vol. 1, 6a.

war period on Huashan. When Xiao Changming died in 1943, it was White Lotus gods that appointed Li his successor. These same gods appear in Tiandijiao texts today, most of which are produced via spirit-writing, and these spirit-writing texts resemble in many details Xiao's talks to his lieutenants at the 1934 retreat.[34]

Nonetheless, while on Huashan, Li Yujie decided that his faith needed a new public foundational text (even if Xiao's *Compass of Life* contained no White Lotus elements either). The history of this decision is not altogether clear. In late 1936, Li had already discussed with other Tiandejiao cadres their collective doubts concerning the Tiandejiao's need for a "central theory." They worried that the twenty characters and the promise of spiritual healing might not be enough to attract the well-educated elite.[35] The project may have been fueled by Li's ambition, as well, although this is pure speculation.[36] He appears to have been by far the most successful of Xiao's 18 true lords. While in Xi'an, he used his many party and government contacts to spread Xiao's religion, apparently completely openly. He and Shaanxi Governor Shao Lizi 邵力子 (1882–1967) seem to have had a genuine friendship and complicity that shielded Li and his local Tiandijiao even from central government intervention. In 1937, government authorities shut down the spiritual healing institutes set up by the Tiandejiao, accusing them of practicing superstition. Only Li Yujie was allowed to continue publicly—because Shao Lizi essentially refused to follow orders from Nanjing. This left Li as the most effective Tiandejiao leader in the country, perhaps adding urgency to his notion that the faith required a new charter.

In fact, I suspect that Li Yujie's *The Ultimate Realm*, the new foundational public text, would not have been written in the way it was without Huang Zhenxia, one of Li's disciples, who spent many months with Li on Huashan. Huang seems to have been a true believer and a devoted disciple, and at the same time very skeptical of Xiao Changming and everything that smacked of the "White Lotus." He was also a very quick study and a facile writer, which may well account for the scientific language that pervades *The Ultimate Realm*. The story of the modernizing of Xiao Changming's Tiandejiao thus begins with Huang Zhenxia.

---

34 See for example Jiaoxun zazhishe 教訓雜誌社, ed., *Shiyu xinchuan: Yixinzhai sanniande shengsheng yuanyuan* 師語心傳：一心齋三年的聲聲願願 (Taipei: Dijiao chubanshe, 1999).

35 See Liu Wenxing, *Li Yujie xiansheng nianpu changpian*, 107–108.

36 Li Yujie's diaries, three volumes that cover the much later period between 1973 and 1983, do not give the impression that Li had ego-control issues or possessed consuming personal ambitions. See Li Yujie, *Tianming zhi lu* 天命之路 (Taipei: Tiandijiao chubanshe, 2009), 3 vols.

Huang was born in Beijing in 1909 into a well-educated, wealthy family.[37] His father, Huang Xiaoxue 黃效學 (1886–1918), had graduated from a translation college in Beijing (北京譯學) and was fluent in English, Japanese, and French, as well as possessing a solid foundation in Chinese classical studies. Huang Xiaoxue was active in the 1898 reforms, and was a disciple of Kang Youwei 康有為 (1858–1927) (Huang, like Kang, was originally from Guangdong) and a close of acquaintance of Liang Qichao 梁啟超 (1873–1929), Cai E 蔡鍔 (1882–1916), and Yuan Shikai's 袁世凱 (1859–1916) sons. He died at the age of 32 or 33, in 1918, when Zhenxia was nine years old. Huang's mother, whose surname was Tang 湯 (?–1926), was from a well-known scholarly family in Xiaoshan 蕭山, Zhejiang. Ms. Tang was a close friend of the martyr Qiu Jin 秋瑾 (1875–1907) as well as the poet Lü Bicheng 呂碧城 (1883–1943). Like her husband, she was a gifted linguist, and spoke both English and French.

Following her husband's death, Huang's mother moved with her son to Hong Kong, and enrolled Zhenxia in St. Paul's College, where he continued his studies until moving to Shanghai in the mid-1920s. While in Hong Kong, Huang's mother defied the traditional Chinese role assigned to widows and frequented cafés, bars, and restaurants, often with her son in tow, associating mainly with foreigners. Huang remembered this period as the happiest and freest of his life, and it was at this point that he developed his life-long love of Western culture. Unfortunately, Ms. Tang lost her money with the collapse of a French bank,[38] and despite appeals from her husband's family to return to the Huang ancestral home in Shunde, Guangdong, decided to move to Shanghai, where she attempted to earn a living as a live-in tutor. She died in 1926 as a result of appendicitis and peritonitis. Her son was 17 years old.

Huang Zhenxia had already quit school at the age of 16 to help his mother, working as a graphic designer and a clerk, among other jobs. He continued to educate himself, spending endless hours at the Zhabei Dongfang Library (閘北東方圖書館), and turned to journalism and creative writing in the 1920s and 1930s. In 1930, he published an epic poem, "The Blood of the Yellow People" (黃人之血), in *Vanguard Monthly* 先鋒月刊, a short-lived journal devoted to "nationalist literature" and apparently financed by GMD authorities

37 The following biographical information comes from a preface to a reedition of Huang's epic poem, "The Blood of the Yellow People" written by his widow. See Huang Zhenxia, *Huangren zhi xue* 黃人之血 (Taipei: Tianhua chuban shiwu, 1979).

38 The Banque industrielle de Chine failed in 1923; see Hubert Bonin, "French Banks in Hong Kong (1860s–1950s): Challengers to British Banks?" available on line at http://www.hkimr.org/uploads/conference_detail/579/con_paper_0_407_hubert-bonin-paper070503.pdf.

(and accused of "fascism" by left-wing critics).[39] In 1932, Huang published a novel, *The Destruction of Greater Shanghai* (大上海的毀滅), which describes the effects of the Shanghai Incident of early 1932 on the young people of the region. He subsequently turned to journalism and, beginning in the early 1930s, worked for the Shanghai newspaper *Dawanbao* 大晚報, becoming known for his war reporting. Jiang Jianren 蔣堅忍 (1902–1993), a GMD military officer, noticed Huang's work during the Shanghai Incident, and after becoming head of political education at the GMD Air Force Academy, invited Huang to Hangzhou in 1934 to edit the *Air Force Weekly* (空軍週刊), a publication designed to raise morale among the Chinese people by publicizing the patriotic exploits of the air force. After the beginning of the Sino-Japanese War, Huang followed Jiang Jianren to Wuhan, and subsequently to Xi'an, where Jiang worked under General Hu Zongnan. Huang eventually held a number of literary and military positions in the region, including editor of the Northwest New China Publishing Company (西北新中國出版社社長) and of the *Xinjiang Daily Newspaper* (新疆日報社長). After the war he moved to Hong Kong and became a well-known journalist (writing under the pen name Dong Fanghe 東方赫), specializing particularly in Chinese Communist military affairs.[40]

Li and Huang met in Xi'an (or on Huashan) through their overlapping networks,[41] and developed an easy intimacy almost from the outset. According to Li Yujie's son Li Ziyi, who was also on Huashan at the time, Li Yujie and Huang talked for three days and nights after meeting for the first time, discovering that they shared many points of view. Huang took Li as his master, and in the winter of 1940–1941 they settled in for three months of intense work, during which the composition of most of Li's foundational public text, *The Ultimate Realm*, was completed.

Huang's views on his newly adopted faith are revealed in an extraordinary letter that he wrote to Li after Xiao's death but before the publication of *The Ultimate Realm* in 1944.[42] The letter seems to be part of a longer conversation Li and Huang have been engaged in concerning the "renewal" or modernization

39 See Lawrence Wang-Chi Wong, "A Literary Organization with a Clear Political Agenda: The Chinese League of Left-Wing Writers," in *Literary Societies of Republican China*, ed. Kirk A. Denton and Michel Hockx (Plymouth, England: Lexington Books, 2008), 238.

40 Huang collaborated with William H. Whitson on *The Chinese High Command: A History of Chinese Communist Military Politics, 1927–1971* (New York: Praeger, 1973).

41 One Tiandijiao member told me that Huang had been experimenting with spirit-writing and had been possessed by a spirit. He initially sought Li out for help in ridding himself of the spirit.

42 The letter is reproduced in Liu Wenxing, *Li Yujie xiansheng nianpu changpian*, 145–148.

of Xiao's teachings, in which Huang appears to have been startlingly frank about his greatest fear, which is that Li Yujie is set to propagate something that is largely indistinguishable from the White Lotus teachings:

> In my view, our teachings have been, in the past, those of Master Xiao's system, a system which, in terms of its contents and style, has retained the form of the White Lotus. Consequently, such teachings would only be suitable for people whose educational levels are backward, and we would not be able to propagate them among the elite of society. Even if it worked in the early Republican period, it will no longer work now. My Master has always been an intellectual, and has dedicated himself to national affairs. It is only because of the constraints of master-disciple ties and the limitations of the genealogy of the faith *daotong* 道統 [inherited from Xiao Changming] that Master Li has not carried out a thoroughgoing reform and renewal of the teachings. As a result, today we find that the faith cannot be propagated as we wish, nor can we elevate the talent of the people in it, nor are the beliefs coherent. We can claim that these problems are because the "time is not right," but actually the weakness of our thinking also plays a role in our predicament.
>
> Master Xiao has died, which provides us an occasion to renew the teaching. If we do not painstakingly carry out a thorough renewal, our future is bleak. If the feudal remnants of the faith are not eliminated, then the style of a new religion will not be set up. If we change the soup without changing the medicine in the soup, then people with vision, once they look carefully at our religion, will despise it … Even if my personal beliefs are strong and will not waver, people in society share with me the desire to have nothing to do with the White Lotus.

> 按本教過去為蕭教主之系統，此系統之內容及方式，始終未脫白蓮教之型態，故僅能行於知識落後之各界，不能昌於社會之上流，即在民國初年能行，今日亦不能行。吾師本為知識分子，亦嘗獻身於國事，徒以師生宗法關係之束縛，道統之限制，致未能痛加改革，一新內容，因循而至今日，教務之不能推廣，人品之不能提高，信仰之不能凝固，雖云天運之未昌，亦人謀之不臧有以致之。
>
> 今蕭教主已矣，際此中興之機運，苟不痛予徹底之刷新，則前途之希望固仍渺茫也。封建殘餘之臭味一日不去，新宗教之作風決難樹立，換湯不換藥，明眼人一見便知之而惡之……維道個人信心堅定，始終不渝，然社會人士與維道同具此感想，而不願與白蓮教之型態相親近者，仍比比然也。

Huang is very direct in his criticism, noting that Li's achievements have been "limited to [recruiting] a few military people and politicians, who have engaged in limited philanthropy but whose beliefs are muddled" (不過助長若干軍人政客消極之行善與模糊之信心而已). He advises Li to use "revolutionary means" (革命之手段) to purge the ranks of his followers of such people, replacing them with more "democratic" (民主) believers. He repeats this call several times over the course of the letter, arguing that the group needs quality, not quantity. Future members, in Huang's view, will be "frank, peaceful, open, well-versed in the writings of masters ... and the history of religion. They must study philosophy, and pay attention to scientific advances" (淡泊寧靜，正大光明，諸子教育……熟讀宗教史，勤研哲理，注意科學進度). Twenty years of study should precede joining Li's religion, Huang avers, and those authorized to transmit the Way in the future must "be college-educated, have great understanding of philosophy, and must be recognized inside China and out" (今後傳道教師必須大學資格，神通哲理，曉暢中西者任之).

Huang further argues that the organization of Li's religion should be fundamentally rethought, the "mysterious" nature inherited from the White Lotus dispensed with completely. He prefers the relative ritual simplicity of Christianity and Islam, and further notes that "mysterious people like Zhang Tianshi [the founder of Daoism] or venerable characters like the lamas [of Tibet and Mongolia] are tomorrow's faded flowers" (張天師式之神秘，喇嘛式之尊嚴，皆是明日黃花).[43]

"The whole notion of *daotong* should be gotten rid of" (道統之觀念須即棄去). Huang continued, "It is hard enough for people today to respect [living] individuals; how can we expect them to respect dead people" (世人能對個人尊敬，已非易事，何能再對死人尊敬)? He says that the Tianrenjiao's charitable organization, the Hongxinzihui 紅心字會, should be scrapped because it is often confused with—and is no better than—the Wanguo daodehui's Hongwanzihui 紅卍字會. The same goes for the Far Eastern Spiritual Healing Clinics, "which exist solely on paper, and make [empty?] gestures like distributing coffins" (有名無實，施捨棺木之小恩小惠). Huang argued that such trivialities were beneath the sort of group whose future he was imagining.

Huang's criticisms are surprising only because he is an avowed follower of Li Yujie, who participated actively in the composition of the group's major scripture. Otherwise, his derision is similar to that of other critics of redemptive societies, such as the anti-superstition elements of the GMD. Happily, the letter also reveals what Huang feels to be the positive points of the religion. Broadly speaking, Huang finds that Li Yujie, and presumably Xiao Changming

43 The reference is to a poem by Su Dongpo entitled *Jiurici* 九日次.

before him—as well as other members of their groups—are in touch with the gods, who dispense valuable teachings. He praises spirit-writing (看光) for facilitating discussion, with the various gods, of the meaning of the Way (道義). He provides a bit more information about these gods, noting elsewhere in his letter that "if our highest gods are solely from the Daoist tradition, we will be unable to achieve our goals and convince the masses. This is crucial—the kind of enlightenment we preach will determine whether we are like the White Lotus (broadly speaking) or a new religion" (僅以道教傳統神佛為最高主宰，不能賢大雅而服中心，此點關係甚大，是否近於白蓮教（廣義的），抑近於信宗教，即基於此最大之覺悟). He cites the names the of two Tianrenjiao gods—Sanqi zhuzai 三期主宰 and Chongren jiaozhu 崇仁教主—who had been assigned to the task of composing *The Ultimate Realm* and thus had been present in spirit-writing sessions. Elsewhere he notes that in addition to putting scientifically educated people in charge of the faith, Li should also "establish relations with American and British spiritualists (靈學會), using the international strength [we will earn from such a gesture] to fend off criticism that we are spreading superstition" (與英美靈學會溝通關係，以國際力量立於不敗之地，堵賽攻擊者謂為宣傳迷信之根據及藉口).[44] This recalls his widow's, Sha Qianmeng's 沙千夢, remark that Huang remained interested in spiritualism throughout his life, and talked about going to England after his retirement to pursue the topic (Huang died before retiring). At the very least, this serves as a reminder of the often shifting boundaries between "superstition" and "religion."

Huang's letter illustrates, in fluent, concentrated form, that modern, well-educated Chinese can be drawn to basic teachings of Chinese salvational religion in spite of elite culture's general embrace of secularism and that they are uncomfortable with much of the language and symbols surrounding these teachings. Even if this letter was drafted after the writing of *The Ultimate Realm*, it is surely revealing of conversations Li and Huang had during the process of writing. Clearly, Li and Huang were searching for a new way to present the key ideas that had drawn Li to Xiao and Huang to Li. In writing (or transcribing) the volume they did not opt for the frank criticism of the White Lotus found in

---

44 Huang Ko-wu's fascinating research sheds light on the shifting boundaries between science, religion, and superstition during the Republican period, when spiritualism was seen as linking science and religion, while hypnotism was spurned as a parlor trick. See Huang Ko-wu 黃克武, "Kexue, zongjiao yu mixin de zai sikao: Minguo chunian de lingxue yanjiu 科學，宗教與迷信的再思考： 民國初年的靈學研究," paper presented at the conference on "Wenhua yu kexue de bianzou: Jindao Zhongguo jiushi tuanti, xinyang wenhua de fazhan yu weilai 文化與科學的變奏：近代中國救世團體、信仰文化的發展與未來," Foguang University, Yilan, Taiwan, October 2/3 2012.

Huang's letter, but chose instead to base the new foundational public text on science, hardly surprising given the iconic status of science in modern China.

The resulting volume, *The Ultimate Realm*, is radically different—at least in form and language—from anything that Xiao Changming wrote, although if one can look beyond form and language, the core of Xiao's teachings remains intact.[45] The preface, or overview, provided in part 1 of *The Ultimate Realm* suggests the major themes to be developed in the body of the text. Li begins by evoking the coming end of the world, noting that "this world plunges into turmoil unlike anything seen before, and humanity suffers through the throes of imminent calamity [a reference to World War II]…[resulting in] insanity, desperation, distress, misery, fear and weariness."[46] Religion, Li asserts, has always been a response to such events and the discomfort such events produce, and has evolved to meet the needs of the time. "For instance, Buddhism arose to counter the rigid castes of Brahmanism, and thus taught equality and the possession of Buddha-nature by all beings. The Christian Martin Luther founded Protestantism to resist oppression by the Pope in Rome, allowing the liberation of European thought and ushering in Western civilization as we have known it for four hundred years."[47] The current task before religion, the author continues, is to transcend the "received notion" of the "mind-matter distinction" and acknowledge that "the distance between Heaven and man lessens as the wheel of time advances."[48] This claim is linked to Li's notion of the historical evolution of religion, developed elsewhere in the volume, according to which primitive man saw the deities as possessing awesome power, traditional man saw God as his savior, and earned his salvation through meritorious service to a benign father, and modern man, who, through scientific advances, has

45 The original edition of the text is Hanjing Li Yujie 涵靜李玉階, *Xin zongjiao zhexue tixi* 新宗教哲學體系 (Xi'an: Shaanxisheng zongjiao zhexue yanjiushe, 1944). Subsequent editions include: Li Yujie, *Xin jingjie: Xin zongjiao zhexue tixi* 新境界: 新宗教哲學體系 (Taipei: Wenxing, 1961); Li Yujie, *Tiandijiao jiaoyi: Xin jingjie* 天帝教教義: 新境界 (Taipei: Tiandijiao shiyuan, 1982); Li Yujie, *Tiandijiao jiaoyi: Xin jingjie* 天帝教教義: 新境界 (Taipei: Tiandijiao shiyuan, 1985); Li Jichu (Li Yujie) 李極初, *Tiandijiao jiaoyi: Xin jingjie* 天帝教教義: 新境界 (Nantou: Dijiao chubanshe, 1997). The English-language translation is *The Ultimate Realm: A New Understanding of Cosmos and Life: Doctrines of T'ienti Teachings*, translated by Denis C. Mair (Taipei: Dijiao chubanshe, 1994). It is not clear which edition served as the basic for the translation. A comparison of the 1944 and 1985 editions found minimal changes to the text. All quotations of the text are to the heroic English-language translation by Denis Mair.

46 *The Ultimate Realm*, 1. Since I am citing from the English translation, I will no longer include the Chinese text.

47 *The Ultimate Realm*, 1–2.

48 *The Ultimate Realm*, 2–3.

come to understand that “divine power ultimately is no more than a mediation between matter and Nature.”[49] *The Ultimate Realm*, composed via spirit-writing, is presented as an example of such communication between the human and divine realms.

The goal of Li’s text is thus to explore “the principles of compatibility between science and philosophy, and in one’s own effort of cultivation and practice.”[50] This guide will allow the cultivated man to “contact and bond with the non-physical spirit realm, to exchange culture between Heaven and man.”[51] Such “bonding” is not new, and has been practiced by Confucians, Buddhists, and Daoists across the centuries. *The Ultimate Realm* aims to provide another explanation for the effectiveness of such bonding, a scientific explanation that is traced in outline in the overview and developed at greater length in the text itself.

The preface also provides the only biographical elements to be found in the volume, which otherwise is almost completely impersonal in tone. Speaking of Li in the third person, the preface notes that Li had been imbued with the rudiments of religious faith by his mother, and subsequently “helped across to the other shore” by his master (who remains nameless).[52] During his spiritual quest, Li was often “guided by an invisible spiritual force, which was a recompense [or a response, a contact, a form of ‘bonding’] given by enlightened beings and immortals who sent down *yang* rays from high-level space.”[53] In 1936, such enlightened beings directed Li to take up residence on Huashan where among mists and sunset clouds he would

> pore over books or foster his ch’i[*qi*], and visit back and forth to talk of mysteries with sacred beings. In the cloud-covered back country, secluded in an ancient cave, [Li] reached up to pristine cosmic *ch’i* and bridged the culture of Heaven and man; below he received it all into his body, a vessel of stillness, and elucidated [the] truths of the cosmos. He revealed the origin and formation of celestial bodies, and how the substance of the universe is a oneness with dual function of mind (harmonons) and matter (e-tropons). Basing his discussion on scientific theory, he methodically addressed the ultimate questions of life, examining spiritual refuge, stages of striving, and the ultimate direction of the world.[54]

49 *The Ultimate Realm*, 91–92.
50 *The Ultimate Realm*, 3.
51 *The Ultimate Realm*, 4.
52 *The Ultimate Realm*, 6.
53 *The Ultimate Realm*, 6.
54 *The Ultimate Realm*, 7–8.

On this foundation, the prelude to *The Ultimate Realm* concludes with a series of points summarizing the authors' "key ideas concerning politics and world vision" which attempt to link Li's spiritual quest to GMD political doctrines.[55] The first of these concerns the achievement of the "self-determination of a people" (民族自決) by providing optimistic and positive religious guidance. Religion must lead the people to "battle for justice and fight against all demonic things."[56] The second is to "sacrifice for one's country … and meet death bravely" so as to exhibit the "spirit of a people" (民族精神).[57] The third insists (citing Mencius) that "Mankind is born into this world to act … [so as to] seek the ultimate goal between the sacred and mundane," which is the "eventual promise of the principle of People's Rights (民權, human rights)."[58] The fourth is to prepare to "strive with Nature" once the war is over so as to develop the nation. "Anyone who is dedicated to co-existence and shared livelihood, who can strive with nature for the benefit of all, is really a 'spirit-intermediary' between Nature and matter. This is what we mean by 'labor is sacred,' and it is the true meaning of the People's Livelihood (民生)."[59] The fifth and final point evokes the utopia that will evolve out of the positive effort put in motion by Li's religion.

> From this, nations will advance to true freedom and equality. By degrees they will mutually assimilate and form federations on every continent. They will approve a head for their league of nations, to guarantee collective security. Thenceforth mankind's ethnic wars will be gone forever; science and philosophy will flourish to their ultimate reaches … Naturally there will be a 'unity of Heaven and man.' Precisely for this reason, the fulfillment of our nation-building and church-building ideals and the completion of our edification in the moral, psychological sense, all depend on the mutual influence and furthering of Heaven and man.[60]

The links to Sun Yat-sen's Three People's Principles, and to the founder of the Chinese revolution's optimism and call for action, are obvious and new (Xiao Changming never attempted such links, at least not in writing), even if it is not clear what Sun Yat-sen or a GMD political theorist might have made of such links. In any event, *The Ultimate Realm* declares itself to be—in part—a political text from the outset, presumably written in large measure for the

55 *The Ultimate Realm*, 8.
56 *The Ultimate Realm*, 8.
57 *The Ultimate Realm*, 9.
58 *The Ultimate Realm*, 9–10.
59 *The Ultimate Realm*, 10.
60 *The Ultimate Realm*, 11.

political elite of which Li was himself a member. Quite clearly, *The Ultimate Realm* belongs to a different cultural world than *The Compass of Life*.

Part 2 of *The Ultimate Realm* is entitled "A Natural View of Matter" and consists of three chapters: "Substance of the Cosmos," "The Origin of the Universe," and "Formation of Celestial Bodies." These chapters are meant to establish the material, scientific basis for the larger religious and philosophical synthesis Li Yujie was aiming for in the writing of this text, and he returns to the basic concepts and arguments developed in part 2 in his discussion of "A Human View of Spirit," which makes up part 3 of the volume. The concepts and arguments deployed in part 2 are also meant to complement traditional Chinese cosmological explanations of the origin of the universe by providing scientific explanations for many of the elements of these traditional explanations. Once again the goal is not to discredit Chinese tradition, but to affirm it by absorbing it into a modernized comprehensive whole.

Part 2 begins by identifying the two basic substances that make up the universe: electropons (電子, or e-tropons, for short) and harmonons (和子).[61] E-tropons are described as the basic components of matter in the universe, but which contain no life force: "E-tropons combine to form atoms, atoms form molecules, molecules form materials."[62] E-tropons are further divided into *yin* e-tropons, which are "coarse, heavy, and high in density" and *yang* e-tropons, which are "fine, light and low in density." Li does not explain why concepts like yin and yang remain necessary to the function of e-tropons and harmonons, but notes simply that rocks are made up chiefly of *yin* e-tropons, and human beings (the most evolved living creature) chiefly *yang* e-tropons.[63] "If the universe had only e-tropons with no harmonons, it would manifest the most rudimentary phenomena of nature (only light, gases, and water). Animals, plants and minerals could not come into existence."[64]

Harmonons are the vital, spiritual component of nature, "what Taoists call 'spirit-nature,'... what Buddhists call 'Alaya consciousness,' and what Christians and Muslims call the 'soul.'"[65] Harmonons are "the prime constituents of all

61 電子 is the accepted translation for "electron." 和子 does not, to my knowledge, exist outside of Li Yujie's writings. I suspect that the translator of *The Ultimate Realm*, Denis Mair, had assistance from Tiandejiao practitioners, some of whom are very well educated in the hard sciences, in arriving at the translations of these central concepts.

62 *The Ultimate Realm*, 12–13.

63 *The Ultimate Realm*, 14.

64 *The Ultimate Realm*, 15.

65 *The Ultimate Realm*, 15. The reference to Christians and Muslims illustrates that Li Yujie continues to embrace world religions as did other redemptive society leaders.

phenomena ... which are *yang*, active, self-determining or self-aware."[66] At the most basic level, harmonons combine with e-tropons to create the beings that inhabit the universe, be it humans (the result of the combination of harmonons with high-quantity *yang* e-tropons) or minerals (the result of the combination of harmonons with low-quantity *yang* e-tropons).[67] The rest of Li's discussion of harmonons is more difficult to follow. He argues that harmonons are made up of hydrogenic essences, oxygenic essences, e-tropic substances, heat, and a special factor X, which "represents spiritual consciousness of a certain kind."[68] Although references to "hydrogenic" and "oxygenic" essences clearly suggest a relationship to basic chemistry and a desire to present harmonons in scientific terms, Li subsequently defines hydrogen as having to do with "functions of touch and smell" and oxygen with "functions of taste and discrimination."[69]

The e-tropic substance is in turn linked to "senses of hearing and sight" and the "special factor X" to "functions of intention and will" (and all four substances are further defined in Buddhist terms, either as "gunas" or "manas").[70] Humans come into being through the "union of harmonons (spirit) and e-tropons (matter) formed by the father's sperm and the mother's ovum."[71] At the same time, he argues that harmonons "spirally descend" through a spot on the top of the human head (頂旋), thus providing the functions of perception and consciousness. The decrease in e-tropic substance over time explains the fact that people's sense of sight and hearing diminish with age. When a person dies, his harmonons abandon the body and are released into the universe, where they will bond again to form other life forms.[72]

Beyond their applications in human biology, harmonons and e-tropons are also at the origin of all "natural forces." Since the two basic components work in harmony to give rise to all phenomena in the universe, this dynamic state is called a "harmonizing force," and "when such harmonizing force expands into an immense spiral force, it becomes [a] spiral harmonizing force, which is fundamental in forming celestial objects in the cosmos."[73] In other words, the union of e-tropons and harmonons explains the formation and movement of celestial bodies as well as the principles of physics and human biology.

66 *The Ultimate Realm*, 15.
67 *The Ultimate Realm*, 17.
68 *The Ultimate Realm*, 15.
69 *The Ultimate Realm*, 16.
70 *The Ultimate Realm*, 16.
71 *The Ultimate Realm*, 16.
72 *The Ultimate Realm*, 16.
73 *The Ultimate Realm*, 17–18.

Li concludes the first chapter of part 2 of *The Ultimate Realm* by noting that "everything in the universe is in a dynamic state. At the large end is the spiral harmonizing force which forms the universe's celestial bodies; in the middle is the force of e-tropons and harmonons acting on each other, as in the human body; and at the small end is the ceaseless movement of e-tropons found even within a cup of water."[74]

In the remaining sections of part 2, Li Yujie attempts to explain the origin of the universe and the formation of celestial bodies (stars, planets, earth). Part 3, "A Human View of Spirit," discusses the origin of life, the nature of human life, the realm of the spirit, the relationship of bonding and harmonizing forces, the powers of spiritual entities, and the equality of the sacred and the worldly, among other things. In these sections, Li attempts to broaden his discussion of e-tropons and harmonons and the harmonizing forces that bind them into a unified field theory explaining the origins of the cosmos, the nature of human life, and the relations between god and man. The language is relentlessly scientific (or pseudo-scientific). In the introduction to part 3, Li describes the argument in part 2 as "mainly an explanation of a new sort of natural science." Part 3, in Li's words, "is an effort to expound cosmic truth from a scientific perspective ... its aim is to establish a new sort of spiritual science, to illumine the true Tao of the cosmos."[75]

Unfortunately, if Li's intentions are clear, his concepts and explanations are not, and I despair of at arriving at a thumbnail sketch of Li's theories and arguments. My impression is that Li and Huang made a good faith effort to digest recent advances in the natural sciences (particularly physics) and apply this knowledge to religion and spiritual cultivation. It is not immediately clear if the opaqueness of *The Ultimate Realm* is due to fanciful or incomplete understanding of scientific concepts by Li and Huang, to translation problems,[76] or to the limits on my own scientific knowledge.

In any event, the following paragraphs will give the reader a brief sample of Li's arguments. In his discussion of the formation of spiral harmony systems (galaxies?), we find analyses of the "primordial phenomenon of chaos," the "evolution ... in e-tropicity and cosmic *ch'i*," the "coalescence of the rhomboid cosmic *ch'i*," the "origination of the spiral harmonizing force," the "workings of the law of spiral harmony," and the "dynamics of primordial nebulae." Drawings

74 *The Ultimate Realm*, 18–19.

75 *The Ultimate Realm*, 39.

76 Denis Mair seems to have done a masterful job in translating a difficult text, but I have not yet examined the Chinese-language physics texts Li and/or Huang must have read on Huashan. Perhaps the strangeness of their language originates in efforts by others to render the abstractions of relativity theory and quantum mechanics in Chinese.

in this section include: "locus of centripetal movement in a spiral harmony system," "rising rhomboid bodies of cosmic *ch'i* encounter vortical wind, then descend in a spiral," "formation of spiral harmony system" and "types of movement in the law of spiral harmony." The conclusion of this section is:

> Thus celestial bodies of this area evolve from chaos into a new spiral harmony system. After its formation the new system depends on a supply of hydro-electropic force from above, below and all sides (all 'below' in the broad sense), to maintain its workings as a spiral harmony system. The supply from above and below maintains its position and that from all sides insures its revolution. If the *aqua essentia* in the system is ever exhausted, the celestial bodies of this area will go back to chaos, its landforms will disintegrate into e-tropic *ch'i* and diffuse through space.[77]

In discussion of the creation of life on earth, we find the following passage:

> 1. In minerals, assume that there is one harmonon for each 4.32 square inches of area. The attraction will be as follows: a. The uppermost portion of minerals can absorb harmonons within one cubic meter; the middle layer can absorb harmonons within a volume of 10.38 cubic inches; the lowest layer can absorb harmonons within a volume of 2.07 cubic inches. b. For any harmonon absorbed into an organism, except in mankind, the direction will be downward. 2. In plants, whenever a seed is sprouting (i.e., its e-tropons are in a ferment), then its atoms will absorb a harmonon. Attraction is possible for any harmonon within a volume of one thousand cubic feet. 3. When an ape is first born, it can attract harmonons from anywhere within a volume of three thousand cubic feet. (The first harmonon absorbed into the object takes predominance).[78]

In a discussion of self-nature and physical desire (subjects often encountered in the writings of Xiao Changming, among other religious specialists), we find the following passage:

> The crux of self-nature and physical desire: All charged bodies exert a force which attracts others with incomparable speed. The push and pull of feelings and physical desire are a response to attraction by e-tropicity. In the human body there is a distinction between *yin* and

77 *The Ultimate Realm*, 27.
78 *The Ultimate Realm*, 48.

> *yang* e-tropicity. When such e-tropicity is emitted, it becomes an initiator of thoughts and a manifestation of character. That which is emitted from the e-tropic substance in harmonons is *yang* e-tropicity, representing kindness and compassionate feelings; what is emitted from e-tropons in *yin* e-tropicity, representing feelings of greed, resentment, and delusion. Love is a feeling that compromises the two … When Christianity takes love as an expression of the highest state of feeling, it is based on this. As for Buddhism, it takes nothing other than *yang* e-tropicity as its 'right mindfulness.'… Emanations of *yang* e-tropicity are straight, intuitive and thus most likely to get a direct response.
>
> Emanations of *yin* e-tropicity are indirect and curved. When a human being has evil thoughts, a great degree of vacillation, hesitation or violent mental disturbance will certainly occur. At this time the e-tropic substance in his harmonons will undergo an electrochemical change; the *yang* e-tropic substance will transform into a *yin* e-tropon. The emanation from this *yin* e-tropon will become determination that stems from this evil thought, and action will follow. Therefore if human beings often have evil thoughts, their harmonons will repeatedly go through *yin* e-tropon transformation, and will become harmonons containing great numbers of *yin* e-tropons. Evil actions will then become habitual, and though one may wish to suppress them, it will be impossible.[79]

Such examples could be multiplied many times over. Above and beyond the scientific language and arguments that make up the lion's share of *The Ultimate Realm*, the text still conveys the basic messages which presumably made Xiao Changming's teachings appealing to his followers. First, spiritual healing is affirmed, if accorded a lesser space than in Xiao Changming's writings. This healing is explained as a result of the mutual attraction between "pleading emanations of *yin* e-tropicity" (i.e., the suffering patient who sincerely desires to be healed) and the "compassionate emanations of *yang* e-tropicity" (i.e., the sincere desire of the healer to help the patient). The bonding and harmonizing forces emanating from these two people produce a "critical energy" that calls force god's primordial *qi* and the patient is cured.[80] But bonding and harmonizing forces, and indeed the whole notion of communication between man and heaven, are discussed at much greater length than spiritual healing, which is presented as part of this larger subject. Such "sympathetic forces" exist between human beings, between humans and harmonons, and between

79 *The Ultimate Realm*, 56–58.

80 *The Ultimate Realm*, 80, figure 17.

humans and deities. For the practitioner desiring to develop his capacity to make use of such forces, the "key is that both patient and healer need to put forth the utmost sincerity,"[81] which is defined in a thoroughly conservative fashion:

> Methods for humans to nurture the bonding and harmonizing forces between themselves and higher beings fall into three types: 1. Do deeds of merit and virtue in this world, and become a freed spirit after death. [Elsewhere in *The Ultimate Realm* those who become freed spirits are described as "those who acted meritoriously in the world," such as religious leaders, philosophers, politicians and educators; "those who contributed something to human society" (such as scientists and philanthropists); and "those who were dutiful and loyal to parents and their country, who practiced chastity and integrity, and acted righteously"[82]]; 2. Increase one's bonding force to attract harmonizing force from the deity or Buddha that one wishes to approach ... 3. Temper the spirit and seek to arrive at a new natural environment after passing away.[83]

Harmonizing and bonding forces are also used to explain the mediumship of the planchette, the mediumship of light (i.e., the projection of characters on the yellow cloth practiced by Xiao Changming and Li Yujie), the mediumship of the pen as well as auditory mediumship. In other words, *The Ultimate Realm* seeks to provide a scientific explanation of spirit-writing and other related practices:

> Mediumship of the planchette is receiving a broadcast from the spirit realm to the human world. The spirit-medium is the transmittal force, the planchette localizes the e-tropic force, and the deity serves as the broadcasting force. Transmitted force (bonding force) reaches out to the broadcasted force (harmonizing force) above. The two stimulate each other, initiating e-tropic kinesis in the planchette.[84]

At the same time, Li argues that the spirit-medium should be a virgin child, should possess "personal qualities of devotion and constancy," and should

81 *The Ultimate Realm*, 79.
82 *The Ultimate Realm*, 64–65.
83 *The Ultimate Realm*, 75.
84 *The Ultimate Realm*, 76.

have "a certain degree of intelligence."[85] The scientific functions of virginity, devotion, constancy and intelligence are not identified (children's harmonons, by contrast, are noted to contain relatively strong e-tropic substances), and the idea that spirit mediums should be young, virginal, and morally upright was widely shared in traditional Chinese religion. As *The Ultimate Realm* moves away from the origin and physical functioning of the universe and toward areas of discourse that touch practitioners' lives more directly, there is more discussion of familiar spiritual and religious tropes and less discussion of science, although science rarely disappears completely. Quiet contemplation (common to both Xiao Changming's and Li Yujie's teachings and practices) is described as "sitting meditation, as in Ch'an, carried to the highest level. It proceeds through settling, quietude, tranquility, and reflection to the true realm of attainment. This is what Taoists call 'penetrating the spirit' and Buddhists call 'seeing one's own nature.'"[86] Success in quiet sitting requires curbing physical desires and purifying the heart. Subsequently, one learns to circulate his *qi*: "an ultra-*yang* heat flow produced after high- level e-tropic substance from harmonon blends with bodies of static e-tropicity ... This practice is what Taoist scriptures call seizing the dragon and taming the tiger, or drawing out the lead and blending in the mercury."[87] The subsequent discussion of Daoist *neidan* practices includes scientific explanations, but Daoist discourse generally takes pride of place.[88] Li concludes this discussion by advocating the "dual cultivation of self-nature and the body" (性命雙修), the lived practice of the unity of matter and spirit which leads to human-divine communication and eventually convergence.[89] "Sacred and mundane share the same origin;/Mundane and sacred have the same foundation./Their foundation and their origin/Are in spiral harmony./Master spiral harmony;/Turn your striving toward Heaven./With arduous training, rough tempering,/Transcend the mundane and be the sacred."[90] Throughout the latter half of *The Ultimate Realm* there are many references to Buddhist and Daoist terms and deities (alongside occasional

85 *The Ultimate Realm*, 76.

86 *The Ultimate Realm*, 79.

87 *The Ultimate Realm*, 85–86.

88 An exception is Li's discussion of a "raydon embryo," which Li notes is his addition to these teachings: "A raydon embryo is a concentration of the universe's great motive force and energy. It is attained by further cultivation of a sacred embryo. In any instance where radiation of e-tropic force reaches an extremely high energy level, the e-tropons will undergo intense excitation and become radioactive. This is what is called a thermonuclear reaction, and what Taoist alchemy calls 'fostering by warmth.'" *The Ultimate Realm*, p. 88.

89 *The Ultimate Realm*, 89.

90 *The Ultimate Realm*, 94–95. This is a poem.

references to Christian and Muslim practices), as well as to gods and practices drawn from popular religion. Thus, even if Li's text does not mimic the well-worn, homey cadences of Xiao's writings, there are still comfortable references to Chinese tradition, its relevance, utility, and power.

A final point of commonality between *The Ultimate Realm* and the teachings of Xiao Changming is a shared positive emphasis on striving. Both thoroughly reject what they see as the passive resignation associated with faiths that preach "non-action" (無為) and argue for positive engagement with the world. The final chapter of part 3 of *The Ultimate Realm* is entitled "The Way of Striving," and Li insists that practitioners "strive toward heaven, strive with nature, and strive within oneself." Those who strive toward heaven "must harbor great enduring will and boundless vows to pursue eternal life. Only this is sufficient to escape the travail of reincarnation, to extricate oneself from the predicament of sin and hasten the manifesting of cosmic truth for later ages—only an upstanding person does this!"[91] As for nature, it is "mankind's common enemy. It must be overcome and reined in, before it will let our human civilization be remade as something higher."[92] And to strive with heaven and nature "one must first strive within himself to lay the foundation. This is what Confucians call cultivating sagehood by rectifying the mind and making the will sincere."[93] The endpoint of striving will be equality with sacred beings.

4 Concluding Remarks

If a casual reader happened to peruse Xiao Changming's *The Compass of Life* and Li Yujie's *The Ultimate Realm* one after the other, I doubt that she would notice that the two were products of the same religious tradition. In terms of title, vocabulary, prose style, and basic cultural orientation, Xiao's text clearly belongs to an earlier era where explanatory power lay with classical texts while Li's grounds its discursive muscles in science—even if the science seems to us idiosyncratic and its goal is to explain the wisdom already found in the classical texts. Li's text is strangely divorced from the circumstances of its creation. Although *The Ultimate Realm* discusses various types of "mediumship," including the "mediumship of light," nowhere does it mention that Li, Huang Zhenxia, and Li's son, Li Ziyi, spent months communicating with the gods and

91 *The Ultimate Realm*, 96.
92 *The Ultimate Realm*, 96–97.
93 *The Ultimate Realm*, 97.

transcribing the text from the yellow cloth where the spirit-written characters appeared.

Li's behavior can be explained in part by his relative ignorance of science and by his sincere hope—like that we find in the Shanghai Spiritualist Society studied by Matthias Schumann in this volume—that science would validate the mysteries and powers at the core of religious experience. Yet by omitting his personal experiences and cloaking most of his argument in scientific discourse, Li created a foundational public text that established a brand, or an identity, that was useful to members and authorities alike. Li was delighted when *The Ultimate Realm* was translated into Japanese in the 1980s, and the text was an important part of Tiandijiao's application for legal status in the 1990s. Li mentions the text repeatedly in his diaries, and was always eager to circulate in hopes of finding an audience.

And it worked. The Tiandijiao's application was approved and the group's reputation on Taiwan is generally positive (although they are seen as the "poor cousins" of Yiguandao, to say nothing of massive Buddhist organizations like Tzu Chi). Many current Tiandijiao members are highly educated, including more than a few in the hard sciences, and while they argue that "science has moved on" from the state of knowledge that produced the text in the 1940s, they are happy to accept the mantle of science, sophistication, and modernity that Li and Huang sought to instill in the text.

And yet while the text is a "must read" for members, it is not something they talk about frequently, and in the course of fieldwork in the summer of 2014, one member admitted that the text was hard to read and not helpful in attracting new members. Li wrote a second foundational public text after Tiandijiao achieved legal status. This book, *The Essence of Quiet Sitting* (靜坐要義), contains a few passages inspired by *The Ultimate Realm*, but most of it reads like a Daoist meditation text.[94] Today's Tiandijiao continues to offer spiritual healing, chiefly via *qigong*, but I doubt that healing methods like those used by Xiao Changming have completely disappeared, even if current Tiandijiao members remain sensitive to anything that smacks of superstition. White Lotus gods continue to speak to Tiandijiao members during spirit communications, which appears to bother current practitioners little, largely because few people know anything about the "White Lotus" and its history of heterodoxy and suppression. As mentioned above, the appeal of Tiandijiao now appears to be two-fold: it allows Chinese people from Taiwan (or Los Angeles) to discover

94 Hanjing laoren 涵靜老人 (Li Yujie), *Jingzuo yaoyi* 靜坐要義 (Taipei: Tiandijiao shiyuan, 1989). There is also a newly edited Chinese-English bilingual edition: Jingzuo yaoyi/Zhong-Ying duizhaoban 靜坐要義/中英對照版 (Taipei: Dijiao chubanshe, 2013).

China's traditional culture, which has largely been removed from the educational curriculum; and it promises a richer spiritual life via meditation and access to the gods. Paradoxically, in the case of the Tiandejiao-Tiandijiao tradition, text is clearly related to context, but less so to practice. Li Yujie and Huang Zhenxia propelled Xiao Changming's teachings into the modern era, allowing practitioners to continue to access ancient wisdom under a new and improved cover.

Bibliography

Bonin, Hubert. "French Banks in Hong Kong (1860s–1950s): Challengers to British Banks?" Available online at http://www.hkimr.org/uploads/conference_detail/579/con_paper_0_407_hubert-bonin-paper070503.pdf.

Clart, Philip, and Gregory Adam Scott, eds. *Religious Publishing and Print Culture in Modern China: 1800–2012*. Boston: De Gruyter, 2015.

Goossaert, Vincent. "Daoists in the Modern Chinese Self-Cultivation Market: The Case of Beijing, 1850–1949." In *Daoism in the Twentieth Century: Between Eternity and Modernity*, edited by David A. Palmer and Xun Liu, 123–153. Berkeley: University of California Press, 2012.

Goossaert, Vincent, and David A. Palmer. *The Religious Question in Modern China*. Chicago: University of Chicago Press, 2011.

Hanjing Laoren 涵靜老人 (Li Yujie). *Jingzuo yaoyi* 靜坐要義. Taipei: Tiandijiao shiyuan, 1989.

Hanjing Li Yujie 涵靜李玉階. *Xin zongjiao zhexue tixi* 新宗教哲學體系. Xi'an: Shaanxisheng zongjiao zhexue yanjiushe, 1944.

Hsiao Chang Ming (Xiao Changming 蕭昌明). *The Compass of Life*. Translated by Chung Hing Sin, Marv Goldberg, and Jim Hollander. New Hyde Park, NY: Religion and Philosophy Research Society, 1999.

Huang Ko-wu 黄克武, "Kexue, zongjiao yu mixin de zai sikao: Minguo chunian de lingxue yanjiu 科學，宗教與迷信的再思考： 民國初年的靈學研究." Paper presented at the conference on "Wenhua yu kexue de bianzou: Jindai Zhongguo jiushi tuanti, xinyang wenhua de fazhan yu weilai 文化與科學的變奏：近代中國救世團體、信仰文化的發展與未來," Foguang University, Yilan, Taiwan, October 2/3, 2012.

Huang Zhenxia 黃震遐. *Huangren zhi xue* 黃人之血. Taipei: Tianhua chuban shiwu, 1979.

Jiaoxun zazhishe 教訓雜誌社 ed. *Shiyu xinchuan: Yixinzhai sanniande shengsheng yuanyuan* 師語心傳：一心齋三年的聲聲願願. Taipei: Dijiao chubanshe, 1999.

Lee Fongmao. "Transmission and Innovation: The Modernization of Daoist Inner Alchemy in Postwar Taiwan." In *Daoism in the Twentieth Century*, edited by David A. Palmer and Liu Xun, 196–227. Berkeley: University of California Press, 2012.

Li Jichu 李極初 (Li Yujie 李玉階). *Tiandijiao jiaoyi: Xin jingjie* 天帝教教義:新境界. Nantou: Dijiao chubanshe, 1997.

Li Yujie 李玉階. *Xin jingjie: Xin zongjiao zhexue tixi* 新境界:新宗教哲學體系. Taipei: Wenxing, 1961.

Li Yujie 李玉階. *Tiandijiao jiaoyi: Xin jingjie* 天帝教教義:新境界. Taipei: Tiandijiao shiyuan, 1982.

Li Yujie 李玉階. *Tiandijiao jiaoyi: Xin jingjie* 天帝教教義:新境界. Taipei: Tiandijiao shiyuan, 1985.

Li Yujie 李玉階. *Tianming zhi lu* 天命之路. Taipei: Tiandijiao chubanshe, 2009, 3 vols.

Li Yujie 李玉階. *Jingzuo yaoyi/Zhong-Ying duizhaoban* 靜坐要義/中英對照版. Taipei: Dijiao chubanshe, 2013.

Liu Wenxing 劉文星. "*Decangjing* shumu tiyao《德藏經》書目提要." Available online at http://www.tienti.tw/node/1197.

Liu Wenxing 劉文星. *Li Yujie xiansheng nianpu changbian* 李玉階先生年譜長編. Nantou: Tiandijiao jiaoshi bianzuan weiyuanhui, 2001.

Liu Zhishan 劉至善. "Tianren qigong lishi yan'ge 天人炁功歷史沿革." Available online at http://www.tienti.tw/node/993.

Lu Yuding 盧禹鼎. *Xiao Changming dazongshi zhuan* 蕭昌明大宗師傳. Taipei: printed by author, 1973.

Naquin, Susan. *Millenarian Rebellion in China: The Eight Trigrams Uprising of 1813*. New Haven: Yale University Press, 1976.

Overmyer, Daniel L. *Precious Volumes: An Introduction to Chinese Sectarian Scriptures from the Sixteenth and Seventeenth Centuries*. Cambridge, MA: Harvard University Asia Center, 1999.

Ownby, David, "Sainthood, Science, and Politics: The Life of Li Yujie." In *Making Saints in Modern China*, edited by David Ownby, Vincent Goossaert, and Ji Zhe, 241–271. New York: Oxford University Press, 2017.

Palmer, David. "Dao and Nation: Li Yujie—May Fourth Activist, Daoist Cultivator, and Redemptive Society Patriarch in Mainland China and Taiwan." In *Daoism in the Twentieth Century: Between Eternity and Modernity*, edited by David A. Palmer and Liu Xun, 173–195. Berkeley: University of California Press, 2012.

Pan Shuren 潘樹仁. *Lihai shengge: Xiao Dazongshi Changming chuanqi yisheng* 歷海笙歌:蕭大宗師昌明傳奇一生. Hong Kong: Boxue, 2007.

Qin Shude 秦淑德. *Decangjing: Tiande lüzang, yibulü* 德藏經:天德律藏，一部律. Tainan: Tiandeshengjiao, 1986.

Ter Haar, Barend J. *The White Lotus Teachings in Chinese Religious History*. Leiden: Brill, 1992.

The Ultimate Realm: A New Understanding of Cosmos and Life: Doctrines of T'ienti Teachings. Translated by Denis C. Mair. Taipei: Dijiao chubanshe, 1994.

Tiandijiao jiyuan jiaoshi weiyuanhui 天帝教極院教史委員會, ed. *Tiandijiao jianshi* 天帝教簡史. Taipei: Dijiao, 2005.

Wang Diqing 王笛卿. *Decangjing: Yiqi zongzhu tanjing* 德藏經:一炁宗主談經. Tainan: Zhongguo jingshen liaoyang yanjiuhui 中國精神療養研究會, 1985.

Welch, Holmes, and Chün-Fang Yü. "The Tradition of Innovation: A Chinese New Religion." *Numen* 27, no. 2 (December 1980): 222–246.

Whitson, William H. *The Chinese High Command: A History of Chinese Communist Military Politics, 1927–1971*. New York: Praeger, 1973.

Wong Lawrence Wang-Chi. "A Literary Organization with a Clear Political Agenda: The Chinese League of Left-Wing Writers." In *Literary Societies of Republican China*, edited by Kirk A. Denton and Michel Hockx, 231–257. Plymouth, England: Lexington Books, 2008.

CHAPTER 6

Transmission and Revision: Scripture Production in the Vietnamese Tứ Ân Hiếu Nghĩa Movement

Chung Yun-Ying
Translated by Philip Clart

1 Introduction

In the process of a religion's propagation and development, the production of scriptures marks its gradual maturation and its ability to persevere in its missionary activities. The key functions of religious scriptures are to shape the founding myths and legends, describe the religion's development, and establish its sacredness, but most importantly, scriptures distinguish a religious group from others and represent its believers' devotion and identity.

During the Ming and Qing dynasties, popular religious movements emerged in China in great numbers; in particular groups proclaiming "the unity of the Three Teachings" (*sanjiao heyi* 三教合一), "the final kalpa of the Three Ages" (*sanqi mojie* 三期末劫), and "the three Dragon Flower Assemblies" (*longhua sanhui* 龍華三會) often found themselves in a precarious situation, being subject to persecution by the authorities. Even so, many such groups composed their own scriptures to effect the transmission and convenient propagation of their cultivation methods. Many such scriptures came into being through the rearrangement, revision, or editing of earlier texts, or they were commentaries on canonical texts of the Three Teachings. In particular the spirit-written texts composed by Qing-period phoenix halls continue to exert a strong influence until today. By means of such textual products of religious movements we can not only study their teachings, but also understand the social conditions at that time. Because Chinese societies emphasize the meritorious nature of the printing, copying, and recitation of scriptures, such texts were collated and published as morality books, circulating widely among the common people. They did not only influence Chinese moral values, but also had a profound impact on Vietnamese popular religious movements.

Before Vietnam came under French colonial influence in the nineteenth century, it had always used the Chinese script[1] and had thus been part of

1 Most of the scriptures of Bửu Sơn Kỳ Hương and its branches, which I collected during my fieldwork, were written in Chinese, sometimes in *quốc ngữ*, but never in *Chữ Nôm* (字喃).

 | DOI:10.1163/9789004424166_008

FIGURE 6.1
Ngô Lợi 吳利 (1831–1890)
© NGUYỄN THANH PHONG 阮清風

the East Asian cultural sphere characterized and influenced by the use of Chinese characters. Vietnamese envoys to China would buy large numbers of Chinese books to ship back to Vietnam, which included not just scholarly works, but also popular texts, books of the Three Teachings, and morality books so that Vietnam was not unfamiliar with these types of works.[2] Furthermore, leaders of Chinese popular religious movements were often exiled to remote border regions; by this policy the Chinese authorities not only did not succeed

---

They were found in Chùa Phước Điền 福田寺, a temple belonging to Bửu Sơn Kỳ Hương, located in An Giang province 安江省, in Châu Đốc 朱篤.

2 From surviving book lists we can learn about the circulation and rewriting of Chinese books in Vietnam. These included many books of the Three Teachings and popular religious texts such as *Yinzhiwen* 陰騭文 (Essay on hidden merit), *Lüzu lingqian* 呂祖靈籤 (Patriarch Lü's numinous oracles), *Taishang ganying pian* 太上感應篇 (Treatise of the Exalted One on Response and Retribution), and *Guandi mingsheng jing* 關帝明聖經 (The Thearch Guan's scripture on illuminating sageliness). See Chen Yiyuan 陳益源, "Zhongguo hanji zai Yuenan de chuanbo yu jieshou 中國漢籍在越南的傳播與接受," in *Yuenan hanji wenxian shulun* 越南漢籍文獻述論 (Beijing: Zhonghua shuju, 2011), 71–86.

in eliminating these movements, but even gave them an opportunity to spread to Tonkin (northern Vietnam), especially from the provinces of Guangxi and Guizhou. Numerous members of popular religious movements also fled to Cochin-China (southern Vietnam) to evade the persecution of the Chinese authorities, bringing many of their religions' texts with them.[3]

The tradition at the center of the present chapter, the Tứ Ân Hiếu Nghĩa 四恩孝義 (literally, "The Four Graces, Filial Piety, and Righteousness"), is a southern Vietnamese religious movement that has preserved many scriptures in Chinese characters and thus deserves scholarly attention. Its followers regarded the movement's founder, Ngô Lợi 吳利 (1831–1890; see fig. 6.1) as a savior. While Ngô Lợi and his associate Nguyễn Hội Chân 阮會真 (dates unknown) were literate and knew Chinese characters, most of the believers of this indigenous Vietnamese religion were illiterate peasants. Today, the Tứ Ân Hiếu Nghĩa has over one hundred thousand members. From its main base of operations in An Giang province (tỉnh An Giang 安江省), close to the border with Cambodia, it spread to other provinces, such as Kiên Giang 堅江省, Vĩnh Long 永隆省, Bến Tre 檳椥省, Sóc Trăng 朔莊省, Đồng Tháp 銅塔省, Hậu Giang 後江省, Tiền Giang 前江省, Đồng Nai 同奈省, and Bình Định 平定省.

According to narratives collected during my fieldwork, Ngô Lợi's father was a carpenter named Ngô Nhàn 吳閒. Shortly after Lợi's birth, his father passed away. Ngô Lợi and his mother lived in Mỏ Cày district 梅祺郡, in the province of Kiến Hòa 建和 (today Bến Tre 檳椥省), on the east coast of Cochin-China. According to legend, his mother could not pay his school fees and so he was not able to learn Chinese characters at school. However, it is said that after seven days in a coma-like state, he started learning Chinese characters rapidly, though it is not clear how and where he did so. In 1851, at the age of 20 years, he wrote his "first scripture," *Poluoni jing* 婆羅尼經 *Bà la ni kinh*, and taught people to chant it. This scripture would eventually be included in the *Lingshanhui shangjing* 靈山會上經 *Linh sơn hội thượng kinh*. In 1870, Ngô Lợi was initiated at xã An Lộc 安祿社 (tỉnh An Giang, tổng An Lương 安江省安良總) into the

3 In this manner the Chinese Xiantiandao 先天道 (Way of Anterior Heaven) entered Sài Gòn 西貢 and Chợ Lớn 堤岸 during the 1910s to 1930s. An initiator named Mr. Wen 溫先生 (full name unknown) spread Xiantiandao in the Chinese town. See Takeuchi Fusaji 武内房司, "Jindai Xiantiandao zai Yuenan de chuanbo 近代先天道在越南的傳播," paper presented at the conference "Xiantiandao lishi yu xiankuang yantaohui 先天道歷史與現況研討會" (Center for Studies of Daoist Culture, Chinese University of Hong Kong, September 22, 2009); Yau Chi-on 游子安, "Daomai nanchuan: Cong Lingnan dao Yuenan Xiantiandao de chuancheng yu bianqian 道脈南傳：從嶺南到越南先天道的傳承與變遷," in *Shanshu yu Zhongguo zongjiao: You Zi'an zixuanji* 善書與中國宗教：游子安自選集 (Taipei: Boyang wenhua chuban gongsi, 2012), 277–304.

FIGURE 6.2
Đoàn Minh Huyên 段明暄 (1807–1856)

Kỳ 奇 branch of the Bửu Sơn Kỳ Hương 寶山奇香 (Miraculous Fragrance from the Precious Mountain) movement founded by Đoàn Minh Huyên 段明暄 (1807–1856; see fig. 6.2), where he learned the foundational myth of the Bửu Sơn Kỳ Hương, namely, that of the Đức Phật-Thầy Tây-An 西安德佛師. This myth adopts a cylical, tripartite, and millenarian conception of cosmic time (*tam nguyên* 三元). Before the "end of the world" (*tận thế* 末日), a local manifestation of Maitreya (Di Lặc 彌勒) is said to appear at the place of the Seven Mountains, regenerating virtue and transferring merit to humanity during a great "Dragon Flower Assembly" (*Hội Long Hoa* 龍華會). On the basis of Đoàn's Buddhist-derived cultivation techniques, and broadly speaking of the messianic myth of Phật-Thầy Tây-An,[4] Ngô can be seen to have synthesized the

4 For a theosophical adapation of the myth and cosmogony of Phật-Thầy Tây-An in the Vietnamese context, see Jeremy Jammes, "Theosophying the Vietnamese Religious Landscape: A Circulatory History of a Western Esoteric Movement in South Vietnam," in

(Chinese) Three Teachings with Vietnamese popular religion;[5] claiming to be a "perfected man" (*chơn nhân* 真人),[6] he used talismanic charms to cure diseases and gathered many followers. In the Seven Mountains (Thất Sơn 七山) region,[7] Ngô cleared the wilderness, established villages, built temples, and settled refugees from among the at that time numerous landless migrant population. This approach enabled the Tứ Ân Hiếu Nghĩa to develop rapidly and establish a firm foundation for its further growth. I have already written elsewhere on the branches of the Bửu Sơn Kỳ Hương, Ngô Lợi's creation of the Tứ Ân Hiếu Nghĩa, and his missionary strategies, so that here I will not delve further into these aspects.[8] The present essay will instead focus on the Tứ Ân Hiếu Nghĩa's scriptures in Chinese characters, including Ngô Lợi's writings in the religion's early history and the Tứ Ân Hiếu Nghĩa's transcriptions, propagation, and revisions of Chinese religious texts and morality books.

As existing research on the Tứ Ân Hiếu Nghĩa is quite limited, this essay is based mainly on field research and interviews conducted by the author between 2010 and 2014.

Theosophy Across Boundaries, ed. Hans Martin Krämer and Julian Strube (Albany, NY: SUNY Press, forthcoming).

5 As Trần Văn Quế 陳文桂 and Hà Tân Dân 何新民 described him in their *Phật Giáo Bửu Sơn Kỳ Hương: Hệ phái: Tứ Ân Hiếu Nghĩa* (佛教寶山奇香:四恩孝義派系), date unknown, 11–14.

6 Trần Văn Quế and Hà Tân Dân, *Phật Giáo Bửu Sơn Kỳ Hương*.

7 The Seven Mountains region is located in the Western portion of An Giang province; the mountains are: Liên Hoa Sơn 蓮花山 (Lotus Mountain, a.k.a. Elephant Mountain Núi Tượng 象山), Phụng Hoàng Sơn 鳳凰山 (Phoenix Mountain, a.k.a. Núi Cô Tô 姑蘇山), Thiên Cẩm Sơn 天錦山 (Heavenly Brocade Mountain, a.k.a. Forbidden Mountain Núi Cấm 禁山), Thủy Đài Sơn 水台山 (Water Terrace Mountain, a.k.a. Water Mountain Núi Nước 水山), Anh Vũ Sơn 鸚鵡山 (Parrot Mountain, a.k.a Núi Két), Ngọa Long Sơn 臥龍山 (Reclining Dragon Mountain, a.k.a. as Long Mountain Núi Giài 長山), Ngũ Hồ Sơn 五湖山 (Five Lakes Mountain, a.k.a. Five Wells Mountain Núi Dài Năm Giếng 長五井山); they are regarded as southern Vietnam's "numinous caverns," *linh huyệt* (*lingxue* 靈穴, a geomantic term). The founder of Bửu Sơn Kỳ Hương, Đoàn Minh Huyên, proclaimed Thiên Cẩm Sơn to be the center of the world; many immortals and Buddhas are said to cultivate themselves there and it is where the future Dragon Flower Assembly will take place, making Thiên Cẩm Sơn a pilgrimage site for Bửu Sơn Kỳ Hương believers. Cf. Hue-Tam Ho Tai, *Millenarianism and Peasant Politics in Vietnam* (Cambridge: Harvard University Press, 1983).

8 Chung Yun-Ying 鍾雲鶯, "Yuenan 'Baoshan qixiang' jiaopai ji qi chuanyan: Yi 'Sien xiaoyi' wei tantao hexin 越南寶山奇香教派及其傳衍—以「四恩孝義」為探討核心," *Minsu quyi* 民俗曲藝, no. 190 (2015): 67–127.

2 Religious Practice and Scriptural Synthesis: on Manifest and Hidden Levels of Belief

If we go by religious practice as represented in the layout of Tứ Ân Hiếu Nghĩa shrines and altars, the Lord Guan (Guan Gong 關公 Quan Công) seems to be its principal deity.[9] In the Chùa Tam Bửu 三寶寺 (Three Treasures Temple, erected in 1882, see fig. 6.3) in Ba Chúc 芭祝 commune (Huyện Tri Tôn 知尊縣, An Giang province), for instance, Lord Guan is worshipped together with Guan Ping 關平 and Zhou Cang 周倉.[10] The couplet on the pillars of the main temple hall describes Guan Gong's loyalty and righteousness:

> When fate divided the realm into three, he supported the Han, attacked Wei, and assailed Wu; he suffered many hardships without completing his life's work.

FIGURE 6.3 Chùa Tam Bửu 三寶寺 (Three Treasures Temple)
© CHUNG YUN-YING

9 In Đoàn Minh Huyên's Bửu Sơn Kỳ Hương, Lord Guan is only a secondary deity and was only promoted to chief deity in the Tứ Ân Hiếu Nghĩa. See Chung, "Yuenan 'Baoshan qixiang' jiaopai ji qi chuanyan."

10 This is in the same region as that of the Tứ Ân Hiếu Nghĩa "patriarchal temple," the Chùa Phi Lai 飛萊寺, which was established in 1877.

> Seeking to preserve unified rule, he aided the glorious Han dynasty, quelled demons, and annihilated rebels; his majestic power was great and noble—he was an exemplar of loyalty in his age.
>
> 数定三分扶炎漢剿吳伐魏辛苦備常未了平生事業，
> 志存一統佐熙朝伏魔蕩寇威靈丕振止完當日精忠。

The shrines in the households of ordinary believers also contain painted or printed images of Guan Gong, Guan Ping, and Zhou Cang as principal deities; these shrines describe Guan Gong with a horizontal plaque containing the words "correct qi" (*chánh khí* 正氣) and with the following couplets to the left and right (see also fig. 6.4):

> He was devoted to the *Spring-and-Autumn Annals*, and gained merit in serving the Han.
>
> His loyalty was bright as sun and moon, his righteousness lofty as heaven.
>
> 志在春秋功在漢，忠同日月義同天。

In 1862, the Emperor of Annam, Tự Đức 嗣德, ceded to France the three provinces of Gia Định, Biên Hòa, and Định Tường. In 1867, the French army annexed the provinces of Vĩnh Long, Hà Tiên, and Châu Đốc. The French colony of Cochin-China was officially established in March of 1874. From this date to 1890, Ngô Lợi actively organized his followers into a militia to fight French colonization. In this historical context, the Tứ Ân Hiếu Nghĩa's worship of Guan Gong was likely related to this militia organization.[11] At the same time, the immediate source for the particular arrangement of the gods' images in domestic shrines—with Guan Gong in the center, flanked by Guan Ping and Zhou Cang on his left and right respectively—has certainly to be understood with regard to the other symbolic component of Guan Gong, i.e., his strong moral spirit, which was widely emphasized in the morality book literature.[12]

To the right and below Guan Gong's tablet is placed a tablet with the inscription "Fire tower of the three teachings" (Tam Giáo Hỏa Lầu 三教火樓,

11 As this issue is not directly relevant to this chapter's subject matter, I will not discuss it in detail. See Mai Thanh Hải, "Các 'Đạo' của nông dân châu thổ sông Cửu Long từ Bửu Sơn Kỳ Hương, Tứ Ân Hiếu Nghĩa đến Đạo Lành và đạo Ông Nhà Lớn," *Tạp chí Nghiên cứu Tôn giáo*, no. 1 (2001): 65; Trần Thị Thu Lương and Võ Thành Phương, *Khởi nghĩa Bảy Thưa (1867–1873)* (Nhà xuất bản Thành phố Hồ Chí Minh 1991), 108.

12 This aspect was pointed out to me by Wang Chien-chuan 王見川.

FIGURE 6.4 Tứ Ân Hiếu Nghĩa household shrine
© CHUNG YUN-YING

see fig. 6.5), which represents Nguyễn Hội Chân 阮會真 (more on him below) and is flanked by the couplet "For his merits appointed overseer of fate by the heavenly court; lord of the stove by grace of the Jade Emperor" (受功天庭封司命，承傳玉帝耽灶君).[13] From this we learn that Nguyễn Hội Chân fulfills the

---

13 At first, I had taken this to be the tablet of the stove god; it was only on my fourth field visit in December of 2014 that I learned that "Fire tower of the three teachings" refers to Ngô Lợi's close associate, Nguyễn Hội Chân. According to the oral testimony of Phạm Văn Vinh 范文榮 (1941–), one of Tứ Ân Hiếu Nghĩa's 24 leaders, the movement's scriptures were compiled mostly by Nguyễn Hội Chân, which indicates his important position. According to tradition, Ngô Lợi dispatched followers to Saigon (today's Ho Chi Minh City) requesting Nguyễn Hội Chân to join and help him in An Giang. Nguyễn told them to return first, he would follow once he had put his private affairs in order. However, when the followers

FIGURE 6.5 "The fire tower of the three teachings" (Tam Giáo Hỏa Lầu 三教火樓), a.k.a. Nguyễn Hội Chân 阮會真

arrived back in An Giang, Nguyễn was already sitting with Ngô Lợi, discussing important matters. Believers also tell stories of Nguyễn Hội Chân's supernatural powers; whenever Ngô Lợi or a believer needed him, he would always arrive right away. He was also said to manifest himself in an incense urn, so he was called the "incense urn Buddha" (Phật Lò 爐佛). With some difficulty I obtained permission to photograph the "Illustrated Jade Calendar, with collected annotations" (*Yuli tushu jizhu* 玉曆圖書集註 *Ngọc lịch đồ thơ tập chú*), which is held only by the inner circle of leaders. Inside there is a reference to the "Buddha Fire tower Nguyễn Hội Chân" (Phật Hỏa Lầu Nguyễn Hội Chân 仸（佛）火樓 阮會真), which shows that this important figure in the early history of Tứ Ân Hiếu Nghĩa is venerated as a Buddha. Phạm Văn Vinh reports that in the early 2000s he once worshipped Nguyễn Hội Chân in an ancestral shrine in Ho Chi Minh City, though he could not remember where exactly it was located. I myself one tried to trace the Nguyễn family

function of the stove god among the deities of Tứ Ân Hiếu Nghĩa, supervising believers' words and deeds. This hypothesis is supported by the fact that the feast of the fire tower of the three teachings on the eleventh and twelfth days of the sixth moon is primarily devoted to the worship of Nguyễn Hội Chân and the recitation of the "Buddha stove scripture" (*Fozao jing* 佛灶經 *Phật táo kinh*), alternatively titled the "Perfected scripture of the overseer of fate and lord of the stove" (*Siming zaojun zhenjing* 司命灶君真經 *Tư mạng táo quân chân kinh*). Below Guan Gong is placed a tablet inscribed "Nine-graded lotus" (九品蓮花), accompanied by the couplet "Willow branches sprinkle sweet dew; above the lotus seat fragrance rises" (楊柳枝頭甘露灑，蓮花座上蕙香生). According to one interpretation, this tablet represents the bodhisattva Quan Âm (Guanyin 觀音); another view holds that, since Vietnam is part of a religious sphere focusing on the worship of goddesses, this tablet collectively represents all female deities.

The very name of the movement signals the great importance of filial piety in the Tứ Ân Hiếu Nghĩa. Thus, to both sides of the gods are placed ancestral tablets, with the male household head's ancestors placed on the right and framed by couplets such as "Ancestral merit and virtue flourish for a thousand years, the descendants' piety and worthiness give honor to ten-thousand generations" (祖功父德千年盛，子孝孫賢萬代榮), or "Filial parents are blessed with filial sons, worthy ancestors are rewarded with worthy descendants" (福至孝親生孝子，祿來賢祖出賢孫). On the left is placed the tablet for the female household head's ancestors, with couplets such as "The debt to one's father is heavier than mountains, gratitude to one's mother is deeper than oceans and rivers" (父道生成山岳重，母恩鞠育海河深), or "Blessings produce wealth

---

in Ho Chi Minh City, but at first was not successful. However, finally in August of 2018, I found a rather derelict Three Treasures Temple 三寶寺 in a remote corner of Huyện Bình Chánh 平政縣, a county adjacent to Ho Chi Minh City. Now only Nguyễn Hội Chân's grandson, Nguyễn Văn An 阮文安 (1963–), remains to perform the sacrifices. His father, Nguyễn Văn Phúc 阮文福, was an adopted son of Nguyễn Hội Chân and the genealogical information provided confirmed that Nguyễn Hội Chân was his birth name (rather than a religious title) and that he was of Vietnamese ethnicity. According to his grandson, Nguyễn Hội Chân once went to Cambodia to practice Buddhism and then returned to Vietnam to assist Ngô Lợi.

The layout of the Three Treasures Temple is similar to the Hongqing Temple 紅清寺 (Chùa Hồng Thanh) in the eleventh district of Ho Chi Minh City. There is a tablet to "36 men" 三十六人, and patriotic couplets indicating that Nguyễn Hội Chân participated in activities against the French colonialists. Some Tứ Ân Hiếu Nghĩa temples contain tablets to the "36 men," and after the visit to the Three Treasures Temple we now understand this to commemorate Nguyễn Hội Chân. However, this is not common in Tứ Ân Hiếu Nghĩa temples, and is typically seen only in fairly remote ones. More commonly an image of Nguyễn Hội Chân is the object of veneration.

and position and the family will prosper; good fortune brings honor and the descendants will be worthy" (福生富貴家堂盛，祿進榮華子孫賢). The veneration of the wife's ancestors in her husband's household is one of the unique characteristics of the Tứ Ân Hiếu Nghĩa.

From the arrangements of Tứ Ân Hiếu Nghĩa temples and household shrines we might assume that the movement focuses primarily on the worship of Guan Gong and ancestors and on filial piety, which ought also to be reflected in their internally circulating Chinese-script texts. However, a survey of these texts reveals that such texts are not numerous at all. Of Guan Gong scriptures, we find only the *Taoyuan jing* 桃園經 *Đào viên kinh* (Peach garden scripture), the *Yuhuang gusui zhenjing* 玉皇骨髓真經 *Ngọc hoàng cốt tủy chân kinh* (Bone-marrow scripture of the Jade Emperor), and the *Guan Sheng Dijun shengjing* 關聖帝君聖經 *Quan Thánh Đế Quân thánh kinh* (True scripture of the divine lord Sage Guan).[14] According to the highest leader of Tứ Ân Hiếu Nghĩa at the time of field research, Nguyễn Hữu Nghi 阮有儀 (1950–2015), the organization has 36 scriptures for internal and 47 for general use; scriptures devoted to the main deities and spirits worshiped in Tứ Ân Hiếu Nghĩa sanctuaries make up only one sixth of the total. This shows us that an analysis of a popular sect's belief system based on the representations of spirits worshiped alone will yield only partial and superficial results; if we want to access the deeper layers of a belief system, we need to begin with the internally circulating scriptures.

Based on the internal document *Gongwen zazhu* 恭文雜注 *Cung văn tạp chú* (Miscellaneous notes on revered texts), Đặng Văn Tuấn 鄧文俊 has provided a list of 36 texts in Chinese script, which matches the number given by Nguyễn Hữu Nghi, but does not completely match my field data (see appendix).[15] Among these texts we find both scriptures produced in Vietnam and scriptures of Chinese origin; examples of the former are the following: *Xiaoyi jing* (孝義經 *Hiếu nghĩa kinh*), the *Foshuo tiandi jing* (佛說天地經 *Phật thuyết thiên địa kinh*, Sūtra on heaven and earth spoken by the Buddha), *Wugong bore jing* (五公般若經 *Ngũ công bát nhã kinh*, Wisdom sūtra of the five lords),

14 This text is bound together in one volume with the *Taishang gan zhenjing* 太上感真經 (True scripture of the Most High's actions).

15 Đặng Văn Tuấn, "Đạo Tứ Ân Hiếu Nghĩa và ảnh hưởng của nó đối với tín đồ Tứ Ân Hiếu Nghĩa ở Nam Bộ hiện nay" (Luận văn Thạc sĩ ngành Chủ nghĩa Xã hội học, Trường Đại học Khoa học Xã hội và Nhân văn TPHCM, tháng 8 năm 2011). My own edition of this text was published by Phạm Văn Vinh 范文榮 and has the title *Gongwen heyi ben* 功文合一本 *Công văn hợp nhất bổn* (Meritorious texts in one volume) on its first page. It contains the announcement and petition texts (*shuwen* 疏文) used in various sacrificial rites and also titles of the scriptures to be recited as part of the rituals, but it does not refer to the internal scriptures mentioned by Đặng Văn Tuấn.

and the *Wuyue zhenjing* (五岳真經 *Ngũ nhạc chân kinh*, True scripture of the five marchmounts). The latter category includes morality and prognostic texts such as *Taoyuan jing*, *Wugong tiantu jing* 五公天圖經 *Ngũ công thiên đồ kinh* (Scripture of the five lords' celestial chart), *Fozao jing* 佛灶經 (Buddha stove scripture), and *Dimu jing* 地母經 *Địa mẫu kinh* (Scripture of the earth mother). We also find many (Chinese) Buddhist texts, especially those connected with Guanyin, such as *Guanyin bore jing* 觀音般若經 *Quan Âm bát nhã kinh* (Guanyin's wisdom sūtra), *Pumen jing* 普門經 *Phổ môn kinh* (Sūtra of the universal gate), *Gaowang jing* 高王經 *Cao vương kinh* (Sūtra of King Gao), *Dabei shizhou jing* 大悲十咒經 *Đại bi thập chú kinh* (Sūtra of the ten mantras of great compassion); in fact, the majority of internal texts are concerned with Guanyin. This poses the question why there are so few Guan Gong texts, if he is supposedly the Tứ Ân Hiếu Nghĩa's principal deity. This issue needs to be addressed from the perspective of Vietnam's history of hidden or underground religious culture.

During the Lý dynasty (1010–1224), Buddhism was the official state religion, and the succeeding Đinh dynasty also promoted Buddhism in Tonkin and in the subsequently colonized southern regions (Annam and Cochin-China).[16] Owing to this official support and the close connection between government and religion, Buddhism became a core component of the Vietnamese worldview. Confucianism played a role at the level of the ruling elite and government institutions, while the cultural basis of Vietnamese daily religious life remained Buddhist, with a particular focus on the cult of Guanyin, whose image as a savior dominates both the broader religious culture of Vietnam and the textual production of the Tứ Ân Hiếu Nghĩa. This is perhaps best exemplified in the Tứ Ân Hiếu Nghĩa internal text *Lingshanhui shangjing* 靈山會上經 (Upper sūtra of the spirit-mountain assembly).[17]

Therefore, when studying scriptures of religious movements within the cultural sphere defined by the use of Chinese script, we need to pay attention to both the cultural basis and the external manifestations of their beliefs (such as the architecture and arrangement of temples, deities worshiped, rituals, etc.), to the hidden and manifest contents of these beliefs, and in particular to the notions and ways of life shaped by the cultural basis. As the hidden dimension of a religion expresses itself in scriptural doctrines, modes of thought, and ways of life, it is not easy to discern from the religion's external form; ordinarily these external forms serve a self-marking function, i.e., they demonstrate

16 Shi Shengyan 釋聖嚴, "Yuenan Fojiao shilüe 越南佛教史略," in *Xiandai Fojiao xueshu congkan* 現代佛教學術叢刊, no. 83 (Taipei: Dasheng wenhua 大乘文化, 1980), 271–299.

17 See Chung Yun-Ying, "Yuenan 'Baoshan qixiang' jiaopai ji qi chuanyan."

sectarian affiliation and religious identity. Hence we can only avoid one-sided misinterpretations by paying equal attention to the hidden and manifest aspects of a religious movement.

Applied to Tứ Ân Hiếu Nghĩa, this insight means that we must not merely deal with its external self-labels while neglecting the hidden Buddhist cultural basis. The internal scriptures show us that one of the fields of great creativity in popular society is its ability to adapt cultural elements to its own needs and views. "Guan Gong" as the Tứ Ân Hiếu Nghĩa's main deity is a marker that distinguishes the new religion from its parent tradition, the Bửu Sơn Kỳ Hương, and may have fulfilled a function in its early militia organization, but the major role in the rituals and scriptures of Tứ Ân Hiếu Nghĩa seems to be given to Guanyin rather than Guan Gong. In comparison with another new Vietnamese religious movement—Caodaism—we could also understand the relationship of Guan Gong and Guanyin in the pantheon as a local adaptation of the male (yang)/female (yin) dyad and its symbolic complementarity.

> The Cao Đài pantheon is as immense as the Three Teachings pantheon can be. [...] All the divinities of this pantheon are considered followers of the Master living on the 'high terrace' or 'the high tower' (*Cao Đài*), another name of the Chinese Jade Emperor, the supreme almighty and ubiquitous divinity. In accordance with a Daoist cosmological interpretation, both the Master Cao Đài (symbolising the *dương* or *yáng* 陽 by an opened left eye) and the Golden Mother of the Jade Pond, Diêu Trì Kim Mẫu (symbolising the *âm* or *yīn* 陰) are theologically described to have breathed life into the universe.[18]

Thus, Tứ Ân Hiếu Nghĩa expresses its participation in the deeply-rooted Buddhism of Vietnam by the copying and recitation of Buddhist scriptures, thereby combining the identity of a Guan Gong-centered religious group with Vietnamese Buddhist culture. Although the Tứ Ân Hiếu Nghĩa has received many scriptures and morality books from Chinese sects, these have acquired new meanings after being grafted onto the Vietnamese religious cultural basis. It is only against this background that we can properly understand the religious messages of the Tứ Ân Hiếu Nghĩa's Chinese-script texts.

18 Jeremy Jammes, "Đại Đạo Tam Kỳ Phổ Độ (Cao Đài)," in *Handbook of East Asian New Religious Movements*, ed. Lukas Pokorny and Franz Winter (Leiden: Brill, 2018), 576.

3 Transmitters and Creators of Scriptures: Ngô Lợi and Nguyễn Hội Chân

The Tứ Ân Hiếu Nghĩa's internal scriptures can be divided into three categories. The first embraces the early texts composed by Ngô Lợi and Nguyễn Hội Chân themselves, which can be subdivided into two kinds: One consists of those scriptures accessible only to the 24 members of the movement's leadership, such as the *Gongwen* (*Cung văn* or the "Revered Texts"), which records rituals and ritual texts, and the *Yuli tushu jizhu* 玉曆圖書集註 (*Ngọc lịch đồ thơ tập chú*), which contains doctrines, cultivation methods, and instructions for temple construction and siting; the other comprises all texts available to ordinary believers for recitation and copying, such as *Xiaoyi jing, Lingshanhui shangjing, Foshuo tiandi jing, Wuyue zhenjing*, and *Wugong bore jing*.

The second category contains Buddhist scriptures of Chinese origin, such as *Pumen jing, Gaowang jing,* and *Mituo jing* 彌陀經 (Amitābha sūtra); the third category are Chinese popular scriptures and morality books, such as *Taoyuan jing, Chaosheng jing, Yuhuang jing* 玉皇經 (Scripture of the Jade Emperor), *Wugong tiantu jing*, and *Dimu jing*. The texts in the third category have sometimes been modified to better accord with Vietnamese conditions and Tứ Ân Hiếu Nghĩa teachings. In fact, after repeated copying, all internal scriptures contain both scribal errors and deliberate emendations, but this needs to be regarded as a by-product of the vitality of a living tradition.

In the course of my investigations, Ngô Lợi and Nguyễn Hội Chân emerged as the key figures in the Tứ Ân Hiếu Nghĩa's creation, transmission, and preservation of scriptures. In the course of spreading his teachings, Ngô Lợi had two mystical experiences, which mark key stages of his mission. In the *Xiaoyi jing* we find the following passage:

> Heaven has preordained that I was to be born in the Southern celestial nation [*Nam thiên quốc*],[19] and so I received this celestial grace in early summer, at the noon hour of the fifth day of the fifth moon in the *xinmao* year [1831]. By the four mercies after which our school is named I accomplished its way; I nourished my parents like the mother of the Brahma king so that they reached a high age. In the *dingmao* year [1867] on the day of my birthday, Heaven changed my body and removed everything profane from it; for seven days and nights I lay unconscious until I awakened tranquilly. I had escaped [from saṃsāra] and cleansed my worldly

19 The Southern land (Nam Kỳ 南圻) can designate Cochin-China (or southern Vietnam) between 1834 and 1945, or "Vietnam land" (Southern China) and its people.

> mind. I taught people to follow the way of goodness and my discourses spread widely. On the fifteenth day of the ninth moon in the *gengwu* year [1870] my name became known to the Perfected Celestial Woman of Marvelous Talent (Diệu Tài Chân Thiên Nữ); I conferred the three treasures on those who took refuge and selected worthy followers among the rich and poor, noble and humble. On the twenty-eighth day of the fourth moon in the *jimao* year [1879] I brought forth an enlightened mind (*Bồ Đề tâm thụ ký*) and attained assurance of Buddhahood, widely teaching and saving all sentient beings.
>
> 佃然先了定，南天國寶生。辛卯年五月，初五日午時，夏長受天恩。吾本宗所號，繼道所成能，養親梵王母，享世壽如山。向上丁卯歲，五月日午誕，轉我身去俗，七日夜低迷，寂然回喚醒，解脱洗塵心，教人從善道，口說普流傳。庚午年九月，十五日出名，妙才真天女，三寶派皈依，不論貧與富，貴賤擇賢人。己卯年四月，二十八日生。菩提心授記，普教度眾生。[20]

In 1867, at the age of 37, Ngô Lợi is said to have experienced a mystical experience of his body being transformed from an ordinary into a sacred one;[21] after awakening, he began his lifelong mission of preaching moral reform and saving others. Three years later, in 1870, having become enlightened through the instruction of the Heavenly Woman (天女 Thiên Nữ) and having received the Three Treasures, he formally founded his religion and began to spread the cultivation method of the Tứ Ân Hiếu Nghĩa. The *Yuli tushu jizhu* states that

> in the ninth moon of the *gengwu* year [1870] he set up his own teaching for refuge; in the *xinmao* year [1871] he conferred his teachings on those who had taken refuge; on the fifteenth day of the first moon of the *renshen* year [1872] with clerical and lay disciples he traveled by boat [to An Giang province]; in An Giang province […] he taught all sentient beings to recite the buddhadharma.
>
> 庚午年九月十五出号皈依，辛未年有給派皈依善男女，壬申年正月十五，僧眾徒弟船艘就，在安江省……教人眾生念佚法."[22]

20 *Xiaoyi jing, shangjuan* (print copy held at the Chùa Linh Bửu 靈寶寺 in Thị trấn Ba Chúc 芭祝鎮, An Giang province), 5–6, 60.

21 Cf. Chung, "Yuenan 'Baoshan qixiang' jiaopai ji qi chuanyan," 94–95.

22 *Yuli tushu jizhu* (Phạm Văn Vinh version), 8.

From this we can surmise that it was in 1870 that Ngô Lợi formally established his own organization and was regarded by believers as the legitimate successor of Đoàn Minh Huyên. Because he was believed to have received a celestial revelation and also because he cured many people by means of herbal medicine and talismans, Ngô Lợi was widely revered and had already gathered a significant number of followers by 1871. For their instruction, he began in 1872 to formally teach them the recitation of Buddha's name; that his proselytizing activities were carried out by boat served on the one hand to evade the French authorities, and but was also due to the fact that he did not yet have a fixed sacred space for the propagation of his teachings. 1879 was the year of the Tứ Ân Hiếu Nghĩa's most rapid growth. Evidence found in the *Yuli tushu jizhu* provides concrete information about Ngô Lợi's transmission of existing scriptures and creation of new ones. Relevant information for the years 1872 to 1879 is contained in the following passages:

> On the fifteenth day of the ninth moon of the *renshen* year [1872], the Master made the Pangu board. […] In the *jiaxu* year [1874], […] the Master saved men and women of this world by means of the great board. […] In the *bingzi* year [1876], he instructed all sentient beings and established a settlement named Anh Định thôn at Elephant Mountain; there he gathered his followers to recite the Buddha's name with a mind of goodness. […] In the *dingchou* year [1877], […] on the twelfth day of the third moon, the Master published the *Zhuanzhi jing*. In the *wuyin* year [1878], […] on the first day of the tenth moon he taught the *Wuyue jing* and *Wuhu jing* (in one volume). In the *jimao* year [1879], […] the Master expounded on the bodhi mudrā and the nirvāṇa mudrā and on the eighteen beads of the *Fenzhu jing*. […] On the twenty-eighth day of the first month, the Master on four occasions expounded the teachings and transmitted them widely, allowing all sentient beings, good men, and pious women to obtain the merit of reciting bodhi, holding the dharma with both hands while uttering the mantra. […] On the thirteenth day of the tenth moon in the *gengchen* year [1880], the teachings and mudrās of our Master of the orthodox, sangha, and Dao traditions were recorded in the *Yinzhi jing*.
>
> 壬申年師造盘古板……甲戌年……師以大板乾坤世度……丙子年……教許眾生設立村邑，在象山号安定村，逯聚良人善心念佛……丁丑年……三月十二日師出轉直經……戊寅年……十月初一教五岳五湖經一卷。己卯年……師說菩提手法，涅槃出法手，分珠經十八顆。……依月二十

FIGURE 6.6 Pangu board
© CHUNG YUN-YING

八日，師四說教普傳，許眾生善男信女等，奉念菩提功攄，[23] 兩手執法口念咒……。庚辰年十月十三日，正僧道師說，傳印入在陰騭經一卷。[24]

This passage enumerates Master Ngô Lợi's writings, which included not just scriptures, but also deity tablets and mudrā charts for cultivation purposes. The "Pangu board," for example, is a chart representing the creation of heaven and earth from the body of Pangu, and is accompanied by the phrase "homage to Amitābha Buddha," the twelve horary characters, the twelve zodiac signs, and a mantra for rebirth in the Pure land (see fig. 6.6). Almost all Tứ Ân

23 攄 *cớ* is a character occurring only in Tứ Ân Hiếu Nghĩa texts; according to the leader Nguyễn Văn Bạc 阮文泊, "功攄 *công cớ*" means "the hands gripping the Buddha beads." 攄 *cớ*'s meaning is "to grip"; 功 *công* means to practice cultivation in daily life.

24 *Yuli tushu jizhu* (Phạm Văn Vinh version), 5–12.

Hiếu Nghĩa temples display a Pangu board, using it to explain the creation of heaven and earth and to justify their proselytizing, as the *Yuli tushu jizhu* states that "the master used the great board to save all the world" (師以大板乾坤世度)—which demonstrates the combination of Buddhist and popular religious elements in Tứ Ân Hiếu Nghĩa.

From the biographical data summarized above we can extrapolate that Ngô Lợi began to compose scriptures in Chinese characters only in 1877; before that year he had been using existing texts which he recompiled, edited, and revised, and to which he added lists of deities. This is why the *Lingshanhui shangjing*, which is regarded as supremely important by believers, is an amalgam of familiar Chinese texts, such as the *Taiyang jing* 太陽經 (Great yang scripture), *Taiyin jing* 太陰經 (Great yin scripture), *Poluoni jing* 婆羅尼經 (Dhāraṇī[25] sūtra), *Zhunti zhou* 準提咒 (Mantra of Cundī), and of Guanyin-related texts such as *Ximao jing* 洗毛經 (Hair-washing sūtra), *Guanyin jiuku jing* 觀音救苦經 (Sūtra of Guanyin saving from distress), *Jin'gangshan jing* 金剛山經 (Diamond mountain sūtra), *Jin'gang shenzhou* 金剛神咒 (Diamond divine mantra), and *Guanyin jingzan* 觀音經讚 (Guanyin sūtra and hymns). At that time the missionary focus lay on "meritoriously assembling good people and with a heart of goodness reciting the Buddha's name" (逮聚良人善心念佛). The *Yuli tushu jizhu* passages also show that Ngô Lợi completed the *Zhuanzhi jing* 轉直經 *Chuyển trạc kinh* in 1877, and that in 1878 he taught two texts authored (in Chinese characters) by Nguyễn Hội Chân, the *Wuyue jing* and the *Wuhu jing* 五湖經 *Ngũ hồ kinh* (Scripture of the five lakes),[26] and other internal scriptures (see below). In 1879, he taught cultivation methods involving mudras (手印), mantras, and talismans;[27] he also composed in Chinese characters the *Fenzhu jing* 分珠經 (*Phân châu kinh*, Scripture on dividing the pearls), which is accompanied by a chart explaining recitation and cultivation by means of the eighteen beads of the Buddhist rosary. Thereafter the use of mudrās, mantras, and talismans became the principal cultivation method of Tứ Ân Hiếu Nghĩa, and followers firmly believe that the mudrās and mantras can help them escape calamities. By 1880, Ngô Lợi had assumed the title of *Zheng seng dao shi* 正僧道師 *Chánh Tăng Đạo Sư* (Master of the orthodox, sangha, and Dao traditions), i.e., he was a savior combining the Three Teachings. He orally expounded on the Tứ Ân Hiếu Nghĩa's mudrās, mantras, talismans, and sitting

25 Reading 陀羅尼 for 婆羅尼.

26 A note in the map depicting the Zhulingsi 珠靈寺 in the *Yuli tushu jizhu* states that among the scriptures to be recited are the *Wuyue jing* and the *Wuhu jing*, which confirms that these are two separate scriptures.

27 Data drawn from 玉曆圖書集註 *Ngọc lịch đồ thơ tập chú* and 功文 *Công văn*.

meditation methods; these lectures were transcribed by Nguyễn Hội Chân and assembled under the title *Yinzhi jing* 陰騭經 *Âm chất kinh* (Scripture of hidden merit).[28] Thus, the *Zhuanzhi jing* and the *Fenzhu jing* were authored directly by Ngô Lợi, while the *Yinzhi jing* is based on his ideas, but was transcribed and edited by Nguyễn Hội Chân. The charts, mantras, talismans, and the *Fenzhu jing* are all included in the *Yuli tushu jizhu*, and they all carry phrases such as "the master said" (*sư thuyết* 師說), "the transmission of the master" (*sư truyền* 師傳), "the teachings of the master" (*sư giáo* 師教), which shows that while this work was compiled by Ngô Lợi, his disciples inserted the honorific "master" in later versions. The other internally transmitted text, the *Gongwen*, which contains liturgical texts and the list of deities, was probably also composed by Ngô Lợi.

In the history of Tứ Ân Hiếu Nghĩa, Nguyễn Hội Chân was an important associate of Ngô Lợi. The current Tứ Ân Hiếu Nghĩa leader Phạm Văn Vinh states that most of its scriptures were given their final shape by Nguyễn. This statement is supported by the following passage in the *Wuyue zhenjing*:

> The marvelous method of Mt. Fire Tower [*Hỏa Lầu Sơn*] lets fall sweet dew, a book to bring relief to the world and escape from saṃsāra. [...] On the fifteenth day of the second moon he [Nguyễn Hội Chân] descended from Heaven to dwell in the nation of the South. [...] Day and night I heard pleas and vows, which moved my heart so that I descended on Mt. Fire Tower. As a master who goes to expound the teachings to others, who does good and accumulates merit, you have the roots of goodness and will reap the proper rewards. I have the Tripiṭaka in 35 sections and 5048 chapters. [...] Day and night I taught you, selecting several [from this vast repository of] scriptures. Among the scriptures appeared the Marvelous Method of Limitless Communication with all Buddhas and Devas, whereby the Buddha vanquishes all demons and robbers and widely saves all sentient beings. In the *bingzi* year [1876], I taught the *Diamond*

28 In August of 2018, I obtained a copy of the *Yinzhi jing* from a female devotee, named Trần Thị Rang 陳氏[火+郎], in Thị trấn Ba Chúc 芭祝鎮, An Giang province. This book details 86 mudras and the appellations of many gods. The excessive wealth and complexity of religious information led to its being hard to memorize for practice, and hence its circulation among the faithful declined. The fact that the invocation "Great Master of True Hidden Merit, completely eradicate all demons" (真陰騭大師，盡滅除妖怪) seems to indicate that the cultivation of mudras served primarily apotropaic purposes. Ms. Trần Thi Rang avows that while she is still familiar with all mudras in the Tứ Ân Hiếu Nghĩa tradition, fewer and fewer people possess that knowledge nowadays.

> *sūtra*, in the following three years[29] the *Xitian yingjing*, the *Nirvāṇa sūtra*, the *Zheng falun jing*, the *Bodhisattva sūtra*, the *Great Wisdom sūtra*, the *Enyi jing*, the *Mahāprajñāpāramitā sūtra*, the *Jueding jing*, the *Sūtra of the bodhisattva precepts*, the *Avataṃsaka sūtra*, the *Fo benxing jing*, the *Baozang jing*, the *Śūraṅgama sūtra*, the *Diamond sūtra*, the *Zhenglü wen jing*, and the *Yinzhi jing*. [Nguyễn Hội Chân] bowed low and took refuge, making a pious vow that the Sagely Mother Cundī [Chuẩn Đề Thánh Mẫu] may manifest herself; she descended into the world to deliver people and open the Great Way [*giáng thế độ nhân khai đại đạo*]. The Orthodox Method of the Celestial Turtle, the Heavenly Writ of the Method of the Three Teachings all descended into the world as limitless methods for the people's deliverance.
>
> ……火樓山妙法澍甘露，濟世脫身一部書。……二月十五日降居大南國……日夜聞請願，配動至我心，降在火樓山。假邁人說教，積善陰隲師，汝善根正果，我有三藏經，共三十五部，各部計五千零四十八卷，……日夜我教明，擇教諸號經。經中即出現無量百千佛神通妙法，佛滅妖怪狂賊，普度眾生安。丙子金剛經，丑寅卯三卷，西天應經、涅槃經、正法輪經、菩薩經、大般若經、恩意經、大智度經、決定經、菩薩戒經、花（案:華）嚴經、佛本行經、寶藏經、首楞嚴經、金剛經、正律文經、陰隲經。稽首皈依，虔誠願準提聖母現全身，降世度人開大道，天竜正法，三教法天書，護國四恩真，降世度人無量法……[30]

Furthermore, the *Wugong bore jing* states:

> The marvelous method of Mt. Fire Tower lets fall sweet dew, a book to bring relief to the world and escape from saṃsāra. [...] Chapter 1 contained the *Guanyin* and *Wugong* scriptures, chapter 2 the *Wuyue* and *Wuhu* scriptures, and chapter 3 the *Dabei* and *Puan* scriptures—together these form the *Scripture of Truth and Longevity*. On the fifteenth day of the *dingchou* year [1877] at the sacred banquet to worship the Gods, the Lord on High said: It is heaven's virtue to love living beings; evil conduct originates from humans, [not Heaven]. I [*thượng đế* or "god"] have

29 Reading 年 for 卷.

30 *Wuyue zhenjing* (manuscript copy held at the Chùa Tam Bửu 三寶寺 in Thị trấn Ba Chúc 芭祝鎮, An Giang province), 12–15. Authorship of the text is ascribed to Nguyễn Hội Chân, but there clearly is some confusion in this text excerpt as to who is speaking to whom. The subject seems to shift between Nguyễn Hội Chân and a deity instructing him. Interviews with Tứ Ân Hiếu Nghĩa devotees cleared up this confusion.

> ordered the Mahasattva Guanyin, the Patriarchal Master Puan, the Four Great Celestial Kings, the Five Lords, and various bodhisattvas to admonish the world. Wenchang, Divine Lord of Zitong, ordered that an assembly be established at Mt. Fire Tower [... whose members were to] make donations, listen to the dharma, save good people, ... respect the writing of scriptures and books ... Nguyễn Hội Chân revered lettered paper. On his journeys from the *jiazi* to the *bingzi* year [1864–1876], he was able to communicate with deities. He studied the ancient language[31] and wrote and expounded the *Yinzhi jing*. Good deeds will not remain unremarked and so with a thunderclap a celestial text descended ... [this] True Scripture of Mt. Fire Tower saves good people ... this text was sent by Heaven on the fifteenth day ... many sages were assembled to compose this scripture so as to rescue sentient beings from disaster.
>
> 火樓山妙法澍甘露，濟世貧寒一部書。……。觀音五公為一卷，五岳五湖為二卷，大悲普菴為三卷，即是真寔長生經。丁丑十五嘉聖筵……上帝曰:天德本好生，寔人自惡行。下令付觀音大士、普菴祖師、四大天王、五公諸菩薩戒世，文昌梓童帝君令生，立會在火樓山……施才聞法度善人……奉敬經書字……阮會真奉敬續字紙，甲子至丙子，行得真感應，下學曾古語，寫論陰隲經，為善必有靈，雷聲天書降……火樓山真經度善人，……天上此書十五降，……此經聖賢會，為救眾生災。[32]

1877 thus was an important year in the scriptural production of the two founders; it appears that Nguyễn Hội Chân's authorial efforts predate those of Ngô Lợi by one year. Like Ngô Lợi, Nguyễn also began by adapting familiar sūtras and morality books, and only later composed his own scriptures.

The *Wuyue zhenjing* contains an itemized list of scriptures ("I have a Tripiṭaka canon in 35 sections and 5048 chapters" 我有三藏經，共三十五部，各部計五千零四十八卷); except for the *Yinzhi jing* the items of this list are drawn from chapter 98 of the *Journey to the West* 西遊記.[33] While these

---

31 According to my informants, this refers to the so-called celestial language (*thiên ngữ* 天語).

32 *Wugong bore jing* (Võ Tô's 武蘇 manuscript copy held at the Chùa Phi Lai 飛萊寺 in Thị trấn Ba Chúc 芭祝鎮, An Giang province), 12–17.

33 Figures and themes from the *Journey to the West* appear in a number of internal texts of the Tứ Ân Hiếu Nghĩa; for example, the *Xiaoyi jing* begins with a story of the monk Xuanzang 玄奘 traveling west to obtain sūtras. In response to my question, Nguyễn Hữu Nghi opined that internal texts imitate the *Journey to the West* because this work focuses on cultivation. In my view, this may only be one general factor—I plan to explore the

listed texts are all of Chinese origin, the *Wugong Guanyin jing* 五公觀音經 *Ngũ công Quan Âm kinh* (Five lords and Guanyin scripture), *Wuyue jing*, *Wuhu jing*, *Puan jing* 普庵經 *Phổ yểm kinh* (Scripture of Puan), *Shousheng jing* 壽生經 *Thọ sanh kinh* (Long life sūtra), and the *Yinzhi jing*, which is based on the oral teachings of Ngô Lợi, were completed by Nguyễn Hội Chân. We find narratives in the texts that deify and mythologize Nguyễn Hội Chân who, as we have seen, was called "Fire Tower of the Three Teachings" (Tam Giáo Hỏa Lầu 三教火樓, see fig. 6.5); although he was not the head of the religion, he was chosen by the Celestial Emperor to compose texts that were to save people, so his contributions to Tứ Ân Hiếu Nghĩa were not inconsiderable. This important salvific function of Nguyễn's works, especially for those who do good, is expressed in phrases such as "[the scripture] brings relief to the world and offers escape" (濟世脫身), "brings relief to those suffering from poverty and cold" (濟世貧寒), "it widely saves and brings peace to all sentient beings" (普度眾生安), "the true scripture saves the good" (真經度善人), and "[it] rescues all sentient beings from disaster" (救眾生災). The deification of Nguyễn Hội Chân and his mystic experiences serve to sacralize his written works. The *Wugong bore jing*'s opening gātha states, "The highest, most profound, sublime and marvelous dharma.... first repay the ruler's grace and Phan Mỹ Bộ,[34] then take refuge in the buddhadharma and Nguyễn Hội Chân" (無上甚深微妙法……前報君恩潘美部，後逩（歸）佚法阮會真).[35] This passage equates Nguyễn's transmitted teachings with the buddhadharma, and his works with the Buddhist sūtras; thus these texts deserve the utmost veneration. Between 1874 and 1876 by divine grace he is said to have learned the "ancient language" 古語 and became able to communicate with deities; when it is said that the texts composed by him "descended as celestial writings accompanied by the sound of thunder" (雷聲天書降), this emphasizes the authority of his works. To further heighten Nguyễn Hội Chân's status, the Tứ Ân Hiếu Nghĩa opened a new sanctuary in

---

question of the *Journey to the West*'s influence on Vietnamese popular religious movements in a separate paper.

34 The life dates of Phan Mỹ Bộ 潘美部 are uncertain. According to the testimony of Mr. Phạm Văn Vinh 范文榮, one of Tứ Ân Hiếu Nghĩa's 24 leaders, Phan Mỹ Bộ and Nguyễn Hội Chân are one and the same person, Phan Mỹ Bộ being merely an alternative appellation of Nguyễn. However, another member of the leadership, Mr. Nguyễn Văn Bạc 阮文泊, stated that Ngô Lợi had two assistants: Nguyễn Hội Chân, who was responsible for the inner teachings and texts, and Phan Mỹ Bộ, who was responsible for political matters such as resistance against the French from 1874 to 1890, the independence cause, and the protection of the people. Thus, the phrase, "first repay the ruler's grace and Phan Mỹ Bộ, then take refuge in the buddhadharma and Nguyễn Hội Chân," might express Ngô Lợi's wish that his followers should obey the joint leadership of Phan and Nguyễn.

35 *Wugong bore jing*, 11.

Cochin-China at Hỏa Lầu Sơn 火樓山 (Mt. Fire Tower) which was ranked with the movement's other sacred mountains. It is here that Nguyễn composed his texts and it is said that the Celestial Emperor commanded the gods to congregate there and protect Nguyễn Hội Chân's work. Such narratives did not just establish the sacredness and authority of Nguyễn's texts, but also gave him the epithets Hỏa Lầu and Tam Giáo Hỏa Lầu under which he is honored among the gods of the Tứ Ân Hiếu Nghĩa.

4 Transmission and Revision of Traditional Scriptures by Ngô Lợi and Nguyễn Hội Chân

As we have seen, during the early phase of Tứ Ân Hiếu Nghĩa's history Ngô Lợi and Nguyễn Hội Chân worked mostly with and on traditional Chinese sūtras and morality books. In the course of their missionary endeavor, they reworked the original texts to make them better fit Vietnamese conditions and customs. This kind of borrowing, reworking, and appropriation of the scriptures of other religions is not uncommon among popular religious movements. I will investigate the particular approach of Ngô Lợi and Nguyễn Hội Chân with regard first to Buddhist sūtras, then to morality books.

4.1 *The Continuation of the Sūtra Form*

As mentioned earlier, Buddhism is an important element in Vietnam's cultural basis, with the cult of Guanyin being particularly significant. The Tứ Ân Hiếu Nghĩa thus has preserved to the present day the custom of copying and reciting sūtras. I have collected the following sūtras (with the titles used in Tứ Ân Hiếu Nghĩa): *Bayang jing* 八陽經 *Bát dương kinh* (Eight yang sūtra), *Pumen jing* 普門經 *Phổ môn kinh* (i.e., *Pumen pin* 普門品, the "chapter on the universal gate" from the *Lotus Sūtra*), *Shousheng jing* 壽生經 *Thọ sanh kinh* (Long life sūtra), *Mituo jing* (i.e., the *Foshuo Amituo jing* 佛說阿彌陀經, "Amitābha sūtra spoken by the Buddha"), *Gaowang jing* (i.e., *Gaowang Guanshiyin zhenjing* 高王觀世音真經, "King Gao's true sūtra of Guanshiyin"), *Puan jing* (i.e., *Puan zhou* 普庵咒, "Puan mantra"), *Yulanpen jing* 盂蘭盆經 *Vu lan bồn kinh* ("Ullambana sūtra"), and the internal text *Lingshanhui shangjing*, which contains a collection of various sūtras and mantras. These sūtras are the ones most familiar to believers and shape their understanding of the "scriptural form."

As the Tứ Ân Hiếu Nghĩa stresses requiting the four kinds of kindness received from (1) ancestors and parents, (2) the nation, (3) the Three Treasures, and (4) humanity and compatriots, we find these concerns represented by incantatory phrases in its sūtra copies. The back of the title page or the first page typically contains the phrase, "Above we pray for the reigning king's longevity, below may [this sūtra] help the civil and military officials gain promotion" (上祝當令國王聖壽無疆， 下資文武官僚高增位品), and "homage to the original teacher, Śākyamuni Buddha 南無本師釋迦牟尼佛." Furthermore, the Tứ Ân Hiếu Nghĩa sūtra versions contain a series of preparatory formulae not found in the original texts: incense hymn (*luxiang zan* 爐香讚), mantra for cleansing karma caused by the body (*jing shenye zhenyan* 淨身業真言), mantra for cleansing karma caused by speech (*jing kouye zhenyan* 淨口業真言), mantra for cleansing karma caused by thought (*jing yiye zhenyan* 淨意業真言), mantra pacifying the earth [god] (*an tudi zhenyan* 安土地真言), mantra for feeding all [ghosts and spirits] (*pu gongyang zhenyan*普供養真言), vow (*fayuan wen* 發願文), opening gātha (*kaijing ji* 開經偈), and various other prayers and mantras. These formulae serve to express piety and still the mind preparatory to the recitation of the sūtra proper.

The Tứ Ân Hiếu Nghĩa's own scriptures are clearly influenced by the example of the Buddhist sūtras: The *Lingshanhui shangjing* requires recitation of a lamp-lighting mantra (*diandeng zhou* 點燈咒), incense vow mantra (*yuanxiang zhou* 願香咒), bell ringing mantra (*kaizhong zhou* 開鐘咒), mantra for the singing bowl (開楪咒), incense hymn (*luxiang zan* 爐香讚), request for sincerity and worthiness (*qing chengxian* 請誠賢), making offerings to the scripture (*gongyang jing* 供養經), dharma protecting mantra (*hufa zhou* 護法咒), praising the willow branch (*zan yangzhi* 讚楊枝), and an opening gātha (*kaijing ji* 開經偈), before getting to the *Poluoni jing* and concluding its recitation with a hymn on the *Guanyin jing* (*Guanyin jing zan* 觀音經讚). In the *Xiaoyi jing*, the list of formulae includes an opening hymn (*kaijing zan* 開經讚), the mantra of the Good Celestial Woman (*shan tiannü zhou* 善天女咒), opening gātha (*kaijing ji* 開經偈), venerating the eight tathāgatas (*fengbai ba rulai* 奉拜八如來), a gātha (*ji yue* 偈曰), honoring the hymns and worshiping the vows (*fengzan baiyuan* 奉讚拜願), prostrating oneself to the 24 vows [of Amitābha Buddha] (*fu da dingli ershisi yuan* 伏大頂禮二十四願), a hymn on concluding the scripture (*zan shoujing* 讚收經), and the invocations "homage to mahāprajñāpāramitā" (*namo mohe boreboluomi* 南無摩訶般若波羅蜜) and "homage to Amitābha Buddha of the Blissful Land" (*namo jile guoshi Amituofo* 南無極樂國世阿彌陀佛). The *Wugong bore jing* lists an incense hymn (*luxiang zan* 爐香讚), a mantra for cleansing karma caused by speech (*jing kouye zhenyan* 淨口業真言), a mantra pacifying the earth [god] (*an tudi zhenyan* 安土地真言), a mantra for cleansing the three kinds of karma (*jing sanye zhenyan* 淨三業真言), a mantra for feeding all [ghosts and spirits] (*pu gongyang zhenyan* 普供養真言), an invitation to the eight celestial worthies (*fengqing ba tianzun* 奉請八天尊), an invitation to the bodhisattvas of the ten directions (*fengqing shifang pusa* 奉請十方菩薩), a vow (*fayuan wen* 發願文), and an opening gātha (*kaijing ji* 開經偈). In all these cases, the Tứ Ân Hiếu Nghĩa scriptures clearly follow the pattern of Buddhist sūtras (or, rather, their widely circulating popularized versions).

Aside from the liturgical formulae, the opening narrative passages of scriptures also closely imitate the tone of Buddhist sūtras. A good illustration is provided by the opening of the *Foshuo tiandi jing*:

> At one time the World-Honored One was staying in the city of Rājagṛha,[36] together with a gathering of bhikṣus and bhikṣuṇīs, twelve hundred fifty in all, who had come to listen to the dharma together. Again, the World-Honored One said: You all know how heaven was created and earth established. These disciples placed their palms together and kneeled, reverently paid obeisance and with a faithful mind turned to[37] the Buddha. Homage to the Buddha, homage to the Dharma, homage to the Sangha.
>
> 爾時世尊在玉舍城，與比丘、比丘尼眾，一千二百五十人俱會同聽法。世尊又曰，造天立地，大眾同知。合掌白跪，恭敬禮拜，信心命佛。南無佛、南無法、南無僧。[38]

The imitative character of another Tứ Ân Hiếu Nghĩa scripture, the *Jin'gang shouming jing* 金剛壽命經, is even more obvious:

> The dhāraṇī[39] sūtra of all tathāgatas on diamond-like longevity, spoken by the Buddha [...] Thus I have heard, at one time the World-Honored One was together with many bhikṣus and great bodhisattvas at the banks of the Ganges river [...] they only wished for the World-Honored One to propound this dharma for all sentient beings. At that time the World-Honored One faced east ...
>
> 仸說一切如來金剛壽命陀羅來經……如是我聞，一時仸在情殑伽河側，與諸比丘及大菩薩……唯願世尊為眾生故宣設是法。爾時世尊面向東方……[40]

36 Reading 王舍城 for 玉舍城.

37 Reading 向 for 命.

38 *Foshuo tiandi jing* (Võ Tô's 武蘇 manuscript copy held at the Chùa Phi Lai 飛萊寺 in Thị trấn Ba Chúc 芭祝鎮, An Giang province), 1.

39 Reading 陀羅尼 for 陀羅來.

40 *Jin'gang shouming jing* (manuscript copy held at the Chùa Mã Châu 馬珠寺 in Thị trấn Ba Chúc 芭祝鎮, An Giang province), 1–2.

We find similar diction in the *Xiaoyi jing*:

> At that time the dharma-master Tripiṭaka and the great sage Sun Wu, accompanied by Dragon-Horse, Sand-Monk, and Eight-Precepts, received the decree of Tang emperor Taizong to go to the western realm.
>
> 爾時三藏法師，孫悟大聖、隨護龍馬、沙僧、八戒，奉詔大唐太宗皇帝勅往西天。[41]

.... and in the *Yuhuang gusui zhenjing*, which is based on the Chinese *Yuhuang xinyin zhenjing*:

> At that time the World-Honored One, the most high Jade Emperor dwelt in emptiness ... mantra for cleansing karma caused by speech, [...], with a determined mind take refuge, bow three times.
>
> 爾時世尊高上玉皇虛空……淨口業真言，唵修唎修唎摩訶修唎修修唎娑婆訶，志心皈命禮，三拜三遍。[42]

The *Sanyuan jishan jing* 三元積善經 *Tam nguơn tích thiện kinh* (The Three Primes' scripture on accumulating goodness) is divided into three sections, titled respectively the "Upper," "Middle," and "Lower Prime's scripture on accumulating goodness" (上、中、下元積善經). In imitation of other scriptures, each section begins with an incense hymn (*luxiang zan*):

> When the Buddha spoke the *Upper Prime Scripture*, he uttered mantras and said: The Lord-on-High in the Numinous Empyrean gathered his sagely court so that together they may examine punishments and blessings in the human world. By weighing the innumerable good and bad deeds, the good obtain good rewards, while the evil fall into purgatory. (same phrasing for the *Middle* and *Lower Prime Scripture*).

41 *Xiaoyi jing* (print copy held at the Chùa Linh Bửu 靈寶寺 in Thị trấn Ba Chúc 芭祝鎮, An Giang province), 3.

42 *Yuhuang gusui zhenjing* (manuscript copy held at the Mộc hương Chùa Phi Lai 飛莱寺木香 in Thị trấn Ba Chúc 芭祝鎮, An Giang province), 11.

> 佛說上元經，即說咒曰，靈霄上帝具會聖朝。公同照鑒罪福人間。河沙善惡較量罪人。善得善果，惡隨地獄。……佛說中元經，即說咒曰……佛說下元經，即說咒曰……[43]

This imitative approach seeks to integrate the indigenous sectarian scriptures into the Buddhist scriptural tradition, stressing that they deserve the same degree of respect in handling, copying, and recitation. The sacredness of the scriptures is further bolstered by the notion of divine punishment for those treating them disrespectfully. Popular scriptures sometimes include retribution stories to enhance the respect for the scripture and assist in its spread and preservation. The presence of such imitative features in Tứ Ân Hiếu Nghĩa scriptures is, of course, partly due to the pervasively Buddhist nature of Vietnamese culture, but they are also the result of a consciously pursued strategy thereby to enhance the sacredness of the texts. The strategy's success is apparent in the fact that they are still being piously copied by Tứ Ân Hiếu Nghĩa believers to the present day.

4.2 *Rewriting of Popular Morality Books*

Aside from Buddhist sūtras, we also find in the Tứ Ân Hiếu Nghĩa collections many hand-copied Chinese morality books. Obviously, hand-copying brings with it the possibility of either inadvertent transcription errors or deliberate editing. Among the internal texts, the *Taoyuan jing, Dimu jing*, and *Siming zaojun zhenjing* contain relatively few alterations in the main text; the principal difference to Chinese versions is the addition of a few Tứ Ân Hiếu Nghĩa incantatory formulae at the beginning and end of the text; these refer specifically to the initial "homage to the original teacher, Śākyamuni Buddha" (南無本師釋迦牟尼佛) and an instruction in the end that the practitioner should "in addition recite the *Heart Sūtra* once and the mantra thrice" (補缺心經一遍，補缺真言三遍).[44] By contrast, the *Wugong tiantu jing*, *Chaosheng jing*, and *Yuhuang gusui zhenjing* differ significantly from their Chinese models; while they largely preserve the original text, they add much further material specifically related to Tứ Ân Hiếu Nghĩa teachings. Let me explain this using the case example of the *Yuhuang gusui zhenjing* (see figs. 6.7 & 6.8).

---

43 *Sanyuan jishan jing* (manuscript at the Chùa Tam Bửu 三寶寺, in Thị trấn Ba Chúc 芭祝鎮, An Giang province), 18, 35, 49.

44 The *Heart Sūtra* is a familiar and widely known text from the Buddhist canon; the "mantra" is a confession text: 菴背字囉。邁字過。語不真。漏字多。意不專。心即差。謬誦經。添減他。香花淨水。誠心意。補缺圓滿。罪消磨。諸佛龍天。求仍（懺）悔，南無求仍（懺）悔菩薩摩訶薩。

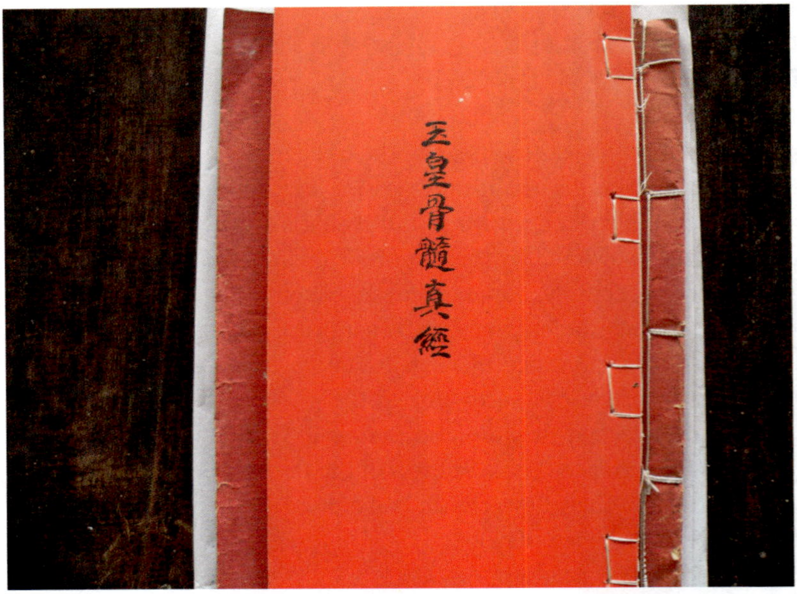

FIGURE 6.7 *Yuhuang gusui zhenjing* 玉皇骨髓真經 *Ngọc hoàng cốt tủy chân kinh* (cover)

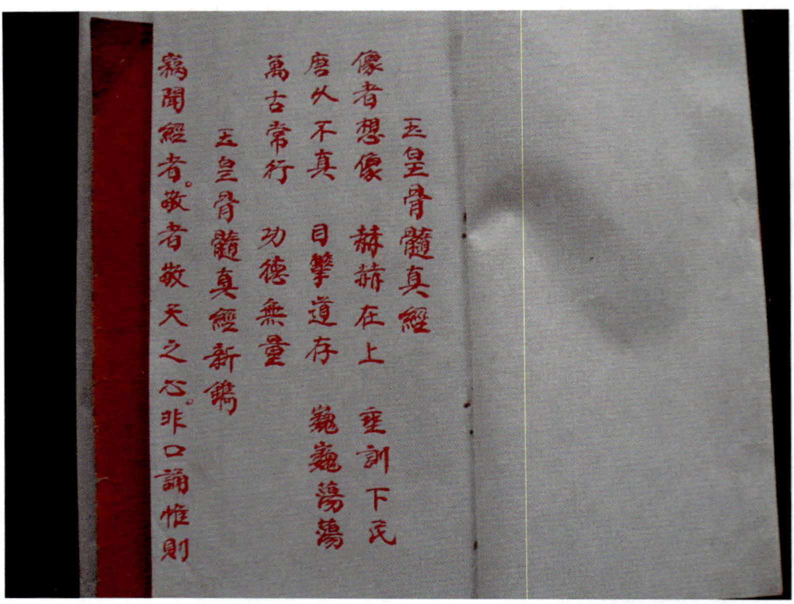

FIGURE 6.8 *Yuhuang gusui zhenjing* 玉皇骨髓真經 *Ngọc hoàng cốt tủy chân kinh* (opening page)

The *Yuhuang gusui zhenjing* is based on the *Yuhuang xinyin zhenjing* 玉皇心印真經, to which a new section is added, whose title became the name of the combined scripture.[45] On this editorial process we find the following information in the *Yuhuang gusui zhenjing xinjuan* 玉皇骨髓真經新鐫 (Newly carved bone-marrow true scripture of the Jade Emperor):

> The Jade Emperor's Perfected Scripture ... is a teaching sent down by the Lord on High ... and contains nothing that has not been proven. Ever since the Lý dynasty, our nation of the South [*Nam quốc*] has been venerating scriptures and canons. For other scriptures there exist printed editions, but for this scripture we have only manuscripts and it has not yet been printed. If one wishes to spread it to innumerable people, one needs to supplement this shortcoming. ... Why should North and South differ in this? The reason why I had it printed, was to express my reverence towards it, so as to widen its distribution. On the twenty-third day of the tenth moon in the *gengchen* year of the Tự Đức reign period [1880], I composed this preface for it. Whether at home or in the temple, one should burn[46] incense in front of the altar while reciting it. Having recited it reverently and sincerely, one must place it on the altar. Do not treat it with disrespect! The printing blocks are stored in the Zhenwuguan (Trấn Vũ Quán) in Hanoi. All those wishing to reprint it should obtain the printing blocks from this temple. Their merit will be beyond measure!
>
> ……玉皇真經……上帝之垂訓由來以矣，……無不明驗者矣。我南國自李朝，崇尚經典以來，他經各有藏板，而此經但有抄板，未遑錄梓，欲傳於無窮者，可不因其缺以補之乎？……豈以北南異此？所以特付梓匠，蓋相主敬，以廣其傳，云辰嗣德。庚辰年梅月望八日，謹序此經。或在寺，或在家，誦時樊香按(案)前，宜篤齋誠，誦後安置按(案)上，勿可輕慢。其藏板在河內省鎮武觀，諸君子有心敬送，請就靈觀印板，功德無量無邊。.[47]

The Vietnamese references are noteworthy in that they give readers the impression that they are looking at an indigenous text. The phrases "Why should North and South differ in this?" and "the printing blocks are stored at

45 According to Xiao Dengfu, the *Yuhuang xinyin miaojing* was composed at the latest by the end of the Tang or beginning of the Song dynasty. See Xiao Dengfu 蕭登福, "*Yuhuang xinyin miaojing* yu Daojiao zhi neidan xiulian xinfa 《玉皇心印妙經》與道教之內丹修鍊心法," *Xing yu ming* 性與命, no. 12 (1997): 100–113.

46 Reading 焚 for 樊.

47 *Yuhuang gusui zhenjing*, 1–4.

the Zhenwuguan in Hanoi" tell us that the *Yuhuang xinyin zhenjing* spread from Cochin-China (south) to Tonkin (northern Vietnam), again intimating that the text has a local history and is not culturally foreign to its Vietnamese readers. The readership likely consisted of two major groups, one being local Vietnamese literati, the other Chinese immigrants. The latter had been settling in An Giang province since the sixteenth century, and many of them had maintained Chinese-language education for their descendants.

To the fundamental text of the *Yuhuang xinyin zhenjing*, Tứ Ân Hiếu Nghĩa added a "mantra for cleansing karma caused by speech" (*jing kouye zhenyan*), a refuge text (*zhixin guiming li* 志心皈命禮) with a list of the titles of eleven popular deities, and of course, the text of the Tứ Ân Hiếu Nghĩa's own *Yuhuang gusui zhenjing*, which then became the title of the compilation. After the opening statement that "at that time the World-Honored One, the most high Jade Emperor dwelt in emptiness," the *Yuhuang gusui zhenjing* expounds about cosmogony and cosmology, citing the sequence of Great Change, Great Origin, Great Beginning, Great Simplicity, and Great Ultimate, and then describing the successive emergence of the Eight Trigrams, twelve hours, 28 constellations, sun and moon, Three Primes, Four Great Celestial Kings, Eight Vajras, ten courts of hell, the twelve plague spirits, the spirit-officials of the three disasters, the spirit-officials of the three poisons, the spirit-officials of the five sounds and five natures, the spirit-officials of the residence and earth, the spirit-officials stopping noxious influences, the 80,000 divine numina and sagely rulers, the four *yakṣa* demon kings, Mt. Sumeru and the great ocean, the dragon kings and aquatic species, the river earl and aquatic officials, the city god and magistrate of the earth altar, the orthodox spirit of the earth, and finally all kings, loyal ministers, and valorous generals throughout history.[48] The text concludes with a call for "all to come quickly, be certified as disciples, and piously practice [the teachings of this scripture]" (公同速來，証明弟子，信受奉行).

This text explains that everything in the cosmos, the stars, the gods of heaven, the underworld, land, sea, and air, and also the human realm, originates from

48 爾時世尊高上玉皇虛空，自然運轉，三才八封。太易、太初、太始、太素、太極，一天二地三人。……轉八卦……。混十二時晨（辰）……，轉天干……，轉二十八宿……轉北斗九皇解厄星君。…… 轉日宮太陽月宮太陰，轉梵玉帝釋護法善神，轉上元賜福天官。中元赦罪地官，下元解厄水官，轉四大天王，轉八部金剛。…… 轉內外主宅土公神官，轉建破住煞神官，轉東西南北四維上下神祇等處。轉八萬神靈聖主，轉四部夜叉鬼王，轉山河大地，轉須彌大海，轉東海龍王，轉王水族，轉河伯水官，轉城隍社令，轉土地正神，轉歷代國王忠臣勇將。*Yuhuang gusui zhenjing*, 11–19.

the Jade Emperor; everything has its origin and emerges through repeated processes of transformation (*zhuan* 轉 *chuyển*). In the Tứ Ân Hiếu Nghĩa's worldview, everything is interconnected, but also arranged in oppositional relationships. Based on the notions of *yin* and *yang*, the consequence of this worldview for moral cultivation is that since good and evil coexist, one must harbor no devious schemes as the good will be protected by good spirits and the evil crushed by evil spirits. While the Jade Emperor is the originator of this morally ambivalent world, he is filled with compassion and will dispatch worthy emissaries to bring order to human society; if only humans can maintain good thoughts in their minds, all calamities will be transformed (*zhuan*). This doctrine is also emphasized in the Tứ Ân Hiếu Nghĩa's *Zhuanzhi jing*.

After these preliminaries, let us now look at the overall structure of the *Yuhuang gusui zhenjing*:

1) [Prefatory phrase]: [The Jade Emperor] is to be visualized as an awesome presence above who bestows his instructions on the people. If there are bold ones who regard this as false, [this scripture] serves as witness that the Dao exists. Majestic and great, it has been practiced since ancient times. Its merit is beyond measure.
像者想像，赫赫在上，垂訓下民，唐以不真，目擊道存，巍巍蕩蕩，萬古常行，功德無量。
2) [Title]: Bone-Marrow Scripture of the Jade Emperor, Printed from Newly Engraved Blocks 玉皇骨髓真經新鐫
3) [Hymns for various deities]: Hymn for Guanyin Buddha, hymn for Great Emperor Zhenwu, hymn for Emperor Wen, also: hymn for Emperor Guan, Emperor Lü, and the Old Man of the Moon 玉皇骨髓真經列聖讚，觀音佛讚、真武大帝讚、文帝讚、又曰、關帝讚、呂帝讚、月老先讚
4) Mantra for cleansing karma caused by speech 淨口業真言
5) Formula for taking refuge 志心皈命禮
6) Bone-Marrow Scripture of the Jade Emperor 玉皇骨髓真經
7) *dhāraṇī* 咒曰
8) Repentance 又志心懺禮
9) Golden elixir handed down by the Jade Emperor 玉皇垂訓金丹
10) *Gāthā* by the Divine Lord Fuyou 孚佑帝君偈語

Item #9, the "golden elixir handed down by the Jade Emperor" is, in fact, the text of the *Yuhuang xinyin zhenjing*. The fact that the hymns, and mantras are placed before the *Yuhuang gusui zhenjing* relegates the *Yuhuang xinyin zhenjing* to an appendix of the former. It is the *Yuhuang gusui zhenjing* that clearly stands at the center of this compilation. This downgrading of the *Yuhuang xinyin zhenjing*'s status is also reflected in its renaming, omitting the term "scripture," thereby stressing that the core (or "marrow," *gusui*) and only "scripture" in the compilation is, indeed, the *Yuhuang gusui zhenjing*.

The Tứ Ân Hiếu Nghĩa's approach of appropriating Chinese religious texts by adding new content and restructuring them demonstrates a combination of continuity and innovation. It can also be seen as a form of cultural appropriation that might be interpreted in terms of P. Steven Sangren's "social reproduction."[49] In the Tứ Ân Hiếu Nghĩa, deities such as the Jade Emperor and Guan Gong are shared Sino-Vietnamese cultural codes, but the reworking of their sacred texts further indigenizes them; as a result, these Tứ Ân Hiếu Nghĩa scriptures become part of Vietnamese religious culture more generally, thus emphasizing the cultural authority of Vietnamese religions to continue to rework, develop, and recreate the resources provided by its traditional culture, both Chinese or Vietnamese. Whether we regard them as transmitters, revisers, or creators, the texts produced by Ngô Lợi and Nguyễn Hội Chân are documents of their religious ideas, which allow us to study them and to assess their impact on Vietnamese culture.

5 Conclusion

This chapter examined scriptures of the Tứ Ân Hiếu Nghĩa from the perspectives of transmission and revision. Accumulated tradition and new creation characterize all religious movements. Guan Gong clearly serves as a distinguishing marker for Tứ Ân Hiếu Nghĩa, combining his worship with that of the Jade Emperor. The *Yuhuang gusui zhenjing* analyzed above provides a very clear example of this process. At the same time, because of the long-standing and profound influence of Buddhism in Vietnam, the cultural basis of Tứ Ân Hiếu Nghĩa belief remains Buddhist, in particular with reference to the cult of Guanyin. I tried to conceptualize this fact in terms of visible and hidden dimensions religious belief, but also as a synthesis of Buddhism and Daoism. Such efforts can be considered as a continuation of Bửu Sơn Kỳ Hương millenarianism, inaugurating a serial process of reincarnation of the Buddha Maitreya—from Đoàn Minh Huyên to Ngô Lợi and later to Huỳnh Phú Sổ 黄富楚 (1920–1947) with Hòa Hảo Buddhism in the 1930s. At the same time, the ritual and textual compositions offered by Tứ Ân Hiếu Nghĩa are much more

49 See P. Steven Sangren, *History and Magical Power in a Chinese Community* (Stanford: Stanford University Press, 1987), cited in Ding Renjie 丁仁傑, *Dangdai Hanren minzhong zongjiao yanjiu: Lunshu, rentong yu shehui zaishengchan* 當代漢人民眾宗教研究：論述、認同與社會再生產 (Taipei: Lianjing, 2009), 74.

elaborate than those of Bửu Sơn Kỳ Hương, prefiguring an original and rational syncretism of Daoism and Buddhism that Cao Đài would fully realize in 1920s Cochin-China.[50]

This hidden level becomes apparent in the movement's scriptures, which also allow us to ascertain that Ngô Lợi and Nguyễn Hội Chân were its true founders and shapers. In particular, they throw into sharper relief the importance of Nguyễn Hội Chân, about whose life we otherwise know very little; deified under the title Tam Giáo Hỏa Lầu, his former sanctuary at Fire Tower Mountain has become one of the sacred sites of the Tứ Ân Hiếu Nghĩa. Ngô Lợi and Nguyễn Hội Chân's scriptural production primarily employs an imitative approach in utilizing Buddhist phrases, structural elements, and concepts; but they also reworked non-Buddhist morality books and scriptures, infusing them with their own Daoist and millenarian ideas and thereby appropriating Bửu Sơn Kỳ Hương theogony and modi operandi for Tứ Ân Hiếu Nghĩa's agenda in mid and late nineteenth century Cochin-China.

The present chapter provides only a preliminary investigation of the texts in Chinese script preserved and revered by the Tứ Ân Hiếu Nghĩa; further studies on ritual, and the history and development of the movement and its leaders, for instance, will enable us to better understand the transmission of Chinese religious texts into Vietnam, as well as the processes of indigenization they underwent there. Such research will also contribute to the comparative study of Chinese and Vietnamese religious movements and increase our knowledge of Vietnamese religions in the nineteenth and early twentieth centuries in particular.

Bibliography

Primary Sources

Đặng Văn Tuấn. "Đạo Tứ Ân Hiếu Nghĩa và ảnh hưởng của nó đối với tín đồ Tứ Ân Hiếu Nghĩa ở Nam Bộ hiện nay." Luận văn Thạc sĩ ngành Chủ nghĩa Xã hội học, Trường Đại học Khoa học Xã hội và Nhân văn TPHCM, tháng 8 năm 2011.

Foshuo tiandi jing 佛說天地經 *Phật thuyết thiên địa kinh*. Võ Tô's 武蘇 manuscript copy held at the Chùa Phi Lai 飛萊寺 in Thị trấn Ba Chúc 芭祝鎮, An Giang province.

Jin'gang shouming jing 金剛壽命經 *Kim cương thọ mạng kinh*. Manuscript copy held at the Chùa Mã Châu 馬珠寺 in Thị trấn Ba Chúc 芭祝鎮, An Giang province.

Sanyuan jishan jing 三元積善經 *Tam nguơn tích thiện kinh*. Manuscript at the Chùa Tam Bửu 三寶寺, in Thị trấn Ba Chúc 芭祝鎮, An Giang province.

50 For more on this process, see the chapter by Jammes and Palmer in the present volume.

Wugong bore jing 五公般若經 *Ngũ Công bát nhã kinh*. Võ Tô's 武蘇 manuscript copy held at the Chùa Phi Lai 飛萊寺 in Thị trấn Ba Chúc 芭祝鎮, An Giang province.

Wuyue zhenjing 五岳真經 *Ngũ nhạc chân kinh*. Manuscript copy held at the Chùa Tam Bửu 三寶寺 in Thị trấn Ba Chúc 芭祝鎮, An Giang province.

Xiaoyi jing 孝義經 *Hiếu nghĩa kinh*. Print copy held at the Chùa Linh Bửu 靈寶寺 in Thị trấn Ba Chúc 芭祝鎮, An Giang province.

Yuhuang gusui zhenjing 玉皇骨髓真經 *Ngọc lịch đồ thơ tập chú*. Manuscript copy held at the Mộc hương Chùa Phi Lai 飛萊寺木香 in Thị trấn Ba Chúc 芭祝鎮, An Giang province).

Yuli tushu jizhu 玉曆圖書集註 *Ngọc lịch đồ thơ tập chú* (Phạm Văn Vinh version).

Secondary Sources

Chen Yiyuan 陳益源. "Zhongguo hanji zai Yuenan de chuanbo yu jieshou 中國漢籍在越南的傳播與接受." In *Yuenan hanji wenxian shulun* 越南漢籍文獻述論, 71–86. Beijing: Zhonghua shuju, 2011.

Chung Yun-Ying 鍾雲鶯. "Yuenan 'Baoshan qixiang' jiaopai ji qi chuanyan: Yi 'Sien xiaoyi' wei tantao hexin 越南寶山奇香教派及其傳衍—以「四恩孝義」為探討核心." *Minsu quyi* 民俗曲藝, no. 190 (2015): 67–127.

Ding Renjie 丁仁傑. *Dangdai Hanren minzhong zongjiao yanjiu: Lunshu, rentong yu shehui zaishengchan* 當代漢人民眾宗教研究：論述、認同與社會再生產. Taipei: Lianjing, 2009.

Jammes, Jeremy. "Đại Đạo Tam Kỳ Phổ Độ (Cao Đài)." In *Handbook of East Asian New Religious Movements*, edited by Lukas Pokorny and Franz Winter, 565–583. Leiden: Brill, 2018.

Jammes, Jérémy. "Theosophying the Vietnamese Religious Landscape: A Circulatory History of a Western Esoteric Movement in South Vietnam." In *Theosophy Across Boundaries*, edited by Hans Martin Krämer and Julian Strube. Albany, NY: SUNY Press, forthcoming.

Mai Thanh Hải. "Các 'Đạo' của nông dân châu thổ sông Cửu Long từ Bửu Sơn Kỳ Hương, Tứ Ân Hiếu Nghĩa đến Đạo Lành và đạo Ông Nhà Lớn." *Tạp chí Nghiên cứu Tôn giáo*, Hà Nội, No. 1, 2001.

Shi Shengyan 釋聖嚴. "Yuenan Fojiao shilüe 越南佛教史略." In *Xiandai Fojiao xueshu congkan* 現代佛教學術叢刊, no. 83, 271–299. Taipei: Dasheng wenhua 大乘文化, 1980.

Tai, Hue-Tam Ho. *Millenarianism and Peasant Politics in Vietnam*. Cambridge: Harvard University Press. 1983.

Takeuchi, Fusaji 武内房司. "Jindai Xiantiandao zai Yuenan de chuanbo 近代先天道在越南的傳播." Paper presented at the conference "Xiantiandao lishi yu xiankuang yantaohui 先天道歷史與現況研討會" (Center for Studies of Daoist Culture, Chinese University of Hong Kong, September 22, 2009).

Trần Thị Thu Lương and Võ Thành Phương. *Khởi nghĩa Bảy Thưa (1867–1873)*. Nhà xuất bản Thành phố Hồ Chí Minh. 1991.

Trần Văn Quế 陳文桂 and Hà Tân Dân 何新民. *Phật Giáo Bửu Sơn Kỳ Hương: Hệ phái: Tứ Ân Hiếu Nghĩa*. Date unknown.

Xiao Dengfu 蕭登福. "*Yuhuang xinyin miaojing* yu Daojiao zhi neidan xiulian xinfa 《玉皇心印妙經》與道教之內丹修鍊心法." *Xing yu ming* 性與命, no. 12 (1997): 100–113.

Yau Chi-on 游子安. "Daomai nanchuan: Cong Lingnan dao Yuenan Xiantiandao de chuancheng yu bianqian 道脈南傳：從嶺南到越南先天道的傳承與變遷." In *Shanshu yu Zhongguo zongjiao: You Zi'an zixuanji* 善書與中國宗教：游子安自選集, 277–304. Taipei: Boyang wenhua chuban gongsi, 2012.

Appendix: Scriptures of the Tứ Ân Hiếu Nghĩa

No.	Titles in Đặng Văn Tuấn's book	Titles collected by Chung Yun-Ying	Notes
1	*Lingshanhui shangjing* 靈山會上經 *Linh sơn hội thượng kinh*	*Lingshanhui shangjing* 靈山會上經 *Linh sơn hội thượng kinh*; *Lingshanhui shangjing yijuan* 靈山會上經一卷 *Linh sơn hội thượng kinh nhất quyển*; *Lingshan jing* 靈山經 *Linh sơn kinh*	
2	*Xiaoyi jing* 孝義經 *Hiếu nghĩa kinh*	*Xiaoyi jing* 孝義經 *Hiếu nghĩa kinh*	3 volumes (上、中、下三卷)
3	*Pudu chaosheng jing* 普渡超昇經 *Phổ độ siêu thăng kinh*	*Chaosheng jing* 超昇經 *Siêu thăng kinh*; *Chaosheng jing yijuan* 超昇經一卷 *Siêu thăng kinh nhất quyển*	
4	*Pudu chaosheng pantao jing* 普渡超昇蟠桃經 *Phổ độ siêu thăng bàn đào kinh*	*Chaosheng pantao jing* 超昇蟠桃經 *Siêu thăng bàn đào kinh*	

Scriptures of the Tứ Ân Hiếu Nghĩa (*cont.*)

No.	Titles in Đặng Văn Tuấn's book	Titles collected by Chung Yun-Ying	Notes
5	*Tiandi jing* 天地經 *Thiên địa kinh*	*Foshuo tiandi jing* 佛說天地經 *Phật thuyết thiên địa kinh*	
6	*Fozao jing* 佛灶經 *Phật táo kinh*	*Fozao jing* 佛灶經 *Phật táo kinh*; *Siming zaojun zhenjing* 司命灶君真經 *Tư mạng táo quân chân kinh* (*Fozao zhenjing* 佛灶真經 *Phật táo chân kinh*)	
7	*Mulu jing* 目錄經 *Mục lục kinh*	×	A list of Tứ Ân Hiếu Nghĩa scriptures, which is buried with the bodies of deceased adherents.
8	*Zhuanzhi jing* 轉直經 *Chuyển trạc kinh*	*Zhuanzhi jing* 轉直經 *Chuyển trạc kinh*	
9	*Huanshengyu huanhun jing* 還生與還魂經 *Toàn sanh* dữ *toàn hồn kinh*	*Huansheng zhenjing* 還生真經 *Toàn sanh chân kinh*	Both versions contain two scriptures, the *Huansheng jing* and the *Huanhun jing.*
10	*Puan jing* 普奄經 *Phổ yểm kinh*	*Puan jing* 普奄經 *Phổ yểm kinh*	
11	*Shengzhu shiming jing* 聖主釋明經 *Thánh chúa thích minh kinh*	*Shengzhu shiming jing* 聖主釋明經 *Thánh chúa thích minh kinh*	
12	*Foshuo xiaozai jing* 佛說消災經 *Phật thuyết tiêu tai kinh*	×	

Scriptures of the Tứ Ân Hiếu Nghĩa (*cont.*)

No.	Titles in Đặng Văn Tuấn's book	Titles collected by Chung Yun-Ying	Notes
13	*Wugong Guanyin jing* 五公觀音經 *Ngũ Công Quan Âm kinh*	*Wugong bore jing* 五公般若經 *Ngũ công bát nhã kinh* (also called *Wugong Guanyin jing* 五公觀音經 *Ngũ Công Quan Âm kinh*)	
14	*Guanyin bore jing* 觀音般若經 *Quan Âm bát nhã kinh*	*Guanyin bore boluomi jing* 觀音般若波羅密經 *Quan Âm bát nhã ba la mật kinh*	
15	*Wuhu wuyue jing* 五湖五岳經 *Ngũ hồ ngũ nhạc kinh*	*Wuyue zhenjing* 五岳真經 *Ngũ nhạc chân kinh*; *Wuhu zhenjing* 五湖真經 *Ngũ hồ chân kinh*	According to the *Yuli tushu jizhu* (p. 31), the *Wuhu jing* and the *Wuyue jing* are separate scriptures
16	*Ganying jing* 感應經 *Cảm ứng kinh*	*Taishang ganying jing* 太上感應經 *Thái thượng cảm ứng kinh*	
17	Tiantu jing 天圖經 *Thiên đồ kinh*	*Wugong tiantu jing* 五公天圖經 *Ngũ công thiên đồ kinh*	
18	*Jin'gang yunzhuan jing* 金剛運轉經 *Kim cang vận chuyển kinh*	×	
19	*Tiandi jin'gang jing* 天地金剛經 *Thiên địa kim cang kinh*	*Foshuo tiandi jing* 佛說天地金剛經 *Phật thuyết thiên địa kim cang kinh*	
20	*Sanjiao helun jing* 三教合論經 *Tam giáo hợp luận kinh*	*Helun jing* 合論經 *Hợp luận kinh*	

Scriptures of the Tứ Ân Hiếu Nghĩa (*cont.*)

No.	Titles in Đặng Văn Tuấn's book	Titles collected by Chung Yun-Ying	Notes
21	*Dabei tuoluoni jing* 大悲陀羅尼經 *Đại bi đà la ni kinh*	×	Not clear yet whether this is the same text as the *Poluoni jing* 婆羅尼經 included in the *Lingshanhui shangjing* (see above No. 1)
22	*Sanyuan jishan jing* 三元積善經 *Tam nguơn tích thiện kinh*	*Sanyuan jishan jing* 三元積善經 *Tam nguơn tích thiện kinh* (includes: *Shangyuan jishan jing* 上元積善經 *Thượng nguơn tích thiện kinh* & Xiayuan jishan jing 下元積善經 *Hạ nguơn tích thiện kinh*)	
24	*Yinzhi jing* 陰騭經 *Âm chất kinh*	×	
25	*Yuanhui jing* 願會經 *Nguyện hội kinh*	*Yuanhui jing* 願會經 *Nguyện hội kinh*; *Yuanhui* 願會 *Nguyện hội*; *Da yuanhui* 大願會 *Đại nguyện hội*	
26	*Pumen jing* 普門經 *Phổ môn kinh*	*Pumen jing* 普門經 *Phổ môn kinh*; *Pumen jing yijuan* 普門經一卷 *Phổ môn kinh nhất quyển*	
27	*Bayang jing* 八陽經 *Bát dương kinh*	*Foshuo tiandi bayang jing* 佛說天地八陽經 *Phật thuyết thiên địa bát dương kinh*; *Foshui bayang jing di'er* 佛說八陽經第二 *Phật thuyết bát dương kinh đệ nhị*	

Scriptures of the Tứ Ân Hiếu Nghĩa (*cont.*)

No.	Titles in Đặng Văn Tuấn's book	Titles collected by Chung Yun-Ying	Notes
28	*Yuhuang jing* 玉皇經 *Ngọc hoàng kinh*	*Yuhuang gusui zhenjing* 玉皇骨髓真經 *Ngọc hoàng cốt tủy chân kinh*; *Yuhuang jing* 玉皇經 *Ngọc hoàng kinh*	
29	*Taoyuan jing* 桃園經 *Đào viên kinh*	*Taoyuan jing yijuan* 桃園經一卷 *Đào viên kinh nhất quyển* (*Guansheng dijun yingyan taoyuan mingsheng jing* 關聖帝君應驗桃園明聖經 *Quan Thánh Đế Quân ứng nghiệm đào viên minh thánh kinh*); *Taoyuan mingsheng jing* 桃園明聖經 *Đào viên minh thánh kinh*	
30	*Dabei shizhou jing* 大悲十咒經 *Đại bi thập chú kinh*	*Dabei shizhou yijuan* 大悲十咒一卷 *Đại bi thập chú nhất quyện*	
31	*Shousheng jing* 壽生經 *Thọ sanh kinh*	*Shousheng jing* 壽生經 *Thọ sanh kinh*; *Foshuo shousheng jing* 佛說壽生經 *Phật thuyết thọ sanh kinh*; *Shousheng jing yijuan* 壽生經一卷 *Thọ sanh kinh nhất quyển*	
32	*Shouming jing* 壽命經 *Thọ mạng kinh*	*Jin'gang shouming jing* 金剛壽命經 *Kim cang thọ mạng kinh*	
33	*Hongming jing* 宏名經 *Hồng danh kinh*	×	
34	*Taishang huangting jing* 太上黄庭經 *Thái thượng huỳnh đình kinh*	×	Same as the Chinese scripture *Huangting jing* 黄庭經
35	*Gaowang jing* 高王經 *Cao vương kinh*	*Gaowang jing xiajuan* 高王經下卷 *Cao vương kinh hạ quyển*	

Scriptures of the Tứ Ân Hiếu Nghĩa (*cont.*)

No.	Titles in Đặng Văn Tuấn's book	Titles collected by Chung Yun-Ying	Notes
36	*Mojie jing* 末劫經 *Mạt kiếp kinh*	*Dasheng mojie zhenjing* 大聖末劫真經 *Đại thánh mạt kiếp chân kinh*	
		Further texts collected by author:	
37		*Pudu zhenjing* 普渡真經 *Phổ độ chân kinh*	
38		*Yulanpen jing* 盂蘭盆經 *Vu lan bồn kinh*	
39		*Dimu zhenjing yijuan* 地母真經一卷 *Địa mẫu chân kinh nhất quyển*	
40		*Mituo jing yijuan* 彌陀經一卷 *Di Đà kinh nhất quyển* (*Foshuo Amituo jing* 佛說阿彌陀經 *Phật thuyết A Di Đà kinh*)	
41		*Pudu jing yijuan* 普度經一卷 *Phổ độ kinh nhất quyển*; *Pudu zhenjing diyijuan* 普度真經第一卷 *Phổ độ chân kinh đệ nhất quyển*	
42		*Gongwen heyiben* 功文合一本 *Công văn hợp nhất bản*	A collection of liturgical texts, available only to the 24 leaders of the movement.

Scriptures of the Tứ Ân Hiếu Nghĩa (*cont.*)

No.	Titles in Đặng Văn Tuấn's book	Titles collected by Chung Yun-Ying	Notes
43		*Yuli tushu jizhu* 玉曆圖書集註 *Ngọc lịch đồ thơ tập chú*	Contains the hagiography of Ngô Lợi, patterns for the architectural layout of temples, mudras, mantras, etc.; available only to the 24 leaders of the movement.
44		*Xianzai xianjie qianfoming jing* 現在賢劫千佛名經 *Hiện tại hiền kiếp thiên Phật danh kinh*	
45		*Guoqu zhuangyanjie qianfoming jing* 過去莊嚴劫千佛名經 *Quá khứ trang nghiêm kiếp thiên Phật danh kinh*	

CHAPTER 7

The *Bible of the Great Cycle of Esotericism*: From the Xiantiandao Tradition to a Cao Đài Scripture in Colonial Vietnam

Jeremy Jammes and David A. Palmer[1]

1 Introduction

Caodaism or Cao Đài, established in French Indochina in 1926, is now the third largest religion in Vietnam, with growing congregations in diasporic Vietnamese communities around the world. Cao Đài has been the subject of many social and historical studies, focusing on its crucial role in Indochina as a social player and cultural mediator in the process of decolonization.[2] Academic accounts of Cao Đài usually stress the colonial context of its emergence, in which the clash between modern and traditional culture led to a spiritual crisis conducive to the emergence and rapid growth of a new religion that combines the worship of traditional Eastern divinities and Western saints and literary figures. Scholarship has noted how revelations in the 1920s–1950s were often composed in French, and how the original Cao Đài spirit-writing group in 1925 was influenced by French Spiritism, a pseudo-scientific technique for communicating with the souls of the dead, which became popular in France in the second half of the nineteenth century[3]—a phenomenon that can be compared to the popularity of spiritualism in Shanghai, as discussed in Matthias Schumann's chapter in this volume.

However, previous scholarship on Cao Đài and on other modern Vietnamese religions such as the Minh (*ming* 明) religious associations, has largely ignored

1 The order of authors' names is alphabetical, and authorship should be considered equal.

2 Jayne Susan Werner, *Peasant Politics and Religious Sectarianism* (New Haven: Yale University Southeast Asia Studies, 1981); Jérémy Jammes, *Les Oracles du Cao Đài: Étude d'un mouvement religieux vietnamien et de ses réseaux* (Paris: Les Indes savantes, 2014); Janet Hoskins, *The Divine Eye and the Diaspora: Vietnamese Syncretism Becomes Transpacific Caodaism* (Honolulu: University of Hawaiʻi Press, 2015).

3 Jammes, *Les Oracles*, 169–173; Marion Aubrée and Jérémy Jammes, "Développements et mutations du spiritisme kardéciste: Brésil/Viêt Nam," *Politica Hermetica* 26 (2012): 70–94; Nicole Edelman, *Voyantes, guérisseuses et visionnaires en France, 1785–1914* (Paris: Albin Michel, 1995).

 | DOI:10.1163/9789004424166_009

the links between them and Chinese religious movements.[4] In this chapter we argue that, comparable to earlier religious movements such as the Tứ Ân Hiếu Nghĩa dealt with in the previous chapter of this volume, Cao Đài and the Minh associations emerged from a distinctly Chinese religious culture, producing salvationist and spirit-writing groups which can clearly be situated within a wave of new religious movements that appeared in early twentieth-century China and have been designated as "redemptive societies" in recent scholarship.[5] Simultaneously, Caodaism emerged from an occultist colonial culture,[6] generating a movement and some practices which are clearly linked to French Spiritism, but also to Freemasonry and the Theosophical Society. Western Occultism and Chinese redemptive societies constitute two major waves of religious innovation that emerged in the late nineteenth and early twentieth century, in France and in China. Both contributed to the spawning of subsequent waves of religious innovation in Vietnam. Cao Đài and some of its predecessor Minh spirit-writing groups in Vietnam can be considered to be products of the intersection and conjugation of these two religious currents—Chinese redemptive societies and French Occultism. In the effervescent sociopolitical, cultural, and idiomatic context that characterized Cochin-China under French colonialism, Cao Đài can be seen as a unique circulatory product of the confluence of Chinese, French, and Vietnamese religious responses to modernity, a hybrid expression of spiritual universalism as well as a vehicle for a distinctly Vietnamese religious construction of ethnic and national identity.

In this chapter, we begin by reconstructing the genealogy of the Cao Đài religion, showing how it emerged out of the Xiantiandao matrix of Chinese salvationist movements which had spread from Chinese migrant networks into Sino-Vietnamese and Vietnamese communities. We then outline the history of the emergence and spread of Caodaism in a social milieu of Vietnamese

4 Except the seminal study of Ralph B. Smith, "An Introduction to Caodaism," *Bulletin of the School of Oriental and African Studies* 33 (1970): 335–349, and 33 (1971): 573–589.

5 For a historical discussion of redemptive societies in the context of the political and religious changes of Republican China, see Vincent Goossaert and David A. Palmer, *The Religious Question in Modern China* (Chicago: The University of Chicago Press, 2011), chapter 4; see also Rebecca Nedostup, *Superstitious Regimes: Religion and the Politics of Chinese Modernity* (Cambridge, MA: Harvard University Asia Center, 2009), 56–66. For a sociological analysis, see David A. Palmer, "Chinese Redemptive Societies and Salvationist Religion: Historical Phenomenon or Sociological Category?" *Minsu quyi* 民俗曲藝 172 (2011): 21–72, part of a double special issue (nos. 172–173) on redemptive societies.

6 For a comprehensive definition of the "occultist" research field, see Jean-Pierre Laurant, *L'Ésotérisme chrétien en France au XIXe siècle* (Lausanne: Éditions l'Âge d'Homme, 1992); Jean-Pierre Brach, Antoine Faivre, Wouter J. Hanegraaff and Roelof van den Broek, eds., *Dictionary of Gnosis and Western Esotericism* (Leiden: Brill, 2005).

colonial civil servants who circulated in both the Xiantiandao-derived movements and among circles of practitioners of French occultism and spiritism. We show that, within this "occulto-redemptive" landscape of colonial Vietnam, Cao Đài was a key node in both the traditional salvationist milieu and in networks of theological, political, and social innovators.[7]

In the second part of the chapter, we investigate the textual productions of this encounter through the "translingual practices" at play in the production of Cao Đài spirit-medium texts. Lydia Liu defines translingual practice as "the process by which new words, meanings, discourses, and modes of representation arise, circulate, and acquire legitimacy within the host language due to, or in spite of the latter's contact/collision with the guest language," in which the "host" and "guest" languages represent that of the colonized and the colonizer, respectively.[8] We will thus propose a close examination of the translingual practices (translations, rhetorical strategies, naming practices, and legitimizing processes) that led to the production and usage of the *Đại Thừa Chơn Giáo*, one of the four canonical scriptures of Caodaism, each of which was composed through spirit-writing.[9] Our analysis will demonstrate that while Caodaism can be linked to Chinese redemptive societies in its genealogy, religious matrix, and textual forms, its unique features can be linked to the French colonial context of its appearance, involving specific translingual practices and transnational religious circulations and interpenetrations.

2 The Xiantiandao Matrix of the Cao Đài Religion

For the historian Ralf B. Smith,[10] Caodaism finds its roots in "secret societies" (*hội kín* 會覲) inspired by the local lodges of the Chinese Heaven and Earth Association (Thiên địa hội 天地會 Tiandihui).[11] Recent scholarship on Chinese

7 Jammes, *Les Oracles*, 510.

8 Lydia H. Liu, *Translingual Practice: Literature, National Culture, and Translated Modernity—China, 1900–1937* (Stanford, Calif.: Stanford University Press, 1995), 26–27.

9 For a fuller discussion of the concept of "translingual practice" and its application to Cao Đài texts, see Jeremy Jammes and David A. Palmer, "Occulting the Dao: Daoist Inner Alchemy, French Spiritism, and Vietnamese Colonial Modernity in Caodai Translingual Practice," *Journal of Asian Studies* 77 (2018): 405–428.

10 Smith, "An Introduction to Caodaism."

11 In this article, we have kept Vietnamese terms but converted them into Chinese characters for the convenience of both Vietnamese and Sinophone readers. Chinese characters are followed by the pinyin romanization for the convenience of non-Sinophone readers. Note that Chinese characters are rarely used in the original Cao Đài sources, and pinyin romanization is never used.

religion, however, has unpacked the category of Chinese "secret societies"[12] and identified several widely differing types of groups often lumped together by the Chinese state and European colonial authorities; most important are the sworn brotherhoods such as the Heaven and Earth Association, and the salvationist movements which, by the early twentieth century, had become the matrix for modern redemptive societies.

Many Chinese redemptive societies—notably Tongshanshe 同善社 (Society for Goodness) and Yiguandao 一貫道 (Way of Pervasive Unity)—were offshoots of an earlier wave of salvationist movements, the Xiantiandao 先天道 (Way of Anterior Heaven).[13] This matrix appeared in the eighteenth century, expanded into numerous branches in the mid-nineteenth century, and spread to overseas Chinese communities in the late nineteenth and early twentieth centuries.[14] Xiantiandao groups practiced vegetarianism and charity, and their temples provided shelter and a social role for orphans, single women, and the elderly. The other main matrix for the emergence of redemptive societies was spirit-writing groups, also known as "phoenix halls" (*luantang* 鸞堂).[15] Spirit-writing revelations often included instructions on Daoist inner alchemy, morality books, and exhortations to practice charity and good deeds. Several redemptive societies, such as the Daoyuan 道院 (School of the Dao)

12 David Ownby and Mary F. Somers Heidhues, eds., *"Secret Societies" Reconsidered: Perspectives on the Social History of Early Modern South China and Southeast Asia* (Armonk, NY: M.E. Sharpe, 1993); David A. Palmer, "Tao and Nation: Li Yujie: May Fourth Activist, Daoist Reformer and Redemptive Society Patriarch in Mainland China and Taiwan," in *Daoism in the 20th Century: Between Eternity and Modernity*, ed. David A. Palmer and Xun Liu (Berkeley: University of California Press, 2011), 173–195; David A. Palmer, "Heretical Doctrines, Reactionary Secret Societies, Evil Cults: Labeling Heterodoxy in Twentieth-Century China," in *Chinese Religiosities: Afflictions of Modernity and State* Formation, ed. Mayfair Yang (Berkeley: University of California Press, 2008), 113–134.

13 For a sociological conceptualization of historical waves of salvationist movements, see David A. Palmer, "Chinese Redemptive Societies and Salvationist Religion."

14 On Xiantiandao, see J.J.M. de Groot, *Sectarianism and Religious Persecution in China* (1903–1904; repr., Shannon, Ireland: Irish University Press, 1973), 176–196; Marjorie Topley, "The Great Way of Former Heaven: A Group of Chinese Secret Religious Sects," *Bulletin of the School of Oriental and African Studies* 26 (1963): 362–392; Yau Chi On 游子安, "Daomai nanchuan: ershi shiji cong Lingnan dao Yuenan Xiantiandao de chuancheng yu bianqian 道脈南傳：20世紀從嶺南到越南先天道的傳承與變遷," in *Zongjiao renleixue di'er ji* 宗教人類學第二輯, ed. Jin Ze 金澤 and Chen Jinguo 陳進國 (Beijing: Shehui kexue wenxian chubanshe, 2010), 232–256.

15 David K. Jordan and Daniel L. Overmyer, *The Flying Phoenix: Aspects of Chinese Sectarianism in Taiwan* (Princeton: Princeton University Press, 1986); Philip Clart, "The Phoenix and the Mother: The Interaction of Spirit-Writing Cults and Popular Sects in Taiwan." *Journal of Chinese Religions* 25 (1997): 1–32. See also chapter 8 of the present volume.

and Dejiao 德教 (Teachings of Virtue) were established through instructions received from the gods in spirit-writing séances.

Similarly, Xiantiandao halls and spirit-writing groups are the direct root of Cao Đài—more specifically, the Chinese-Vietnamese spirit-writing groups named Minh, meaning "light." After the seventeenth century, with the decline of the Chinese Ming dynasty, a large number of small Minh societies started to emerge in Cochin-China, especially around Saigon.[16] The first of the Minh societies were established by Chinese emigrants in Cochin-China for around three or four generations. The other Minh societies were the fruit of later initiatives in the late nineteenth and early twentieth centuries, involving both Chinese and Sino-Vietnamese participants.

At that time, Chinese guilds or native-place associations seemed to effectively control these Minh associations which, until the early twentieth century, limited their activities to the scale of their respective temples. The latter comprised places where urban, peripheral, as well as provincial cults were practiced, acting like autonomous structures and building up their local authority through divination and/or spirit-writing activities. All these religious communities, many of which were driven by philanthropy or literary pursuits, worshiped the deities of the *tam giáo* ("Three Teachings," 三教 *sanjiao*) pantheon, which includes Confucius, Laozi, and Buddha. They were autonomous yet often clandestine, and their esoteric interpretations of old sutras or new oracles were strongly linked to an embryonic Vietnamese nationalism against colonial domination.

The Minh networks largely overlap with those of the Xiantiandao in Vietnam; indeed, during field work in Ho Chi Minh City in 2013 we found, for example, that the Quang Nam Phật Đường 光南佛堂 Guangnan Fotang, a Chinese temple which is mentioned in Yau Chi On's study of Xiantiandao in Vietnam,[17] and which has close ties with the Minh Lý *đạo* (明理道), self-identifies as both Xiantiandao and Minh Sư. The specific geographic and historic mapping of these overlapping networks remains to be done; Yau Chi On has, however, traced the spread of Xiantiandao from Guangdong to Vietnam in the late nineteenth century and early twentieth century. In 1863, the Xiantiandao lineage of the Hidden Glow (Cangxia 藏霞) first established its Guangdong base, namely the Cangxiadong (藏霞洞 Temple of the Hidden Glow Cavern) in Qingyuan 清遠. The Cangxiadong later became the "ancestral cavern" (祖洞 *zudong*) of other Xiantiandao offshoots in Guangdong, Hong Kong, and Cochin-China. In Saigon, the Cangxia jingshe 藏霞精舍 (the Hidden Glow

16 Ownby and Heidhues, eds., *Secret Societies*.
17 Yau, "Daomai nanchuan," 238.

Abode) is known as the root from which the Xiantiandao movement spread in Vietnam. Established in 1949 and based in Saigon, the Abode supported the maintenance and building of other Xiantiandao halls; more notably, it built a Xiantiandao cemetery and set up a branch in Cambodia. Its founder claimed the Cangxiadong in northern Guangdong as its origin, where the deceased masters of the Abode were worshipped. In addition, the other major Xiantiandao halls—namely Yongdetang 永德堂, Yuegengtang 月庚堂, Yong'antang 永安堂, Anqingtang 安慶堂, Jingshengtang 敬聖堂, Baofutang 寶福堂, Guangnan Fotang 光南佛堂, and Miaonantang 妙南堂, all originated in Guangdong province. And the deities worshipped by the Vietnam halls, such as the Yuncheng qisheng 雲城七聖 (Seven Saints of the Cloud City), are very similar to those worshipped by the Xiantiandao temples in Guangdong province.[18]

These networks gave birth around the 1850s to local congregations known as the Minh Sư ("Enlightened Master," 明師 *Mingshi*) societies, which continued their links with the Xiantiandao branches in Guangdong and Hong Kong. The Minh Sư religious associations, in turn, spawned a number of Sino-Vietnamese sects, namely Minh Đường ("Enlightened Hall," 明堂 *Mingtang*, 1908), Minh Thiện ("Enlightened Goodness," 明善 *Mingshan*, 1915), Minh Lý ("Enlightened Reason," 明理 *Mingli*, 1924), and Minh Tân ("Enlightened Renewal," 明新 *Mingxin*, 1925).[19]

The Cao Đài religion, whose members were mostly Vietnamese, was founded in the years of 1925–1926, as described below; it eventually absorbed the Minh Đường, Minh Thiện, and Minh Tân, and collaborates closely with Minh Lý. Minh Sư federated several temples that would affiliate themselves, after 1926, as Cao Đài oratories or literally "holy houses" (*thánh thất* 聖室 *shengshi*).

3 The Emergence of Cao Đài in the Colonial Context

Caodaism emerged in the early 1920s through the spirit-writing activities of Ngô Văn Chiêu 吳文昭 (1878–1932), a Vietnamese civil servant of the French colonial administration in Cochin-China. Following instructions he received from the Chinese deity Guan Gong 關公 at spirit-writing séances held in the Minh-Sư-derived Minh Thiện temple in Thủ Dầu Một, Northern Saigon, in

18 See Yau, "Daomai nanchuan," 237–238, 239–240, 246–246, 253.

19 For a more detailed study of the Xiantiandao-derivated Minh genealogy and roots of Caodaism, see Huệ Nhẫn, *Ngũ Chi Đại Đạo (Nam chi Đạo họ Minh)* [The Five branches of the Great Way, named Minh] (Ho Chi Minh City: internal edition of the Cơ Quan Phổ Thông Giáo Lý Đại Đạo, 1999); Jammes, *Les Oracles*, 52–62, 89–92, 163–169; Smith, "An Introduction to Caodaism."

Xiantiandao in Guangdong 廣東先天道
(late nineteenth century movement)

↓

Minh Sư societies in Vietnam 越南明師道
(late nineteenth century, early twentieth century Chinese movement)

↓

Minh Lý 明理 (1924); Minh Đường 明堂 (1908), Minh Thiện 明善 (1915), Minh Tân 明新 (1925)
(early twentieth century Chinese and Sino-Vietnamese movement)

↓

Cao Đài religion 高臺教
(1925–1926—Vietnamese and Sino-Vietnamese movement)

FIGURE 7.1 Xiantiandao genealogy of Cao Đài religion

1902, Ngô Văn Chiêu spent twenty years visiting Daoist and Minh temples, learning spirit-writing, studying commentaries on the *Daodejing* 道德經, and improving his skills in Daoist meditation, talismans, and oracles.[20]

In 1920, he was appointed colonial district head of Phú Quốc, a remote island in the Sea of Siam. At the Xiantiandao-affiliated Quan Âm (觀音 Guanyin) Chinese temple, he devoted himself to training youth in mediumship through spirit-writing.[21] The Daoist master Tùng Ngạc, a member of the Minh Sư, guided him in his learning of meditation techniques.[22] In one spirit-writing session, on the Lunar New Year (8 Feb.) of 1921, one deity revealed himself as Master Cao Đài, *Thầy* Cao Đài (偨[23]高臺[*Thầy*] *Gaotai*), "the Master [living on] the Highest Platform," an abbreviation of Cao Đài Tiên Ông Đại Bồ Tát Ma Ha Tát (高臺天皇大菩薩摩訶薩 Gaotai tianhuang dapusa mohesa), the "Heavenly Emperor of the Supreme Platform and Great Bodhisattva Mahasattva." This deity also identified himself as the Jade Emperor (Ngọc Hoàng Thượng Đế 玉皇上帝 Yuhuang shangdi). Ngô Văn Chiêu was given the mission to reveal

20 Huệ Nhẫn, *Ngũ Chi*, 22–27.

21 Huệ Khải, *Ngô Văn Chiêu: Người môn đệ Cao Đài đầu tiên* [Ngô Văn Chiêu: The first Cao Đài adept] (San Martin (California): Nxb Tam Giáo Đồng Nguyên, 2008), 20.

22 Op. cit., 21.

23 The character 偨, pronounced *thầy*, is from the Vietnamese vernacular *chữ nôm* writing system, meaning "teacher, master, father." There is no equivalent for this character in Chinese.

and propagate a universal "new Dharma" (*tân pháp* 新法 *xinfa*). Ngô began to worship this deity regularly.

Later, on 20 April 1921, as he sat under a willow tree and gazed at the sun shining over the ocean in the coastal village of Dương Đông ("The Sun Rises in the East"), he saw a gigantic left eye floating in the sky above the north star and the moon. Petrified by this vision, he asked it to disappear. It did so, but appeared again at his request. Master Cao Đài instructed Ngô to represent him with the image of this eye. A second, similar vision was received while he meditated at Dinh Cậu (the westernmost temple in Cochin-China, based on a small rock in Phú Quốc island). He thus believed to have confirmation that the Left Eye was the "Celestial Eye" (*Thiên Nhân* 天眼 *tianyan*) and the new icon to worship.

Soon afterwards, the teachings of Master Cao Đài made their way into the urban millenarian networks of the Xiantiandao-affiliated temples in Saigon and its Chinese neighboring city, Chợ Lớn. In 1925, Ngô was posted back to Saigon, where he regularly visited the Minh Sư (明師 *mingshi*) Jade Emperor temple in Đa Kao district,[24] and began to recruit some adepts among Vietnamese colonial administrators. He was contacted by a group of younger Vietnamese civil servants who had been practicing spirit-writing by tipping tables. Revelations were often composed in French and the original spirit-writing group was influenced by Spiritism, which was popular in France in the late nineteenth and early twentieth centuries. Between November and December 1925, in a séance, the Golden Mother of the Jasper Pool (Diêu Trì Kim Mẫu 瑤池金母 Yaochi jinmu) instructed this group to switch from using French spiritist methods (the oui-ja board) to the Chinese technique of "phoenix writing" (*phò loan* 扶鸞 *fuluan*), in which a bird-headed basket is held by one or two mediums to write on a surface.[25] The mediumistic use of the "beaked basket" is a set of divinatory practices whereby the visit of a spiritual entity enables the written revelation of messages. The basket, and the prayer spoken in Vietnamese (which summons the spirit of the Cao Đài Master or of the deities of the pantheon to descend into it), were borrowed from the Minh Thiện (明善 *mingshan*) religious association, which had originally borrowed them from Minh Lý *đạo* (明理道 *minglidao*), itself a new offshoot of the Xiantiandao/Minh Sư

24 See a contemporary picture of this Minh Sư temple in Jeremy Jammes, "Cao Đài Acceptance in Contemporary Vietnam: Tightrope Walking between Past and Future," *Gis-Reseau-Asie*, 2016. Online at www.gis-reseau-asie.org/monthly-articles/reconnaissance-caodaisme-dans-viet-nam-contemporain-jeu-equilibriste-entre-passe-avenir (accessed September 15, 2016).

25 Jordan and Overmyer, *The Flying Phoenix*, 36–88. This "automatic writing" is renamed *cơ bút* (乩筆 *jibi*), "the brush," by the Minh and Cao Đài followers.

tradition.[26] Sometimes the Cao Đài séances modified the Chinese technique of phoenix writing to use a Vietnamese alphabetic board and receive messages in Romanized Vietnamese and French. In this case, the technique is clearly inspired by the oui-ja board and inscribes Caodaism into the French spiritist tradition.[27]

On Christmas eve of 1925, a mysteriously erudite and philosophical spirit, known to them only by the first three letters of the Romanized Vietnamese alphabet (*quốc ngữ* 國語 *guoyu*)—A, Ă, Â—revealed to the spirit-writing group that he was "Master Cao Đài," indeed the Jade Emperor, who had previously sent Buddha, Confucius, and Laozi, and was also the father of Jesus. And in the night of December 31, Master Cao Đài instructed the group to seek and meet Ngô Văn Chiêu to learn how to establish a worship to Himself. Ngô had also received instructions from Master Cao Đài to give guidance to this spiritist group. In a new series of joint séances, Master Cao Đài indicated that Ngô should lead a world religion. From then on, the new religion began to spread rapidly in the cities and suburbs of Cochin-China.[28]

In November of 1926, a huge celebration was held in Tây Ninh city (west of Saigon, close to the Cambodian border), to officially present to the colonial authorities the "Great Way of the Third Cycle of Universal Salvation." For the occasion were performed a great number of spirit-writing séances in which new disciples were called on by name, and each received a poem relating, often somewhat enigmatically, to his own biography. Thousands of participants received prophetic and apocalyptic visions, convincing them to convert to the so-called Vietnamese-born but universal faith.[29]

Mediums, businessmen, and landowners at the head of the church's hierarchy recruited thousands of the colonized peasant population in the space of ten years only. By 1930, "the Great Way" had converted more disciples in the southern colony of Cochin-China than the Catholic Church had in over 300 years of missionary activity.[30]

Caodaism had appeared in a milieu of spirit-writing groups of scholars, intellectuals, and petty colonial officials who were able to implement this pyramidal structure in only a few months' time. Caodaism was officially registered (under the redemptive name of *Đại Đạo Tam Kỳ Phổ Độ*, see below) as a religious association with the French colonial authorities in November of 1926. As the first mass conversion movement in French Indochina, born during

26 Huệ Nhẫn, *Ngũ Chi Đại Đạo*, 25.
27 Aubrée and Jammes, "Développements et mutations."
28 Jammes, *Les Oracles*, 94.
29 Jammes *Les Oracles*, 98–100.
30 Jayne S. Werner, "The Cao Dai: The Politics of a Vietnamese Syncretic Religious Movement" (PhD diss., Cornell University, 1976), 60.

a period of anti-colonial resistance, Cao Đài established its own army during the Japanese occupation and the ensuing war of independence, and directly governed a large part of Cochin-China and later on of South Vietnam. With its own theology, its own flag, and even its own army,[31] Caodaism is a case in point of what Prasenjit Duara has called the "traffic" between the religious and the secular.[32] The political aims of Caodaism gradually gained substance and momentum to the point where it was ultimately able to offer a genuine project of a religious society, a theocracy that aimed to become the "State religion" (*quốc đạo* 國道 *guodao*) of Vietnam. As such, Caodaism has created a strict hierarchical organization and a unique disciplinary framework in the hands of a group of mediums, hence turning the religion into either a potential rival or an ally of anti-colonial nationalist forces. Such national aspirations were combined with a religious language, Cao Đài prophecies emphasizing that the Vietnamese people were chosen for a special spiritual but universal mission.[33]

Cao Đài membership expanded rapidly, as both the economic crisis of 1930–1931 and the foundation of new Cao Đài denominations attracted the peasantry to the religious solidarity structures offered by the new religion. Ngô Văn Chiêu, who enjoyed solitude, was worried by the growing number of followers. As early as May 1927, he decided to withdraw from the world and to follow a path of cultivation based primarily on meditation. A few years before his death, in 1932, he founded his own branch, the Chiếu Minh Tam Thanh Vô Vi (照明三清無為 *zhaoming sanqing wuwei*, Radiant Light of Non-Interference of the Three Purities). This denomination was focused on the meditative and divinatory quest for "non-interference" or "non-action" (*vô vi* 無為 *wuwei*), whereas the main branch of Cao Đài, based at the "Holy See" of Tây Ninh, was more focused on social activity and "universal salvation" (*phổ độ* 普度 *pudu*).

The politics of the Cao Đài religion later brought it into tension with the State of South Vietnam. After 1975 and unification under the Socialist Republic of Vietnam, some Cao Đài leaders suffered from repression and Caodaism

31 Jérémy Jammes, "Caodaism in Times of War: Spirits of Struggle and Struggle of Spirits," *SOJOURN: Journal of Social Issues in Southeast Asia* 31 (2016): 247–294; Trần Mỹ Vân, "Japan and Vietnam's Caodaists: A Wartime Relationship (1939–1945)," *Journal of Southeast Asian Studies* 27 (1996): 179–193.

32 Prasenjit Duara, *The Crisis of Global Modernity: Asian Traditions and a Sustainable Future* (Cambridge: Cambridge University Press, 2015), 195–238.

33 Đức Nguyên, *Cao Đài Từ Điển, Quyển I, II, III* [Dictionary of Caodaism, vol. I, II, and III] (Ho Chi Minh City: private printing, 2000), "*quốc đạo*" (online version, accessed January 10, 2015); Jammes, *Les Oracles*, 126–130; Jérémy Jammes, "Đại Đạo Tam Kỳ Phổ Độ (Cao Đài)," in *Handbook of East Asian New Religious Movements*, ed. Lukas Pokorny and Franz Winter (Leiden: Brill, 2018), 569, 571; Janet Hoskins, "God's Chosen People: Race, Religion, and Anti-Colonial Struggle in French Indochina" (Singapore: ARI Working Paper No. 189, 2012).

became a "religion in exile,"[34] formed in overseas communities in the United States, Europe, and Australia (with about 15,000–20,000 adepts abroad). The "Cao Đài religion" was officially legalized in 1997 and is now Vietnam's third largest organized religion after Buddhism and Catholicism, with at least 3 to 4 million followers among the 94 million Vietnamese (according to the 2009 National census, which typically undercounts the number of adepts in the "atheist" and communist land of Vietnam).[35]

4 Cao Đài as a Vietnamese Redemptive Society

Caodaism emerged in a Sino-Vietnamese religious milieu in Cochin-China, in which both Xiantiandao offshoots and spirit-writing groups were actively expanding and interlinked. Born out of this religious culture, the core of Cao Đài doctrine is essentially the same as that of the Xiantiandao-influenced redemptive societies: worship of the Golden Mother of the Jasper Pool (Diêu Trì Kim Mẫu 瑤池金母 Yaochi jinmu), as the supreme female deity; the universalist syncretism of the Three Teachings; and the three-phase eschatology (*tam kỳ mạt-kiếp* 三期末劫 *sanqi mojie*) with the first dispensation associated with Moses and Fu Xi 伏羲, the second associated with Buddha, Confucius, Laozi, Jesus, and Mohammad, and the third to be ushered in by Maitreya (or Master Cao Đài, alias the Jade Emperor, Ngọc Hoàng Thượng Đế 玉皇上帝 Yuhuang Shangdi). Indeed, the full name of the Cao Đài religion—"Great Way of the Third Cycle of Universal Salvation of the Higher Platform" (Cao Đài Đại Đạo Tam Kỳ Phổ Độ 高臺大道三期普度 *Gaotai dadao sanqi pudu*)—is an explicit reference to the realization of these prophecies.

Like most Chinese salvationist groups, Caodaism propagated the doctrine of the Unity of the Three Teachings *tam giáo hợp nhất* (三教合一 *sanjiao heyi*) and millenarian expectations of Maitreya's arrival and of the Dragon Flower Assembly (*hội Long Hoa* 龍華會 *Longhuahui*) to be ruled by him. However, the traditional notion of the Union of the Three Teachings was modernized and universalized with the aid of a more modern language and by incorporating explicitly Christian figures from the French spiritist pantheon (Jesus, Victor Hugo, Joan of Arc, etc.).[36]

The Cao Đài religion developed its own scriptures, philosophical systems, liturgies (an intentional assemblage of Confucian, Buddhist, and Daoist sources), congregational modes of participation, missionary and conversion strategies,

34 Hoskins, *The Divine Eye and the Diaspora*, 212–216.

35 Jammes, *Les Oracles*, 237–238; Jammes, "Cao Đài Acceptance in Contemporary Vietnam."

36 Jammes, *Les Oracles*, 197–208, 307–309.

and its own religious administration. Like modern Chinese redemptive societies, Cao Đài founded national modern-style organizations that registered with the state as religious, philanthropic, or public interest associations, with a national and centralized head office (the "Holy See" of Tây Ninh near the Cambodian border), overseeing provincial and municipal branches. The Cao Đài religion's main difference from the Chinese redemptive societies was its organizational style, which drew its inspiration from the Catholic Church, with its own Holy See and cathedrals, and an ecclesiastical hierarchy of deacons, priests, bishops, cardinals (for both men and women), and a pope (rank restricted to men only). The model of the Catholic church had actually become the new paradigm of "religion" in Cochin-China and Vietnam (as Protestant Christianity had in China),[37] rather than the traditional Buddhist, Daoist, or Confucian institutions. At the same time, a series of Vietnamese hierarchical terms were invented in order to depart from the Catholic model and to propose another and properly Vietnamese idiomatic way to arrange this hierarchy, delimiting a specific Cao Đài identity through this invention process.

Emerging out of the theological, political, and sociological framework of Chinese redemptive societies, Cao Đài leaders inscribed their religion into a new civilizational discourse which, in a variety of forms throughout Asia, advocated an Eastern solution to the problems of the modern world. While integrating Christianity, and even evolutionary theories, into its cosmology, Cao Đài religion would eventually adopt forms of organization and social engagement which resembled other modern religious and morality promotion societies around the world. This included hospitals, orphanages, refugee centers, schools, periodicals, libraries, factories and farms for the poor, and, in the contemporary diasporic situation of Caodaism in California, disaster relief and drug rehabilitation projects.[38] This social and missionary engagement was motivated by a profoundly religious program of self-cultivation.

The Caodaism of the 1920s shares with the Minh associations the same political, territorial, and nationalist concerns as well as many common religious activities, including spirit-writing. These connections displayed a long-lasting mediumistic production and unveiled a hidden side of Caodaism. Although the Minh associations descend from Chinese late-imperial Xiantiandao traditions, they also represent a specific response to the challenges and opportunities afforded by the collapse of the imperial order and the irruption of modernity in a colonial context. Cao Đài in fact attempted to organize networks of Minh spirit-writing groups, offering them regional and national levels of leadership

37 Goossaert and Palmer, *The Religious Question in Modern China*, 73–79.

38 Jammes, *Les Oracles*, 476–478.

with a universal and missionary agenda.[39] Through spirit-written messages and Vietnamese translations of Minh prayers and texts, Cao Đài thus adopted the cosmology, theology, and eschatology of the Xiantiandao tradition and adapted it to the decolonization agenda and Sino-Vietnamese culture. Since the colonial period, the Minh Lý religious association has occupied a crucial place in Cao Đài activities.

5 The Minh Lý Dao: the Key Link between the Xiantiandao Tradition and Cao Đài Religion[40]

The founder of Minh Lý, Âu Kiệt Lâm 歐傑林 (1896–1941), was an intellectual of half Chinese, half Vietnamese origin, and thus he belonged to the colonial category of the Sino-Vietnamese *métis*, *minh hương* (明鄉 *mingxiang*).[41] In the period between 1916 and 1926 he became a renowned medium in spirit-writing and demonstrated an ability to transcend cultural barriers. Swiftly bridging the Chinese and the Vietnamese cultures, he was capable of merging the two social and cultural systems by bringing them into contact. His translation of Chinese or *chữ nôm* (字喃 *zinan*—an indigenous Vietnamese writing system that looks like Chinese characters but is pronounced in Vietnamese language) holy texts into modern Vietnamese *quốc ngữ* (國語 *guoyu*) writings provides fine examples of this ability.

The Minh Lý community erected its own temple in 1924 in a suburb of Saigon (Bàn Cờ district). This temple is now well known as the Tam Tông Miếu (三宗廟 *Sanzongmiao*), "the Temple of the Three Doctrines." Among the main activities of the Minh Lý were therapeutic sessions (acupuncture and "magnetism"), divination and the production of oracles using multiple methods such as astrology, chiromancy, and physiognomy. According to Nguyễn Văn Miết 阮文懱,[42] a Minh Lý dignitary, Âu Kiệt Lâm carried out in-depth research into magnetism (*nhân diễn* 人電 *rendian*, literally "electric energy in the human body") and constructed a body of knowledge based on French spiritism and Chinese spirit-writing.

In 1926, before Cao Đài had begun to spread among the peasant community and the Vietnamese elite, Lê Văn Trung 黎文忠 (1875–1934), a senior

39 Jérémy Jammes, "Divination and Politics in Southern Vietnam: Roots of Caodaism," *Social Compass* 57 (2010): 357–371; Jammes, *Les Oracles*, 162–169.

40 This section is largely derived from Jammes, "Divination and Politics."

41 Jammes, *Les Oracles*, 163–164.

42 Nguyễn Văn Miết, *La religion "Minh-Lý", pagode "aux trois religions"* (Saigon: Tam Tông Miếu internal publication, 1960), 7–10.

Vietnamese official, was appointed head of Caodaism with the title of Cardinal (*Đầu Sư* 頭主 *touzhu*, Head-Master) and soon of "interim pope" (*quyền giáo tông* 權教宗 *quan jiaozong*). Lê Văn Trung owed a large part of his legitimacy to a mediumistic message received in September 1925 by the Tam Tông Miếu mediums, to whom he was presented by his maternal cousin Nguyễn Hữu Đắc 阮友得, a former city councilor of Chợ Lớn and translator of French occultist texts.

In order to compose its first corpus of prayers, the Cao Đài clergy headed by Lê Văn Trung and Phạm Công Tắc 范公稷 (1890–1959) turned to the Minh Lý association, which had, at that time, just begun its own project of translating Chinese religious texts into Vietnamese. The majority of Cao Đài prayers are thus sourced from the Minh Lý corpus of prayers, including the prayer of Opening (*Khai kinh* 開經 *kaijing*), the prayer of Incense Offering (*Niệm hương* 念香 *nianxiang*), the prayer celebrating the Jade Emperor (*Ngọc Hoàng kinh* 玉皇經 *Yuhuangjing*), the prayers of Repentance (*Sám hội* 懺悔 *chanhui*), of Praise (*Xưng tụng* 頌榮 *songrong*), of the Dead (*Cầu siêu* 求超 *qiuchao*), and so on.[43] The transmission of scriptures from Minh Lý to Cao Đài was further endorsed by means of spirit-writing orders received at both Minh Lý and the Cao Đài Holy See of Tây Ninh. As such, Minh specialists were regarded as the legitimate elders responsible for training young Cao Đài spirit-writing groups.[44] Owing to their mediumistic competence, the content of these messages established Minh associations as both the depositories and the guardians of the knowledge of Master Cao Đài.

To explain these borrowings, we should recall that the initial Cao Đài group around Lê Văn Trung and Phạm Công Tắc was oriented towards mass proselytism and sought to gather religious texts in Vietnamese that would not require the learning of Chinese, hence targeting the broadest possible audience and reaching out to the peasant community. And Minh Lý, between January 1924 and November 1925, had already begun the same process of Vietnamization, translating into *quốc ngữ* religious texts previously available in Minh Sư circles only in Chinese characters.

The visibility of the Cao Đài religion, the presence of its dignitaries in the government, and the involvement of some of them in the Sûreté coloniale were all reassuring factors for Minh dignitaries, who felt that they would guarantee the continuity of their religious practices after the 1916 suppression of secret society revolts by colonial authorities.[45] At the same time a cooperative

43 Jammes, "Divination and Politics," 361–362; Jammes, *Les Oracles*, 162.

44 Phạm Công Tắc, *Le Caodaïsme* (*La Vérité*, Phnom Penh, 1937).

45 Jammes, *Les Oracles*, 57.

network between Minh and Cao Đài religions was established that would last until the present day.

6 Cao Đài and the Occultist Colonial Culture

The Cao Đài religion is, in many ways, an ideal-typical redemptive society with its Xiantiandao roots, its salvationist message, its practice of spirit-writing, its expanded syncretic universalism, and its adoption of modern forms of religious organization and philanthropic action. At the same time, it emerged from a distinctly occultist colonial culture, producing a movement and some practices which clearly fall into the same category as Western Esotericism, Spiritism, Freemasonry, and Theosophy. Caodaism brought the Minh groups "out of the shadows and into the clear light of day" (to quote a Franco-Vietnamese newspaper of the time, *Écho Annamite*),[46] but also fused them with the occultist interests of Vietnamese employees of the French colonial state.

The Western use of these two neologisms—esotericism and occultism—comes from the transformations in the rationalist thought of the Christian West at the end of the nineteenth century. The term "esotericism" was used for the first time by Jacques Matter in his *Critical History of Gnosticism*.[47] It indicated here a type of timeless spiritual quest according to a set of more or less hidden traditions. In other words, esotericism refers to a secret teaching requiring an initiation; *lato sensu*, it can apply to almost all the divination and religious practices in the world, such as esotericism in Daoism or Buddhism in Asia.[48]

The term "Occultism" indicates a specific movement in the West, characteristic of the end of the nineteenth century and beginning of the twentieth century. A person, a group or an institution can be regarded as "occultist" when they find, under cover of a scientific or scientistic discourse, "the lost unity of science and religion: the science of the new times."[49] Thus, supernatural phenomena, traditional spirit-mediumship activities, theology, and several bodies of religious knowledge and philosophical ideas were re-interpreted and recast

46 Paper published by Nguyễn Phan Long, a reputed political leader (of the so-called Constitutionalist party), Cao Đài follower, and manager of the *Écho Annamite* (see Jammes, *Les Oracles*, 86, 172).

47 Jacques Matter, *Histoire critique du gnosticisme* (Paris: F.G. Levrault, 1828), 83.

48 Benoytosh Batthacharya, *An Introduction to Buddhist Esotericism* (London: Oxford University Press, 1932); Paul Lévy, *Buddhism: A "Mystery Religion"?* (New York: Schocken Books, 1968 [1957]).

49 Laurant, *L'Ésotérisme chrétien*, 21.

through the filters of modern scientific methods and instruments. Moreover, French Occultism can be described "as heterodox Christian and universalist, informed by an unconventional reading of the Bible"; their literature borrows "from many other religious and philosophical traditions, and seeks to spread its message to all peoples."[50] The *fin-de-siècle* occultist movements included Spiritist groups, the Rosicrucian brotherhood, the Martinists, the Theosophical society, and Perennialist groups around René Guénon and Frithjof Chuon.[51] French occultist networks spread to Cochin-China under the colonial regime, disseminating through books, magazines, and spirit-séances the *mission civilisatrice* of a positivist France.[52] Among these networks were those that practiced what was known in French as *Spiritisme*. Spiritism arose directly from its first theoretician, the French teacher and medium Hippolyte L.D. Rivail (1804–1869), who had taken the Celtic name of Allan Kardec. His principal works are *The Book of the Spirits* (1857), *The Book of the Mediums* (1861), *The Gospels According to Spiritism* (1864), *Hell and Paradise* (1865), and *Genesis* (1868). The goal of the work of Kardec and his successors was to offer a study of the invisible world, highlighting doctrines of reincarnation and a rational communication with the dead, re-defined as the "non-incarnated souls." Kardec's work also expresses a social project, wishing to build a spiritist pedagogy for a reformed new social order. Spiritism proposed a reform of Catholicism and used modern techniques (telegraph, photography, radiography, X-ray, etc.) as vehicles for a new hope in the afterlife. As with Caodaism sixty years later, Spiritism is presented by its founder as the third revelation of God on Earth, after Moses and Jesus Christ.[53] The third period opened by spiritism is described by Kardec himself as an "alliance between science and religion,"[54] a union of both a material and a "spiritual science,"[55] a period dedicated to the "Instructions from Spirits."[56]

In the years 1920–1930, in Cochin-China, spiritist brochures, books, and circles, as well as all of Kardec's doctrines and spiritist-mediumship techniques,

---

50 David A. Harvey, "Beyond Enlightenment: Occultism, Politics, and Culture in France from the Old Regime to the Fin-de-Siècle," *The Historian* 65 (2003): 667.

51 Laurant, *L'Ésotérisme chrétien*; Wouter J. Hanegraaff, *New Age Religion and Western Culture: Esotericism in the Mirror of Secular Thought* (Leiden: Brill, 1996); Brach, Faivre, Hanegraaff, and van den Broek, eds., *Dictionary of Gnosis*.

52 Harvey, "Beyond Enlightenment," 668.

53 Allan Kardec, *Genesis: The Miracles and the Predictions According to Spiritism* (Boston: Colby & Rich, 1883 [1868 in French]), 44–45.

54 Allan Kardec, *The Gospel According to Spiritism. Contains Explanations of the Moral Maxims of Christ in Accordance with Spiritism and Their Application in Various Circumstances in Life* (London: The Headquarters Publishing Co LTD, 1987 [1864 in French]), 26.

55 Kardec, *Genesis*, 114.

56 Kardec, *The Gospel According to Spiritism*, 27.

were made available to French-speaking Vietnamese people. The presence of famous French practitioners of Spiritism in Saigon and their close relationship with Caodaism were noticed in many sources. Spiritism is translated into Vietnamese as *thần linh học* (神靈學 *shenlingxue*), "study of the spirits" or *thông linh học* (通靈學 *tonglingxue*), "study of communications with spirits." The doctrine of Kardec is thus designated in Vietnamese as a discipline that would give access to knowledge by the means of a communication established with the spiritual entities. The first Caodaists actually practiced the "turning tables" of French-derived Spiritism, which they conceived as more "rational" and "scientific" than the traditional Vietnamese spirit-possession practices (*lên đồng* 登童 *dengtong*).

The Cochin-Chinese amateurs of French Spiritism also showed themselves to be captivated by the spiritist method of the turning tables (*xây bàn* or *xoay bàn* 旋板 *xuanban*), literally "to turn the table," which consists in decoding the sounds of the spirits, in particular by swings of the table (one leg of the table being shorter than the others) or by "raps" of the table (literally *gõ* 鼓 *gu*). These two methods use the letters of the alphabet to reconstitute the messages, bringing both questions and answers. Vietnamese Spiritists adapted this Western alphabetical process by replacing it with the Romanized modern alphabet of the Vietnamese language (the *quốc ngữ*). The non-incarnated spirits are thus invited to express themselves by "rapping" the table on specific letters to spell words, sentences, and doctrine.

In the global market of Eastern spiritualities and cultural goods in the first part of the twentieth century, the theosophical literature occupies a unique but dynamic position.[57] Founded in New York in 1875, the Theosophical Society seeks to understand the mysteries of universal sacred books by filtering them through a syncretic approach and at the same time a Christian and Buddhist conceptualization. This movement played a political role in India, participating in the training of its religious and political elites during the struggle for independence, after the First World War. Their members became famous through their activist contribution to the rebirth of Buddhism in Ceylon, their traditionalism in India (supporting the Sanskrit language and the Buddhist schools), and their sense of social reform (fighting for an improvement in women's social conditions, of pariahs and prisoners, etc.). For these reasons, the theosophical credo—"There is no religion greater than Truth"—attracted some French, Vietnamese, but also Indian, British, American, New Zealander, and Australian political or religious personalities.

57 Roland Lardinois, *L'Invention de l'Inde: Entre ésotérisme et science* (Paris: CNRS Éditions, 2007), 127.

The 1920s marked the beginning of the Theosophical Society's establishment in Cochin-China:[58] the *Thông thiên học* (通天學 *tongtianxue*), literally, "studies of communications with the heavens"), aimed to revitalize and rationalize Buddhist theology and practices (especially its millenarian, meditative, and philanthropic traditions). The prolific productions of its Vietnamese actors—consisting largely of translations and commentaries of the verbose founders of Theosophical Society such as Blavatsky, Leadbeater, and Besant—were rationalist insertions into the dialogue between Eastern and Western civilizations and those between religions and science. This theosophical enterprise to build up an "edifying science" or a "savant religiosity"[59] was perfectly integrated into the intellectual fabric of its time, and exerted influence on the production of Cao Đài texts, which emerged at the same time among the cosmopolitan milieu of Cochin-China. Caodaism found many areas of agreement with the Theosophical society, as both shared a similar millenarian vision, within a familiar Christian and Buddhist theology, as well as a common religious and comparative literature. It is not surprising that many Caodaists attended theosophical circles until their prohibition in 1975; at the same time, many theosophists came to preach in Cao Đài temples. Moreover, the numerous connections and overlaps between the Theosophical Society, Caodaism, and the reformed lay Buddhist movements in the 1930s–1950s in Cochin-China remain relatively uncharted terrain for future studies.

We can also note in passing the presence of Vietnamese freemasons in the Cao Đài leadership, such as Nguyễn Hữu Đắc 阮友得 (1897–1974), who translated Pourvourville's *La Voie Rationnelle* (The Rational Way) as *Đạo Giáo* (道教 *daojiao*, literally the "Religion of the Dao" or "Daoism") in 1935.[60] However, his membership in freemasonry is not emphasized in the Cao Đài literature, which prefers to remind us that Nguyễn Hữu Đắc is the cousin of the Cao Đài pope, Lê Văn Trung, and the one who introduced the latter to the Minh Lý temple where he converted to Caodaism. Among other vocal Cao Đài freemasons, we can also mention the names of Cao Triều Phát 高朝发 (leader of Minh Chơn Đạo branch [Dao of the Enlightened Truth 明真道 *mingzhendao*] and a Việt Minh military commander), of Nguyễn Văn Ca 阮文歌 (Pope of the Minh Chơn Lý branch [the Reason of the Enlightened

58 A forthcoming paper focuses specifically on the settlement in Cochin-China of the Theosophical Society: Jeremy Jammes, "Theosophying the Vietnamese Religious Landscape: A Circulatory History of a Western Esoteric Movement in South Vietnam," in *Theosophy Across Boundaries*, ed. Hans Martin Krämer and Julian Strube (Albany, NY: SUNY Press, forthcoming).

59 Pierre Bourdieu, *Choses dites* (Paris: Éditions de Minuit, 1987), 110.

60 Jammes, *Les Oracles*, 482.

Truth 明真理 *mingzhenli*]), and of Cao Sĩ Tấn 高仕晋, a doctor and spirit-medium at Cầu Kho temple, Saigon.[61]

The Cao Đài and Minh libraries we visited during our different field trips (2000–2013) contained large collections of occultist literature in French, especially of the spiritist and theosophical varieties, published between the 1910s and the 1930s. In the library of the Minh Lý's main temple in Ho Chi Minh City,[62] for instance, few new titles have been placed on its dusty shelves since the 1930s; it contains a comprehensive collection of French esoteric and occultist texts, as well as a rich trove of Chinese scriptures, morality books, and spirit-writing texts, a large proportion of which were printed in the late nineteenth and early twentieth centuries by a Xiantiandao temple, the Chaoyuandong 朝元洞, located at Luofushan 羅浮山in Guangdong, founded in 1873 and venerated as "ancestral court" of the Dongchu branch (東初派) of Xiantiandao, that spread to various parts of Southeast Asia.[63] We found a similar collection of Chinese texts (but no French or Vietnamese ones) at a decrepit Minh Sư/Xiantiandao temple in Saigon, the afore-mentioned Quang Nam Phật Đường 光南佛堂 Guangnan Fotang, established in 1920. These collections are evidence of the Xiantiandao-Minh networks and of the rapid development of the printing business during the late imperial period throughout the Chinese overseas communities.[64]

On the other hand, the library of a major Cao Đài research institute in Ho Chi Minh City, the "Centre for the Diffusion of the Doctrine of the Great Way" (Cơ Quan Phổ Thông Giáo Lý Đại Đạo 機關普通教理大道*jiguan putong jiaoli dadao*), a Minh-Tân-derivated temple established in 1965,[65] in addition to its substantial collection of holdings in Vietnamese, contains much the same collection of French esoteric and occultist titles as the Minh Lý Dao, but no Chinese texts. The distinctions and overlaps between these libraries are traces of the translingual textual circulation of religious ideas in the colonial and post-colonial era: from the purely Chinese corpus of a Minh Sư temple founded in 1920, to the Chinese, French, and Vietnamese resources of the Minh Lý Dao

61 See Jammes, *Les Oracles*, 167–168, citing Jacques Dalloz, *Francs-maçons d'Indochine (1868–1975)* (Paris: Éditions Maçonniques de France, 2002), 10.

62 Jammes, *Les Oracles*, 468–474; Jammes, "Divination and Politics," 365–366.

63 Wei Dingming 危丁明, *Shumin de yongheng: Xiantiandao ji qi zai Gang'ao ji Dongnanya diqu de fazhan* 庶民的永恆：先天道及其在港澳及東南亞地區的發展 (Taipei: Boyang wenhua, 2015), 487.

64 Yau Chi On, "The Xiantiandao and Publishing in the Guangzhou-Hong Kong Area from the Late Qing to the 1930s: The Case of the Morality Book Publisher Wenzaizi," in *Religious Publishing and Print Culture in Modern China (1800–2012)*, ed. Philip Clart and Gregory Adam Scott (Boston, Berlin: De Gruyter, 2014), 187.

65 Jammes, *Les Oracles*, 260–262.

founded in 1924, to the exclusively French and Vietnamese holdings of the Cao Đài library established in 1965.

7 The *Đại Thừa Chơn Giáo* (大乘真教): the Cao Đài Context of an Esoteric Textual Production

In the following section, we examine the idiomatic "traffic" of "translingual practices" generated in these already trans-national, trans-ethnic, trans-generational, and trans-temple networks through a study of the production and translation of the core esoteric scripture of Caodaism, the *Đại Thừa Chơn Giáo* (大乘真教 *Dacheng zhenjiao*), "The True Teachings of the Great Vehicle," hereafter referred to as *ĐTCG*.

The *Đại Thừa Chơn Giáo* is one of the four canonical scriptures of Caodaism, each of which was composed through spirit-writing. Three of the scriptures focus on the religious life and community organization of the followers. They were compiled at the Holy See of Tây Ninh between 1926 and 1927, based on a preliminary selection of spirit-writing texts. They are the *Thánh Ngôn Hiệp Tuyển* (聖言集全 *shengyan jiquan*, "Compilation of Holy Words"), translated into French by Caodaists as *Les Saintes Paroles* ("The Holy Words") or *Recueil des saints messages spirites* ("Compilation of Holy Writings of the Spirits"); the *Pháp Chánh Truyền* (法正傳 *Fazhengchuan,* "the Orthodox Dharma," translated by francophone Caodaists as *Constitution Religieuse*, "Religious Constitution"); and the *Tân Luật* (新律 *xinlü*, "New Code"), which deals with conversion rituals (*cầu đạo* 求道 *qiudao*, literally, "to seek the Way") and other administrative topics. The fourth canonical text, the *ĐTCG,* deals primarily with esoteric practices.

The *ĐTCG* is not structured as a coherent and organized dogmatic treatise, but rather as a collection of moral guidance and teachings proclaimed by "instructors of the invisible." The *ĐTCG* presents itself as an archetype of the omniscient knowledge transmitted by the spirits. The Daoist notion of self-cultivation (*tu luyện* 修煉 *xiulian*) through techniques of the body and meditation is one of the core themes of the book. The messages of the spirits elaborate on the tradition of the Three Teachings of Confucianism, Buddhism, and Daoism (*Tam Giáo* 三教 *sanjiao*), while claiming that they have lost their power in this era of the third kalpa. These doctrinal elements directly echo the millenarian themes of the Chinese salvationist tradition and especially the contents of the seventeenth-century *kinh Long Hoa* (龍華經 *Longhuajing*, "Dragon Flower Sutra"). According to this tradition, the human race is subject to a final trial or "Dragon Flower Assembly" (*hội Long Hoa* 龍華會 *Longhua hui*), in which only the most virtuous will pass the exam, attain salvation, and eventually find a place beside the Golden Mother of the Jasper Pool—and the Jade Emperor in the Cao Đài context.[66]

The revelation of the teachings in the ĐTCG had been announced during a séance in 1932, organized by the Chiếu Minh branch, following the death of Ngô Văn Chiêu, its founder. The author of the ĐTCG preface, Trần Văn Quế 陳文桂, assisted Liên Hoa, the medium at the séances who had been trained by Ngô Văn Chiêu himself, in reading the spirit messages. A mathematics teacher at the Lycée Pétrus-Ký elite high school, Trần Văn Quế (1902–1980) joined Cao Đài in 1929 and immediately got involved in the struggle against schisms in the movement, considering unity as crucial to counter colonial power.[67]

We have noted above that the Chiếu Minh denomination was described by the Tây Ninh Holy See as the "esoteric" branch of Caodaism, which practices "heart-to-heart transmission through non-interference" (*nội giáo vô vi tâm truyền* 內教無為心傳 *neijiao wuwei xinchuan*). This branch was considered as the trustee of the "secret law of esoteric exercises" (*tâm pháp bí truyền luyện đạo* 心法密傳煉道 *xinfa michuan liandao*) which should not be transmitted outside of the small circle of initiates. The latter would be released from the law of karma and would attain to high positions in the afterlife after this intense "effort" (*công phu* 功夫 *gongfu*).

The notion of "exotericism" (*ngoại giáo công truyền* 外教公傳 *waijiao gongchuan*), on the other hand, is often used by Caodaists to refer to the ideas and actions of the Tây Ninh Holy See. From the 1920s until today, the Tây Ninh Holy See instrumentalizes the original schismatic division by according to itself the monopoly of proselytism and social action, and by presenting itself as the sole possessor of the Dharma for the new kalpa (*kiếp pháp* 劫法 *jiefa*), while it recognizes Ngô Văn Chiêu's dissident branch as a method of individual self-cultivation.

The production of the ĐTCG by the Chiếu Minh aimed, on the other hand, to reinforce its authority in matters of esoteric cultivation. When, on 19 November 1936, Trần Văn Quế wrote the text which would become the preface to the 1950 ĐTCG, he was positioning himself directly in reaction to the Tây Ninh Holy See, whose leader, the prolific medium Phạm Công Tắc,

66 Đức Nguyên, *Cao Đài Từ Điển*, "*Tiến hóa*"; Jammes, *Les Oracles*, 109–113. According to the theological perspective, but also to the believer, there is a debate whether the highest deity would be the Jade Emperor, the Golden Mother, or both (following the Daoist dyad or yin/yang dynamics).

67 For more details on the production of these texts in the context of sectarian rivalries between Cao Đài branches, see Jammes and Palmer, "Occulting the Dao"; on the commitment of Trần Văn Quế to the union of the Cao Đài branches, see Jammes, "Caodaism in Times of War," 274–279.

had been publishing esoteric teachings, undermining the complementarity between the "esoteric" and "exoteric" branches of the Cao Đài religion.[68] Phạm Công Tắc played the role of medium during séances at which messages were specifically received, in French, from Lenin (25 February 1934), Joan of Arc (24 February 1933), Jean de la Fontaine (14 March 1933), Shakespeare (29 December 1935), and recurrently Victor Hugo (between 1927 and 1959).[69] These messages engaged Caodaism in the political discourses of the time through the intermediary of these European figures.

In 1946, Phạm Công Tắc had returned to Cochin-China after having been jailed for five years in Madagascar by the French authorities. The French forced him to support them and to join the war against the Communists. Seeking to unite the masses of believers who were dispersed in different branches, and having gained an intense meditation experience during his exile, he began to compete directly with the Chiếu Minh branch on the terrain of its own specialty: esoteric meditation. He eventually managed to convince the members of the Minh Thiện redemptive society to join his meditation centers, in which the spirits would be able to teach "the spiritual and secret exercises" (*bí pháp luyện đạo* 密法煉道 *mifa liandao*).[70] His meditation practice inspired his homilies, written between 1946 and 1959 in Vietnamese prose, and compiled into eight published volumes.[71] His spirit-writing sessions had at the same time generated an original esoteric body of knowledge, directly produced in French, that was politically engaged and legitimated the power of this medium and the orthodoxy claims of the Tây Ninh Holy See.

The publication of the ĐTCG in 1950, in response to these initiatives, aimed to consolidate the authority of the Chiếu Minh denomination in esoteric matters. In the ĐTCG, the Chiếu Minh branch is thus described as the guardian of the "Great Dao of the Highest Platform" (*Cao Đài Đại Đạo* 高臺大道 *Gaotai dadao*), while the branch of the Tây Ninh Holy See, under the name of the "Great Way of the Third Cycle of Universal Salvation" formed the "Cao Đài religion" (*Cao Đài Tôn Giáo* 高臺宗教 *Gaotai zongjiao*) focused on evangelizing the masses (*cơ Phổ hóa* 幾普化 *jipuhua*).[72]

68 Jammes, "Divination and Politics," 362–374.

69 Jammes, *Les Oracles*, 529–539.

70 Đức Nguyên, *Cao Đài Từ Điển*, "*Trí huệ cung.*"

71 See the publications of Phạm Công Tắc in our bibliography.

72 Phái Chiếu-Minh, *Đại Thừa Chơn Giáo—Le Grand Cycle de l'Ésotérisme*, "Cao Đài Đại Đạo" [Great Way of Cao Đài or Caodaism] Series (Saigon: Nguyễn-Văn-Huấn Printing House, 1950), 6–7.

8 A Translingual Study of the *ĐTCG*

The *ĐTCG* is a collection of 51 spirit-writing messages attributed mostly to the Jade Emperor, Li Bai 李白, Guan Gong 關公, Laozi, and so on, revealed in Vietnamese at the end of 1936; to these texts were added 22-odd messages produced by the divinized spirits of former Chiếu Minh disciples (two in 1926, two in 1934, two in 1935, five in 1937, one in 1938, two in 1939, two in 1941, two in 1945, one in 1948, two in 1949, one in 1950). It is symptomatic of the spirit-writing origin of this volume and of its supposed role in the self-cultivation of the followers that the last pages (530–531) list the divine titles of Chiếu Minh members who passed away—the so-called pioneers (*tiên phong* 先鋒 *xianfeng*), translated as "angels" (*les anges*), and "the elected men and women" (*les élus* and *les élues*).

The collection was compiled as a 538-page volume in thematic (and not chronological) order with a print run of "2,000 copies, not for sale" in 1950, in a bilingual, Vietnamese-French version.[73] It was printed by a company run by Nguyễn Văn Huấn 阮文訓, a famous and active member of the Theosophical Society.[74]

The book contains both the original Vietnamese text and a French translation heavily laden with the idioms of French Occultism, itself based on a reappropriation and reinterpretation of the symbols and tropes of Roman Catholicism. The 1950 edition carries the French title of *La Bible du Grand Cycle de l'Ésotérisme*—"The Bible of the Great Cycle of Esotericism"; the Vietnamese preface refers to it as "a manual of the pill of immortality" (*kinh sách luận về Đơn-Kinh* 經書論於丹經 *jingshu lunyu danjing*).[75] These two designations reveal the two distinct idioms in which the teachings are presented in the book: as a Daoist manual of immortality in the Vietnamese version, and as an "Esoteric Bible" in the French version.

The publisher of the *ĐTCG*, Nguyễn Văn Huấn, was possibly involved at least in the proofreading process, imprinting his theosophical and occultist influence on some terms and concepts. However, the inner cover pages (pages 2–3) of

73 The 1950 edition ("Nguyễn Văn Huấn Printing house") is mentioned as the "second edition"; we have not been able to locate earlier edition(s) of this text and assume the "first edition" was circulated internally and in Vietnamese only.

74 A lay Buddhist, art professor, and publisher, Nguyễn Văn Huấn was the first secretary of the Theosophical branch for "Việt Nam" in 1949. See Jammes, "Theosophying." On the community of Cao Đài exegetes, journalists, and publishers, see Jeremy Jammes, "Printing Cosmopolitanism, Challenging Orthodoxies: Cao Đài Journals in Twentieth Century Vietnam," *Vienna Journal of East Asian Studies* 10 (2018): 175–209.

75 Phái Chiếu-Minh, *Đại Thừa Chơn Giáo*, 8–9.

the *ĐTCG* state that the translation was carried out by "a group of disciples of the Chiếu Minh Cenacle." The production and the publication of this book are the work of a milieu of Cao Đài editors and exegetists who were very experienced in Vietnamese-French translation. We can speculate with a reasonable degree of confidence that the following Caodaists actively participated in this translation: Trần Văn Quế (signatory of the preface), Nguyễn Hữu Đắc[76] (1897–1974, signatory of a note at the beginning of the book), and probably Phan Trường Mạnh 潘長孟 (1895–1967), prolific author and chief editor of the bilingual *Revue caodaïque/Cao Đài Giáo Lý* (高臺教理 *Gaotai jiaoli*, "the Doctrine of Cao Đài," publishing in 1930–1933 and 1947–1949), which makes ample reference to the spirit-writing production of the Chiếu Minh denomination. This "Caodaic Journal" actively participated in "Vietnamizing" the knowledge emanating from spirit-writing séances. It was run and hosted by the "Caodaic Institute. Psychological, philosophical, metaphysical studies" (Institut Caodaïque. Études psychologiques, philosophiques, métaphysiques). This institute (Học viện Cao Đài 學院高臺 *xueyuan gaotai*) aimed to bring studies on Caodaism to the status of a true theological discipline.

In our study, we have employed the following method to compare the meanings of the original Vietnamese and French versions of the text. We selected a number of stanzas from the two sections of the *ĐTCG*, which are representative of some of the core concepts of the text and exemplify the passage from a Chinese religious lexicon to French occultist and Catholic ones. The 1950 edition of the *ĐTCG* is a bilingual version, with the Vietnamese original on each left-hand page and the French translation on the facing page. For the purposes of the present English-language publication, we translated the French version of the selected passages into English. We also compared the original French translation from the 1950 version with a new, slightly revised French translation published by a Cao Đài group in 2013—the first revised French version to have been published since the 1950 edition.[77] The 2013 edition, in an obvious effort to adapt to a different cultural and religious context, has watered down

76 Nguyễn Hữu Đắc was a follower of the Minh Lý Dao and the maternal cousin of Lê Văn Trung, the pope of Caodaism.

77 Cao Đài Đại Đạo Cénacle Ésotérique de Chiếu Minh, *Le véritable enseignement du grand cycle caodaïste* (*Đại Thừa Chơn Giáo*), translated into French from Vietnamese by Quách Hiệp Long (Hanoi: NxB Tôn Giáo, 2013). This revised version was published by the "Centre for Diffusing the Doctrine of the Great Way" (Cơ Quan Phổ Thông Giáo Lý Đại Đạo), a Cao Đài ecumenical and missionary group founded in 1965 by Trần Văn Quế, a member of both Minh Lý and Cao Đài who, fifteen years earlier, had written the foreword of the *ĐTCG*.

the occultist and Catholic flavor of the 1950 version, sometimes instead using terms with more connotations of "New Age" spirituality.

The first English translation of the *ĐTCG* was published in 2015.[78] To our knowledge no Chinese translation has ever been attempted or published. It is interesting to note, however, that these recent translations, especially the English one, have largely removed the theosophical and spiritist language of the 1950 edition. Here, the translator attempted to tailor "Cao Đài" as a scientific and religious doctrine, which becomes "a profoundly mystic science"[79] driven by spirit-mediumship. This English translation departs substantially from the 1950 and 2013 French versions. Although there are still some clear references to Western occultist terms (spiritism, the Spirit of Truth, the disincarnated) or concepts (evolutionism, dematerialization ...), they occur much less than in the French versions; the translator(s) tried to stay close to the literal meaning while maintaining a more generic tenor, in which both the specific spiritist and Daoist/Chinese salvationist flavors are attenuated. Interestingly, the 2015 English translation lists several Vietnamese-English, French-English and English-English dictionaries in a bibliography, but no Chinese dictionary was consulted by its translator(s).[80] In the section below, while we quote the 2015 English translation for reference and comparison, our focus is on the 1950 bilingual Vietnamese-French edition.

We thus laid the different versions side by side: (1) the original Vietnamese; (2) the 1950 French translation;[81] (3) our English literal translation of the 1950 French version; (4) the 2013 French translation; and (5) the 2015 English translation. We then proceeded to "convert" the Vietnamese version into Chinese characters. We started with the hypothesis that the classical, religious, and poetic idiom of the *ĐTCG* could be converted into Chinese characters on a word-by-word basis (rather than translating the meaning of full verses into modern Chinese), for the following reasons: (1) the basic structure and pattern of the verses appears to be very similar to typical Chinese spirit-writing texts; indeed, the *ĐTCG* was revealed through spirit-writing techniques in basic continuity with Chinese methods, and in the tradition of the Xiantiandao branches within

78 Cao Đài Đại Đạo "Chiếu Minh" Séance, *The Grand Cycle of Esoteric Teaching* (San Jose, CA: Cao-Dai Temple Overseas, 2015).

79 Cao Đài Đại Đạo "Chiếu Minh" Séance, *The Grand Cycle of Esoteric Teaching*, 113.

80 Cao Đài Đại Đạo "Chiếu Minh" Séance, *The Grand Cycle of Esoteric Teaching*, 223.

81 Quotations from the text are references according to the date of production, i.e., year/month/day (in the text, the year is according to the Gregorian calendar and the month and day are according to the lunar calendar).

which the early founders and leaders of Cao Đài religion were active; (2) the text was produced at a time when the *quốc ngữ*—the modern romanization/alphabet system for Vietnamese—had only begun to be the dominant writing system, while the traditional writing system based on Chinese characters, formally abolished only in 1918 together with the Confucian mandarinate exams, retained a residual influence; (3) the Vietnamese language has many similarities with some Southern Chinese dialects such as Cantonese. Methodologically, then, we treated the Vietnamese text as if it were the romanization of a Chinese dialect, which could be converted into Chinese characters.

Converting the Vietnamese into Chinese characters was not an easy task—similar to the Chinese *Hanyu pinyin* romanization system, romanized Vietnamese contains a large number of homophones and there were often several plausible possibilities of equivalents in Chinese characters. Chinese characters were chosen based on the meaning and pronunciation of individual Vietnamese words (often similar to Cantonese or many other Chinese dialects demonstrating relatively systematic variations in pronunciation compared with Mandarin), placed in the context of the overall meaning of the verse and bearing in mind the use of specialized religious terminologies. We were unable to convert into Chinese about 15 percent of the selected Vietnamese verses, either because the meanings were too obscure, or because the terms were too purely or locally Vietnamese, without any equivalent Chinese characters with similar sound and meaning. In such cases, as in the first verse cited below, it is possible to convert the words into the *chữ nôm* logographic script of the Vietnamese language, derived from Chinese characters and used in vernacular texts prior to the introduction of modern Vietnamese romanization.

The outcome of this process fully confirmed our hypothesis—the Chinese text of the ĐTCG reads in style and content like a rather typical Chinese scripture produced through spirit-writing. It is particularly resonant with texts associated with Chinese redemptive societies of the early twentieth century, with an emphasis on both personal spiritual cultivation through Daoist inner alchemy and Confucian morality, and on universal salvation in the context of the sectarian eschatology of the three kalpas. Apart from a few syntactical structures distinct from standard Chinese, there is little in the text to indicate its Vietnamese provenance, and even few specific indications of a "uniquely" Cao Đài revelation. A reader familiar with Chinese spirit-writing texts and unaware that the text had been revealed in Vietnamese, could be forgiven, without studying the ĐTCG in depth, for assuming that our Chinese version was simply another of the myriads of texts produced by the thousands of spirit-writing altars in China and diasporic Chinese communities in the late imperial or modern era.[82]

An example of the stylistic similarity between the ĐTCG and Chinese spirit-writing texts is the literary practice, common in Chinese poetry and spirit-writing texts, in which the first word of each horizontal verse can be read vertically as a meaningful phrase. In the first stanza, for example, the three first Vietnamese words *ĐỘNG ĐÌNH HO* can be converted, based on the sound and meaning in the context of the verses, into the Chinese characters 洞頂蝴 (*dong ding hu*).[83] These characters, in turn, are homophones of the characters 洞庭湖 (*dong ting hu*)—Dongting Lake, which has strong associations with the famous Chinese Tang dynasty poet Lý Thái Bạch (Li Taibai 李太白), who is here referenced as the deity who authored this revelation, and who is venerated by Caodaists as the (spiritual) pope (*giáo tông* 教宗 *jiaozong*) of their religion.

[Original Vietnamese version]
ĐỘNG lòng thương xót buổi đời nguy,
ĐÌNH hội Phật Tiên đã mấy kỳ,
HO điệp mê mang chưa tỉnh thức,
ĐẠI TIÊN TRƯỞNG giáng hoát vô-vi.[84]

[Conversion into Chinese characters]
洞悉傷悴眲代危[85]
頂[庭]會佛仙達每期
蝴[湖] 蝶迷夢未顛醒
大仙將降活無為

[English translation of the Chinese version]:
My heart is pained by the calamities of this era
Buddhas and Immortals arrive for the assembly at each cycle
[The people are] Not yet awakened from their butterfly dream
The Great Immortal will come down, moving in non-action

82 Indeed, we showed the text to some Chinese readers unaware of its origin, and their reaction was the same: they saw our Chinese version of the ĐTCG text as a collection of Chinese poems.

83 Phái Chiếu-Minh, *Đại Thừa Chơn Giáo*, 16 (message of September 24, 1936).

84 Boldface in this and in the following extracts follows the original text.

85 This verse includes *chữ nôm* characters (underlined) for vernacular terms that do not have equivalents in Chinese characters.

[French version in the 1950 edition]:
Les malheurs de ce monde m'ont profondément ému.
Des Anges et des Bouddha se sont manifestés à maintes reprises pour son salut.
Mais, hallucinés par le Rêve des Papillons, ses hôtes ne veulent pas se réveiller ...
Je viens en Esprit leur ouvrir la Bible Caodaïque de la Délivrance.

[English literal translation of the 1950 French version]:
The calamities of this world have profoundly moved me.
Angels and Buddhas have manifested themselves on numerous instances for its salvation.
But, hallucinated by the Dream of the Butterflies, its hosts do not want to awaken ...
I come in Spirit to open for them the Caodaic Bible of Deliverance.

[English translation published in 2015]:
Touched by miseries of this world,
Divine Beings manifest many times to save it.
Yet humans are still deeply wallowing in reveries,
The GREAT IMMORTAL descends to teach them Self-Deliverance.

The meter and structure of *ĐTCG*'s verses read like a typical Chinese spirit-writing text. What makes the *ĐTCG* distinctive is the fact that it was revealed in romanized Vietnamese, *not* in Chinese characters—allowing it to cast a veil over the Chinese origin and content of its teachings, a veil that has become thicker with each generation of Vietnamese becoming increasingly ignorant of Chinese writing and civilization. Lacking the Chinese linguistic knowledge and Daoist terminology, a reader would find parts of the text to be simply incomprehensible.

The "occultation" of the Chinese religious roots of the *ĐTCG* was carried a stage further by the French edition, which overlaid an interpretation—onto the entire text—based on the categories of European esoteric and occultist re-appropriations of Catholic, Buddhist, and Daoist words and concepts. Since many of the early Cao Đài leaders and believers were educated in French colonial schools, they were often more literate in French than in Chinese or even Vietnamese, and used the French version as a key to understanding the obscure Vietnamese original with its stylistic roots in classical Chinese poetry. The bilingual edition of the *ĐTCG* was certainly published with this first purpose in mind. Moreover, the French edition helped to legitimize and convert the ĐTCG into both the language of modern rationality (through the idiom of Occultism) and the language of religious hegemony (through the idiom of Catholicism re-mixed by Occultism). But this "occultization" process of conversion and transformation, nearly completely "occulted" or eclipsed the Chinese and, especially, the Daoist roots of the text. This linguistic overlay is evidenced in the French title of the ĐTCG—*La Bible du Grand Cycle de l'Ésotérisme* ("The Bible of the Great Cycle of Esotericism"), which shifts the terminology from the generic Chinese Buddhist connotation of the original title, "The True Teachings of the Great Realization" or "The True Teachings of the Great Vehicle [Mahāyāna]" to an explicit combination of Biblical and esoteric references.

An archetypal example of the conversion of Daoist concepts into Christian terms with an explicit reference to Master Cao Đài that is absent in the original text is the fourth verse of the stanza revealed on 24 September 1936 and cited above. In the Vietnamese original, the line "*Đại-Tiên-Trưởng giáng hoát vô-vi*," converted word-by-word into Chinese characters, becomes 大仙將降活無為 (*daxian jiangjiang huo wuwei*), which may be rendered into English as "The Great Immortal shall come down, moving in non-action"—a rather generic expression of the process of spirit-writing by Daoist immortals in Chinese religion (the poet Li Taibai in this text). But in the French version—*Je viens en Esprit leur ouvrir la Bible Caodaïque de la Délivrance* ("I come in Spirit to open for them the Caodaic Bible of Deliverance")—the Daoist terminology of the original is replaced by Christian tropes ("I come in Spirit," the "Bible of Deliverance") in the name of Cao Đài.

Indeed, much of the original version of the ĐTCG can be read in the original like a relatively typical Chinese spirit-writing text, with the recurrent themes of a syncretic view of self-cultivation referring to the Three Teachings of Confucianism, Daoism, and Buddhism, associated with specific techniques of Daoist inner alchemy, and a message of universal salvation in the eschatological framework of the three kalpas of the Chinese salvationist (sectarian) tradition. The term "Cao Đài" rarely appears in the original; but is inserted repeatedly throughout the French translation, together with Christian and occultist terms. The French-mediated translingual practice of Cao Đài religion would appear to play an important role in articulating a Cao Đài identity that is distinct from Chinese popular religion and spirit-writing—the Vietnamese original version of the scripture containing little to distinguish it from the broader genre of Chinese spirit-writing.

It is interesting to note that in the new 2013 French translation of the scripture, the Christian terminology is removed from the translation of the aforementioned verse, which becomes: "The superior Spirit of the Great Immortal

Li Taibai manifests itself and opens the era of Spirituality" (*L'Esprit supérieur du Grand Immortel Li T'ai Pe se manifeste et ouvre l'ère de la Spiritualité*), perhaps indicating an alignment with a more "New Age" discourse of "spirituality," all the while explicitly naming the "Great Immortal" as Li Taibai.[86] And the 2015 English version is rather generic: "The GREAT IMMORTAL descends to teach them Self-Deliverance."[87]

In the next stanza, we find what again reads as a relatively generic spirit-writing text, with the exception of a specific reference to the "South"—which can, in the context of this scriptural production, be interpreted as either Vietnam, being located to the South of China, or as South Vietnam—given that the Cao Đài religion appeared in the Mekong delta and has been associated with South Vietnamese religious culture and identity. In the French translation, several of the implicit nuances of the stanza are rendered into explicit interpretations, again using Chinese sectarian, Christian, and occultist references. The reference to the third cycle of salvation, a mainstay of Chinese sectarian eschatology, is interpolated into the first line; the "Great Virtue" is named as the "Comforter," which is understood by Christians as referring to the Holy Spirit.[88] The Vietnamese sentence "educate the souls" (*giáo dục hồn dân* 教德魂人 *jiao de hun ren*), largely influenced by a Chinese conception of cultivation, was translated into French with a Christian-driven formula, "Angelic education."

In the third verse, the vaguely Daoist notion of the "return to one's spiritual nature" (*chuyển qui linh tánh* 轉歸靈性 *zhuangui lingxing*) is translated into strongly dualistic Biblical imagery as "fishing out the divine soul entangled in the flesh," while the generic "true transmission of Dao," *Chơn truyền đạo* (真傳道 *zhenchuan dao*), is rendered as "Caodaic esotericism." The Cao Đài practice of spirit-writing, "holding the divining stylus," *thừa cơ mật nhiệm* (乘乩密驗 *chengji miyan*) is rendered as "by means of psychography" with its Western spiritist and modernist connotations of a "writing of the psyche" or "photography of the soul."

> [Original Vietnamese version]:
> **ĐẠI** đức Nam Phương hóa Đạo Huỳnh,
> **THỪA** cơ mật nhiệm thức tâm linh,
> **CHƠN** truyền đạo chuyển qui linh tánh,
> **GIÁO** dục hồn dân trí huệ minh.

---

86 Cao Đài Đại Đạo Cénacle Ésotérique, *Le véritable enseignement du grand cycle caodaïste (Đại Thừa Chơn Giáo)*, 17.

87 Cao Đài Đại Đạo "Chiếu Minh" Séance, *The Grand Cycle of Esoteric Teaching*, 11.

88 See John 14:16, John 14:26, John 15:26.

[Conversion into Chinese characters]:
大德南方化道黃
乘乩密驗篤心靈
真傳道轉歸靈性
教德魂人智慧明

[English translation of the Chinese version]:
The Great Virtue generates an emperor of Dao in the South.
Holding the divining stylus to secretly activate the souls.
The true transmission of Dao returns to the spiritual nature.
Educate the souls and people to understand the wisdom.

[French version in the 1950 edition]:
Le consolateur prêche le 3ᵉ Salut Universel au Viet-Nam.
Au moyen de la psychographie, Il réveille les âmes dévoyées.
L'Ésotérisme Caodaïque *repêche l'Âme Divine enlisée dans la chair.*
Cette Éducation Angélique rallume la flamme Sacrée des cœurs humains.

[English literal translation of the 1950 French version]:
The comforter preaches the 3rd Universal Salvation in Vietnam.
By means of psychography, He awakens the lost souls.
Caodaic Esotericism *fishes out the Divine Soul entangled in the flesh.*
This Angelic Education re-ignites the Sacred flame of the human hearts.

[English translation published in 2015]:
GOD preaches the Saintly Doctrine in Vietnam;
HE reveals the mystic science to wake human spirits,
HE shows them the method to return to their spiritual nature,
And teaches them the doctrine to cultivate their mind.

A few lines down, Chinese salvationist apocalyptic themes are again translated into Christian terms: the "True Dao" (*Chơn Đạo* 正道 *zhengdao*) becomes "the Gospel of the Spirit of Truth"; the "end of the kalpa" (*mạt kiếp* 末劫 *mojie*) becomes "the prophesied end times"; the "Dragon Flower Assembly" (*hội Long Hoa* 龍華會 *Longhuahui*) becomes the "coming judgment of God." It seems that the main inspiration in the translation came from the spiritist reform of Catholicism. Indeed, by mentioning the role of the "Spirit of Truth" announced to "the Incarnates," we have a clear-cut reference to one of the key concepts of Kardec's spiritist doctrine. In his *Book of the Spirits* (*Le Livre des Esprits* in its 1857 original French version), Kardec referred to "The Spirit of Truth" as a group of spirits who taught the new doctrine during spiritist séances in the 1850s. In volume II of *The Book of the Spirits*, Kardec dedicated chapter 2 to the "Incarnation of Spirits" and explained why spirits "incarnate" in material bodies, justifying later the necessary "disincarnation" process taught by the spiritist doctrine itself.

> [Original Vietnamese version]:
> Minh Chơn-Đạo thời kỳ mạt-kiếp,
> Thức tỉnh đời cho kịp Long-Hoa,
>
> [Conversion into Chinese characters]:
> 明正道吹起末劫
> 學省俗至及龍華
>
> [English translation of the Chinese version]:
> Enlightening the True Dao at the end of the kalpa
> Awakening from the profane world will allow one to reach the Dragon Flower Assembly.
>
> [French version in the 1950 edition]:
> *L'Évangile de l'Esprit de Vérité s'ouvre aux derniers temps prédits*
> *Pour annoncer aux Incarnés le prochain Jugement de Dieu.*
>
> [English literal translation of the 1950 French version]:
> *The Gospel of the Spirit of Truth is opened in the prophesied end times*
> *To announce to the Incarnates the coming Judgment of God.*
>
> [English translation published in 2015]:
> *The Spirit of Truth is elucidated in this late Era of Destruction,*
> *To warn the incarnate of the upcoming Judgment.*

A little further down,[89] the DTCG does mention Cao Đài explicitly, referring not to the Master here but rather to a specific "set of teachings," *Cao Đài giáo* (高臺教 *Gaotai jiao*). The original verses use a generally Buddhist imagery to speak of guiding sentient beings to deliverance through self-cultivation, although the term "Second Person," *Ngôi Hai* (位二 *wei er*) can refer, in Vietnamese Catholicism, to the Son, i.e., to the second person of the Holy Trinity. In the French version, this incarnation-related and messianic theme is

89 Phái Chiếu-Minh, *Đại Thừa Chơn Giáo*, 18.

expanded to convert the stanza into a fully Christian eschatological structure, speaking of the "lambs," the "manger," the "children of God," and the "Darkness of Satan" (albeit with the "Three Nirvanas" thrown in, which do not appear in the original version). The mention in French of "the Era of Incarnation" sets up again a spiritist framework of understanding and translation. The extensive use of Christian terminology has to be comprehended within this spiritist perspective.

[Original Vietnamese version]:
CAO-ĐÀI-GIÁO lưu hành phổ tế,
Pháp chánh truyền cứu thế thoát nhân,
Bốn phương phát triển tinh thần,
Gội nhuần võ lộ hồng ân **CAO-ĐÀI**.
Gần tận thế **NGÔI-HAI** ra mặt,
Đặng toan phương dìu dắt chúng-sanh,
Chỉ tường cội phước nguồn lành,
Giác mê tỉnh ngộ tu hành siêu thăng.
Cuộc tang thương dữ dằn trước đó.

[Conversion into Chinese characters]:
高臺教流行普渡
《法正傳》救世脫人
四方發展省清
溉濕霧露鴻恩**高臺**
近旦夕**位**二出面
當痛方調度眾生
指通概福慷恩
覺夢醒悟自行超升
局疼痛暴壓速逃

[English translation of the Chinese version]:
The Cao Đài teachings spread universal salvation far and wide
The Orthodox Transmission of the Dharma saves the world and delivers humanity
In the four directions, consciousness shall develop
Moistened by the blessed mist and dew of the grace of [Master] Cao Đài
Approaching the Last Day [End of the World], the **Second Person [the Son]** appears
And suffers in order to guide all sentient beings
Points through the root of abundant blessings

To be awakened and enlightened, and to rise to salvation through one's own cultivation
When suffering pushes you to escape.

[French version in the 1950 edition]:
Le CAODAISME *prêche le Salut Universel*
Cette Doctrine Unique enseigne: « Sauvez-vous vous-mêmes en sauvant les autres »
Des 4 points du globe, les consciences se raniment
Sous le souffle du Saint-Esprit qui se répand du **CAO-DAI**
Aux termes de l'Ère de l'Incarnation, **DIEU LE FILS** *se révèle à nouveau*
Pour ramener ses brebis au Bercail d'En-Haut.
Son Évangile montre les 3 Nirvana
D'où les Enfants de Dieu partaient pour y revenir.
Les Ténèbres de Satan dissipés, la Voie de Dieu réapparaît.

[English literal translation of the 1950 French version]:
CAODAISM preaches Universal Salvation
The Unique Doctrine teaches: "Save yourself by saving others."
From the 4 points of the globe, conscious souls are coming back to life
Through the breath of the Holy Spirit that spreads from the **CAO-DAI**
At the term of the Era of Incarnation, **GOD THE SON** reveals himself again.
To bring his lambs to the Manger Above.
His Gospel shows the 3 Nirvanas
From which the Children of God left and now return.
The Darkness of Satan dissipated, the Way of God re-appears.

[English translation published in 2015]:
CAODAISM promulgates the new doctrine,
The true method of self-deliverance to liberate mankind;
It revives this spirit throughout the world,
So that everyone receives the great favor of CAO-ĐÀI,
Near the end of the Cosmic Cycle, GOD THE SON reveals Himself,
To lead humans back to their original nature;
He points out their Saintly Origin,
Waking them from illusion, focusing them on self-attainment.

Much of the second part of the *DTCG* is devoted to the esoteric spiritual practice of Caodaism, describing a nine-stage method that is titled in French as the "nine initiations of Caodaic esotericism."[90] Converted to Chinese characters, the original text of the name of the method, "Tam Thừa Cửu Chuyển" (三乘九轉 *sancheng jiuzhuan*), "three vehicles in nine cycles," evokes the terminology of Daoist inner alchemy; following the conventions of Daoist studies, it might be also rendered in English as the "Three Vehicles of Nine Reversions,"[91] or as "Ninefold transformation"[92] or "Nine reversals."

Indeed, the description of the method over the following sections clearly refers to inner alchemical practices. But the "pre-natal realm" or *tiên thiên* (先天 *xiantian*, also often translated by scholars as "anterior heaven"), a core concept in Daoist cosmology and alchemical practice, is translated as "Occult life" (i.e., the hidden life which requires an initiation); while the process of alchemical refinement of the *hồn* (魂 *hun*) and *phách* (魄 *po*) souls on the path of immortality (*tiên* 仙 *xian*), is rendered as "Cleans[ing] the soul and the body of the Elect who aspire to the Bliss of the Angels." In the 2013 revision, those terms are replaced by the more New-Age theosophical connotations of "creating the astral body."[93] Indeed the founders of the Theosophical Society extensively based their argumentation on the existence and definition of this astral body, especially the 1902 book *Man Visible and Invisible* by Charles Webster Leadbeater (1854–1934).

> [Original Vietnamese version]:
> Đại thừa Đạo chánh Tiên-Thiên,
> Luyện hồn chế phách đăng Tiên hưởng nhàn.
> Trong cửu chuyển phải tàng tâm-pháp,
> Phải y hành cho hạp phép tu,
>
> [Conversion into Chinese characters]:
> 大乘道長先天
> 練魂制魄登仙享閒
> 純九轉恰藏心法
> 恰依行才合法修

90 Phái Chiếu-Minh, *Đại Thừa Chơn Giáo*, 384 (message of August 19, 1936).

91 Louis Komjathy, *The Way of Complete Perfection: A Quanzhen Daoist Anthology* (Albany: State University of New York Press, 2013), 309.

92 Kristofer Schipper and Franciscus Verellen, eds., *The Taoist Canon: A Historical Companion to the Daozang* (Chicago: University of Chicago Press, 2004), 399.

93 Cao Đài Đại Đạo Cénacle Ésotérique, *Le véritable enseignement du grand cycle caodaïste (Đại Thừa Chơn Giáo)*, 299.

[English translation of the Chinese version]:
The Way of the Great Vehicle is eternally located in the Pre-Natal realm
Refine the heavenly (*hun*) souls and control the earthly (*po*) souls, ascend to the bliss of the Immortals
In the nine pure cycles is stored the method of the inner heart
You must follow the right rules and train with the right principles

[French version from the 1950 edition]:
Le Grand Cycle de l'Ésotérisme révèle la Vie Occulte,
Assainit l'âme et le corps des Élus qui aspirent à la Félicité des Anges.
Au cours des 9 spires d'évolution, pénétrez-vous des Lois Occultes
Selon lesquelles vous pratiquez vos Exercices Spirituels.

[English literal translation of the 1950 French version]:
The Great Cycle of Esotericism reveals the Occult Life,
Cleanses the soul and the body of the Elect who aspire to the Bliss of the Angels.
During the 9 stages of evolution, immerse yourself in the Occult Laws
According to which you practice your Spiritual Exercises.

[English translation published in 2015]:
The Grand Cycle of Esotericism reveals the Way of the Pre-Genesis,
To forge the soul and create the double-body for the spiritual ascension.
You should know the method of heart in the Nine Initiations,
And scrupulously exercise them in accord with the rules of self-perfection.

Further down,[94] we find a typical piece of advice on nurturing the triad of *tinh* (精 *jing*), *khí* (氣 *qi*), and *thần* (神 *shen*) in Daoist inner alchemy—three terms usually translated in English-language scholarship as Essence, Qi (or vital breath), and Spirit; these, here, are rendered as "sperm," "breath," and "the Holy Spirit." The Chinese terms are impossible to translate adequately—*jing*, *qi*, and *shen* each referring to different forms of vital energy, *jing* being the most "material" and *shen* the most "spiritual," externally associated respectively with sperm, breath, and the mind, but internally the object of subtle circulations and transformations within the body, each being transformed into the other through alchemical meditation aiming to refine the *jing* into *qi*, the *qi* into *shen*, and the *shen* back into the void *xuwu* 虛無 (*hư vô* in Vietnamese). Given the impossibility to fully render the terms into European languages—and the

94 Phái Chiếu-Minh, *Đại Thừa Chơn Giáo*, 386 (message of August 19, 1936).

opacity of the terms to anyone not familiar with inner alchemy—it is interesting that the Cao Đài translators chose two terms that reflect an extreme dualism of body and spirit, rendering *jing* into its most materialized expression as "sperm" and *shen* into a Christian term associated with the absolutely transcendental God, as the "Holy Spirit." (The 2015 version translates *jing* and *shen* as "quintessence" and "spirit" respectively, a choice of terms that most scholars would probably find appropriate.)

> [Original Vietnamese version]:
> Nhứt là dưỡng khí, tồn tinh,
> Tinh khô, khí tận, thần linh chẳng còn.
>
> [Conversion into Chinese characters]:
> 一來養氣存精
> 精枯、氣竭，神靈將乾
>
> [English translation of the Chinese version]:
> Most important is to nurture the *Qi* and preserve the Essence
> When the Essence is dried and the *Qi* is exhausted, the Spirit will disappear.
>
> [French version from the 1950 edition]:
> Ménagez d'abord le Souffle de vie et économisez le Sperme.
> Quand le Sperme s'épuise et le Souffle se gaspille, le Saint-Esprit disparaîtra.
>
> [English literal translation of the 1950 French version]:
> First nourish the Breath of life and conserve your Sperm.
> When the Sperm is drained and the Breath is wasted, the Holy Spirit will disappear.
>
> [English translation published in 2015]:
> Especially you should nurture Energy and conserve Quintessence,
> If you expend Quintessence and exhaust Energy, the Spirit no longer exists.

The dualistic framework appears again a few verses below on the first reversal, in which the "communication between *shen* (spirit) and *qi* (vital breath)" (*thần khí giao thông* 神氣交通 *shenqi jiaotong*) is rendered as "union of the

Soul and Body," and the "elimination of worries and malice" (*Diệt trừ phiền não lòng không* 滅除煩惱心空 *miechu fannao xinkong*) is translated as their "dematerialization." This Chinese conception of the body is fully "Caodaized" in the French translation, as the Daoist alchemical process is here said to be conducted "according to the Caodaic Code," a specification that is absent in the original.

[Original Vietnamese version]:
Sơ **Nhứt Chuyển** lo tròn luyện kỹ,
Xây đắp nền thần khí giao thông,
Diệt trừ phiền não lòng không,
Thất tình lục dục tận vong đơn thành.

[Conversion into Chinese characters]:
初一**轉**耐圓煉意
升台基神氣交通
撇除煩惱心罡
七情六慾殆忘丹成

[English translation of the Chinese version]:
In the first cycle, remember to wholeheartedly train with intention.
Raise the foundation for the communication between *qi* and spirit.
Eliminate all worries and malice.
Extinguish the emotions and desires to form the elixir [of immortality].

[French version from the 1950 edition]:
A la 1ère spire d'évolution (1ère INITIATION) forgez et trempez vaillamment vos 3 âmes.
Bâtissez les assises du Temple où l'Âme et le Corps s'unissent selon le Code Caodaïque.
Dématérialisez-les des soucis et des chagrins.
La pilule d'immortalité se forme dès que les instincts et les passions se taisent.

[English literal translation of the 1950 French version]:
At the first stage of evolution (FIRST INITIATION) valiantly forge and soak your 3 souls.
Build the foundations of the Temple where the Soul and the Body are united according to the Caodaic Code.

Dematerialize them of anxieties and worries.
The pill of immortality is formed as soon as the instincts and passions are quieted.

[English translation published in 2015]:
In the FIRST INITIATION you should accomplish self-perfection,
To build the foundation for Energy-Spirit alliance,
Also to abolish all grieves (*sic*) and maintain the emptiness of heart,
Once the seven emotions and six passions are shut, serenity emerges.

A few verses down, "Caodaic consciousness" is interpolated into the text where the original *Tâm Đạo* ("The Dao of the Heart" 心道 *xindao*) makes no mention of Cao Đài and carries a generic coloration; and the "sublime *qi*," *khí hạo nhiên* (氣浩然 *qi haoran*), which evokes the Confucian philosopher Mencius and the poet Su Dongpo 蘇東坡 (1037–1101),[95] is rendered with the yogic and Sanskrit term of "prana" (the vital principle).

The last verse of this stanza expresses the essence of Daoist inner alchemical practice: the harmonization of *tánh* (性 *xing*) and *mạng* (命 *ming*)—terms that are also very difficult to translate but generally refer to one's spiritual nature or essence (*xing*) and to the life of the body (*ming*)—each of which is the subject of training regimens in Daoism; the relationship between the two of them has been the subject of protracted debates in Daoist discourse over the centuries, with a general consensus, however, that *both* the practice of techniques of the body (*ming*) *and* the pursuit of spiritual purity (*xing*) are essential and should be harmonized.[96] The second part of the last verse refers to the metaphors of lead and mercury in inner alchemy, which are respectively associated with water and fire, denoting energies within the body whose circulation must be inverted and conjoined to form the elixir. This complex Daoist cosmology of the body is here rendered in terms of "sublime *qi*" being described as the

95 See the *Mencius: Gongsunchou* I: 2 孟子：公孫丑上: "I am good at nourishing my sublime *qi*" (我善養吾浩然之氣). And in the melody "Prelude to the Water: In the Happy Pavilion" 水調歌頭：快哉亭作, included in *The Poems of Dongpo* 東坡樂府 (edited in the Yuan dynasty), verse 34, the poet Su Dongpo wrote, "A little bit of sublime *qi* senses a thousand miles of blissful wind" (一點浩然氣，千里快哉風). (https://ctext.org/wiki.pl?if=gb&chapter=616023).

96 For a detailed discussion of this issue, see Fabrizio Pregadio, "Destiny, Vital Force, or Existence? On the Meanings of Ming 命 in Daoist Internal Alchemy and its Relation to Xing 性 or Human Nature," *Daoism: Religion, History and Society* 6 (2014): 157–218.

"Holy Spirit" acting as the "hyphen" linking the "Spirit of Light" and the "Spirit of Darkness." While the translation does convey the sense of conjoining dual opposites, the notions of "Spirit of Light" and "Spirit of Darkness" have rather different, spiritist-driven connotations.

[Original Vietnamese version]:
Tâm Đạo phát thanh-thanh tịnh-tịnh,
Dưỡng Thánh-thai chơn bỉnh Đạo Huyền,
Ngày đêm cướp khí hạo nhiên,
Hiệp hòa tánh mạng, hống diên giao đầu.

[Conversion into Chinese characters]:
心道合神神靜靜
養聖胎貞秉道玄
日夜豁氣浩然
協和性命、汞鉛交投

[English translation of the Chinese version]:
The Dao of the Heart becomes calm and pure
Nurture the Holy Foetus and hold to the mystery of Dao
Day and night, expand the sublime *qi*
Harmonize spiritual nature and bodily life, inducing the intercourse of Mercury and Lead.

[French version from the 1950 edition]:
La CONSCIENCE CAODAIQUE s'épanouit dans le calme et la pureté.
Nourrissez le SAINT-FŒTUS selon les règles strictes de l'Ésotérisme du Maître.
Nuit et jour, captez vaillamment le PRANA.
Qui est le Saint-Esprit ou Trait d'Union entre l'Esprit de Lumière et l'Esprit des Ténèbres symbolisés par le HG et le PB.

[English literal translation of the 1950 French version]:
The CAODAIC CONSCIOUSNESS expands in stillness and purity.
Nourish the HOLY FŒTUS according to the Master's strict rules of Esotericism.
Night and Day, valiantly capture the PRANA.
That is the Holy Spirit or Hyphen between the Spirit of Light and the Spirit of Darkness symbolised by HG and PB.

[English translation published in 2015]:
Develop the Conscience of DAO in serenity and quietude,
Nurture the Saintly Fetus in accord with the mystic laws;
Day and night, capture the primordial energy of life,
To harmonize soul and body, to unite mercury and lead.

A few lines further—"*Âm dương thăng giáng điều hòa*" (陰陽升降調和 *yinyang shengjiang tiaohe*), literally "Yin and Yang rise and fall in coordination"—we find an intriguing translation of the *yinyang* dyad—*âm* (陰 *yin*) and *dương* (陽 *yang*) as the "Spiritual and the Temporal," which "rise and descend according to the rhythm of Providence," providing a strong Kardec-inflected Catholic flavor to what, in Chinese, is an ordinary statement on the basic cosmological operation of yin and yang cycles.

[Original Vietnamese version]:
Âm dương thăng giáng điều hòa,
Huân chưng đầm ấm tam hoa kiết huờn.

[Conversion into Chinese characters]:
陰陽升降調和
熏蒸潭温三華結還

[English translation of the Chinese version]:
Yin and Yang rise and fall in coordination
Steam and distil the three essences [essence, *qi*, and spirit] back to the origin

[French version from the 1950 edition]:
Le Spirituel et le Temporel montent et descendent selon le rythme de la Providence.
Le Syncrétisme des Fluides amène l'Harmonie des 3 Âmes.

[English literal translation of the 1950 French version]:
The Spiritual and the Temporal rise and descend according to the rythm of Providence.
The Syncretism of the Fluids brings about the Harmony of the 3 Souls.

[English translation published in 2015]:
The Yin and Yang concertedly rise and fall,
And the Three Treasures rhrythmically harmonize and sublime.

Next we find another pair of verses that express, in typical inner-alchemical terms, some basic processes of alchemical cultivation. While "Opening the nine orifices" (*khai cửu khiếu* 開九竅 *kai jiu qiao*) is open to different interpretations,[97] the ĐTCG translates them as the "nine chakras," drawing on Western esoteric interpretations of Indian tantra. Indeed, the Theosophical Society published extensively on these terms and this literature circulated in Cochin-China. The book *The Chakras* (1927) of Charles W. Leadbeater, one of the founders of the Theosophical Society, notably included a series of colored drawings, which contributed to the popularization of his interpretation in Cochin-China.[98] This theosophical literature was stored and explored in the Minh Lý and Cao Đài libraries, but also in various bookshops in Ho Chi Minh City that we visited during our fieldwork (2000–2013).

The second verse refers to the operation of the Five Elements or Five Phases (*ngũ hành* 五行 *wuxing*: wood, fire, earth, metal, and water) and to the circulation, in inner alchemy, of the yang and yin forces of Heaven and Earth, *Càn-Khôn* (the *qian* 乾 and *kun* 坤 trigrams). The translator(s) of the ĐTCG here interpreted the *wuxing* as the "five senses" and once again used the "union of the spiritual and the temporal" to render the circulation and rotation of *qian* and *kun*.

> [Original Vietnamese version]:
> Khai cửu khiếu kim-đơn phanh-luyện,
> Vận ngũ hành lưu chuyển Càn-Khôn,
>
> [Conversion into Chinese characters]:
> 開九竅金丹返煉
> 運五行流轉乾坤
>
> [English translation of the Chinese version]:
> Open the nine orifices for the reverse refinement of the golden elixir
> Operate the Five Phases to rotate the Heaven and Earth [Qian and Kun]

97 For example, the "Wonderful Instructions on the Golden Elixir of the Nine Cycles 大洞煉真寶經九還金丹妙訣," a Tang-dynasty text preserved in the Daoist Canon (no. 891), links the "nine orifices" to "nine stars." See Schipper and Verellen, eds., *The Taoist Canon*, 383–384.

98 In the year of his death (1934), the Cochin-Chinese branch of the Theosophical Society, based in Saigon, was named after him. See Jammes, "Theosophying."

[French version from the 1950 edition]:
En ouvrant les 9 CHAKRAS (sens spirituels) la pilule d'immortalité se chauffe et se forge.
En convergeant les 5 sens, le Spirituel et le Temporel s'unissent intimement.

[English literal translation of the 1950 French version]:
By opening the 9 CHAKRAS (spiritual sense organs) the pill of immortality heats up and is forged.
By converging the 5 senses, the Spiritual and the Temporal conjoin intimately.

[English translation published in 2015]:
Activate the nine corporal energy centers to elaborate the golden pill,
Operate the Five Elements to circulate the micro-cosmos

The stanza below[99] describes the inner-alchemical process of reversing the aging process to preserve the body, cultivating the birth of an immortal spirit-embryo within one's abdomen. This process is largely occulted in the ĐTCG translation, which speaks of "purifying and lightening the Superior Self."

[Original Vietnamese version]:
Gom vào tư tưởng trong ngoài,
Luyện phanh trong sạch Thánh-Thai nhẹ nhàng.

[Conversion into Chinese characters]:
歸化思想內外
煉反存身聖胎輕閒

[English translation of the Chinese version]:
Collect your thoughts from the inner and outer realities.
Practice to revert and preserve the body and the Holy Foetus will become ethereal.

[French version from the 1950 edition]:
Concentrant le Mental et le Causal, l'initié sélectionne ses pensées.
Il les analyse et les synthétise en vue de purifier et d'alléger le Moi Supérieur.

99 Phái Chiếu-Minh, *Đại Thừa Chơn Giáo*, 388 (message of August 19, 1936).

[English literal translation of the 1950 French version]:
Concentrating the Mental and the Causal, the initiate selects his thoughts.
He analyzes and synthesizes them in order to purify and to lighten the Superior Self.

[English translation published in 2015]:
Converge all inside and outside thoughts,
Forge and purify them so that the Saintly Fetus becomes lighter.

And in the following verse, opening the "seventh initiation,"[100] the alchemical refinement of the "true spirit" is rendered in both theosophical terms, by a Hindu and cosmic representation of the fluid as *prana*, and Biblical terms ("enthrones the Holy Spirit on the Throne of Glory").

[Original Vietnamese version]:
Thất Chuyển pháp hạo nhiên chi khí,
Luyện Chơn-Thần qui vị hưởng an.

[Conversion into Chinese characters]:
七轉法浩然之氣
煉真神歸位享安

[English translation of the Chinese version]:
The seventh cycle is the method of the Majestic Spirit.
Refine the True Spirit and return to the position of peace.

[French version from the 1950 edition]:
À la 7e INITIATION, l'initié condense le fluide cosmique ou le Prana.
Et intronise le Saint-Esprit sur son Trône de Gloire.

[English literal translation of the 1950 French version]:
At the 7th INITIATION, the initiate condenses the cosmic fluid or Prana.
And enthrones the Holy Spirit on its Throne of Glory.

[English translation published in 2015]:
The SEVENTH INITIATION is the method for the energy of life,
To forge your true spirit into its original state.

100 Phái Chiếu-Minh, *Đại Thừa Chơn Giáo*, 388 (message of August 19, 1936).

9 Conclusion

Scholarship on Caodaism has only begun to explore the key role of Western Occultism and Chinese redemptive societies as contexts for Cao Đài history and identity. In this chapter, we have begun to trace how Minh Lý and Cao Đài appeared as redemptive societies at the point of convergence of the Chinese Xiantiandao salvationist tradition and French Occultism.

In our research, we have found that the core cosmology and practices of all the Minh and Cao Đài religious groups can be clearly identified as related to the Chinese spirit-writing tradition, and especially to the salvationist eschatology and practices of the Xiantiandao tradition—with a core Daoist cosmology and inner alchemical meditation techniques, vegetarianism, the basic Xiantiandao pantheon, and three-stage millenarianism. As for French Spiritism, it seems to have played a role both as an initial trigger before a switch to the Chinese-style "flying phoenix," and later as a "modernist" discursive and interpretive device. It was used to reformulate and explain the teachings and practices in a more legitimate, scientific and Christian-sounding language, and, through the translation process, to obscure the traces of Caodaism's Chinese genealogy.[101]

But Vietnamese redemptive societies are not a simple combination or synthesis of the Chinese and European traditions. The structural position of both elements is not identical. Both movements—Occultism and redemptive societies—bear the imprint of the socio-cultural conditions and concerns of their period and their place of origin. Reconsidering Caodaism within the context of European occultist culture and Chinese redemptive societies brings into focus the specific features of this religious movement at a crucial moment in Vietnamese history, without getting locked into old scholarly categorizations ("secret societies," "folk religious cults," "sectarian rebels," "new religious movements," …) which have obscured the academic understanding of Caodaism until now. These semantic shifts allow us to focus on the intrinsic characteristics of Caodaism and move away from these categories.

In this chapter, we have engaged in an exercise of *reverse translation*, converting sections of the core Cao Đài esoteric scripture into Chinese characters. This has revealed that the original Cao Đài *text* was little different from typical Chinese spirit-writing productions. But the French colonial and Vietnamese nation-building *context* of Cao Đài's emergence was quite different from that of redemptive societies in China, and this led to significantly different results in terms of its textual production in the Vietnamese and French languages—a

101 For a further discussion of these issues, see Jammes and Palmer, "Occulting the Dao."

process that was shaped by, and shaped in turn, the religious identity construction and institution building of Cao Đài religion.

If spiritist literature was widespread in Cochin-China, it seems to not have been institutionalized but rather followed the model of recreational circles. On the other hand, the Theosophical Society created an organizational, publishing, and translating infrastructure "that was perfectly integrated into the intellectual fabric of its time."[102] The Vietnamese Theosophical Society's production—books, brochures, magazines, visuals, neologisms, and "foreignisms"—was supportive of the Cao Đài publication and translation agenda.

The Kardec-ish (spiritist) and Leadbeater-ish (theosophical) style of the Cao Đài translation certainly implies an intentional transformation of the text by the translators, a repackaging of Vietnamese and Chinese indigenous religious cosmologies and practices into equivalents or alternatives to Christian churches (through the occultist lens). Within the Vietnamese cultural contextualization of Chinese sacred texts occurring in late nineteenth and early twentieth centuries Cochin-China (as discussed in chapter 6 of this volume about the Tứ Ân Hiếu Nghĩa movement and its production of new and hybrid Buddhist texts), it appears as if the Cao Đài translators deliberately downplayed the Chinese-ness of the spirit-writing text, opting for a French translation that could serve their agenda of universalizing the Cao Đài scriptural corpus and of offering an Asian (Vietnamese) counterpart to Western knowledge.

We see here the limit of a structural logic which suggests a dual and complementary alternative and opposition between the Self and the Other (Vietnam/China or Vietnam/France). On the contrary, it would be fruitful to approach the ĐTCG production as a sort of paradoxical logic that interpenetrates the ambivalences of each categories of thinking, manages in a constructive and creative way the theological contradictions, and ultimately re-evaluates the forms of classification, the symbolic forms, the categories and universes of meaning.[103] In the colonial context, this *bricolage* or creolization makes possible and viable what the French anthropologist Roger Bastide, in his studies of syncretism, called "the cohabitation [and] the alternation, among an individual or a sociological group, of some logics and categories of thinking that are themselves incompatible and irreducible."[104]

102 See the conclusion in Jammes, "Theosophying."

103 See Roger Bastide, *Le prochain et le lointain* (Paris: Cujas, 1970), 137; Bastide, "Le principe de coupure et le comportement afro-brésilien," *Anais do XXXI Congresso Internacional de Americanistas (São Paulo, 1954)* 1 (1955): 493–503.

104 André Mary, *Les anthropologues et la religion* (Paris: Presses Universitaires de France, 2010), 129.

This article opens questions for further research on the significance of European occultist culture and Chinese redemptive societies in the social, political, and intellectual history of modern and contemporary Vietnam. In the context of the intersection of these two waves, Caodaism provides an excellent case to understand religious innovation at the interface between Chinese religious culture, indigenous identity, and Western influences in a non-Chinese and colonial context.

Acknowledgments

This article is an output of the Chiang Ching-kuo Foundation-funded project on "Text and Context: Redemptive Societies in the History of Religions of Modern and Contemporary China," and the Universiti Brunei Darussalam (UBD)-funded project on "Vietnamese Religious Connectivity: a Multi-Sited, Anthropological and Historical Approach." We are grateful to the CCKF, to the Hong Kong Institute for the Humanities and Social Sciences at the University of Hong Kong, and to UBD for supporting the research leading to this article. Our sincere thanks are also extended to Vito Yu and Martin Tse, research assistants at the University of Hong Kong, for their assistance with data collection and translations.

Bibliography

Aubrée, Marion, and Jérémy Jammes. "Développements et mutations du spiritisme kardéciste: Brésil/Viêt Nam." *Politica Hermetica* 26 (2012): 70–94.

Bastide, Roger. "Le principe de coupure et le comportement afro-brésilien." *Anais do XXXI Congresso Internacional de Americanistas (São Paulo, 1954)* 1 (1955): 493–503.

Bastide, Roger. *Le prochain et le lointain*. Paris: Cujas, 1970.

Batthacharya, Benoytosh. *An Introduction to Buddhist Esotericism*. London: Oxford University Press, 1932.

Bourdieu, Pierre. *Choses dites*. Paris: Éditions de Minuit, 1987.

Brach, Jean-Pierre, Antoine Faivre, Wouter J. Hanegraaff, and Roelof van den Broek, eds. *Dictionary of Gnosis and Western Esotericism*. Leiden: Brill, 2005.

Cao Đài Đại Đạo Cénacle Ésotérique de Chiếu Minh. *Le véritable enseignement du grand cycle caodaïste (Đại Thừa Chơn Giáo)*. Translated to the French from Vietnamese by Quách Hiệp Long. Hanoi: NxB Tôn Giáo, 2013.

Cao Đài Đại Đạo "Chiếu Minh" Séance. *The Grand Cycle of Esoteric Teaching.* Translated to the English from Vietnamese and French by Anh-Tuyet Tran. San Jose: Cao-Dai Temple Overseas, 2015.

Clart, Philip. "The Phoenix and the Mother: The Interaction of Spirit-Writing Cults and Popular Sects in Taiwan." *Journal of Chinese Religions* 25 (1997): 1–32.

De Groot, J.J.M. *Sectarianism and Religious Persecution in China.* Reprint, Shannon, Ireland: Irish University Press, 1973 [1903–1904].

Duara, Prasenjit. *The Crisis of Global Modernity: Asian Traditions and a Sustainable Future.* Cambridge: Cambridge University Press, 2015.

Đức Nguyên. *Cao Đài Từ Điển, Quyển I, II, III* [Dictionary of Caodaism, vol. I, II, and III]. Hochiminh City: private printing, 2000. Available online at http://www.daotam.info/booksv/CaoDaiTuDien/CaoDaiTuDien(v2012)/index.html.

Edelman, Nicole. *Voyantes, guérisseuses et visionnaires en France, 1785–1914.* Paris: Albin Michel, 1995.

Goossaert, Vincent, and David A. Palmer. *The Religious Question in Modern China.* Chicago: University of Chicago Press, 2011.

Hanegraaff, Wouter J. *New Age Religion and Western Culture: Esotericism in the Mirror of Secular Thought.* Leiden: Brill, 1996.

Harvey, David A. "Beyond Enlightenment: Occultism, Politics, and Culture in France from the Old Regime to the *Fin-de-Siècle.*" *The Historian* 65, no. 3 (2003): 665–694.

Hoskins, Janet. "God's Chosen People: Race, Religion, and Anti-Colonial Struggle in French Indochina." Singapore: ARI Working Paper No. 189, 2012. http://www.ari.nus.edu.sg/wps/wps12_189.pdf (accessed January 10, 2015).

Hoskins, Janet. *The Divine Eye and the Diaspora: Vietnamese Syncretism Becomes Transpacific Caodaism.* Honolulu: University of Hawai'i Press, 2015.

Huệ Khải (Lê Anh Dũng). *Ngô Văn Chiêu: Người môn đệ Cao Đài đầu tiên* [Ngô Văn Chiêu: The first Cao Đài adept]. San Martin (California): Nxb Tam Giáo Đồng Nguyên, 2008.

Huệ Nhẫn (Võ Thành Châu). *Ngũ Chi Đại Đạo (Nam chi Đạo họ Minh)* [The Five branches of the Great Way, named Minh]. Hochiminh City: internal edition of the Cơ Quan Phổ Thông Giáo Lý Đại Đạo, 1999.

Jammes, Jérémy. "Divination and Politics in Southern Vietnam: Roots of Caodaism." *Social Compass* 57, no. 3 (2010): 357–371.

Jammes, Jérémy. *Les Oracles du Cao Đài. Étude d'un mouvement religieux vietnamien et de ses réseaux.* Paris: Les Indes savantes, 2014.

Jammes, Jérémy. "Cao Đài Acceptance in Contemporary Vietnam: Tightrope Walking between Past and Future." *Gis-Reseau-Asie,* 2016. Online at www.gis-reseau-asie.org/monthly-articles/reconnaissance-caodaisme-dans-viet-nam-contemporain-jeu-equilibriste-entre-passe-avenir (accessed September 15, 2016).

Jammes, Jérémy. "Caodaism in Times of War: Spirits of Struggle and Struggle of Spirits." *SOJOURN: Journal of Social Issues in Southeast Asia* 31, no. 1 (2016): 247–294.

Jammes, Jérémy. "Đại Đạo Tam Kỳ Phổ Độ (Cao Đài)." In *Handbook of East Asian New Religious Movements*, edited by Lukas Pokorny and Franz Winter, 565–583. Leiden, Boston: Brill, 2018.

Jammes, Jérémy. "Printing Cosmopolitanism, Challenging Orthodoxies: Cao Đài Journals in Twentieth Century Vietnam." *Vienna Journal of East Asian Studies* 10 (2018): 175–209.

Jammes, Jérémy. "Theosophying the Vietnamese Religious Landscape: A Circulatory History of a Western Esoteric Movement in South Vietnam." In *Theosophy Across Boundaries*, edited by Hans Martin Krämer and Julian Strube. Albany, NY: SUNY Press, forthcoming.

Jammes, Jérémy, and David A. Palmer. "Occulting the Dao: Daoist Inner Alchemy, French Spiritism, and Vietnamese Colonial Modernity in Caodai Translingual Practice." *Journal of Asian Studies* 77, no. 2 (2018): 405–428.

Jordan, David K., and Daniel L. Overmyer. *The Flying Phoenix: Aspects of Chinese Sectarianism in Taiwan*. Princeton: Princeton University Press, 1986.

Kardec, Allan. *Genesis: The Miracles and the Predictions According to Spiritism*. Boston: Colby & Rich, 1883 [1868 in French].

Kardec, Allan. *The Gospel According to Spiritism. Contains Explanations of the Moral Maxims of Christ in Accordance with Spiritism and Their Application in Various Circumstances in Life*. London: The Headquarters Publishing Co Ltd., 1987 [1864 in French].

Komjathy, Louis. *The Way of Complete Perfection: A Quanzhen Daoist Anthology*. Selected, translated, and with an Introduction by Louis Komjathy. Albany: State University of New York Press, 2013.

Lardinois, Roland. *L'Invention de l'Inde: Entre ésotérisme et science*. Paris: CNRS Éditions, 2007.

Laurant, Jean-Pierre. *L'Ésotérisme chrétien en France au XIXe siècle*. Lausanne: Éditions l'Âge d'Homme, 1992.

Lévy, Paul. *Buddhism: A "Mystery Religion"?* New York: Schocken Books, 1968 [1957].

Liu, Lydia H. *Translingual Practice: Literature, National Culture, and Translated Modernity—China, 1900–1937*. Stanford, Calif.: Stanford University Press, 1995.

Mary, André. *Les Anthropologues et la religion*. Paris: Presses Universitaires de France, 2010.

Matter, Jacques. *Histoire critique du gnosticisme*. Paris: F.G. Levrault, 1828.

Nedostup, Rebecca. *Superstitious Regimes: Religion and the Politics of Chinese Modernity*. Cambridge, MA: Harvard University Asia Center, 2009.

Nguyễn Văn Miết. *La religion "Minh-Lý", pagode "aux trois religions."* Saigon: Tam Tông Miếu internal publication, 1960.

Ownby, David, and Mary F. Somers Heidhues, eds. *"Secret Societies" Reconsidered: Perspectives on the Social History of Early Modern South China and Southeast Asia*. Armonk, NY: M.E. Sharpe, 1993.

Palmer, David A. "Heretical Doctrines, Reactionary Secret Societies, Evil Cults: Labeling Heterodoxy in Twentieth-Century China." In *Chinese Religiosities: Afflictions of Modernity and State* Formation, edited by Mayfair Yang, 113–134. Berkeley: University of California Press, 2008.

Palmer, David A. "Dao and Nation: Li Yujie—May Fourth Activist, Daoist Cultivator, and Redemptive Society Patriarch in Mainland China and Taiwan." In *Daoism in the Twentieth Century: Between Eternity and Modernity*, edited by David A. Palmer and Liu Xun, 173–195. Berkeley: University of California Press, 2012.

Palmer, David A. "Chinese Redemptive Societies and Salvationist Religion: Historical Phenomenon or Sociological Category?" *Minsu quyi* 民俗曲藝, no. 172 (2011): 21–72.

Phái Chiếu-Minh [Chiếu Minh Branch]. *Đại Thừa Chơn Giáo—Le Grand Cycle de l'Ésotérisme*. "Cao Đài Đại Đạo" [Great Way of Cao Đài or Caodaism] Series. Saigon: Nguyễn-Văn-Huấn Printing House, 1950.

Phạm Công Tắc (*Hộ Pháp*). *Le Caodaïsme* (*reportage inédit*), *La Vérité*, Phnom Penh, 1937.

Phạm Công Tắc (*Hộ Pháp*). *Bí Pháp* [The Secret Doctrine]. Tây Ninh: Holy See of Tây Ninh, 1949.

Phạm Công Tắc (*Hộ Pháp*). *Lời thuyết đạo năm 1946, 1947, 1948* [Sermons]. Tây Ninh: Holy See of Tây Ninh, 1970–1973.

Phạm Công Tắc (*Hộ Pháp*). *The Divine Path to Eternal Life, Con Đường Thiêng Liêng Hằng Sống*. Translated by Đào Công Tâm and Christopher Hartney. New South Wales, Australia: Sydney Centre for Studies in Caodaism, 2004.

Phan Trường Mạnh. *Qu'est-ce que le Caodaïsme?* Saigon: éd. Phan-Trường-Mạnh, 1949.

Phan Trường Mạnh. *Đường Cứu Rỗi Đạo Cao-Đài—La voie du Salut Caodaïque* (version bilingue). Saigon: éd. Phan-Trường-Mạnh, 1950.

Pregadio, Fabrizio. "Destiny, Vital Force, or Existence? On the Meanings of Ming 命 in Daoist Internal Alchemy and its Relation to Xing 性 or Human Nature." *Daoism: Religion, History and Society* 6 (2014): 157–218.

Schipper, Kristofer, and Franciscus Verellen, eds. *The Taoist Canon: A Historical Companion to the Daozang*. Chicago: University of Chicago Press, 2004.

Smith, Ralph B. "An Introduction to Caodaism, 1. Origins and early history." *Bulletin of the School of Oriental and African Studies* 33, no. 2 (1970): 335–349.

Smith, Ralph B. "An Introduction to Caodaism, 2. Beliefs and Organization." *Bulletin of the School of Oriental and African Studies* 33, no. 3 (1971): 573–589.

Topley, Marjorie. "The Great Way of Former Heaven: A Group of Chinese Secret Religious Sects." *Bulletin of the School of Oriental and African Studies, University of London* 26, no. 2 (1963): 362–392.

Trần Mỹ Vân. "Japan and Vietnam's Caodaists: A Wartime Relationship (1939–1945)." *Journal of Southeast Asian Studies* 27 (1996): 179–193.

Wei Dingming 危丁明. *Shumin de yongheng: Xiantiandao ji qi zai Gang'ao ji Dongnanya diqu de fazhan* 庶民的永恆：先天道及其在港澳及東南亞地區的發展. Taipei: Boyang wenhua, 2015.

Werner, Jayne Susan. "The Cao Dai: The Politics of a Vietnamese Syncretic Religious Movement." PhD diss., Cornell University, 1976.

Werner, Jayne Susan. *Peasant Politics and Religious Sectarianism: Peasant and Priest in the Cao Dai in Viet Nam*. New Haven: Yale University Southeast Asia Studies, 1981.

Yau Chi On 游子安. "Daomai nanchuan: ershi shiji cong Lingnan dao Yuenan Xiantiandao de chuancheng yu bianqian 道脈南傳：20世紀從嶺南到越南先天道的傳承與變遷." In *Zongjiao renleixue di'er ji* 宗教人類學第二輯, edited by Jin Ze 金澤 and Chen Jinguo 陳進國, 232–256. Beijing: Shehui kexue wenxian chubanshe, 2010.

Yau Chi On 游子安. "The Xiantiandao and Publishing in the Guangzhou-Hong Kong Area from the Late Qing to the 1930s: The Case of the Morality Book Publisher Wenzaizi." Translated by Philip Clart. In *Religious Publishing and Print Culture in Modern China, 1800–2012*, edited by Philip Clart and Gregory Adam Scott, 187–232. Boston, Berlin: De Gruyter, 2014.

CHAPTER 8

Text and Context in the Study of Spirit-Writing Cults: A Methodological Reflection on the Relationship of Ethnography and Philology

Philip Clart

1 Introduction

Thirty-three years ago, David K. Jordan and Daniel L. Overmyer published their landmark monograph, *The Flying Phoenix: Aspects of Chinese Sectarianism in Taiwan* (Princeton University Press 1986). In his "personal introduction," Jordan gives the following account of the motivation and aim of this collaboration between an anthropologist (Jordan) and a historian of religion (Overmyer):

> Overmyer, it developed, was working with *pai-luan* texts from Taiwan. The texts he found fascinating, he explained. But he was concerned about the ethnographic context in which they were created and in which they functioned. He was not trained in fieldwork, he told me, and spoke no Hokkien. And this created a problem in describing the people who used the texts he was writing about.
>
> The solution he proposed was obvious: we would coauthor a book, with him doing the texts and me doing the fieldwork. This would take advantage of our skills and help to compensate for the weaknesses of both of us, and it would allow us to create a book that would consider contemporary *pai-luan* sectarianism both through its texts, in a way parallel to the way in which we must study it in earlier periods, and also ethnographically.[1]

In his own "personal introduction," Overmyer concurs:

> Our goal has been to combine our strengths and supplement our weaknesses, in the hope of producing a comprehensive study that would deal with texts and history as well as contemporary activities. The complexity

1 David K. Jordan and Daniel L. Overmyer, *The Flying Phoenix: Aspects of Chinese Sectarianism in Taiwan* (Princeton: Princeton University Press, 1986), xv–xvi.

 | DOI:10.1163/9789004424156_010

> of the sects themselves demands nothing less. I have long believed that anthropology, history, and textual studies need each other, and hope that our present effort will encourage such cooperation.[2]

In practice, this cooperation took the form of a core section of three case-studies (chapters 4–10), framed by introductory and background material (chapters 1–3), a conclusion (chapter 11), and five appendices containing translations and descriptions of sectarian texts. The case-studies concerned a spirit-writing cult in Madou 麻豆 (southern Taiwan, chapters 4–5), a Compassion Society (Cihuitang 慈惠堂) branch hall in Tainan (chapters 6–8), and the "Way of Pervasive Unity" (i.e., Yiguandao 一貫道, chapters 9–10). For the purposes of the present paper, I will focus on the case-study of the Madou cult group, called "Hall of the Wondrous Dharma" (Aofatang 奧法堂) by Jordan and Overmyer, and will try to assess whether or not the dual textual and contextual perspectives on this cult group produced specific insights unavailable to each perspective in isolation.

Chapter 4, presumably composed by Jordan, is primarily based on interviews and participant observation and traces the cult's development from first dabblings in spirit-writing in 1946, over its revival and heyday in the context of Madou's bid to compete with Nankunshen 南鯤鯓 as a major center for the worship of the "Five Kings" (*Wufu qiansui* 五府千歲) from 1956 through the 1960s, to its virtual demise by 1976. The only written source used extensively in this chapter is a history of Madou's main Five Kings temple, the Daitianfu (*Madou Daitianfu Wufu qiansui yan'ge* 麻豆代天府五府千歲沿革, no date). The impact of some of the events described by Jordan in texts produced by the Hall of the Wondrous Dharma is mentioned but not followed up on. Presumably, this task was left to Overmyer whose handwriting is all over the next chapter on the "Papers of the Hall of the Wondrous Dharma" (chapter 5). These papers include two texts: a varied collection of spirit-written texts (*The Great Enlightenment Dragon-Phoenix Precious Mirror for Awakening the Lost, Dajue longfeng xingmi baojian* 大覺龍鳳醒迷寶鑑) and a scripture (or "liturgical text," as Overmyer terms it) with the elaborate title *Marvelous Scripture of the Most High Mystery Penetrating Divine Treasure, Which Cultivates the Real, Refines the Nature, Rescues [Those in] the Realm of Darkness, and Saves [Those in] the Realm of Light* (*Taishang dongxuan lingbao xiuzhen lianxing duyou jixian miaojing* 太上洞玄靈寶修真煉性度幽濟顯妙經). Overmyer provides a careful description and analysis of the two texts, marking textual traces of events and issues described in the previous chapter based on Jordan's field

2 Jordan and Overmyer, *The Flying Phoenix*, xix.

observations, such as the excavation of the dragon pool (*longchi* 龍池), the loquacity of female cult members, and the conflict between the planchette-medium and speaking mediums (*tang-ki* 童乩). These two descriptions of texts are supplemented by a brief discussion of unpublished "personal revelations," presumably again provided by Jordan.

What is striking is the degree to which the ethnographic and textual perspectives remain separate; by setting them side by side, the reader does get a more complete picture of the cult group, its religious notions, and activities than she would get from either account by itself. However, while the two accounts supplement each other for the reader, they do not illuminate each other for the researchers as much as one might have expected. Jordan and Overmyer's case-study of the Hall of the Wondrous Dharma shows that in their cooperation information flowed mainly from Jordan to Overmyer, who used ethnographic data to elucidate specific references in the spirit-written texts. However, it is hard to detect what benefit Jordan might have derived from Overmyer's textual studies. In fact, the two scholars' attitude towards the texts is already apparent at the outset in Jordan's "personal introduction." Jordan starts out with a somewhat contradictory, but overall less than enthusiastic estimation of the research value of the texts:

> The revelations themselves struck me as valuable—how often do informants not only produce projective material, but edit it and print it and present the ethnographer with a bound copy? But beyond the texts (which on closer examination struck me as both trite and trivial in content), and the intriguing sociological problem of the organizations which this style of divination spawned, there was the fascinating question of the nature of the attraction which it seemed to exercise for Chinese participants.[3]

As Overmyer found the texts "fascinating," Jordan was certainly open to the possibility that the texts were not as trivial as they appeared to him,[4] but ultimately his main focus remained an ethnographic one on the things people do and think; the written record was a secondary projection of these actions and thoughts and could not add anything substantial to the data derived from participant observation and interviews. Thus, in the *Flying Phoenix*, ethnography serves on the one hand as a handmaid to philology, while at the

3 Jordan and Overmyer, *The Flying Phoenix*, xiii.

4 "How 'trite' were the texts really? Why? Did the Chinese think of them that way? What *did* they think of them? How important were they to the participants? Which participants? …" Jordan and Overmyer, *The Flying Phoenix*, xiii.

same time pursuing its own research agenda quite independent from philological insights.

Some degree of disjunction is to be expected as Jordan and Overmyer did not conduct the research together; in fact, they very rarely (if ever) met in person during the writing of the book, each completing his portion of the project as divided up by mutual agreement. The purpose of the present paper is to consider ways in which ethnographic and philological approaches may be integrated more closely so as to produce substantial added value when compared to their separate use. Before I set about this task, let me stress that this is not intended as a criticism of Jordan and Overmyer's monograph. *The Flying Phoenix* was tremendously important for me personally as it stimulated my interest in spirit-writing cults when I first bought a Taiwan reprint of the book in the Caves Bookstore in Taichung 臺中 in 1990. It opened to me a research field that promised a golden opportunity to combine ethnography and philology. That was something I had been looking for since finishing my master's degree in Chinese Studies with a minor in Social Anthropology in 1989. I eventually ended up pursuing my PhD degree with a project on a Taichung spirit-writing cult under Dan Overmyer's supervision and with the explicit purpose of achieving a closer integration of philological and ethnographic perspectives; David K. Jordan ended up serving as the external reader of the dissertation so that both co-authors of *The Flying Phoenix* eventually were involved in guiding and evaluating my research.

A couple of decades having passed since the completion of the original research, this seems a good time to reflect on whether possibilities for a closer integration of ethnography and philology have emerged in the course of my long-term studies of Taiwanese spirit-writing cults. Below I will discuss one such area (the production of scriptures by means of spirit-writing) where such an integrated approach has, in my view, provided "added value" to the study of this particular form of religious group. This is merely a case example to provide a basis for discussion and for further methodological consideration; the insights drawn from this are applicable to other aspects of spirit-writing cults and, *mutatis mutandis*, perhaps also to other thematic fields in the study of Chinese religions.

2 The Meaning, Role, and Function of Scriptures (*jing*)

Scriptures (*jing* 經) are in a category of their own among the textual output of spirit-writing cults (a.k.a. "phoenix halls," *luantang* 鸞堂) and are clearly distinguished from "books" (*shu* 書). A celestial mandate to compose a scripture is a major indicator of divine favor for a spirit-writing cult and attendance during the séances when a scripture is being written produces more merit than for séances during which non-scriptural texts are produced. While *shu* such as the Hall of Wondrous Dharma's *Precious Mirror for Awakening the Lost* are produced in regularly scheduled séances on an ongoing basis, the revelation of a new *jing* is a much rarer event; indeed, many spirit-writing halls never compose a scripture of their own. The cluster of cult groups in central Taiwan on which my research has focused is a bit unusual in that it has produced several such scriptures. At the center of my field studies stood the Wumiao Mingzhengtang 武廟明正堂 (Temple of the Martial Sage, Hall of Enlightened Orthodoxy; short: Mingzhengtang) in the city of Taichung. It emerged in the 1970s from the Shengxiantang 聖賢堂 (Hall of Sages and Worthies) and produced in the 1990s an offshoot of its own, the Xuyuantang 虛原堂 (Hall of Origin in Emptiness). The personnel involved in the scripture revelations overlapped to some extent so there exists a continuity among these three cults and we can and should look at them as a single line of transmission. Let us start with a quick overview of the scriptures produced by the three groups up to 2003:

Cult group	Scripture	(Title in English)	Medium	Date of completion
Shengxiantang	*Yuhuang pudu shengjing* 玉皇普度聖經	*The Jade Thearch's Sacred Scripture for Universal Salvation*	Yongbi 勇筆	1972
Shengxiantang	*Taishang wuji hunyuan zhenjing* 太上無極混元真經	*The Most High's True Scripture of the Limitless and Primordial Beginning*	Yongbi 勇筆	1972
Mingzhengtang	*Wuji Huangmu huanxing tianjing* 無極皇母喚醒天經	*The August Mother of Limitless Heaven's Celestial Scripture for Awakening* [*Her Children*]	Yongbi 勇筆	1982
Mingzhengtang	*Shun Di quanxiao jing* 舜帝勸孝經	*The Thearch Shun's Scripture Admonishing to Filial Piety*	Zhengbi 正筆	1984

(*cont.*)

Cult group	Scripture	(Title in English)	Medium	Date of completion
Mingzhengtang	*Wuji zhengdao xuanmiao jing* 無極證道玄妙經	*Mysterious and Marvelous Scripture of Limitless Heaven for Realizing the Way*	Mingbi 明筆	1987
Mingzhengtang	*Dimu puhua zhenjing* 地母普化真經	*The Earth Mother's True Scripture for Universal Transformation*	Mingbi 明筆	1996
Xuyuantang	*Guanyin miaodao lianhua jing* 觀音妙道蓮華經	*Guanyin's Lotus Sutra of the Marvelous Dao*	Xubi 虛筆 (= Mingbi 明筆)	2000
Xuyuantang	*Ba Xianweng ling-ying zhenjing* 八仙翁靈應真經	*Perfected Scripture of the Eight Immortals' Numinous Responsiveness*	Xubi 虛筆 (= Mingbi 明筆)	2003

The two Shengxiantang scriptures were revealed shortly after the official opening of the cult's new building and its emergence as an independent group no longer under the tutelage of the Caotun 草屯 based phoenix hall Huidegong 惠德宮 (Palace of Kindness and Virtue). The two scriptures together develop a specific theological profile for the new cult group as a mixture of a few innovations and of items for which a broad consensus already existed at the time among Taiwanese phoenix halls. The most significant innovation is the *Yuhuang pudu shengjing*'s elevation of Guan Sheng Dijun 關聖帝君 to the exalted position of Jade Emperor.[5]

5 On the history of this mythological innovation, see Wang Chien-chuan 王見川, "Cong 'Guandi' dao 'Yuhuang' tansuo 從「關帝」到「玉皇」探索," in *Jindai de Guandi xinyang yu jingdian: Jiantan qi zai Xin, Ma de fazhan* 近代的關帝信仰與經典：兼談其在新、馬的發展, ed. Wang Chien-chuan, Soo Khin Wah 蘇慶華, and Liu Wenxing 劉文星 (Taipei: Boyang wenhua, 2010), 107–121; Zhang Jialin 張家麟, "Lun Huaren minjian zongjiao shenqi de shen'ge zhuanhua: Yi Guangong jinsheng Yuhuang dadi wei jiaodian 論華人民間宗教

The Mingzhengtang's first scripture comes not shortly after its founding in 1976, but six years later as a charter for a major theological innovation, the introduction of the worship of Wuji Laomu 無極老母 (the Venerable Mother of the Non-Ultimate). This is closely related to the Mingzhengtang's strategic shift from an alliance with the Yellow Emperor Religion (Xuanyuanjiao 軒轅教) to a competitive adoption of elements of Cihuitang and Yiguandao doctrine. The 1987 revelation of the *Wuji zhengdao xuanmiao jing* in turn is related to another innovation, this one as much theological as ritual: the establishment of the "Academy for Realizing the Way" (Wuji Zhengdao Yuan 無極證道院), where the faithful could enrol their ancestors so that they would find it easier to cultivate the Dao and be appointed to divine offices in Heaven. The *Wuji zhengdao xuanmiao jing* codified the soteriology underlying and legitimating the Academy's operation.

While the two scriptures just mentioned marked crucial turning points in the history of the Mingzhengtang, the other two scriptural texts revealed at the Mingzhengtang had a less marked impact. They primarily signify attempts to push specific deities to the forefront, thus diversifying the Hall's "portfolio" of major deities worshipped on a regular basis. However, in both cases these seem to have been projects supported by only a minority of believers with a special affinity for the deities in question. The *Shun Di quanxiao jing* 舜帝勸孝經 was primarily promoted by the revealing medium, Zhengbi, and apparently never caught on among the Mingzhengtang's followers. Soon after the completion of the scripture, Zhengbi left the Mingzhengtang to set up his own phoenix hall. These days, the *Shun Di quanxiao jing* is rarely (if ever) recited at the Mingzhengtang. The *Dimu puhua zhenjing* was revealed by Mingbi to accompany the installation of a new image of the Earth Mother beside the Venerable Mother on the third floor of the temple building. This new focus upon the Earth Mother was another pet project by a leading member of the Hall, in this case one of the deputy chairmen. He initiated the fund-raising project for the new Earth Mother image and afterwards repeatedly requested the gods to reveal an Earth Mother scripture. After some procrastination, Mingbi finally received a mandate to channel the scripture. There are some similarities here with Zhengbi's attempt to establish an individual cult for Shun Di in 1984 in that the Earth Mother also seemed to lack a broad basis of support among the phoenix disciples and was pushed mainly by a small faction supporting her. Different from the *Shun Di quanxiao jing*, however, the new Earth Mother

神祇的神格轉化—以關公晉昇玉皇大帝為焦點," in *Taiwan zongjiao ronghe yu zaidihua* 臺灣宗教融合與在地化 (Taipei: Lantai, 2010), 310–351.

scripture has taken hold in the ritual activities of the Mingzhengtang, though it has not ushered in a theological reorientation of the Hall.

As I have argued elsewhere, the two Xuyuantang scriptures were intended to serve as charter texts for the liturgy of the new phoenix hall and to set it apart from its parent cult, the Mingzhengtang. But why the Eight Immortals and Guanyin? Mingbi/Xubi[6] had felt a special affinity to the Eight Immortals ever since one of them, Han Xiangzi 韓湘子, had become his spiritual teacher. Every planchette medium honors a particular deity as his or her "immortal teacher" (*xianshi* 仙師). It is this deity that guides the candidate through the training that qualifies him or her as a medium for the first time. Through his immortal teacher Han Xiangzi, Mingbi/Xubi's destiny is connected with the rest of the group of the Eight Immortals. The link with Guanyin is less obvious, but may have to do with the fervent Guanyin devotion of at least one vice-chairman of the Xuyuantang. Furthermore, while the Eight Immortals are well known in Taiwanese popular culture, they rarely are objects of intense religious veneration; Guanyin on the other hand has a wide following among Taiwanese and would seem to offer a devotional focus for the new phoenix hall that could attract new members to the cult. Thus, in a sense, the Eight Immortals by dint of their unusualness as objects of worship seem to function as markers of the Hall's unique and separate identity, while the cult of Guanyin serves the double purpose of setting the Xuyuantang off from the Mingzhengtang, while at the same time tapping into the strong current of Guanyin devotionalism in Taiwanese popular culture.[7]

As this overview shows, the revelation of a scripture is usually tied to a major organizational and/or doctrinal shift in a spirit-writing cult's development; as a *sui generis* type of authoritative text, scriptures serve as charters legitimating these shifts. Their relative impact on the cult group (and beyond) depends on the magnitude of the shift and the degree of support for it. As we saw, the Shun Di and Dimu scriptures had a limited impact as they arose in response to the religious interests of only a minority among the cult membership, while the other two Mingzhengtang scriptures as well as the Shengxiantang ones have shown staying power along with the innovations they legitimated and have even spread beyond the cult group that produced them. The prospects of the two Xuyuantang scriptures are still uncertain and will depend on the

6 Mingbi used the name "Xubi" at the Xuyuantang.

7 Philip Clart, "Anchoring Guanyin: Appropriative Strategies in a New Phoenix Hall Scripture," *Minsu quyi* 民俗曲藝 / *Journal of Chinese Theatre, Ritual and Folklore*, no. 173 (2011): 101–128. See also my "The Eight Immortals between Daoism and Popular Religion: Evidence from a New Spirit-Written Scripture," in *Foundations of Daoist Ritual: A Berlin Symposium*, ed. Florian C. Reiter (Wiesbaden: Harrassowitz Verlag, 2009), 84–106.

one hand on the fate of the cult group itself, which recently completed a major building project, and on the other hand on whether the Xuyuantang develops a corporate doctrinal identity in which these two scriptures and their deities (Guanyin and the Eight Immortals) play a central role (as with the introduction of Wuji Laomu in the Mingzhengtang in the early 1980s). As the medium of these two scriptures, Xubi, has meanwhile passed away, it remains to be seen if his successors will build on the foundations laid by him or will rather take the group in new directions.

3 Ethnography and Philology in the Study of Spirit-Written Scriptures

The above summary is based on both my dissertation research and on the follow-up studies I have undertaken since then; the implications are followed up in greater detail elsewhere.[8] The purpose of the present paper is to reflect on the methodology employed to arrive at the analysis summarized above. Let us therefore take a look at the approaches employed when dealing with the scriptures and their historical and social contexts. As canonical texts, scriptures are intended to be "timeless" and hence tend to contain few references to particular circumstances of their revelation. In a scripture, the researcher will rarely find the kind of specific pronouncements on the activities or internal affairs of a phoenix hall that may be discovered in spirit-written texts of the *shu* type. Thus, data on the context of a scriptural text must be gathered outside of the text itself. One major contribution of ethnography to textual study is to identify circumstances and motivations of the scripture's composition, but in the text-centered environment of phoenix halls, the researcher is not limited to interviews and observations to establish context. The steady stream of documentation produced by active "sectarian-type" phoenix halls such as those in the Mingzhengtang network is a veritable mine of information that allows us to reconstruct much of the network's development from its texts alone; its magazines are especially important, as they carry all kinds of service announcements and personalized compositions that usually do not get republished in book format. A careful study of the *Shengxian* 聖賢, *Luanyou*

8 See the articles cited in the previous footnote, and my dissertation, "The Ritual Context of Morality Books: A Case-Study of a Taiwanese Spirit-Writing Cult," University of British Columbia, 1997; also, "Competition, Entrepreneurship, and Network Formation among Taiwanese Spirit-Writing Cults," in *Jindai Huaren zongjiao huodong yu minjian wenhua: Song Guangyu jiaoshou jinian wenji* 近代華人宗教活動與民間文化—宋光宇教授紀念文集, ed. Li Shi-wei 李世偉 (Taipei: Boyang, 2019), 197–163.

鸞友, and *Xuyuan* 虛原 magazines provides exact dates for the revelations of the scriptures, information on rituals in the course of which they are employed, and some indications of factors involved in the decision to produce a scripture (such as laudatory poems for members particularly active in the promotion of the scripture). In revelations preceding the composition of the scriptures, we can also trace the beginnings of the doctrinal and/or organizational shifts the scripture serves to legitimate. Thus, in the highly "textualized" context of phoenix halls a philologically-minded researcher can get a lot of empirical mileage out of the study of texts. In my own experience, detailed analysis of the textual production of an active sectarian phoenix hall is the foundation of any meaningful research on this type of religious group; it yields a wealth of data and helps the researcher formulate the questions for his or her field research. Field research then supplements the data derived from textual study in at least two ways:

1) It provides information on the interpersonal and group dynamics behind the revelation of a scripture. While careful study of the magazine issues before, during, and after the revelation of the scripture gives us glimpses of individuals and interests involved in the process, only field studies can clarify their positions in the cult and the underlying group dynamics. In particular the question of the degree of support within the group for a reorientation represented by a scripture requires longer-term observation of the cult group. The intricate weighing of diverging interests in a cult group that Jordan emphasizes for the case of Hall of the Wondrous Dharma as a key task for a successful planchette medium leaves visible traces in the texts, but these can only be brought into focus by field study. Thus, in the cases of the Dimu and Guanyin scriptures produced by the Mingzhengtang and Xuyuantang respectively, the role of an activist minority surrounding a particular member of the cult leadership does not become clear enough from the written record alone.
2) Beyond adding detail to outlines already known from the texts, the ethnographic record also contains data that either are not represented at all in the written record or only in such heavily encoded form that they are unintelligible without an ethnographic "key." An example is the absence of new scriptures in the first six years after the Mingzhengtang's secession from the Shengxiantang. The written record allows us to identify the new cult's alliance with the Xuanyuanjiao as a key factor in restraining efforts to create a new profile for itself.[9] However, another important factor

9 And this interpretation is strengthened by field data made available by another scholar who studied the Yellow Emperor Religion; see Christian Jochim, "Flowers, Fruit, and Incense

is much harder to detect in the written record, namely the temporary unavailability and overall unreliability of the cult's main medium, Yongbi, which eventually led to his expulsion in 1985. Here ethnography provides important new data that allow us to explain the particular timing of the scripture revelations.

In the case of *shu*-type writings, the data and insights derived from ethnography may be crucial in arriving at a correct reading of at least some portions and aspects of the texts themselves if the latter contain hidden references to persons and events within or surrounding the cult group. In the case of the less contextualized scriptures (*jing*), the ethnographic contribution helps not so much in reading the texts themselves, but in analyzing the context of their production and usage, as well as their overall impact in the originating cult group. Here ethnography performs the "handmaid" function for philology that we already saw in *The Flying Phoenix*.

Now, let us switch perspective and ask about the contributions of textual study to ethnographic research. What kind of information can flow from textual study to ethnographic inquiry? As already pointed out above, study of the textual output of a phoenix hall enables the researcher to formulate relevant questions for field research; in a sense, here philology serves as handmaid to ethnography by providing a foundational knowledge of the group to be studied and shaping the research design by identifying specific areas of interest. In my view, more important and perhaps even a key source of philological "added value" for ethnography is, however, another aspect. As "projective material" the texts produced by a spirit-writing cult are not just field notes nicely printed up for the ethnographer, data that he or she could also, though more laboriously, collect by means of interviews. Textual production involves a level of reflexivity and systematization that is rarely fully accessible in interviews. Thus, spirit-written texts are not just records of what people do and think, but they are documents of actions and thoughts at a level removed from the immediate context of the knowledge-in-action accessible in interviews. That does not mean that interviews are not able to produce information on more abstract and systematic formulations of cultural knowledge, but in this regard the projective material of spirit-written texts is clearly a much more promising primary source for at least those cult members closely involved with textual production. Among all its textual output, scriptures such as the ones described above are the most systematic and abstract formulations of doctrinal systems available in a spirit-writing cult. The Xuyuantang's Guanyin scripture in particular

Only: Elite versus Popular in Taiwan's Religion of the Yellow Emperor," *Modern China* 16, no. 1 (1990): 3–38.

is a carefully crafted text that integrates a core of fundamental phoenix hall beliefs with Buddhist devotional practices. The doctrinal structure emerging from the philological analysis would not have been available to me by means of interviews with the revealing medium, a notoriously taciturn man who preferred to express himself in writing. Even if Xubi had been more forthcoming in conversations, I doubt that interviews would have elicited data systematic enough to reconstruct the carefully balanced worldview presented in and by the Guanyin scripture. Therefore, a close reading and analysis of spirit-written texts produces data of an order difficult to access by participant observation and interviews alone. Of course, the ethnographer then needs to ask herself how widely these views are shared among the membership, a question that can once again be pursued by means of interviews. However, this question can only be asked after she has given close philological attention to the most authoritative canonical texts of the cult group.

4 Conclusion

In conclusion, once one accepts that spirit-written texts are not (necessarily) "trite and trivial," their philological analysis can produce insights into systematized belief systems, which in turn can help formulate ethnographic questions and approaches for the investigation of the groups that generate the texts in question. In return, the ethnographic study of the groups and individuals involved in the production of the texts produces contextual knowledge to help interpret the texts and gauge their role and impact in the group. Such a dual and mutually enriching approach is in my view indispensable in the study of spirit-writing cults, where a good deal of what people "do and think" involves the creation and consumption of textual material; thus even an ethnographer primarily focusing on the social intra-group dynamics ignores the textual dimension at her own risk. In the *Flying Phoenix*, David K. Jordan acknowledges that "however unimportant the content of the revelations seemed to me (and to many sectarians) to be, *pai-luan* groups *were* text-centered, after all, and some examination of their textual basis seemed to be absolutely necessary."[10] It is the argument of this paper that an examination of their textual basis is indeed absolutely necessary, and if taken seriously can be highly informative for ethnographic research on such groups. Admittedly, owing to their text-centered nature spirit-writing cults are ideal cases to make such an argument for a close integration of ethnographic and philological approaches.

10 Jordan and Overmyer, *The Flying Phoenix*, xv.

However, in a long-standing literate civilization such as China, I would expect that we will find many other subject fields where this argument has validity and a combination of ethnography and philology will together produce more and better results than these academic pursuits would bring about in isolation from each other.[11]

Bibliography

Chau, Adam Yuet. "Modalities of Doing Religion." In *Chinese Religious Life,* edited by David A. Palmer, Glenn Shive, and Philip L. Wickeri, 67–84. New York: Oxford University Press, 2011.

Clart, Philip. "The Ritual Context of Morality Books: A Case-Study of a Taiwanese Spirit-Writing Cult." PhD diss., University of British Columbia, 1997.

Clart, Philip. "The Eight Immortals between Daoism and Popular Religion: Evidence from a New Spirit-Written Scripture." In *Foundations of Daoist Ritual: A Berlin Symposium,* edited by Florian C. Reiter, 84–106. Wiesbaden: Harrassowitz Verlag, 2009.

Clart, Philip. "Anchoring Guanyin: Appropriative Strategies in a New Phoenix Hall Scripture." *Minsu quyi* 民俗曲藝 / *Journal of Chinese Theatre, Ritual and Folklore*, no. 173 (2011): 101–128.

Clart, Philip. "Competition, Entrepreneurship, and Network Formation among Taiwanese Spirit-Writing Cults." In *Jindai Huaren zongjiao huodong yu minjian wenhua: Song Guangyu jiaoshou jinian wenji* 近代華人宗教活動與民間文化—宋光宇教授紀念文集, edited by Li Shi-wei 李世偉, 107–163. Taipei: Boyang, 2019.

11 This is certainly relevant for any study addressing what Adam Yuet Chau calls the "discursive/scriptural" modality, one of five ideal types of "doing religion" in a Chinese setting. See Adam Yuet Chau, "Modalities of Doing Religion," in *Chinese Religious Life*, ed. David A. Palmer, Glenn Shive, and Philip L. Wickeri (New York: Oxford University Press, 2011), 67–84. For instance, it will certainly apply in the case of the Chinese lay Buddhist groups that Gareth Fisher defines as "textual communities," i.e., groups and networks that form around texts and their expositors beyond the control of the official monastic establishment. Here the circulation of texts serves to legitimate masters and establish and maintain links with and among their followers. In the absence of an articulated institutional support structure, it is the circulating texts themselves that provide the main framework of social interaction in these communities. See Gareth Fisher, "Mapping Religious Difference: Lay Buddhist Textual Communities in the Post-Mao Period," in *Recovering Buddhism in Modern China*, ed. Jan Kiely and J. Brooks Jessup (New York: Columbia University Press, 2016), 257–290.

Fisher, Gareth. "Mapping Religious Difference: Lay Buddhist Textual Communities in the Post-Mao Period." In *Recovering Buddhism in Modern China,* edited by Jan Kiely and J. Brooks Jessup, 257–290. New York: Columbia University Press, 2016.

Jochim, Christian. "Flowers, Fruit, and Incense Only: Elite versus Popular in Taiwan's Religion of the Yellow Emperor." *Modern China* 16, no. 1 (1990): 3–38.

Jordan, David K., and Daniel L. Overmyer. *The Flying Phoenix: Aspects of Chinese Sectarianism in Taiwan*. Princeton: Princeton University Press, 1986.

Wang Chien-chuan 王見川. "Cong 'Guandi' dao 'Yuhuang' tansuo 從「關帝」到「玉皇」探索." In *Jindai de Guandi xinyang yu jingdian: Jiantan qi zai Xin, Ma de fazhan* 近代的關帝信仰與經典：兼談其在新、馬的發展, edited by Wang Chien-chuan, Soo Khin Wah 蘇慶華, and Liu Wenxing 劉文星, 107–121. Taipei: Boyang wenhua, 2010.

Zhang Jialin 張家麟. "Lun Huaren minjian zongjiao shenqi de shen'ge zhuanhua: Yi Guangong jinsheng Yuhuang dadi wei jiaodian 論華人民間宗教神祇的神格轉化——以關公晉昇玉皇大帝為焦點." In *Taiwan zongjiao ronghe yu zaidihua* 臺灣宗教融合與在地化, 310–351. Taipei: Lantai, 2010.

Index

Printed in the United States
By Bookmasters